Anstruther Harbour

Chalmers' Church
West Port

LETTERS OF
THOMAS
CHALMERS

LETTERS OF
THOMAS
CHALMERS

Edited by
William Hanna

THE BANNER OF TRUTH TRUST

THE BANNER OF TRUTH TRUST
3 Murrayfield Road, Edinburgh EH12 6EL, UK
P.O. Box 621, Carlisle, PA 17013, USA

*

First published 1853
First Banner of Truth edition 2007

*

ISBN-10: 0 85151 940 7
ISBN-13: 978 0 85151 940 1

*

Printed in the U.S.A. by
Versa Press, Inc.,
East Peoria, IL

THOMAS CHALMERS:
A Biographical Table

1780	Born in Anstruther, Fife.
1791	Begins study at St Andrews University.
1796	Discovers Jonathan Edwards' *On Free Will*.
1799	Licensed to preach the gospel.
1802	Elected minister of Kilmany Parish, Fife (inducted 1803).
1804–5	Unsuccessfully seeks professorships at St Andrews
1811	Experiences evangelical conversion.
1814	Elected minister of the Tron Church, Glasgow (inducted 1815).
1819	Becomes minister of new parish of St John's, Glasgow, and leads experimental work for the relief of the poor.
1823	Professor of Moral Philosophy at St Andrews.
1828	Moves to Edinburgh to become Professor of Theology.

1832   Moderator of the General Assembly of the Church
          of Scotland, leader and symbol of the Evangelical
          party.

1834   Champions cause of Church Extension. Appointed
          Convenor of Committee on Church
          Accommodation, 1834–41. Builds 220 new churches
          at a cost of £290,000.

1842   Presents his plans to the Convocation of a
          Sustentation Fund for the Church.

1843   Disruption takes place. Chalmers elected first
          Free Church of Scotland Moderator and Professor
          of Theology in New College.

1845   Commences 'territorial mission' in the impoverished
          West Port district of Edinburgh.

1847   Gives evidence to the House of Commons on behalf
          of Free Church regarding its principles for reunion.

1847   Dies at home in Edinburgh and is buried
          'amid the tears of a nation and with more than
          kingly honours'.

INTRODUCTION

'Thomas Chalmers, as all the world knows, was born in the Fifeshire town of Anstruther in the year 1780.' If William Beveridge was justified in so expressing himself in 1908, then the passing of another century has surely made a vast difference in the knowledge of professing Christians, let alone 'the world'. An uncleaned statue of Chalmers still looks down on Edinburgh's George Street, yet the man himself, the man who was 'the greatest spiritual force Scotland saw in the nineteenth century', is today scarcely remembered even in his own country. The descendants of those who in 1847 witnessed the burial of Thomas Chalmers, 'amid the tears of a nation, and with more than kingly honours', now have other matters on their minds.

Undoubtedly many great preachers have been overlooked by posterity because they published little or nothing; after all, the living voice has a short span compared with the life of a book. In Chalmers' case, however, one reason for his eclipse may lie in exactly the opposite direction. His literary work was manifold. *The Works of Thomas Chalmers* (Glasgow: William Collins, 1835–42) run to twenty-five volumes, and they do not contain, by any means, all that he wrote! Certainly, to a reader who has the leisure of an early Victorian, these *Works* will convey the size of his mind and the many-sidedness of his thinking, running as it did into such subjects as economics (including savings banks), pauperism, social reform, and education, but for most people, what is great and of abiding value is simply buried amidst a mass of paper.

There is good reason why Thomas Chalmers ought to be remembered today. He was at the centre of a recovery that brought the churches in Scotland from mediocrity, indifference and unbelief, to new conditions of spiritual vitality. To understand Chalmers is to understand *how* that transformation occurred. It is unquestionable that towards the middle of the nineteenth century many parts of Scotland witnessed a profound awakening and that none stood closer to the spiritual influence which brought this about than Thomas Chalmers. Today the works of several of the men who shared in this recovery are being read again across the world. They include those of Robert Murray M'Cheyne, William Cunningham, George Smeaton, Hugh Martin, Andrew and Horatius Bonar, David Brown, and James Buchanan. For those who have discovered the value of these writers there cannot but be cause for interest in the man who was, in many respects, their teacher and leader.

* * * * *

When Chalmers was born in 1780 it was one of the deadest times in the history of the Church of Scotland since the Reformation. The *cause* of that deadness is not hard to trace. Some ninety-two years earlier in 1688, the Church of Scotland had emerged from the persecutions of the Covenanting era and had been reconstituted. Clergy who had been submissive to episcopacy when Christians of Presbyterian conviction were being put to death, now turned Presbyterian and thus kept their places in the national Church. In too many cases they were men who paid lip service to a creed (the *Westminster Confession*) to which they had no heart attachment. A deadening influence was thus continued in the life of the Church of Scotland, and this influence gained increasing sway by an Act of Parliament in 1712, which took away from congregations the right to choose their own ministers. That right was given to patrons, generally the local landowners, who, if they wished, could place a worldly cleric over an evangelical people.

Despite some local revivals during the eighteenth century, evangelical pulpits in the national Church were few in number, while 'the Moderates', as the majority of the men-pleasing clergy were called, dominated the life of that Church. When Chalmers was a youth of thirteen, Lachlan Mackenzie of Lochcarron began an ordination sermon with these words:

> If people go to perdition in these days it is not for want of ministers. The clergy are likely to become soon as plentiful as the locusts in Egypt, and which of them is the greatest plague of the two, time and the experience of the Church will discover.[1]

The Moderates preached morality, with almost nothing of the supernaturalism of true Christianity. They ignored the Fall of man, sneered at the idea of a new birth, and said nothing of the perfection and power of the work of the Son of God. They left their hearers with the impression that man is the author and finisher of his own salvation. Summarizing the results of their influence, Alexander Duff wrote:

> The savour and unction of divine grace was gone; the peculiarities of the gospel were despised as offensive to classic taste and culture, and devotion scorned as fanatical and contemptible . . . Instead of the power and pathos of earnest gospel invitations and appeals, there were substituted cold pretences of academic learning, that froze the generous sympathies of the human heart.

As a consequence of this state of affairs, large areas of the country were left without any gospel preaching. When Robert and James Haldane, members of the Scottish nobility, were converted towards the end of the eighteenth century, and began itinerating all over the country, they spoke to multitudes that had never heard of salvation by grace. One old man of ninety-two years of age told James Haldane that he had prayed eighty years earlier that God

---

[1] *The Happy Man: The Abiding Witness of Lachlan Mackenzie* (Edinburgh: Banner of Truth, 1979), p. 45.

would send the gospel to his part of Scotland, and at his death, as he clasped Haldane's hands in his own, he affirmed, 'I believe, I believe!' It was a striking contrast to many other deathbeds of that period. When one enquiring sinner, not far from death, asked his Moderate minister what he must do to be saved, he was met with shocked silence. In his minister's view, only the committing of some awful crime could explain why anyone should put such a question.

Not all areas in Scotland were equally dead. In the south there were a number of Secession churches that maintained a faithful witness but, at the time when Chalmers was born, true gospel preaching in Church of Scotland parishes was the exception rather than the rule.

Apart from unusual abilities in the fields of mathematics and chemistry, Chalmers' student days followed the common pattern. Before he was twelve years old he entered the University of St Andrews, ten miles from his birthplace in Fife, and at fifteen he commenced the study of theology with a view to making the ministry his profession. At the age of nineteen he was licensed to preach and in 1802 was elected to the country parish of Kilmany, in Fife. In the meantime he had abandoned the beliefs of his godly father and succumbed wholly to the Moderate school. As he later wrote: 'St Andrews was at this time overrun with Moderatism, under the chilling influences of which we inhaled not a distaste only, but a positive contempt for all that is properly and peculiarly gospel.'

One day, while still a student, Chalmers had heard a lecture touching on the subject of Calvinism. Sitting alongside him was another youth by the name of William H. Burns, whom he knew to hold the historic faith of the Church of Scotland. In conversation with Burns after the lecture, Chalmers exclaimed:

> You are a sincere Calvinist. There is none in St Andrews that I know. Come down to Anstruther with me on Saturday, and see my father and Mr Hodges [an old elder]. They all agree with you.

Chalmers' view of the ministry coincided with his Moderatism. The ministry was a helpful profession for a man who wished to make a name in the world. In the case of some of his colleagues, that meant simply being thought a 'good fellow' and taking a leading part in fox-hunting or other less strenuous social engagements. But Chalmers was more ambitious and coveted distinction in the academic world. With this goal in view his main studies remained mathematics, chemistry and geology, and for as long as six months in a year he might be absent from his parish in order to teach in St Andrews. When he was at home he acted on the belief that two days in the week were quite enough for religious duties; sometimes his sermon preparation, such as it was, had to be done on the Sunday morning. In one of his earliest writings, he declared:

> The author of this pamphlet can assert, from what to him is the highest of all authority, the authority of experience, that after the satisfactory discharge of his parish duties, a minister may enjoy five days in the week of uninterrupted leisure, for the prosecution of any science in which his taste may dispose him to engage.

Not surprisingly, for his first seven years at Kilmany Chalmers had no personal conversation with people about their souls, and from the pulpit he would warn his congregation of such evangelical authors as John Newton, from whom they might learn 'fanaticism'. Anything like evangelism he openly nauseated. 'Let us tremble to think that anything but virtue can recommend us to the Almighty' was the sentiment to which his hearers were accustomed to listen.

 Ineffective as Chalmers' ministry was at this period, that fact, if he recognized it, did not lead him to question the worth of his opinions. But in 1808 his plans for his career were singularly stopped. On 23 July we find him writing, 'I purpose setting off for London about the middle of August. My great object is to get introduced into some of the literary circles.' Instead of this, however, August found Chalmers at the bedside of a favourite sister in

Anstruther, and she died before the month was ended. The London visit was abandoned. The next summer, death drew even nearer. First an uncle, to whom he was closely attached, passed suddenly into eternity, being found kneeling in the attitude of prayer. Returning from a visit to this bereaved home, Chalmers encountered inclement weather that exacerbated an illness to which he had already succumbed. For the next four months he never left his room; his life hung in the balance.

* * * * *

It was now that the 'great revolution' began. After six months' absence from his pulpit, the congregation saw a very different minister, and one whose muffled figure, walking slowly to the church in the summer of 1810, revealed him to be the invalid that he was. With sunken and sallow countenance, Chalmers now spoke of new themes, and chiefly of the shortness and insignificance of time and of the nearness and magnitude of eternity. In later years when an opponent in the General Assembly reminded him of his early views on the work of the ministry, from which we quoted above, Chalmers was to confess that he was then blind to the lesson which even his scientific studies should have taught him: 'What, sir, is the object of mathematical science?' he had replied. 'Magnitude and the proportions of magnitude. But then, sir, I had forgotten two magnitudes. I thought not of *the littleness of time*—I recklessly thought not of *the greatness of eternity.*'

Yet when these new truths were first heard from the Kilmany pulpit the greatest change was still going on in secret. Smitten with a sense of sin, Chalmers had begun to pray, 'O God, fit a poor, dark, ignorant and wandering creature for being a minister of Thy Word.' Gradually the way of salvation by faith in the atonement of Christ was opened up to him, and before the close of the year 1811, when he was thirty-one years of age, his journal records the joy of assurance and of full commitment: 'O God, make me feel the firmness of the ground I tread upon, and enable me to give all my mind to Thy Word. Above all, may I never recede by a single inch from my Saviour.'

The change in the ministry of Kilmany was soon widely known. To Moderates it had the appearance of a bout of insanity, and for years the nickname 'Mad Chalmers' was to be common. Evangelicals saw it differently. One who visited Chalmers at this time reported:

> He has long been known as a celebrated philosopher and scorner of the peculiar doctrines of Christianity; now, from conviction and with a warm heart, he preaches the faith he once destroyed. I have had serious conversation with him, and am astonished at a man of such superior powers so modest and humble. He is indeed converted, and like a little child.

At no point did Chalmers' life remain the same. Family prayer was established twice a day, anxiety appeared for the souls of others, parish visitation, formerly accomplished in a fortnight each year, became regular and earnest work, and the impenitent dying were warned with tears. His beloved science books now lay closed; instead there was the *Westminster Confession of Faith*, Jonathan Edwards, John Owen, John Calvin, the once-despised Newton, and supremely, the Bible itself, which he began to read and memorize with an intensity that astonished those who had known his former interests.

Before long a changed spirit also began to appear in Chalmers' parish. In the spring of 1812, as two men were walking away from the church after hearing a sermon on John 3:16, one said to the other, 'Did you feel anything particularly in church today? I never felt myself to be a lost sinner till today, when I was listening to that sermon.' 'It is very strange', replied his companion, 'it was just the same with me.' Both men dated their conversion from that day. The following year, William Carey's friend, Andrew Fuller, visited Kilmany, and after hearing Chalmers preach he declared, 'If that man would but throw away his papers in the pulpit, he might be king of Scotland!'

In 1814, the scene of Chalmers' ministry changed from the quietness of the some one hundred and fifty families of Kilmany to the heart of Scotland's greatest city, Glasgow; here he was to remain for the next eight years, preaching with passionate eloquence to a crowded church. He opposed unbelief with a boldness that awoke many; church laws, which do not come from the Scriptures, he described as 'not worth a straw'. Above all, he laboured to bring the gospel not only to his hearers, but to the multitudes of Glasgow who had no church connection. The fact that the first volume of his Sermons sold nearly 20,000 copies in a year gives some idea of the extent of the influence that he was now given.

* * * * *

Although William Hanna gives the whole of the second volume of his biography to Chalmers' time in Glasgow,[1] his subject had probably not yet commenced his most important work. In 1823, to the surprise of many and contrary to the judgment of some of his best friends, he left the thousands of Scotland's largest city to undertake the professorship of Moral Philosophy in the University of St Andrews. It was certainly a considerable change. Geographically, St Andrews was a backwater and vastly different from Glasgow where, he once complained, 'My bell is ringing every half-minute with inquirers.' Apart from the new-found quiet, there were few advantages. His family, now grown to six daughters, were to enjoy the 'bathing process', and they were all to value the nearness of Anstruther, where his mother was still alive 'as if at the gate of Heaven, and with such a fund of inward peace and hope as made her nine years' widowhood a perfect feast and foretaste of the blessedness that awaits the righteous'. His parents' religion, however, was still as rare in St Andrews as it had been in his student days, and there was nothing which Thomas and Grace

---

[1] William Hanna, *Memoirs of the Life and Writings of Thomas Chalmers*, Vol. 1 (Edinburgh: Sutherland and Knox, 1850). Unhappily the extent of this work (4 volumes published 1850–2) has been against its general usefulness.

Chalmers felt so much as the change in the spiritual climate when they settled in Fife. In one of his letters from his new home Chalmers wrote in February 1824: 'Perhaps there is no town in Scotland more cold, and meagre, and moderate in its theology than St Andrews. I do find the Sabbaths to be very heartless in regard to the public services; and Mrs Chalmers half threatens to be a Seceder upon our hands. I will not hinder her . . .'

Despite the trials that followed his appointment Chalmers never seems to have doubted the correctness of his decision to remove from Glasgow. Two principal considerations had swayed his judgment. The first was his conviction that moral philosophy is vitally related to sound theology: 'Moral Philosophy stands to Christianity in the relation that Law does to Gospel, that the preaching of John the Baptist did to the preaching of the Saviour.' In this John-the-Baptist role Chalmers soon had evidence that he had not misjudged the opening which existed. 'I can lift many testimonies on the side of the Gospel', he wrote to a friend in December 1824, 'my classes give me some precious opportunities.'

A second consideration was more fundamental. For some years he had been convinced that a *changed ministry* was the primary need if there was to be any general renewal in the Church. While he was still at Kilmany his diary reveals this burden:

Thy blessing and thy Spirit, O Lord, be on this parish and neighbourhood. O that a day of power and of refreshing were to come amongst them. I implore thy Spirit on behalf of this county. O may its ministers be turned to the Lord. O send them pastors according to thine own heart . . . Stay not thine arm, O God; make it bare. Come forth in the might of thy all-subduing Spirit, and reveal Christ in many hearts, for His sake.

Certainly some ministers could be changed in the midst of their ministries, as he himself had been, yet the surest hope was for *a new generation of preachers* – men not trained in the aridity and dead scholarship of Moderatism, but in experimental Christianity and in a faith that subordinated everything to the Bible. And as the universities were the only theological schools of the day, it was there, at the 'fountain heads', that a transformation was supremely needed. This was the foremost reason why from 1823 onwards Chalmers was to give the best of his time and thought to helping young men, and why, even amidst the difficulties of St Andrews, he did not return to a parish. In June 1825 we find him writing:

> I have of late had several offers to leave the University and return again to the Church . . . But it was not upon light grounds that I relinquished the clerical for the professorial life; and I am more and more confirmed in the belief that a chair in a college is a higher station on the field of Christian usefulness, than a parish anywhere in Scotland. Could one acquit himself rightly of his duties as a professor, it is incalculable the good which might be done to the guides and the clergy of our next generation.[1]

It was not only in Scotland that the 'next generation' were to see the fruit. Of the three-hundred students who passed through Chalmers' classes in his five years at St Andrews, six—including the eminent Alexander Duff—were to become pioneer missionaries overseas. The great fulfilment of his vision was, however, to come in Edinburgh. When the professorship of divinity in that university was offered to him towards the close of 1827, he accepted, and on a snow-swept November morning in the following year, he gave the first of the many hundreds of lectures which were to be heard by successive classes of students through the next twenty years. William Cunningham, one of the students present on that first occasion was struck most of all by 'the deep, vital consciousness of the glory of the divine presence', and he noted, 'It is impossible not to indulge the hope that the time to favour our Zion, yea, the set time, is come.'

---

[1] See p. 198 of the present volume. The present reprint was originally published as *A Selection from the Correspondence of Thomas Chalmers*, edited by William Hanna (Edinburgh: Constable, 1853).

Chalmers has been variously assessed as a teacher of theology. He was certainly not without deficiencies. In depth and accuracy of learning he is not in the front rank of Scottish theologians. The course of divinity that he set his students embodied the doubtful procedure of beginning with 'natural theology' before advancing to the subject matter of Christianity itself. His lectures were liable to diverge into matters extraneous to the main theme before him. Yet when this has been said, there is a great deal to support the verdict of his biographer when he writes:

> Others have amassed larger stores of learning, and conveyed them to their students in more comprehensive and compendious forms. But who ever lit up the evidences and truths of Christianity with a light so attractive; and who ever filled the youthful breasts of those who were afterwards to occupy the pulpits of the land, with the fire of so generous and so devoted an enthusiasm.[1]

There are many testimonies to support these words of Hanna. John Duncan, who was to serve with Chalmers in New College after the Disruption, spoke thus of his senior:

> Chalmers was not a widely read divine, but as a practical thinker and teacher of the heart he was unrivalled. We have lost much of him for want of a Boswell. Many of his best sayings are gone for ever. As a man of erudition he might have been better. As a heaven-taught man, he needed little.[2]

W. M. Taylor wrote similarly:

---

[1] *Memoirs of Chalmers*, Vol. 4, p. 420.

[2] *Colloquia Peripatetica: Conversations with John Duncan* (Edinburgh: Oliphant, Anderson & Ferrier, 1907), pp. 27–8. 'How did you and Dr Chalmers get on?' a friend once asked Duncan in later years. 'Oh, nobly. Though very inferior, I took the liberty of differing with him sometimes about doctrine. One day, when he came down to my house for a little refreshment. I found fault with his definition of faith. Ah! my doctrine about faith was better than his – but he went to prayer, and his faith was better than mine.' David Brown, *Life of John Duncan* (Edinburgh: Edmonston and Douglas, 1872), p. 484.

To the end of his days he had around him a circle of loving and devoted students, all of whom were fired with enthusiasm which they had caught from his lips . . . He was not so much an instructor as a quickener. The other professors laid the materials in the minds of the students, but he brought and struck the match which kindled these materials into a flame that burned with an energy kindred to his own.[1]

resources

In addition to his more formal class lectures, Chalmers also used what amounted to discussion sessions, class conversations in which he and the students held 'continued parley'. It was probably on these occasions that he did most to direct their minds to the authors that they should master. A few of these authors were contemporaries, such as his friend, the Anglican Charles Bridges, author of *The Christian Ministry*. Among his favourites from the eighteenth century were Edwards, Boston, Newton, Doddridge, and Halyburton. But in their sustained biblical thought and fire it was the Puritans who remained his first love; the books of such authors as Joseph Alleine, John Owen,[2] William Guthrie, and Richard Baxter, which he had first revelled in at Kilmany, he was to press upon successive generations of students:

> There is a closeness, and a pertinency, and a power in the writings of the good old Puritans, of which we fall greatly short in these days of feebleness and degeneracy . . . From them you are most likely to carry away the impression that a preparation for eternity should be the main business and anxiety of time.

Along with such 'practical' writers, which he thought should be a main part of the reading of every minister, he also urged the value of the best Christian biographies (amongst which he gave a high place to the *Lives of Philip and Matthew Henry*, and the *Memoir and Correspondence of Henry Venn*). 'I am thankful to say', he wrote in

---

[1] *The Scottish Pulpit*, 1887, pp. 206–7.
[2] Chalmers seems to have continued reading Owen all his days and with mounting appreciation. 'Have you read Owen on the 130th Psalm?', he said to a friend in 1843. 'This is my last great work, and I would strongly recommend it.'

1835, 'that no reading so occupies and engages me as the biography of those who have made it most their business to prosecute the sanctification of their souls.'

* * * * *

Chalmers' concern for evangelism went beyond giving directions to his students about preaching. He was one of the first nineteenth-century leaders to emphasize that care for the souls of men was not to end in the pulpit. He pressed upon his divinity students what became known as 'the aggressive principle'; that is to say, they must take the gospel to the people. The unchurched must not be left alone; rather they must be pursued wherever they are to be found. And this was to be done methodically, with accurate records and statistics. On Saturday mornings in the 1830s some twelve to twenty of his students would meet for prayer in his vestry at the Divinity Hall, before proceeding in pairs to visit the poorest districts of the city. Robert M'Cheyne has described his shock on the first occasion he joined this 'Visiting Society' and discovered 'what imbedded masses of human beings are huddled together, unvisited by friend or minister!' Chalmers was to make important use of the statistics which his students gathered, and the General Assembly of 1838 heard that in Glasgow and Edinburgh alone there were 100,000 adults who were totally estranged from the Christian faith.

Few professors of divinity have had such students as crowded Chalmers' classroom in the 1830s. Many of them, as their subsequent biographies reveal, were to become men of outstanding usefulness. In part this usefulness was, of course, due to the considerable natural gifts with which they were endowed, but under other influences such talents might have developed in a different direction. As it was, the 'favourite ideas' they imbibed from Chalmers did much to shape their future lives. Four years' divinity under Chalmers and David Welsh (Professor of Church History) 'afforded no ordinary advantages', Andrew Bonar could write from experience. 'New fields of thought were daily opened up.' And of M'Cheyne, his fellow student, Bonar says, 'His notes and his diary testify that he endeavoured to retain what he heard, and that he used to read as much of the books recommended by the professors as his time enabled him to overtake.'[1] David Yeaworth writes, 'In Chalmers, more than any other person, M'Cheyne found the mould for his ecclesiastical and religious thought, and a worthy pattern for his own ministerial life.'

Nor did Chalmers' link with his students end when their course was completed. M'Cheyne was a case in point. The new parish of St Peter's, Dundee, to which he went in 1837, had come about through the exertions of John Roxburgh, who, fired by Chalmers, had gone amongst the spiritually destitute in Dundee in 1831. At the time of M'Cheyne's settlement, Chalmers himself was leading the Church Extension work of the Church of Scotland, and St Peter's was one of the 222 new churches which were provided during the seven years when he had this responsibility. By 1843, Chalmers was able to say that he could travel from one end of Scotland to the other and spend each night in the manse of one of his former pupils. And in that same momentous year—the year of the Disruption and of the formation of the Free Church—Hanna believed that 'nine-tenths' of the men whom Chalmers had taught stood with him.

* * * * *

We have already noted that in the 1820s Chalmers' hopes and prayers centred upon 'the next generation'. By 1842 he could write:

> I am quite sensible that talent is but secondary to piety – that gifts are but secondary to graces in a minister of the Gospel, and I therefore am all the more thankful that, besides being men of

---

[1] Andrew A. Bonar, *Memoir and Remains of R. M. M'Cheyne,* (London: Banner of Truth, 1966, frequently reprinted), p. 31.

power and high scholarship, very many of our young preachers are men of faith and prayer, who preside at fellowship meetings, and have been the instruments of great and promising revivals in various parts of Scotland.[1]

There is, however, one other recurring theme in Chalmers' thought that needs to be stated. It would be a travesty of Chalmers' position to give the impression that his students saw revival in their day merely because they faithfully repeated their teacher's doctrine and copied his example. More than anything else, perhaps, Chalmers insisted that nothing truly effective could be done *without the personal activity of the Holy Spirit*. He had seen enough of a moribund orthodoxy to know that it is not true that, if preachers have a correct knowledge of the truth, then the Holy Spirit's ministry can be *assumed*. Vast though the importance of sound knowledge is—for the Holy Spirit works by the truth—to view knowledge as the *same thing* as supernatural energy was a profound mistake, which had disastrous consequences for preaching. To Charles Bridges he writes in 1834:

> I deeply feel my need of effort and prayer that my whole course may be more and more spiritualized, assured as I am of the possibility of delivering all the lessons of theology in the strictest form of sound words, and with the fullest adherence to the letter of the truth as it is in Jesus, while the real unction and vitality of the Gospel spirit may be altogether wanting.

For Chalmers, theory and intellect were only the starting point. If men possessed those things alone, instead of 'talking religion', they would merely join the numbers who 'talk about religion'. There must be much personal dealing with God himself. 'Read Edwards on Prayer', he would counsel men. 'A season of revival in the Church is generally preceded by a season of prayer.'

There was much intellectual ferment in the decade before the Disruption. A healthy controversy was stirring. Church government and the spiritual independence of the Church were to claim

[1] See p. 237 below.

popular attention, but by the blessing of God the results of
Chalmers' teaching work were men who, in the first instance, were
gospel preachers, and men of, in his phrase, 'deep and decided
piety'. They were no mere imitators or supporters of a movement.
Rather they were themselves taught of God, and if their thought
was akin to that of Chalmers it was through the medium of personal experience and the teaching of the New Testament itself.

* * * * *

Chalmers' primary interest as his life drew to its end was the
same as it had been in those early years of evangelical fervour at
Kilmany. When the Disruption came, he opened his own private
house for a church in Morningside and used his hall staircase as a
pulpit. He lived to see the Free Church College, of which he was
the first Principal, open its splendid building, New College, Edinburgh, in 1846, and declared that the essential equality of human
souls would there be strenuously taught: 'In the high court and
reckoning of eternity, the soul of the poorest of natural children,
the raggedest boy that runs along the pavement, is of like estimation in the eyes of heaven with that of the greatest and the noblest
of our land.' This truth he lived out to the end. Though increas-
ingly disengaged from all the public business of the Church, he
lent his last energies to seeking to advance the gospel in one of the
poorest districts of Edinburgh, where about a dozen adults, most
of them elderly women, had commenced a witness after the Disruption, meeting in a loft. Whatever other duties necessity required
him to lay down, this one he would not abandon, and when, in
February 1847, a church with 132 communicants was opened in
the West Port, he spoke of it as 'the most joyful event of my life'.
    To the last Chalmers also maintained his primary interest in the
young men who would be the future ministers of the Church. In
March 1844, by which time the Free Church had her own divinity
school in Edinburgh, he says, 'I am obliged to teach two classes,
and the whole number of my enrolment is 209.' Declining an

invitation to attend the next General Assembly, he wrote in 1845, 'Truly it is a higher department to have to do with the understandings and consciences of my students than to wear out any more of my life in the outward business of the house of God.' When, latterly, his memory was less dependable, he still kept up his efforts to have personal contact with the many men who attended his classes. The biographer of Alexander Somerville observed: 'The personal kindness of Dr Chalmers, especially to his students, did more for Somerville and his fellows than the whole training of some professors who, however competent intellectually, fail in this.'[1]

Despite his long-held belief that a man in his sixties should give himself chiefly to preparation for heaven—for he liked to think of a parallel between the seventh decade of life and the purpose of the Sabbath rest—Chalmers was not to enjoy a period of quiet retirement. In May 1847, when he was sixty-seven, he made his last visit to England and, against 9 May, his Diary contains the entry, 'Preached with greater comfort than I had ever done before in London.' On his return to Edinburgh at the end of the month he did not seem unduly tired. Sunday, 30 May, found him at his home in Church Hill, Morningside. He did not rise as usual in the morning but when a friend observed he was unwell he denied it with the words, 'I only require a little rest.' To the same friend he proceeded to speak, with the kind of liberty more usual in the pulpit, on the election of God, the sacrifice of Christ, and the freeness of the offer of the gospel. During the morning William Cunningham called, and the two men went together to the afternoon service at the local Free Church. After tea, and a brief note to an old friend, he walked in the garden, where he was overheard by one of the family saying, 'O Father, my heavenly Father!' The same evening he addressed a friend with a question he must have often asked, 'Are you much acquainted with the Puritan divines?',

---

[1] *A Modern Apostle, A. N. Somerville*, George Smith (London: John Murray, 1891), p. 18. Chalmers' interest in his former students is also illustrated by the eager support which he gave to the *Kelso Tracts* written by Horatius Bonar.

and went on to speak of Howe's *Delighting in God*, which he was currently reading. 'Immediately after prayers he withdrew, and bidding his family remember that they must be early tomorrow, he waved his hand, saying, "A general goodnight."' The next morning he was found still in his bed, asleep in Christ.

* * * * *

Although many have written on Chalmers, the best knowledge of the man comes from reading his own words, and there is no better starting point than the volume of his correspondence, carefully put together after his death, by his son-in-law, William Hanna. It has long been unobtainable, and numbers will surely be thankful to see it in print again. The times and the religious scene are greatly changed since Chalmers' day, yet what lay at the centre of his influence remains the church's constant need, and there is here much sound wisdom from which other generations can profit.

IAIN H. MURRAY
January 2007[1]

---

[1] The above is an abridged version of 'Chalmers and the Revival of the Church', in Iain H. Murray, *A Scottish Christian Heritage* (Edinburgh: Banner of Truth, 2006) pp. 73–121.

PREFATORY NOTICE.

MANY of the following Letters were forwarded too late to secure their insertion in the proper order of their dates. The Letter, for instance, addressed to Mrs. Dunlop (p. 131) had passed through the press some weeks before that important series with which the Volume closes, and of which it should have formed a part, came into the Editor's hands. He trusts that this explanation may be accepted as an apology for any want of orderly arrangement that the Volume may present.

EDINBURGH, *May* 1853.

CONTENTS.

CONTENTS.   xxix

CORRESPONDENCE OF DR. CHALMERS.

[So great an interest has been expressed in Dr. Chalmers's Correspondence with Mr. James Anderson and Mr. Thomas Smith, that we commence this volume by completing that Correspondence. Dr. Chalmers's answers to Mr. Anderson's last letters unfortunately have not been preserved, but these letters appeared to have merit enough of their own to warrant their insertion.]

No. I.—Dr. Chalmers to Mr. James Anderson.

Kilmany Manse, 22d February 1812.

My dear Sir,—It grieves me to disappoint the hopes I had myself raised, but the truth is, that I overrated my strength when I last wrote you. I was very much fatigued on the night of my arrival, but expected to be quite fresh and active next day ; instead of which I felt myself quite powerless and exhausted, and am still in a very useless state. I am too well aware of the effects of a Sunday's exertions upon me to think, in these circumstances, of attempting Dundee on Monday at all.

I regret it the less, that I find you have every prospect of matters going on as they should do. Had I been in possession of the requisite strength, I meant to prepare myself for resisting the proposal of a Scottish Bible Society, in case it had been made by Dr. Nichol or others. Be strong, I beseech you, on this head. When I meet you I will go over the mystery of this Society at greater length. In the meantime, it may well be illustrated by the following comparison :—

A

Suppose the town of Dundee to be in want of water, and a general subscription proposed for bringing it in pipes from a good and copious spring at a distance. Each individual subscription tells for the benefit of the whole. Some inferior spring is discovered in the Seagate, which can only supply half the street, with water of less value than the former, and at a superior expense to the individuals benefited. An association in the Seagate for digging wells would not be more ridiculous than a Scottish Bible Society. It would injure the general subscription, and thereby affect the interest of the whole town. And this unlucky diversion would be found to carry along with it more expense, and less benefit, to the very promoters of it. When I say that a separate Society must produce an inferior article, I am quite correct. The power of capital multiplies beyond its own rate of increase. £20,000 a year can effect more than twenty times what £1000 a year can effect. And think of the privilege which the London Society has of working off Bibles at a University press. This explains the cheap rate at which they can afford Bibles.

There is one circumstance which should never be forgotten in the administration of your Society. You may overdo the supply of home objects,—this is the great mischief to be apprehended from the Scottish. To prove its utility, it must do something ; and to manifest its importance, it will make that something as much as possible. The peasants of Scotland purchase Bibles for themselves. This is too fine a habit to be repressed or tampered with. Our people think a Bible worthy of its price. They should be left to make the sacrifice. It endears the Bible more to them. And you may conceive the mischief that must accrue from an officious Society substituting its own bounty, and issuing Bibles from their public repository in the same business style that they would distribute soup, or shoes, or greatcoats, or breeches. The auxiliary Societies in England often detain one-half for home objects. But remember that in England the habit is yet to form. In Scotland the habit is formed already ; and to do anything which can trench upon this habit would be to do an incalculable mischief. If the man who, at this moment, depends upon himself for a Bible, and actually buys one, is led by the indiscreet administration of your funds to depend upon the Society, what becomes of that man when this dependence fails him ? He has lost the habit of purchasing for himself; and the security that Bibles shall be read, and possessed, and valued by our people, is transferred from the deeply-seated principles of their own hearts to the precarious exertions of a Society, irregular in its movements and uncertain in its duration. Send as much as possible to the London Society ; avail yourselves as little of your privilege as Auxiliary Societies as is absolutely necessary.—Yours truly,

THOMAS CHALMERS.

No. II.—MR. JAMES ANDERSON TO DR. CHALMERS.

Dundee, 11*th June* 1812.

MY DEAR SIR,—I am ashamed I have been so long in acknowledging your kindness at Kilmany, and the happiness I enjoyed under your roof. Could I maintain the impressions I there received, I would deem my Christian course rapidly progressive ; but I am here in a widely different scene—little favourable to sober thinking. My mind, distracted with the bustle and cold-heartedness of business, recurs with difficulty to the contemplations of religion ; and the want of a friend with whom I can communicate on these subjects deprives me of that excitement which is the life of every pursuit. I, however, feel myself much more decidedly attached to Christianity, and I hope, by the blessing of God, to attain the stability of a true disciple of Jesus. I every day see more and more the propriety of deriving my religion from the uncommented oracles of God, and of forming my system on the connected declarations of the New Testament. I wish to unshackle myself from the vassalage of text-books, summaries, and human systems. I wish to give the Bible a fair trial ; for if it alone is not sufficient to make a Christian, " we are of all men most miserable." I at present therefore confine myself to the perusal of the Bible, and occasionally some book of practical morality. I find many things which I do not understand—many passages indeed totally unintelligible ; but these difficulties are to be got over, not by a religious commentary, but by a classical criticism. I conceive every duty of a Christian to be comprehended in the single word, translation—a translation of the Scriptures into his own tongue, and a translation of their truths into his own heart and conduct. All we have to do is to ascertain the doctrines, and to believe them ; to ascertain the duties, and to practise them ; to make the Bible our *vade mecum*, our book of reference, our book of trust. I will rejoice, after my opinions are settled, to examine those of others ; but I think it is inverting the process to begin with the latter. My objections to the school of theological orthodoxy are three :—First, its tenets are not authoritative, and therefore may be wrong. Next, its tenets are not progressive. The New Testament gives you Christianity in its *growth ;* a system of divinity displays it at some given step of its progress, or at best at its maturity. The latter is a religion of results. It has been formed by a man who has become unconscious of the steps of his own cogitations, and who, from familiarity with demonstrative truths, now regards them as axioms. He, from the sublime height of his own conceptions, looks down with contempt on the man who complains that he has removed the ladder by which he first ascended ; and, accustomed to the wide ken of his own exalted region, wonders at those whose views rest within a narrower horizon. How different the system of the Bible ! It leads you on step by step, and accommodates its lessons to your capacity. While perusing it, one naturally fixes on the truths which are most congenial ; familiarity with these prepares us for others more remote, until we at length embrace the whole scheme of the Gospel. Thus, I may first delight to dwell on the Gospel morality ; a second perusal may show that faith is also necessary ; a third perusal may convince me that morality and faith must be united, and that it is not a union of separate acts, but of consequential duties ; and, I may finally come to the conclusion, that our salvation resolves itself into a simple and disencumbered act of acceptance. But if you at once come forward with this last proposition, you present me with a system in which I cannot sympathize, and which, however well founded, rests on what must be to me a metaphysical distinction, until I arrive at it by a process of individual experience. My third objection is, that theological orthodoxy is too stimulative. It begets a disrelish for the simple excitement of the Gospel. It urges you by such a multiplicity of motives that you become too passive for a New Testament impulse. It clothes the doctrines in so much metaphysical acumen that you consider their Gospel dress as slovenly, and it anatomizes the precepts so much, that the simple exhibition of a *text* suggests no ideas of vitality. We revel in a kind of religious epicurism, and lose all taste for sober fare.

These and similar considerations have made me resolve to study, in the meantime, only the New Testament. I may not thus so well prepare myself for classing with a particular sect ; but I will have greater security in my own principles, and in my intercourse with others I will be more ready to observe the maxim, " I have yet many things to say unto you, but you cannot bear them now."

I will soon write you again. And requesting your prayers for my progress,—I remain, my dear friend, yours,

JAMES ANDERSON.

No. III.—Mr. James Anderson to Dr. Chalmers.

Dundee, 16th July 1812.

My dear Sir,—I have expected a letter from you for two or three weeks past, but have been disappointed. I wish our correspondence could assume a more decided and regular form, and that I might be able to leave the generalities, which have hitherto occupied me, and proceed to the characteristic parts of Christianity. I must, however, once more beg of you to permit me to state the sentiments under which I peruse my Bible, for even on this point I feel perplexed, and I see it occupying so prominent a place in the systems of matured Christians as to disconcert me with regard to the very first steps of my progress.

I have resolved then to make the Bible the rule of my opinions and conduct; not so much from any deep sense of sin or consciousness of my own insufficiency, as from a conviction that the Bible is a revelation from God, and a determination to submit to that revelation whatever it may be. I have divested my mind of that repugnance to the adoption of truths which arises from their disagreement with our prior conceptions; but I do this in such a state of passivity, that I would adopt without hesitation, if I found it in the Bible, that scheme of salvation a consciousness of the insufficiency of which is believed by many Christians to be a necessary preliminary in any attempts to become a Christian. As I do not allow my prior conceptions of Divine mercy to obstruct my admission of the declaration that sinners will be condemned to everlasting punishment, so I do not permit my prior conceptions of Divine justice to facilitate my admission of the declaration that there is no salvation but in Jesus. I open the Bible to ascertain the will of God, and so conscious of my inability to judge of His counsels that I would, with perfect security, expect salvation from ceremonial observances, had the Bible declared that with these God would be satisfied. But I at the same time allow that it is possible that such a procedure may be presumptuous, and that God might have declared that He would not permit the truths of the Gospel to be even investigated until we approached them under a conviction of their necessity. Here, then, I feel embarrassed. Had I read only the New Testament, I do not think that such embarrassment would have existed; but I have found, both in books and the conversation of Christians, great stress put on this very question, and I do not know whether to refer it to their being wise above what is written, or to my own imperfect acquaintance with Scripture. There are many topics of a similar nature, concerning which I am reduced to the same state of perplexity. For example:—Lesslie, the bookseller, whom I believe to be a sincere and experienced Christian, asked me a few days ago to write an appendix to a small tract which he is reprinting. I did so; and, having given a short account of the nature and beneficent exertions of the Religious Tract Societies, I concluded with a few exhortations—among other things recommending to the reader frequent prayer to God. When I carried it to him, he (with a frankness which, in a dependent tradesman, I consider no mean proof of the sincerity of his principles) told me that he did not approve of my recommending prayer, " because," to use his own words, "prayer is sinful in the unregenerate." This opinion I heard, at the moment, with extreme disgust; but a little reflection soon convinced me that it is possible his opinion may be true, for the arguments which he used were at least plausible. Although I retain my former opinion, I have a sense of insecurity from these repeated obstacles and difficulties, and I feel a disappointment at not finding the scheme of Christianity so well defined as I expected. I would be ashamed to say it to any one else; but I confess to you, that, at this moment, I have no adequate and well-defined conceptions of the plan of salvation,

or of the economy of that intercourse which subsists betwixt a
Christian and the Godhead. I perceive that there is, if I may
so express it, much more of business in the unseen realities of
the Gospel than I formerly conceived ; and that these realities,
whatever they may be, are something as distinct from my
simple and generic notions twelve months ago, as the ideas
which a clown entertains of the atmosphere are from those of
one acquainted with its chemical analysis. What, however, the
specific peculiarities of the system are I do not yet perceive in
a clear and uniform manner ; and the diversity of opinion,
among conscientious, candid, and enlightened men on this subject, is to me the greatest of all discouragements in my progress. One recommends prayer, another says that faith must
precede prayer; and thus I am left in doubt as to the propriety
of employing such prayers as I at present am most inclined to
use. Do you conceive that this prayer, " O God ! so guide me
in the investigation of thy Gospel, that I may arrive at a distinct knowledge of that faith which is the source of acceptable
prayer,"—do you conceive that such a prayer, put up to the
Deity upon a conviction of His omniscience and omnipotence,
would be heard, although not made in the name of Christ, or
accompanied by a request for the Spirit's operation ; or would
you consider it as an address to the Unknown God ? Or, to
take another instance, do you think that the prayer of that
man would be sinful, who, upon being presented with a Bible,
and told what it professed to be, should pray to God so to
direct him in the investigation of its evidences that he might
detect its falsehood if it was untrue ? Such prayers I should
deem efficacious for the following reasons ; because belief in the
existence and superintendence of a Deity I consider to be
faith,—and, although not that faith which will secure salvation,
yet such a faith as will render a prayer for farther convictions
acceptable ; and because Jesus recommended prayer before (if we

may judge from the arrangement of the history) the scheme of saving faith was unfolded, and when His hearers were so far ignorant of His nature as to be astonished that He used a style more authoritative than the Scribes.

I have many other subjects to discuss with you ; but I will not abuse your patience at present. Of the need I have of assistance, you have ample proof in the unsettled and contradictory nature of my letters. I am still undecided in the very fundamentals of religion, and in moments of gloom I often dread I will relapse into a state of obdurate scepticism.—I am, my dear Sir, yours truly, JAMES ANDERSON.

No. IV.—MR. JAMES ANDERSON TO DR. CHALMERS.

Peterhead, 28th September 1812.

MY DEAR SIR,—I was never more anxious to be with you than since I came here, for my mind has been distracted by the most violent emotions respecting a subject intimately connected with my future happiness, and, perhaps, my eternal salvation—I mean my future profession. . . . My father expresses himself averse to my becoming a clergyman, for many reasons, which he enumerates, and adds, " that a desire to advance the cause of Christianity may be gratified by a well-intentioned and well-informed layman as effectually, and, in many cases, with more effect than by a clergyman." I endeavour to bring my mind to this simple decision—in which way shall I most promote the glory of God ? But a thousand other considerations intrude in spite of me, until at last I get bewildered in questions of personal comfort and worldly estimation. What I most dread is, that my religious progress would not be so great in the situation of a merchant as that of a clergyman ; for, were I able, amid the distractions of business, to acquire and maintain that tone of elevated Christianity, to which the pursuits of a clergyman are so favourable, I believe my exertions in the cause

would be more useful on account of the greater extent of my
means, the absence of professional obligation, and because my
influence would be exerted in a sphere to which clergymen
have little access, and which of course is little pre-occupied.
On all these points I am most desirous to have your opinion.
My father farther says, that if arrangements can be made with
the Bank of Scotland, whose servant I am at present, he is
fully inclined to give me another winter at Edinburgh. " This,"
he says, "may prove useful whatever your future destination
may be, and it will afford time for us all to consider and implore direction for our government in meeting the allotments of
Providence." This is my present situation. We return to
Dundee on the 6th or 7th of October, and I will then either
visit or write you. I have a dependence on your counsel and
friendship which Christianity alone could inspire ; and I feel
grateful to my God that He has brought us together. The
affairs of time are slowly shrinking into their due dimensions—
the realities of an eternal world are gradually expanding before
me—I begin to take refuge from the cares and the prospects of
life in the bosom of my Saviour, and to realize that period
when, through His merits, the faithful shall worship before the
throne of God for ever.

Since I came here I have read " Edwards on Necessity,"
and I have read it with rapture. I have as much confidence
in his theory as in any mathematical proposition ; and I find
that it leads at once to a thorough solution of what appeared
to me the greatest difficulties of the Bible. It is the centre
pillar of Christianity ; and if there is one subject more than
another in which I should like to have my language and conceptions modelled to strict propriety it is this. But as yet, although I see the gross absurdity of the Arminian system, my new
opinions sit uneasily upon me, and it will require some time to
assimilate them with the train of my ordinary conceptions.

What is true, however, must ultimately prove familiar. I see, by to-day's paper, that Wilberforce has refused to stand during the approaching election, and is to retire from public life. This I consider one of the most alarming features of the times. Such a man would not have quitted his post if he had not seen that his exertions were fruitless; and when worth loses its sway over public opinion, a country is near its downfal. His memory will ever be cherished; and, although Britain yield to the fate of nations, his name will emerge from the ruins of her greatness a monument to the heroism and the triumphs of Christian principle. Even at this moment he is known throughout Africa, and his name circulates in their dreary habitations as that of some mysterious being who curbs the fury of the whites.—I ever am, my dear friend, yours most truly, JAMES ANDERSON.

No. V.—MR. THOMAS SMITH TO DR. CHALMERS.

Glasgow, 13th November 1815.

DEAR SIR,—After a week's separation from you, which, to say the least, has been very tedious to me, the slight communication I can produce by writing is very acceptable. The weather, during the last week, has been very bad, and it gives me some comfort to think that only two days have elapsed since you left this, which would have answered for our walk. . . .

I have read with great interest the accounts of the Moravian Missionaries, which you were so kind as lend me. These people seem to have more religion and knowledge of their Creator than any I have ever heard of. The mild description they give of the inhuman conduct of the captain of a vessel who carried some of them 1000 miles from their place of destination, gives an example of forgiveness which, I dare say, is to be found among no other people but themselves. And surely when we read of an instance of forgiveness, so far above what we would count a prodigy of virtue, we need not be surprised to hear of the spiritual enjoyment they feel, which no doubt is the reward of their Christian conduct. From what I have met with in these journals, I see a very strong inducement to a religious life. Indeed, when I consider that it is a people now living who possess spiritual advantages, which make them superior to the pleasures of this world, I feel this inducement presented with such plainness and truth that it is calculated to make a deeper impression upon me than the most elaborate composition : showing to what extent the Christian duties might be performed, and their rewards experienced, founded on the consolations of ancient Christians.

From the consideration of the advantages these Moravians enjoy, I derive great encouragement to proceed on the good work which, I trust, is begun within me ; nor do I derive less when I recognise in each temptation, as it presents itself, a device of the powers of darkness, and know the triumph it produces to a higher order of beings, when they know that their attempts are baffled.—I remain, my dear Sir, with much esteem, yours affectionately,   THOMAS SMITH.

No. VI.—DR. CHALMERS TO MR. THOMAS SMITH.

Edinburgh, 15*th November* 1815.

MY DEAR SIR,—I read, with much affection and pleasure, your very interesting communication. I have been thinking much of you ; and I trust that the tenderness I feel will never be wounded by any woful apostasy on your part to the spirit and the practices of an alienated world. As to its grosser profligacies, it is my delight to think that you are purely and nobly superior to them ; but do all you can to strengthen your abhorrence of them. Let not the withering example of others so much as harden your feelings against the exhibition of them; for it is not enough, my dear Sir, that you keep aloof from the practice of external ungodliness, you should also cherish a most delicate recoilment of mind from the intrusion of every gross and unworthy conception, recollecting that it is to the *pure in* HEART that our kind and amiable Saviour has promised the blessedness of seeing God.

We read in the Bible of the first love—a phrase which has been much commented upon by theologians, and which is supposed to embrace all that peace, and joy, and ecstatic affections that are felt by the heart, on the first admission of confidence in a God, whom it sees through the medium of the Gospel to be a reconciled Father. I wish you every enjoyment of this kind, which consists with our present state; and many may be those sacred hours of communion with Heaven, which give you the blessed proof of experience that the way you have chosen is, indeed, a way of pleasantness, a path of peace. I have great hopes of you. I love the spirit which animates your letter. I sympathize most cordially with all your taste and admiration for those Heaven-born men who have long been the light of the world; and you will put it down to the right cause when you ascribe it to my anxious and tender regard for you that I point your attention to that part of the Bible where certain are charged with leaving their first love. Oh! do, my much loved friend, cultivate a suspicion of yourself. Keep in firm bond of dependence with the Saviour. Pray unceasingly for the progress of His work in your heart; and while you strive mightily, let it be by His grace working in you mightily. Be assured that there is a call and a significancy in the following directions :—Let him that thinketh he standeth *take heed* lest he fall. —Work out your salvation with *fear and trembling.*—Mix *trembling* with your *mirth.*—Pass the time of your sojourning here in *fear*.—Do aspire after a realizing sense of the holy and the heart-searching God. I want you not to be painfully intense in His service;—you are in earnest, and with God's blessing you will feel your way; and, I trust, you will come experimentally to know that the way of sanctification, while a way of watchful, unceasing diligence, is also a way of peace, and that in quietness and in confidence you shall have strength.

May I crave a remembrance from you in your hours of intercourse with God. Give me a part in your daily prayers as you have in mine; and let the affection, which 1 believe to be mutual and equally strong and sincere on your part as on mine, be thus kept alive, and receive its constant augmentations on this side of time, till it ripen to the love of a pure and happy eternity.

I looked into Watts' "Sermons" the other day. I was much struck with the title of one of them, " The hopeful youth falling short of Heaven." I had not time to read it, but presume it will be excellent. You cannot, my dear Sir, you cannot err on the side of caution and extreme jealousy of yourself. It is not a jealousy which will disturb you, but it will direct you to the right source of strength and influence, and to the diligent use of that strength in every matter that comes before you. I should like you to read that sermon, and to have your opinion of it. . . .

Give my kindest compliments to Miss Fortune, when you see her. I intend being at home on Saturday—come and sup with me at night, spending a precious hour with me in my study. Let me know if you can read my letters easily, for, if not, I shall make a more careful exertion afterwards. I beg you will always write me at very great length, as close as you can, and filling up the folded spaces of the last page. Tell Mrs. C. that I have not gotten her promised letter, and am disappointed. You say there have only been two walking days for a whole week in Glasgow. Every day has been fair in Edinburgh, and I have walked every day. But what to me is a still more interesting point of comparison—I have lived in a clergyman's house, and he is suffered to remain in a state of the most enviable tranquillity. None of that feasting and clamouring about attentions, and petitioning about poor, and drudgery with the work of institutions, and hard-driving at a multiplicity of secular and never-ending affairs; all of which, unless simplified and abridged, would disgust any man with a place where mere spiritual work is undervalued, and the demands of a clergyman for leisure are neither understood nor sympathized with.

Be assured of my warmest regard and unceasing prayers for you.—Yours very affectionately,   THOMAS CHALMERS.

No. VII.—DR. CHALMERS TO MR. THOMAS SMITH.

Blochairn, 21st December 1815.

MY DEAR SIR,—Lest we should miss each other to-day, it occurs to me to state to you, in reference to our conversation of yesterday, that you should not make it a capital aim to obtain clear and immediate views on the doctrine of election; and even, though my argument be not thoroughly acquiesced in, I can say, for your comfort, that however luminous my own conceptions may be to my own mind, I have repeatedly failed in my attempts to reach the conviction of others who were men of powerful understanding.

But what I am mainly in earnest about is, that you do not for a single moment slacken or suspend the practical work of sanctification on the solution of any speculative difficulty whatever. If to your faith you add the splendid list of accomplishments set before you in 2 Peter i. 5-7, you will never fall, but make your calling and election sure. You do not see that election inscribed on the records of Heaven; but you are told in plain language what is the instrument by which you make it sure to you on earth. That instrument is *diligence*, (2 Peter i. 5, 10 ;) and I trust you will never let down a diligence of which I trust to see the prints upon your character in time, and to share the rewards along with you in eternity.

See 2 Peter iii. 16. I rejoice that you are so impressed with the reality of a powerful and insidious tempter, and I would have you not to be ignorant of his devices. He may turn an anxiety after Christian doctrine into an engine for his purpose; and I beg that you will be frank enough to let me know, when you judge it for your practical benefit, that our conversation on that particular subject should be suspended.

It would furthermore give me great pleasure that you wrote me an occasional note, though you had time only for half-a-dozen lines : you should not, my dear Sir, stand upon difficulties with me, and I have to entreat a little more confidence from you in this way than I have yet witnessed.

THOMAS CHALMERS.

No. VIII.—MR. THOMAS SMITH TO DR. CHALMERS.

Glasgow, 22*d December* 1815.

MY DEAR SIR,—I read the note you gave me to-day with much interest—this, indeed, has been the case with all I have received from you—but I feel very grateful to discover in your last such a kind and anxious attention to my most substantial welfare. You have placed 'my desire to become acquainted with a particular doctrine of Christianity, in a light in which I think I should myself have viewed it, had I devoted much of my time and thoughts to the subject ; but, as the matter stands at present, I trust I am far from neglecting the very few duties I can perform in obedience to the Divine will, in the pursuit of a subject that must have the same effect on my ultimate salvation, whether I am convinced of the exact manner of its operation or not. These are my present feelings on the subject. I know well, however, that I might become so interested in the business as to attend to it in prejudice of more important duties. It is in this view that I see the importance of your warning voice, and that I beg you to lift it often, and oftener than you think there is occasion for it, because I fear very much that you have formed too high an opinion regarding my present state, both as to my religion and morals. It requires a long acquaintance to discover the exact character of any person. Ours, indeed, has been intimate; but there are circumstances which, I think, may have operated with you too favourably towards discovering the true state of mine; and I hope you may take this hint and act upon it, faithfully pointing out what you see amiss, and I in return shall make it my serious business to reform.

As to the doctrine of predestination, without much anxiety, I have obtained a view of it which most entirely satisfies myself; and I only wait for the explanation of what, I must say at present, appears to me irreconcilable, viz., that under the belief of this doctrine, and its actual operation, it is in the power of a person predestined to be saved, by any misconduct on his part to forfeit his election, or *vice versa*. This really puzzles me a little, and I look to you for assistance. I do not forget, however, that puzzle me as it may, if I act conscientiously in the discharge of my duties to God and man, and possess a firm faith on the merits of my Saviour, both to enable me to accomplish this and to save me from my deficiencies, that I have placed myself in as good a situation to deserve reward as I possibly could; and with this comfort, which I think substantial, I shall quiet my mind, and trusting in my Saviour, I shall not be troubled, though all the questions theologians ever started were brought to bear against me.

I am aware you may think this quite unphilosophical, but

B

I am happy in my ignorance, and have the authority of a sage for saying, that he that increaseth wisdom, increaseth sorrow.

My dear Sir, I must now conclude; and I am happy I can say at present what I should never have said in your presence, that I love you above all my friends on earth. Amid all the changes this world can produce, in this I trust I shall not change, and shall carry it with me to a land beyond the world's influence.   THOMAS SMITH.

No. IX.—DR. CHALMERS TO MR. THOMAS SMITH.

Blochairn, 23d December 1815.

MY DEAR SIR,—Your kind note was highly gratifying to me, and, in addition to every other argument for a frequent interchange of them, I think that one mighty advantage is, that it may reduce to a point many an agitated topic, and facilitate the precise solution of many a question which would not be set at rest by the fading and the desultory conversation of whole weeks.

Your question is, " How comes it that a man predestined to salvation has it not in his power to fall away from it ?" I answer that every man may, *if he will*, commit sin unto perdition ; but the man predestined to salvation wills not, and does not, commit any such sin. God, who decreed His salvation, decreed and foreknew all the steps that went before it. He knew the effect of every one circumstance upon His volitions ; and should the practical effect of our views on predestination be that we turn careless and fall away, then God foresaw this, and knew our final destruction from the beginning, and we shall afterwards know from the event that we are not fore-ordained unto life.

I trust that a thorough and well-grounded faith in this doctrine will at length be formed in you ; but, in the meantime, make a vigorous use of all that is clearly and distinctly understood by you. I am much pleased with your humility in thinking that I have overrated your religion and your morals; but I trust I do not overrate them when I say, that you hunger and thirst after righteousness; that measuring you by others you stand at a wide distance from all the gross and vulgar profligacies of this unhallowed generation; and while I fearlessly offer this tribute of respect to your character, will you permit me further to say, that the effect of all your doings would be hurtful did the consciousness of them go to wean you from dependence on Christ, or turn your eye from Him as all your desire and all your salvation? Go joyfully to God in His name; follow closely in the path of His example; feel your need of His Spirit in every enterprise; have no doubt of your forgiveness through the merits of His blood, coupling with faith in this one testimony, the acceptance of every one saying about the necessity of holiness and self-denial, and the mortification of all that is sinful, and the adornment of the whole man with the graces of the Spirit, and the dedication of the whole life to the will of Him who poured out His soul unto the death for you.

My heart is greatly enlarged towards you, my dearest of all earthly acquaintances; and it is my prayer that God may more and more purify, and exalt, and Christianize, that friendship which it has pleased Him to put into our bosoms.—Yours ever, THOMAS CHALMERS.

No. X.—DR. CHALMERS TO MR. THOMAS SMITH.

Blochairn, 29th December 1815.

MY DEAR SIR,—When I cannot be present with you in person, I find that it in some manner fills up the disappointment to sit down to an exercise in which I feel my heart to be altogether present with and alive about you.

I have been thinking more of your very valuable contribution to our scriptural conference of yesterday, and the use I make of it is to endear me the more to our plan, quite assured that much will result from it. Let it convince us more and more of the prodigious fertility of the Bible ; how much lies hidden and unobserved, even after many perusals ; and surely, if it be true, that a man may read it an hundred times and find something on his next reading which he missed on all his former ones, a joint-reading bids fair for multiplying our lessons, and must give a double advantage to each of them who are embarked in it.

Do, my dear Sir, feel how various and how animating a field lies before the man who has resolved on being the altogether Christian. He may look for indefinite attainments in knowledge, as well as for an ever-increasing lustre of accomplishments and of character ; and my earnest, and fervent, and often repeated prayer for you is, that sanctified wholly by the truth as it is in Jesus we may, after running our destined course as fellow-helpers on earth, mingle with the pure families of Heaven, and be found faultless together in the presence of God with exceeding glory.

My heart is greatly enlarged towards you, and I entreat that you will put up with all my warnings, and all my anxieties, and all my devoted earnestness, in behalf of your best interests. For myself, I have great need of your prayers. May they ascend often, and with affectionate earnestness, to the throne of grace. Be assured that I approve much of your prudence and reserve in the matter of your acquaintances. I trust that the conversation of yesterday will not lead to any precipitate measures on your part. And, on the other hand, that a growing experience as to the best way of walking to those who are without ; and a growing strength and intrepidity of character ; and last, though not least, a growing affection for others in the Christian and spiritual sense of the term, will at length enable you to be of use to some of those deluded, unhappy young men *love for the lost*

—each of whom, let it never be forgotten, has a soul as unperishable as ours ; and none of whom are beyond the reach of
that grace which teaches and enables us to deny ungodliness
and worldly lusts, and to live soberly, righteously, and godly in
the world.—My kindest affection to you, my very dear Sir,

THOMAS CHALMERS.

No. XI.—MR. THOMAS SMITH TO DR. CHALMERS.

Glasgow, 2d January 1816.

MY DEAR SIR,—When we are separated it is my most
agreeable employment to write to you ; and were I once fairly
embarked in the business, I know you would have occasion
rather to complain of the frequency of my letters than the want
of them.

I pursued our yesterday's topic of consideration for a part
of the day with some success, but during the greater part of
the evening I was employed in a manner contrary to the disposition in which we should be employed at the beginning of a
new period of time, and I was thus unfitted for continuing my
beneficial train of thought. At this season of the year I have
been always inclining to the desponding tone, when I think of
the small progress I have made in the different studies in which
I am engaged. But I never, till this time, felt the disappointment at the past, and anxiety for the future, in regard to my
religious improvement so strong as at present. I have, indeed,
felt something of the kind formerly, and have formed resolutions of a good tendency, but this feeling was never very strong,
of course it was not permanent ; and the resolutions, I am
ashamed to say, were formed chiefly in a dependence on myself
to execute them, and thus made, you well know, only to be broken.

It is not so with me now, I hope—my resolutions, founded
on the experience of the fate of the past, are not so extravagant
as not to admit of the probability of these being executed.

This is well; but I have learnt also from what I have already attempted, that in my own strength I cannot accomplish my desires; that the more my dependence is upon myself, the greater the certainty of my failure; and the more my hope rests on the assistance, promised me from a quarter where there is no deceit or weakness to perform, the more the certainty is of my success. It is on this foundation that I now look forward with joy to the progress of my Christian career, and firmly trust to attain that standard of obedience, and high tone of moral sentiment, with the description of which you have often delighted me.—Yours very affectionately,   THOMAS SMITH.

No. XII.—Dr. Chalmers to Mr. Thomas Smith.

Kilmardinny, 3d January 1816.

My dear Sir,—You have not yet arrived at an adequate estimate of the interest I take in you, if you think you can either write me too frequently or at too great length. . . .

You speak of uncongenial business or society in the evening, which broke up in some measure the religious frame of your mind on the preceding part of the day. Now, mark well that there will be no such interruptions in the Millennium; there are none such in a Moravian village at this moment; and there would be much fewer than there are in Glasgow had we a more extensive Christian community. The direct road to this is just to make as many Christian individuals and Christian families as we can; and in the exact proportion of our success shall we be rewarded by a freedom from all these temptations which the deadening and secularizing influence of the great majority of companies brings along with it. Let us ever keep by this object then, as our great aim and purpose of our lives here below, combining, at the same time, all that discretion and skill which are necessary in the important work. Let us pray for that most desirable wisdom, the wisdom of winning souls—not forgetting that He who says, keep thyself pure, also says, lay hands on no man *suddenly ;* and taking care, at the same time, never to convert the latter direction into a shelter for cowardice, or a plea for denying Christ before men. Oh, my dear Sir, you are right to feel your shortcomings, and it is at the same time right to strike the high aim of being perfect even as God is perfect. It is only wrong to conceive such a purpose in a dependence on ourselves—but who shall limit the power of His Spirit ? Who shall question the provisions of the Gospel for the accomplishment of its own avowed object, to redeem us from all iniquity, and to form us again after the image of Him who created us ? Do turn from the contemplation of your own worthlessness, to Him for whose sake God will cover as with a cloud all your past sins, and make no more mention of them ; and by whose power resting upon you He will enable you to wing your ascending way through the career of practical Christianity—He will send a purifying influence into all the services of the inner man—He will bless your solitude with a sense of His holy but reconciled presence—He will adorn your walk in society with all that is graceful and honourable—He will keep you in thought as well as in conduct undefiled by the sickening profligacies of this world—He will work you up to a meetness for the inheritance hereafter, and give you a foretaste of its enjoyment even here, by mingling with all your struggles, and temptations, and difficulties—the smile of an approving God—the radiance of an anticipated Heaven.—Believe me to be, my dear Sir, yours most affectionately,   THOMAS CHALMERS.

No. XIII.—MR. THOMAS SMITH TO DR. CHALMERS.

Glasgow, 3d January 1816.

MY DEAR SIR,—In my note to you of yesterday I mentioned something of my forming resolutions. I have to-day

been thinking that it is a dangerous matter to form resolutions
unless there is a pretty certain prospect of the person who forms
being able to accomplish them.   The consequence of such resolutions as are made without consideration, and soon trespassed
against, is to leave the mind impressed with the facility of
destroying its best intentions, and in a state to overleap its
most serious projects.   I wish you would say something on this
subject when you are at leisure.   Foster, in his Essay on
" Decision of Character," seems to have neglected this means of
destroying the quality he so strongly recommends.—With much
esteem and regard, I am, my dear Sir, yours, &c.,

THOMAS SMITH.

NO. XIV.—DR. CHALMERS TO MR. THOMAS SMITH.

Kilmardinny, 4th January 1816.

MY DEAR SIR,—I feel much interested in your letter of
yesterday's date, as it touches on a truly important subject—
that of resolutions. If you simply mean by a resolution a purpose, it should be your purpose at this moment to forsake all
sin and to attain all righteousness—a purpose which can only
be carried into accomplishment by prayer for the promised aid
believingly preferred, and daily persevered in.   But if, by a
resolution, you understand a purpose accompanied with a vow,
this is a matter of very great caution, and postponing the full
discussion of it to our personal interviews, I shall just observe,
in a hurried way, that there is one set of such resolutions which
it appears to me to be safe and competent for a man to make and
to adhere to, and another set which it would be extremely
hazardous.   I shall illustrate the two sets by examples:—I
could, on a deliberate view of all the effects on my moral character produced by attendance on the theatre, resolve to give
up that attendance, and keep by the resolution. I could, on my
experience of its effects upon my health, resolve never to sup

out at night, and keep by that resolution. These two cases represent a number of others where I might resolve with success, and where the kind of resolution taken might be of the utmost subserviency either to my temporal or eternal interests.

But, again, I would not resolve never to be angry. It is my wish to be delivered from this work of the flesh; but I think I shall the better bring this about by fearfulness, and watchfulness, and humble persevering prayer to God in Christ that He would root this evil thing out of me more and more.

I see symptoms of uneasiness in your letter which most powerfully interest me in the state of my dear and much-loved friend. Should the uneasiness be grounded on any failure in the first set of resolutions, which I believe not to be the case, I would construe it into the token of a declension, from which it should be my most strenuous attempt to recover you. Should it be grounded on any failure in the second set of resolutions, then this uneasiness is an essential step in the progress of a Christian. You are rising in your conceptions of the spirituality and extent of the requirements that lie upon you; and you are making purposes to fulfil them; and you are experiencing your own incompetency to the task; and God is humbling you into a closer dependence on the aids of His grace, and on the promises and provisions of His Gospel. Never let go your aspirings, but know that you must be shut up unto Christ as all your sanctification and strength, ere you shall ever succeed in realizing them. You come short of your aspirings, or, in other words, you come short of duty and contract guilt. A sense of this will lead you daily to Christ for forgiveness; and going to him on the other errand of obtaining reformation also, (1 John i. 9,) you will make constant progress in the joys of the Christian faith, and in the diligence of the Christian practice. Be

c

not restlessly or excessively anxious ; and if I have not
cleared up your difficulties, look forward to our conversations.
—Yours, &c.,   THOMAS CHALMERS.

No. XV.—MR. THOMAS SMITH TO DR. CHALMERS.

Glasgow, 5th January 1816.

MY DEAR SIR,—I am glad you have said so much of resolutions—those which I ever formed were not attended with
enough of solemnity in the making, and thus, perhaps, it is
that they have been less binding, and I have more readily
found the means of avoiding them. I never made a resolution,
or purpose, accompanied with the determination of carrying it
into effect, and at the same time sealed it with a solemn vow.
My resolutions have been made and noted in my journal ; I
have often the reading of them to remind me of them ; I have
my prayers to God to enable me to fulfil them ; and I have the
attempts which I make to resist the habits which might lead
me to forsake them ; and to all these combined, I trust for the
accomplishment of my purpose. As to the subjects of these
purposes, they are such as may be accomplished by perseverance ; and, by the attention of a few weeks, I have sometimes
found myself in a much higher state of obedience to God's will,
in so far as one particular transgression was concerned. These
kind of trials have been my employment for some time past ;
but now I have made a general determination to examine my
conduct as a whole, composed of those things I have attempted
to root out of it, and I find that examining each separately
there is a sad want in it—that I have only reached the mere
surface of the business, and in many respects have remained
satisfied and consoled that I had done as much as I could
accomplish. This has caused me uneasiness, which I am not
unwilling to suffer ; but like a person who knows his accounts
are in confusion, examines them, and finds them ten times

worse than he expected—so, though I knew the examination might be painful to me, yet the extent to which it has been, was never calculated on. And it is in this state of the case that I was induced to give way to my resolution in some degree, although its consequences might have been, and still I hope will be, more productive of good than any I ever yet made. I do not wish to exculpate myself; but since I have told of the uneasiness which the putting of this resolution into effect as a cause of my in part having relinquished it, I must also mention that a great deal of business, and an anxiety to have it finished, has operated heavily upon me, and withdrawn my mind from its more serious occupation.—Yours most sincerely,

THOMAS SMITH.

No. XVI.—MR. THOMAS SMITH TO DR. CHALMERS.

Stockwell Street, January 8th, 1816.

MY DEAR SIR,—This has been a most pleasant day with me, it brought so long a letter from you—the longest I have yet received ;* and to procure another, I shall continue to write to you, trusting in my good fortune to say something which may call forth an answer.

When I sit down to write to you, it is not anything I have previously arranged and thought of which forms the subject, but merely the idea which is uppermost at the moment. I write to you generally in the evening, when I have leisure to review the events of the past day, and it is the impression of this review which is generally communicated to you. After a quiet, retired, and pleasant Sabbath, I find its beneficial effects often during the week, but more especially on the day immediately following it. This has been my condition to-day, confirmed to me by your letter, which left me in the exact state in which I have found myself after some of our most agreeable con-

* For this letter, see Dr. Chalmers's Memoirs, vol. ii. pp. 30-34.

versations ; and I have enjoyed this under a heavy and gloomy atmosphere such as generally has a depressing effect upon my spirits. I have been successful also to-day in contracting my thoughts and bringing them to bear on the subject I chose from my chapter this morning—" If ye had faith as a grain of mustard-seed," &c. ; and when I am successful in confining my thoughts to a good scriptural text, it generally happens that all goes smoothly and successfully along with me ; and the reason of this is obvious. Should a man direct his mind to a state superior and independent of this, it places him high above all the adverse fortune which can beset him, and enables him almost to rejoice in the midst of it, while on the other hand it allows him to enjoy as much as he possibly can the success which may attend him. It will not, indeed, permit him to exult immoderately ; were it to do so, he would feel discontented when the novelty and first charm of his prosperity wore off; but when he enjoys the present happiness subordinately to a greater in store for him, then should his present joy be converted into grief, he still possesses the ulterior prospect, and where his treasure is, there—bursting through the surrounding objects—will his heart be also. This is a temporal reward which is worthy of being purchased at great expense. It is an insurance against losses of all kinds, and there is less danger of failure on the part of the guarantee than in any ever made on earth. Yet this is only a subordinate and one of the most trivial advantages afforded by the Christian religion. It is, indeed, a religion which ought to be highly venerated, and an interest in it is to be desired in preference to everything else.

There are several topics in your letter of to-day which I should like to write you about, but it would branch out into a correspondence too extensive to be carried on at present, and must therefore be declined. I anticipate with much pleasure the renewal of our personal interviews, which have appeared

to me far more valuable since I have experienced their absence.
This will be the last opportunity of my writing to you at Kilmardinny, as I understand you return on Wednesday; until
then, and thenceforth, I remain, my dear Sir, yours very
affectionately,   THOMAS SMITH.

No. XVII.—DR. CHALMERS TO MR. THOMAS SMITH.

Kilmardinny, 9th January 1816.

MY DEAR SIR,—Your letter received this day forms a most
delightful finish to this series of our correspondence. I could
have seen in it the happy Christian frame of the writer, though
he had not announced it to me. In point of expression it is
free and powerful; in point of spirit it breathes a most serene
and tranquil elevation. I am charmed with the growing intelligence it discovers on the highest of all subjects; and, above
all, do I inwardly rejoice in observing that my excellent young
friend is realizing the peace and the pleasantness which are
to be found even here on that way which leads to the felicities
and the glories of Paradise.

Will you believe that, for the last 24 hours, I have been the
victim of a most distempered melancholy, and that you have
been the subject of it? I hesitated for some time whether I
should reveal this to you, on grounds which I shall afterwards
mention; but I have now resolved on the clear and simple
maxim of keeping back from you *nothing;* and I do find that
we have got greatly too far on in our intimacy to stop short of
the most entire, unbounded, and universal confidence in each
other. The ground of my disquietude was an expression in
your note of the 5th, probably ill understood by me, and which
I shall explain more fully to you at meeting. All I shall say
further about it at present is, that your note, received this
evening, has chased from my agitated bosom all its fears and
all its anxieties; and it is with tears of gratitude and delight

that I acknowledge how much I have been reassured and comforted by your kind communication.

My dear Sir, you may think all this extravagant, but it can be accounted for. You are in one sense the child of my anxious efforts to consolidate and Christianize you. I have not the vanity to think that I began the work; but the work has made progress since I knew you, and I have conceived a deep interest in all its steps. I do not know one single dispensation that would more imbitter my heart than that the work should retrograde. I would feel all the grief of a bereaved parent—it would spread a sad desolation over my spirits—it would be the cruellest of all violence to my affections for one, whom I trust I shall long hold sweet counsel with on earth, and rejoice with in Heaven. Such is the state of my feelings towards you; and I hope that it both explains and apologizes for my extreme watchfulness over you—a watchfulness which, I have sometimes feared, you would dislike as obtrusive, and suspicious, and troublesome. O, my dearest of all earthly associates, had the happiness of our friendship been without alloy, it would have been too much for earth; but the malignant tempter, whose power you so firmly recognise, has thrown a mixture of bitterness into it—he has tried to turn the whole to anguish by raising before my fancy the glowing image of your apostasy. Your kind epistle has cleared it away, and I now enjoy a precious interval of repose. All is hushed and tranquillized within me—and I now write from the fulness of a heart which feels no fear and harbours no suspicion.—Yours ever,

THOMAS CHALMERS.

No. XVIII.—MR. THOMAS SMITH TO DR. CHALMERS.

Glasgow, 9th January 1816.

MY DEAR SIR,—I received your letter of yesterday's date, and though I expect to meet you to-morrow, I shall take this method of answering a question proposed in it, which I see has arisen from a most stupid confused note of mine of the 5th current.

I made a general determination at the beginning of this year, strictly to examine the state of my mind. I did so—found it so far below my expectation, that it affected my spirits so much as to make me give up the examination, and thus to transgress my determination or resolution. This, as far as I can make out, is what my note of the 5th would say, but seems ashamed, as no doubt there is reason to be, of the avowal.

You may be thinking that I shall thus be diverted from my attempt. But this is not the case, for I have since resumed my review, and am at present going on successfully with it.

What I would desire at present is to know, what are the errors which I am most liable to fall into, and to apply myself to the business of their extermination one by one. When this is accomplished, I shall cultivate the virtues which ought to exist in their stead, and the bringing these virtues to perfection will form the business of a whole life, and at its close, though the comfort of having succeeded in the attempt will not be enjoyed, yet the consolation of having seriously made the trial will supply its stead. There is nothing I so much delight in, as in the idea of a character refined and ennobled by a whole life's attention to the business. Such a character would, in all probability, enjoy more happiness and peace of mind than any attainments in science could afford. It is a discouraging fact, however, that there is not one in thousands who can boast such a treasure—the road to it is exceedingly unfavourable to those who have only for a short time travelled on it, and to people surrounded by others of different opinions about the reward to be attained, or who pursue a quite contrary course, the temptations to deviate are innumerable. Man, by his own strength, cannot conquer them ; but by dependence on another's, he undoubtedly can, and may realize a finer and purer mind than the ancients ever thought of. From the knowledge of Cowper, which his life and writings give, I think he had attained this character; but it is not in a man who is well known to the public, and whose writings are made with the view of pleasing them—nor in any public character, whose life is handed down to us—that I would be inclined to expect these virtues;—but rather in private characters, who are only known to a few around them, and by whose example the world in general are never benefited.

But, my dear Sir, I must earnestly beg of you to excuse all the deficiencies of my last week's correspondence. Most of my letters were written in the evening when I was very tired, and all of them hurriedly. It was with a view to obtain answers in return, and in compliance to your request, that they were sent to you. Amid all my faults, I shall always be yours most affectionately,　　　　　　　　　　　　THOMAS SMITH.

No. XIX.—MR. THOMAS SMITH TO DR. CHALMERS.

Glasgow, 20th January 1816.

MY DEAR SIR,—I do not intend in this letter to say anything either on one side or the other regarding assemblies for dancing—the subject of our late conversations. I think it better that you should begin the subject, and that I attend you as you prosecute it, and unreservedly give you any objections which may remain with me after the perusal of your letters. And of this freedom of remark, I request you will allow me the unlimited use; for should I be only half-convinced of the danger of attending these parties, if it turns out they are dangerous, it might be a matter of afterthought and deliberation whether the restriction had been properly adopted: and on a tempting invitation being presented, more reasons might appear in favour of the restrictions being injudicious. Thus swayed, I might overturn all my more impartial thoughts on the subject, and commence imperceptibly the business of undermining a proper system of self-denial, which I intend shall be considerately and judiciously planned, and as resolutely and perseveringly adhered to. A few days ago we talked of the frankness which ought to subsist among friends ; and I think you were disposed to blame me for a want of it. If I possess a reserved temper, I am equally insensible of it, as of many of my other faults ; and in our written correspondence, I hope you will soon perceive that all reserve is banished, and that you receive my sentiments upon any subject which comes in our way exactly as they exist, and to the whole extent of their existence. I sometimes am disposed to be very silent in our conversations, and this most probably has given the appearance of reserve to my conduct ; but this silence is of a very different origin indeed, and I blame you for its existence.

Our regular weekly correspondence, I think, will be productive of much advantage. One thing has just now occurred to me, which well demonstrates this :—Should I, when in some unguarded time, be induced to think favourably of any amusement which we have in a proper season examined and condemned—from the mere circumstance of having your reasons stated in writing to recur to, I shall examine what formerly caused me to renounce the favourite object, and the result of the examination will be to set me right and establish me in the path chalked out.—I am, my dear Sir, yours with much affection, THOMAS SMITH.

No. XX.—DR. CHALMERS TO MR. THOMAS SMITH.

20th January 1816.

MY DEAR SIR,—In answer to your much esteemed note of this day, I have to observe, that I do not mean at present to enter into the question of Assemblies for dancing, but shall satisfy myself with a few prefatory remarks. I am quite assured that if you saw it to be against your Christian interest, you would surrender every one inducement you have at present to attend them, and keep studiously and determinedly away from them altogether. I am further assured that could I prove it to be as much your duty to keep away from them, did they expose these interests to the *hazard*, though not to the *certainty* of being injured, you would be as obedient to the second demonstration of duty as to the first.

In a word, I presume (and it is with the most unfeigned pleasure, and a heart filled with affection, that I can declare from all that I have observed in you, how I look on the presumption as one of the surest and strongest I ever conceived on any subject) that should you see it to be your duty, either on the first ground or on the second, to refrain from going to Assemblies, you would not hesitate a single moment to put the principle of forsaking all into effect, and bring your habit of general carefulness to offend in no point whatever to bear on this one point which we have now selected for consideration.

And now, my dear Sir, there is even at this stage of the business a way in which this great initiatory principle of the Christian life may be put into exercise. As you would forsake all in the way of shunning what you knew to be sinful, so you may be in readiness to forsake all whenever what is more doubtful shall be proved to be sinful. In this state of readiness, which it is competent for you at this moment to put on, you will, I am persuaded, resolve against, and strive against, and pray against all partiality and all hypocrisy, it will be the language of your heart—" Lord, teach me thy way that I may walk in it." Cleanse Thou me from the secret fault of all unfair leaning, and all wilful self-deceit. Let me clearly see thy will and hear thy voice ; and here I am in the attitude of a servant to obey thy orders, and be found at the post thou art pleased to assign to me.—It is my business also to be most careful in this matter : wo be unto me if I wilfully mislead you. It is my prayer, my dearest of all earthly friends, that much comfort and direction may be given to us in this correspondence. It may strike out much of what we are not at present anticipating. It may branch into many a devious but important track of inquiry ; and I trust that, walking together as friends over the field of Divine truth, we shall end our every excursion with some new spoils of heavenly doctrine to enrich, and comfort, and adorn us. May God prosper us in this enterprise ; may He smile propitious on our every attempt to find out His will for our salvation ; and may the great and ultimate results of all our converse here be a common mansion in that country of perfect blessedness, where there is no sorrow and no separation.—Yours most affectionately, THOMAS CHALMERS.

No. XXI.—MR. THOMAS SMITH TO DR. CHALMERS.

Glasgow, 23d *January* 1816.

MY DEAR SIR,—I shall still delay entering upon anything which immediately concerns the question of the effect of a dancing assembly upon a Christian character.

In your note, you mention you are quite assured that if I saw it to be against my Christian interests I would not go ; and even go so far as to say, that were they to place these interests even in a hazardous situation, I would be obedient to this second call of duty. This is saying a good deal, and to acquiesce complacently in it, would be going farther, than from the limited knowledge I have of the true state of my mind, would be allowable.

To bring my mind to this subject, totally free of any bias to the one side or other, it would require some little time to consider the value of the recompense, which I place at stake, by acting in such a way as my long-established feelings on the subject would induce me. Surrounded by all the amusements and gaieties of life, I have considered them more in relation to the delight they afforded, than their consistency with the laws of Heaven and my own permanent happiness. But though surrounded on every side by a God and the objects of His creation, I had almost forgotten the Mighty Being from whose presence there is no escaping ; and the objects of His creation, long looked upon merely in reference to themselves, have failed to suggest the remembrance of their invisible Creator. In such a situation and circumstances, I cannot bring my judgment to an impartial determination on the subject. But this need not prevent a determination being adopted, which, if it is a just one, must lean to the side against which my prejudices have hitherto been directed. I see the necessity of this ; and, perhaps, were I to act prudently, I would renounce the whole business from this moment. This would be right in the meantime ; but the great obstacle to this, which I think, however, much to be dreaded, should always be kept in view, is, the danger of a relapse into such a frame of mind as may dispose the person who made his resolutions of doing good, to reject the grounds on which they are founded. It is of great importance, in this event, that these grounds be multiplied and embraced into a general and comprehensive rule of action. And that however trivial any objection may be considered at present, it is of consequence that they should all be brought forward—that there may be no lurking seed of corruption which may spring up in the hour of temptation.

In the course of our correspondence upon this subject, whenever you discover in me an inordinate desire to question anything you advance, I beg you will look upon it as arising from the reasons I have above alluded to. From these reasons, I really believe, that any objections which I shall make will arise, and not from a desire to mix in any company, dangerous to the principles which I am so desirous, for the most weighty reasons, to encourage the growth of, and to preserve them in a state of increasing strength and beauty, till death shall deprive the mind in which they exist of its earthly habitation.

My dear Sir, in this matter we have entered upon, there is much reason to pray to Him whose honour it concerns, that He would give us a distinct view of the case, that the judgment we form may be such as we shall have cause never to be ashamed of.—I remain, my dear Sir, yours very sincerely,

THOMAS SMITH.

No. XXII.—Dr. CHALMERS to Mr. THOMAS SMITH.

Charlotte Street, 24th January 1816.

MY DEAREST SIR,—I would hurry at once into the subject did I not feel that our system of correspondence admitted of that free and excursive method which can stop, and deviate, and be arrested by any one point that happens to be started in the course, either of our writing or our talking communications ; and you will not, I trust, feel impatient, though I should still be lingering among the preliminaries of our argument. May God keep you in health, and prolong our stay here, if it so please Him, that our notes may swell out to thousands and thousands more ; and praying, as I do, that He may give each of us a single eye to His glory, and fill our understandings with the light of His blessed Spirit. I trust that much interesting matter, and much consoling and edifying remark, may pass through each of our hands. You tell me it is saying a good deal to say that you would not wilfully do a thing which put your religious interests to hazard.—It were surely not saying too much of a man, whose ruling principle it was to keep entire the property of his word, to say of him that he would not wilfully put that property to hazard. It is not saying too much of a mother, whose honest anxiety is for the health of her child, to say that she would not wilfully put that health to any hazard. It is not saying too much for your friend, whose earnest aspiring is after the purity and integrity of your religious character, to say that he would not wilfully put you into a situation which hazarded that character. And if for your friend you just substitute yourself, be it your earnest aspiring to keep entire and to advance the reign of Christian principle within you, then I say, what is not less evident than in the three first examples, that you would not wilfully put to hazard your Christian interests.

I suspect, my dear Sir, when you hesitate about pronouncing on yourself in this matter, you complicate the matter by the doubtfulness which still exists in you about the particular question that is betwixt us. But, conceive that doubtfulness done away—conceive it clearly made out, that the act of spending some hours at an Assembly for dancing, carried along with it the chance of one to two, or one to ten, or one to a hundred, that you come away a worse man, and a worse Christian, than you went—then I mistake my dear friend altogether, if I conceive that upon such a hazard being attached to such a big and momentous interest, he would not resolve to shun the temptation altogether, and class this enjoyment among the *all things* which, in the act of taking to the path of his eternal interests, a disciple of Jesus is bound to forsake.

I do not look on this note as lost to the question. I mean to sift it thoroughly, and am sure that it will open up some deeply interesting traits of Christian speculation. But still it will be the power, not so much of argument as of simple principle acting on a single, and affectionate, and impressed heart, that will carry the question to its practical conclusion. It is the darkness of our depraved wills, and of our entangled affections, that makes it so difficult to pull down the strongholds of obstinacy within us. I speak of the general nature of man—for of you I have nothing to say but all that is kind, and tender, and respectful ; and I have to crave of you, my dearest Sir, that you will look again at this matter, and tell me whether you *ought* to run your Christianity in the way of a clearly made out hazard; and if you say you ought not, would you wilfully, and knowingly, and by a self-originating and deliberative step, do that which you ought not to do ?

I hope I shall be able to advance some way into the argument next week—but much is to be done for a clear outset—and, in the meantime, I am highly gratified by the conclusion of your much valued and most interesting note. Oh, that we were more in the habit of carrying all our doubts, and of committing all our ways, and of subordinating all our wishes to that Father who is in Heaven, and whose yoke is easy—not because He permits any relaxation, which is merely of an earthly nature; but because He gives a peace which passeth understanding, and sheds an animating glory over the whole life of him who is devoted to the will of God in all His works and in all His ways. —Yours with the utmost regard,   THOMAS CHALMERS.

No. XXIII.—DR. CHALMERS TO MR. THOMAS SMITH.

Charlotte Street, 28*th January* 1816.

MY DEAR SIR,—I know well that it is a less trial of delicacy to talk on religious opinions than to talk on religious feelings—and the same is true of writing. I have not heard whether my last Sabbath attempt was approved of by my dearest friend ;* but I shall make a second similar attempt this evening, and shall only add at present, that though I should not be surprised at your not answering me in kind, yet I would be highly pleased if you did so answer me ; and I trust that the day is coming when not one barrier shall stand in the way of that full com-

* See Dr. Chalmers's Memoirs, vol. ii. pp. 34, 35.

munion of soul, which I long to be more and more established betwixt us in what remains of our earthly intercourse.

My prayer, then, for you in particular, is, that your health may be firmly restored—that you may, for many years, see much of the goodness of the Lord in the land of the living— that you may get as much prosperity as you will feel inclined to employ to the entire honour of Him who gives it—and may meet with as much adversity as is necessary to refine and exalt your affections away from the vanities of a treacherous world. I pray particularly that God might purge away from your bosom every one reservation you might be disposed to make upon the integrity of His right to all your substance, and to all your services—that not one taint of that conformity to the world, which He bids you abstain from, might remain upon your character— that, with a noble consistency of principle, you might be enabled to make one entire surrender of all you have, and all you are, to His entire claim of authority over you—that all that friendship of the world, which is enmity against God, may be renounced by you as a fair but ruinous temptation—and all that love of the world, which is opposite to the love of the Father, may be extirpated in its very least degrees and remainders from your soul.

And while I thus pray, with all the fervency of a most longing and affectionate regard for you, that you may never, never be brought under the power of those entanglements which would make the latter end worse than the beginning, it would be to me a high matter of gratitude to God, that He speedily accomplished upon you the promise of all that peace, and all that pleasantness, and all that respect and acknowledgment even from those who at first were gainsayers, which are generally found to succeed the first victories of the aspiring Christian, over the trials which thicken around him at the outset of his career.

My prayer extends from yourself to your relations—all of whom I love. May God prolong the life of your brother, and bear up the weight of your father's old age.—May Miss Smith be a distinguished ornament to her family ; and may all the graces of the Spirit form upon her into one lovely assemblage.

In reference to the tenderness which I feel for you, and which it delights me to think is not without a kind return of good-will on your part, I pray that God would subordinate the whole of this unlooked-for intimacy to His own will and His own glory. May He root out all that is idolatrous— all that would occupy His own place in our heart—all that would offer to depose duty from its lawful demand on our time, on our attention, on our talent. May He enable me, in particular, to introduce a little more self-government into this affection, that it might not run away with me—that it might not distress me by vain and needless anxieties—that it might not make me too obtrusive of my own will, or my own way, or him who is the object of it—that I might be preserved from saying anything which may make my brother to offend—that I may, at all times, be enabled to acquit myself with wisdom—and that, as you occupy by far the highest place in the scale of my earthly friendship, the union might be perfected in Heaven, and we be found faultless in the presence of God and before the throne of His glory.—My dear Sir, yours most affectionately,

THOMAS CHALMERS.

No. XXIV.—MR. THOMAS SMITH TO DR. CHALMERS.

Glasgow, 31st January 1816.

MY DEAR SIR,—Your letter goes upon a wrong track when it supposes me to have said in mine, that were the propriety of dancing Assemblies doubtful, I would hesitate about relinquishing all thoughts of attending them. I merely meant you to understand that I might be so influenced by allurements to go

D

to them, that their true hurtful effects upon the character might be obscured, and that thus misled I could go to the Assemblies, though the effect might be dangerous. My intention in saying this was to put you in fair possession of the knowledge that those allurements did exist, and that you might be enabled to write more to the purpose by guarding me against any influence of this kind. And I feel no hesitation in saying, that I shall not go to these companies if I am persuaded there is anything of even a doubtful appearance about their propriety.

At this moment, I am neither more nor less decided on this subject than when it was first started. I am placed, in one respect, in a better situation than I was then. I have undertaken carefully to examine the different grounds of the reasons why I either should go or not, as they concern a Christian life, and by the result of this examination I am resolved to be guided.

The difficult matter appears to be how to judge of the merits of the case. Many go to these Assemblies who possess the best characters, and rank among the most religious in town ; and many do not go to them from reason of their hurtful influence upon the character, and this latter class are at least as far advanced in Christian attainments as the former. If we are to form an opinion of the propriety of these parties from the attendance or absence of the people accounted religious around us, I think it would just land us in the doubtful point. This is what I most anxiously wish to avoid ; and for other reasons it would certainly be much better that this, and any other question of the same kind, was decided on other principles than the example of the world. Its customs and morals vary with every generation ; and if we consider that though we are blinded by the example of others to do good or evil, yet we shall be judged and receive our sentence according to the true nature of our actions, whether done in concert with our neighbours or not, we shall find no great reason to rest satisfied with our conduct merely because that of others is the same.—Yours with much affection,   THOMAS SMITH.

No. XXV.—Dr. CHALMERS TO MR. THOMAS SMITH.

Charlotte Street, 6th February 1816.

the danger of worldly amusements

* *

good arguments

MY VERY DEAR SIR,—You may think it strange that previous to discussing the effects of dancing Assemblies on your own mind, I should resort, as my first argument against them, to the pernicious effect of your example on the minds of others. I do it for a reason which will afterwards evolve itself; and I come direct to the assertion, that within the limits of such a room, the ears of the young are exposed to improper conversation; opportunities are afforded them of beginning and of perfecting improper intimacies; occasions of sin are multiplied; actual parties may be formed for the commission of wickedness; and whether the young, in whose behalf I am anxious to perpetuate the preventive system, be actually drawn into such parties or not, at all events their delicate abhorrence of evil is blunted, and the safeguard of that natural and instinctive repugnance which forms the defence of youth, and which, to my eye, constitutes its finest and its loveliest ornament, is enfeebled by the rudeness of such an exposure. Now, my dear Sir, it is possible for a family party to keep all its members together; but why go to a place where a vigilant and fearful anxiety of this kind is necessary? But, in point of fact, this vigilance is not kept. Young men of decent families are at liberty to expatiate over the whole surface of the room that contains them, and I aver it on what I have learned both from yourself and others, that this liberty cannot be taken without such exposures as serve to harden and familiarize them with what is gross; or, in other words, they are in a far more direct way, by being at an Assembly, to corruption, both of

principle and of practice, than if at home they were surrounded
with the salutary influence of affectionate parents and delicate
sisters, and sober family habits, and religious converse, mixed
up with the judicious tempering of cheerful society, by intercourse among congenial neighbours, a varied and improving
reading, or the vigorous prosecution of some great acquirement
in knowledge, or anything else that can make home agreeable,
and harmonizes with the virtue and the sober-mindedness of a
character still untainted by the profligacies of a world lying in
wickedness.

Now, it is not enough that you say, I would never leave
my party ; I would never go among the half-intoxicated acquaintances I have at the other end of the room ; or even if I
did, I would not be influenced by any example of theirs.
What you would not suffer from all this others would, and you,
by your presence, have sanctioned an avenue of intercourse
between the corrupt and the untainted—have levelled one barrier of defence between the purity of domestic and the danger
of general society—have multiplied the points of contact between the younger and the older in wickedness—and have
contributed your share to the general amount of that mischief
which results from the letting in of a worldly influence on
minds not yet trained to the darkness and deceitfulness of the
world's ways.   More of this in my next.—Yours most affectionately,   THOMAS CHALMERS.

No. XXVI.—MR. THOMAS SMITH TO DR. CHALMERS.

Stockwell Street, 8th February 1816.

MY DEAR SIR,—Your note has afforded me great satisfaction.
I think it has begun a revolution in my sentiments of the consequences which arise from attending Assemblies.

All along I have considered the propriety of my attending
them almost exclusively as it was calculated to affect myself,

and I have paid very little attention to the effect my attendance might have upon others. Your note has opened a new field of objections, arising from this quarter, and I see that they are to have more effect upon my ultimate decision upon this subject than anything which has yet been brought forward. I do not mean to say, that what produces a baneful effect upon the minds of others will not also produce the same upon mine ; but I do not recollect of being thus affected at any amusement of the kind which I have engaged in, nor do I see their improprieties in so strong a light as you have done. I know that such improprieties, and great exposures to depart from every delicate feeling, do exist in an assembly, and which, if not strictly guarded against, may produce the worst consequences to those who expose themselves to its influence. These, I trust, I should be enabled to overcome, but they are such as I would be afraid to expose any person for whom I had a regard to the danger of encountering.

This, I think, ought to decide the question, (whether there is ground to believe that these Assemblies would have a bad effect upon myself or not,) that I perceive there lies danger in them to others who might be influenced to go from my example. Knowing this, were I to go, it would surely evince the most direct disobedience to one of the most generous feelings of the heart—love to our neighbour. Were I to appear at an assembly with the feeling that I myself was safe from its poisonous influence, and knew how to guard myself, and therefore had nothing to do with those around me, it would then be time to fear that all Christian infiuence had departed from me. I should then have reason to believe that my avidity to gratify a taste for worldly amusements had so blinded me to all perception of the dangers resulting from them, that I was gradually indulging myself to an extent from which I could not recover. I would not at any time have gone to any place had such a prospect of its consequences been set before me ; and it is only from considering deliberately any doubtful step that we can arrive at the right conclusion how to proceed. I consider it a fortunate circumstance that this subject was started ; it is dreadful to think that indulgence in this single amusement might have been the origin of sins which would lead to utter condemnation, and that in this uncommon manner I have been diverted from it.—I am, my dear Sir, yours very affectionately,

THOMAS SMITH.

No. XXVII.—DR. CHALMERS TO MR. THOMAS SMITH.

Charlotte Street, 16*th February* 1816.

MY VERY DEAR SIR,—I will not disguise the satisfaction I felt on receiving the information conveyed by your note,—a satisfaction which you have kindly cleared of every alloy by your subsequent assurance that the resolution stated is the unmingled effect of conviction, and that so far from having been led to it by a respect for human authority, the suspicion of such an influence had suspended and kept back your resolution longer than it would otherwise have been. And in return for this most gratifying intimation, I have to assure you that the joy with which I rejoice over the friend of my bosom is not founded on the mere act of his abstaining from Assemblies, but on the evidence which this act affords of a mind fearlessly resolved to take the line of principle, and to follow wherever conscience and revelation shall lead the way.

Your intimation leaves me at entire liberty, in taking up the subject of example, to announce my sentiments not more strongly than I would have done—for sorry should I be did even a respect for your feelings influence me to the suppression of truth—but more strongly than I would have been inclined to do. The delightful spirit which breathes through your last note saves all my delicacy on this point ; and let me express myself as strongly as I may, I rejoice to find that I speak in full harmony with the sentences which have already flowed from your pen.

Suppose, then, a man anxious for his own Christianity to go to an Assembly ; to be aware of the exposures which were to be met within the four corners of the room where it was held ; to wrap himself up in all the defences of that caution and vigilance which are prescribed to him ; to keep studiously aloof from every questionable association ; nay, so far to command his spirit as to put it into trains of pious contemplation, and after having acted his part so nobly and so well, to retire with all the triumph of conscious satisfaction, because his conduct had sustained no injury, and his principles had suffered no pollution. Combine all this gratification at the safety of self with an inconsiderateness and unconcern about the others who had not acted their part as he did, and who have therefore suffered more by their attendance than they would have done had they kept within the inclosure of the family mansion ; and with all the semblance of a Christian does this man exhibit the very essence of selfishness—not confining a trifle to himself which he withholds from others, but satisfied that he alone, of all the people there who have the capacities of an immortal duration as well as he, should bear away his chance for immortality as good and as entire as he brought it, and making it no subject of care or of concern at all, though the people with whom he is surrounded should, by the history of that evening, have made themselves more the children of hell than before, should have drunk in more of the poisonous spirit of the world, should have strengthened the barrier which lies across the path of their return to God, and thrown themselves at a wider distance from the offers of pardon and the calls of repentance than ever. This is not considered by many, but I tremble to think of the awful responsibility which inconsidera-

tion brings along with it. The people who did not consider
were the people whom God pours an exclamation on, and de-
nounces anger against—" Ah! sinful nation"—and note the
clause—" children that are corrupters." These corrupters did
not consider. They did not think of the mischief they were
doing. They felt not the awful weight of criminality and of
condemnation they were bringing upon themselves; but they
did not escape for all this ; and let it never be forgotten that the
frequenters of Assemblies are just such inconsiderate corrupters,
and that their power of corruption is just so much the greater
as their character and credit stand before the world for the
degree of Christianity they have attained. The more an example is looked up to, the more responsible is he who shews it
for every flaw and every deficiency which may be found in it.*
—I am, my dearest Sir, yours with much affection,

THOMAS CHALMERS.

[*Free Church Manse, Hawick, 20th April* 1849.—DEAR SIR,—I beg to
enclose for your inspection a series of letters addressed by our venerated
friend, Dr. Chalmers, to different members of the family with whom he
lodged in Hawick, about the commencement of his ministry, or during the
short period when he officiated as assistant in the neighbouring parish of
Cavers. It is singularly interesting to observe the strong and enduring
grasp which his warm heart had taken of a family who had shewn some
kindness to him in the days of his youth, but who, while moving, comparatively, in circumstances of humble life, were not remarkable for any of
the high mental endowments by which he was himself so eminently distinguished. When his vast mind was most thoroughly engrossed with the
magnificent schemes which are likely to tell on the wellbeing of many
coming generations, he seems never to have lost sight of them. And even
at the period of the Disruption, when great principles were struggling for
the ascendency, and the burden and responsibility of every onward movement were resting almost exclusively upon himself, we find him, like his

---

* This correspondence was interrupted by that illness of Mr. Smith which ended
in his death. See Memoirs, vol. ii. pp. 37-61.

Divine Master at Bethany in the days of old, turning aside from all matters of public and most engrossing concern, that he might sympathize with them in their afflictions, and send to them those brief but precious communications, which fell like the balm of the sweetest consolation over their sorrowing hearts. In this respect alone, these letters are valuable memorials of our venerated father; and if there be few men in the history of this fallen world who have held a larger place than himself in the affections of his brethren of mankind, it is perhaps so far to be accounted for by the fact, that the lovingkindness of his own nature was so childlike in its simplicity, and so active and untiring in all its manifestations, that it seemed scarce possible for the most callous heart to resist it.

These letters, moreover, are possessed of additional interest, inasmuch as they embody in themselves incontestable evidences of the great moral change which, under the teaching of the Divine Spirit, he was made personally to undergo. In the earliest of these communications, there are beautiful traces of the native kindliness of his disposition. At the same time there is nothing to indicate that the love of Christ was constraining him, or that he sought for principles of action, or for elements of enjoyment elsewhere than within the dark and cloudy horizon of this brief and mortal life. But ere long the light breaks upon him. The great realities of the eternal world are brought vividly before him. The wellbeing of the never-dying soul becomes the one thing that is needful. And the correspondence which commences almost, if not altogether, in the spirit of a man who was living without God and without Christ in the world, exhibits him, as it advances, rising step by step in the scale of Christian attainment till it closes at last with the clearest and most impressive discoveries of the unsearchable riches of the Saviour's grace.—Believe me to be, dear Sir, yours very truly, J. A. WALLACE.

Rev. Dr. Hanna.]

No. XXVIII.

St. Andrews, 12th October 1802.

DEAR MRS. KEDIE,*—The bearer of this is Mr. Carstairs, who means, if convenient, to live in your house about a month, or perhaps more. I have been endeavouring to prevail on him to remain till Christmas, at which time I propose being in Hawick myself. You know there was one fault I used to charge you with—too great an anxiety about giving satisfaction. I can

* See Dr. Chalmers's Memoirs, vol. i. p. 58.

assure you, in the case of Mr. Carstairs, such an anxiety is altogether unnecessary.

I will thank you to send one of your daughters to Mr. Armstrong, bookseller, and inquire for a book entitled, "The Economy of Human Life." I intend it for them, and they will find it well worth their attentive perusal. You will deliver them the enclosed sheets,* which they can read over at their leisure. There is one foolish idea which is apt to get into the minds of young people, and which often renders one's instructions less effectual than they would otherwise be, and that is, they sometimes imagine, when you give them advice, it is because you suspect they are worse than others, and therefore require it. With regard to your children, I give them advice, not because I think them worse than others, but really because they are better than others, and I am anxious they should remain so.

We have had much stormy weather here of late. A sloop belonging to my father has been wrecked lately on the west coast of Scotland, and totally lost. She had thirteen passengers, and among the rest, an officer and his lady. All the lives, however, were saved by means of the boat.

By some mistake I received the letter you sent me along with the clothes only a few days ago. I got quite free of my sore throat a few days after leaving Hawick, and have continued so ever since.—With best compliments to your husband, I am, yours sincerely,   THOMAS CHALMERS.

No. XXIX.

Anstruther, 11th *October* 1802.

MY DEAR GIRLS,—You must not suppose from my long silence that I have given over thinking of you. I can assure you there is nothing in which I take greater pleasure than in young people who I have reason to believe are well disposed, and are

---

* The letter marked No. xxix.

careful to preserve themselves from the dangers and temptations of bad company. I hope, on the other hand, that you have not forgotten the many advices I gave you about the necessity of attending to your conduct, and the snares to which the young and thoughtless are exposed. I hope you have not forgotten the solemn promises you both made me, that you would keep yourselves free of all vicious and improper acquaintances. I beg you would both seriously reflect on the awful effects of being led astray by wicked example. What an affliction it would be to your parents in their old age if you disgraced yourselves by folly and misconduct! You would be despised by all who know you; you would live a life of dishonour, and die tormented by the horrors of a guilty conscience. I tremble to think that all this is possible, and must therefore earnestly request you to lay to heart the importance of a sober, and decent, and virtuous life.

You will receive the following advices, not as if I suspected that you are worse than others, and therefore had more need of them. I hope and believe that you are both sincerely resolved to conduct yourselves through life in a manner that is praiseworthy and respectable. But you are young and ignorant of the world—ignorant of its arts and temptations—ignorant of the deceitful villany that abounds in it—ignorant of the dangers which beset the young before they reach the years of reflection and experience. You are therefore unqualified to direct yourselves aright without the assistance of those who are more advanced in life, and who are at the same time sincerely attached to your interests. When I think of you, I cannot help feeling all the anxiety of an affectionate friendship, and beg you would read the following advices with a real disposition to be made wiser and better by them.

You must guard against all temptations to falsehood and deceit. You must scorn the meanness of falsehood, and never

suffer any consideration of fear or interest to deter you from
speaking what you know to be the truth. You must be particularly careful in the choice of your company. Never take
up with those whose conversation is profane, or impure, or corrupting. It is highly proper that you should have companions ;
but let them be equally regular and well-disposed as yourselves.
It is highly proper that you should have cheerful and happy
amusements ; but let them be blameless and innocent.

I must farther request of you to reverence the authority of
your parents ; to pay a sacred respect to religion ; to be regular
and, above all, sincere in your prayers ; to fear and love God
in your youth, that you may enjoy an age of consolation and
peace.

You have often heard me insist on the advantage and propriety of keeping within doors at night. You must both be
sensible that running in the streets at night exposes you to idle
and disorderly companions. I therefore hope that you have
enough of work and amusement to keep you both at home after
it is dark, and that you will, for your own sakes, resist the
pleasure of running about with your acquaintances at such late
hours. You must both give up such a dangerous and corrupting practice, and set about contriving some amusements which
may make you happy within doors. Think not that to be sober
and religious you must give up all play, and amusement, and
cheerfulness. This is by no means necessary or even proper.
Be happy, and enjoy the company of your acquaintances—only
let these acquaintances be well chosen, that you may suffer
nothing from their conversation or example. I am not sure if
both of you can write. I expect a letter from your mother in
a few days ; I will thank one of you to write me at the end of
her letter, and in particular tell me if you can read my hand.
I have been at some pains in making this letter as plain and
distinct as possible, and I am much afraid, after all, that you

will feel some difficulty in making it out.* I am engaged in constant and busy employment for the whole winter, which will prevent me from writing you as often as I could wish. I, however, will grudge no time or trouble that may have a useful effect in preserving you from corruption, and in improving the purity of your characters. I hope you are getting on in understanding the meaning of words. When I next come to Hawick, I mean to put you both upon a method which I think will be of great use to you in that respect. If Miss Brown is still with you, give her my best compliments, and tell her, that though she refused to accompany me to Fife, I am determined to see her in Hawick before the year is done, which is now less than the space of three months. You may also give my advice to your brother, that he be diligent and attentive to his learning. Remember me to William Walker, if he has yet returned from the west country, where I understand he went to spend a few weeks. My sincerest wishes attend you. May Heaven preserve the purity and innocence of your youthful years ! May He defend you from the pollutions of the world, and prepare you for a life of usefulness and honour.—I am, your wellwisher and friend, THOMAS CHALMERS.

No. XXX.

Elie, 26th July 1816.

DEAR MRS. KEDIE,—I am now on a visit to my friends in Fife ; but, before I left Glasgow, I received your kind letter and present. I was grieved to hear of your daughter's illness, and sincerely hope that she has now completed her recovery. Mrs. Chalmers had just got a daughter a few days before your parcel arrived, and I have great reason to be thankful for the very expeditious recovery she has met with. She joins me in

---

* The original letter extends over twelve quarto pages, and is written in half-text and in the plainest handwriting.

thanking you for your welcome remembrance of me; and I can assure you that my eldest daughter, Anne, was not long of trying your biscuits, and did most heartily approve of them.

My whole family consists of two daughters. Give my best compliments to both your daughters and your son. I retain a very warm remembrance of Hawick and its neighbourhood; and I am hopeful, that before other twelve months have gone, I may again have it in my power to visit it.

I trust your son-in-law will never be in Glasgow without seeing me, and giving me all the news of the place and of your family.

It is my prayer that you may long be spared in health and comfortable circumstances amongst them; that you and your children may receive an abundant blessing from Him who is the giver of every good and of every perfect gift; that you may receive an interest in the sure mercies of our great and all-sufficient Saviour; and that redeemed by His blood, and sanctified by the power of His Spirit, you may all be made perfect in holiness, and meet for an inheritance of glory.—Believe me to be, my dear Mrs. Kedie, yours with much regard,

THOMAS CHALMERS.

No. XXXI.

Edinburgh, 6th September 1831.

MY DEAR MR. KEDIE,—If your mother be still in the land of the living, tell her from me, that the blood of Christ cleanseth from all sin—and why not from her sin? Tell her to lean the whole weight of her dependence on the foundation which God hath laid in Zion, and she will find it broad enough, and strong enough to bear her. Tell her to look unto Jesus, who poured out His soul unto the death, that she and all who trust in Him may live, and may find rest and rejoicing in her soul.

I feel the deepest sympathy with you and your afflicted

family on this occasion. I pray that you may have that comfort which God alone can give; and, above all, that this chastisement from His hand may yield both to you and to your sisters the peaceable fruits of righteousness.

It is now twenty-nine years since I lodged in your house, and I have still a pleasant and a grateful recollection of all the kindness I received from your mother, and of all the affection which both she and her family bore to me.

Give my kindest regards to your married sister, Janet; and tell your younger sister, Betty, that from her childhood, when I used to hear her read in my room, I have always remembered her, and with feelings of very great regard.

Let us think that our time is coming when we shall lie on our dying beds, and let us make no delay in seeking our peace with God, and keeping all His commandments.—Believe me, my dear Sir, yours very truly, THOMAS CHALMERS.

No. XXXII.

Edinburgh, 6th October 1840.

DEAR MR. KEDIE,—I have just now received your kind letter, and both I and Mrs. Chalmers feel very much obliged by your remembrance of us. Is it your elder or younger sister who has lost her husband? Give my best regards to them both; and let it be the care of us all to perfect holiness in the fear of God. Give it as my charge to your dear sisters, Janet and Betty, that they mind the one thing needful, which is the care of their souls—the guilt of which the blood of the Saviour alone can wash away, but whose grace will never fail those who put their trust in Him. Oh, that we received the Spirit from on high, who might enable us to purify ourselves even as Christ is pure.

If you have any parcel to send in, address it to Edinburgh, No. 7, Inverleith Row. We are very grateful to you for your generous offer of some Hawick bakes, which have long been famous.—I am, dear Mr. Kedie, yours very truly,

THOMAS CHALMERS.

No. XXXIII.

Edinburgh, 22d January 1843.

MY DEAR MR. KEDIE,—I am very much concerned to hear of your poor sister's illness. My memory is failing me, and I don't recollect the name either of her husband or that of your younger sister, though I shall ever retain a very affectionate remembrance of themselves. I understand it is your elder sister whom you represent as now sinking in the arms of death. It is my earnest prayer that she may fall asleep in Jesus; and if she be still alive, assure her from me that the blood of Christ cleanseth from all sin—and why not from her sin? We are all of us by nature great sinners; but Christ is a great Saviour, and there is no sin beyond His atonement. Tell her to cast all her care and all her confidence on Him; and so may she look with joyful expectation to that eternal life which is the gift of God through Jesus Christ our Lord. He casts out none who come unto Him, and all who come unto God by Him shall be saved to the uttermost.

Read to her the 23d Psalm, some of the first verses of the 14th chapter of John, and some of the last verses of the 5th chapter of 2d Corinthians; and should God, by this time, have been pleased to take her to Himself, these passages and reflections will not be thrown away upon her surviving relatives. Tell Betty, your younger sister, how much I desire both your and her salvation. I was not so earnest as I ought to have been in pressing this great concern upon you when I lived under your roof. But better late than never; and it mightily concerns us to know, that in turning to Christ we must turn from all our iniquities, that we must give up the sins both of our hearts and of our lives, and become holy creatures, else we shall not enter the kingdom of God.

Give my best regards to your sisters, also to your wife and daughter, whom I expected to see in my house here last summer. But we all went to Ireland; and, indeed, I am so very much taken up that I have no time to show that attention to my friends which I would like.—I am, my dear Sir, yours very truly,   THOMAS CHALMERS.

No. XXXIV.

Edinburgh, 17th June 1844.

MY DEAR SIR,—I feel greatly obliged by your kind letter of the 17th June, and have much value for the strong and unabated friendship which you have ever shown towards me.

I fear I shall not be able to avail myself of your welcome invitation to Hawick, as I have much to do which necessarily detains me at home. Give my best regards to your son. You speak of a former communication of his, which I hope I acknowledged at the time. I rejoice to understand from you that he is a deacon of Mr. Wallace's, and am persuaded that he will make a duty, not only of doing all he can for the good of his own particular Church, but that through the medium of the Hawick Association he will exert himself for the good of the Church at large.

Give my most cordial remembrance to your only surviving sister, dear Betsy, of whom and of all your family I pray that we may meet in Heaven, after a life of faith and holiness upon earth.—Ever believe me, my dear Mr. Kedie, yours very affectionately,   THOMAS CHALMERS.

No. XXXV.

Edinburgh, 5th April 1846.

MY DEAR MR. KEDIE,—I very much grieve to hear of your sister's illness, and, from the concluding part of your letter, I

can infer your great earnestness about her soul. It is most true
that it is a very serious, solemn thought when one thinks of
meeting with an angry God; and had we only ourselves and
our own merits to trust in, there would be nothing for any of
us but a fearful looking for of judgment. But tell your dear
sister, Elizabeth—dear to myself as to you—that when she
thinks of herself, what we all ought, as a great sinner, she
should also think of Christ as a great Saviour, whose blood
cleanseth from all sin—and why not from her sin? In and
through Him the anger of God is turned away even from the
chief of sinners. O that you, and she, and we all could be led
to place full confidence in Him, to cast our burden upon the
Lord, who is both willing and able to sustain it. It is true that
a work must be wrought in us as well as for us, that the clean
heart and the right spirit must be created; for without holiness
no man can see God. But still let us go to Him for all our
wants, for all we stand in need of, and go *as we are.* His
blood can atone for all our guilt; His grace can wash away all
our pollutions, and sanctify us wholly. He is able, and as
willing as He is able, to do all for us.

Let the following texts be pointed out to your dear sister :—
John iii. 16; Luke xi. 13; Matt. xx. 28; Rom. iii. 24-26;
Rom. x. 13; 2 Cor. v. 18-21; 2 Cor. xii. 9; 1 John iv. 8, 9, 10,
16, 19; Isaiah xxx. 15.

Give my kindest regards to your dear sister, and let me hear
soon of her again.—I ever am, my dear Sir, yours very truly,

THOMAS CHALMERS.

No. XXXVI.

Edinburgh, 13*th December* 1846.

MY DEAR MR. KEDIE,—It gives me real concern to hear from
you of your wife's serious illness. May God prepare us for the
whole of His will. He afflicts not willingly, and makes all

things work together for good to them who love Him. It is my earnest prayer that you and yours may be prepared for the whole of God's will; and let us never forget that our best preparation is to be found in Christ, who casteth out none who come unto Him. May the Holy Spirit draw yourself, and all who are near and dear to you, to His well-beloved Son, in whom all is safety, and peace, and joy.

Give my kindest regards to your dear wife, and also to your sister, my very old friend, Betty. I felt much at parting with her when I drove off in the coach after her affectionate farewell. —I ever am, my dear Sir, yours most truly,

THOMAS CHALMERS.

LETTERS TO THE REV. DR. JONES OF EDINBURGH.

No. XXXVII.

Kilmany Manse, 14th November 1812.

MY DEAR SIR,—I owe you much gratitude for your good services, and though not able for much exertion in preaching, I look upon myself as bound to make you a plentiful repayment for your most friendly and seasonable assistance to me. You ascribed my illness to the right cause when you laid it upon the Dundee kirks;* and this may serve as a lesson against too much exertion, or too many engagements, in all time coming. I shall certainly make up for my deficiencies, in as far as the Destitute Sick Society is concerned,† if God spare me in health and strength for it—though I would certainly prefer the summer-side of the year for any undertaking of that kind. My complaints have left me for the present, and I regret, from the shortness of their duration, that I should have had them at so unseasonable a time.

* See Memoirs, vol. i. p. 304.   † See Memoirs, vol i. p. 328.

My prayer to God is, that you may have many seals of your usefulness—that you may be the instrument of reclaiming many from darkness to the marvellous light of the Gospel—and that the seed scattered around you in the course of your ministrations, may fall upon hearts prepared by Divine grace to receive it. I wish you the truest of all enjoyments to an evangelical mind, when I wish that you may see the pleasure of the Lord prospering in your hand—sons and daughters turned unto righteousness—and the extensive field, which Providence has assigned to your labours, growing richer every year in the fruits of faith, and charity, and all righteousness.

I owe you much gratitude, not merely for your substantial services, but for your full and friendly communication of them. Your letter gave me great relief; and while I admit only your two first claims upon me for a sermon early, I can assure you that I shall always look upon you as having the first title to my future services. And, *ceteris paribus*, I shall always, in my journeys to Edinburgh, be decided by the time of your sacrament. I have no immediate prospect, however, of being in the city.—My best compliments to Dr. Fleming, and believe me, my dear Sir, yours most truly, THOMAS CHALMERS.

No. XXXVIII.

Kilmany Manse, 12th February 1813.

MY DEAR SIR,—I should certainly prefer preaching for you at one of your little sacraments; and as to my not being able to assist Dr. Fleming, you have perhaps forgot my former assurance to you, that one engagement during one visit to Edinburgh is all that I can answer for at present. I hope that in time I shall be able to make up for the actual disappointments I have already given you both—but I must be cautious not to lay the foundation of future disappointments ; and, be assured, that though greatly and decidedly better, I am still too frail a subject, and live at too great distance from you, to have any regular dependence upon.

I am glad to observe, by a note from Mr. Wright, subjoined to your letter, that he has begun the penny-a-week operation in his parish; and it gives me still greater pleasure to understand that this mighty instrument has been put into action in Edinburgh, in behalf of the Missionary Society. There is something very animating in the stir that is now abroad; and it is my hope and prayer, that it may speedily redound to the furtherance of the Messiah's kingdom. But while so much is doing to push forward the limits of the visible church among heathen, let it never be forgotten, that even within these limits there are many, and very many, who still stand without, and let us not relax our efforts in the cultivation of the home territory. It is my delight to observe, that so far from there being any interference in the two concerns, they give life and energy to one another, and that, generally speaking, those clergy, who are most assiduous in the way of vitally Christianizing their own districts, are ever readiest to give their assistance and their testimony to Missionary enterprises. It is the same with the great body of the people—give them a share and an interest in the cause, and though the object be foreign, I contend that it is accompanied with a home influence, and that the inference is not merely understood but felt among them. If so much is to be done for sending the Bible to others, with what consistency can we neglect it for ourselves, or suffer it to lie beside us unread, unopened, and unattended to?

My best compliments to Dr. Fleming when you see him. Mr. Tait will be a rare accession to the ministry in Edinburgh. He may be deficient in splendour, but he has a hearty good will to the business, and is, to a great degree, experimentally conversant in the work of close dealing with souls; and a single human being called out of darkness, though he lives in some

putrid lane or unheard of obscurity in your great city, is a
brighter testimony than all the applauses of all the fashionables.
—Yours with much regard,   THOMAS CHALMERS.

No. XXXIX.

Kilmany Manse, 17th January 1814.

MY DEAR SIR,—I arrived here in safety on Wednesday, and
am not in the slightest degree fatigued or worse by my excursion. This I attribute, in a great degree, to the very polite
system which obtains in Hanover Street. The truth is, that
any complaints I have are chiefly dependent upon the stomach ;
and I have the misfortune to be extensively connected with a
set of people who worry you with what they absurdly think
kindness, and are so outrageous in pressing you to this one
thing and that other thing, that you have neither peace nor
liberty in their presence. I have just been telling my wife that
I enjoyed a most delicious exemption from all this, and that I
was never more happy than in the bosom of your easy and enlightened family.

I looked in upon Mr. Wright of Markinch, on my road homewards, and find him to be as you represented him—altogether
a man of our own spirit. It is most refreshing to meet with
such, and grievous to think how thinly scattered they are
over the surface of our Establishment. . . .

Since seeing you, I have been looking into the last Number of
the Moravian Accounts, and am quite delighted with the gentleness, unction, and simplicity which pervade it. This is Monday ;
and to give you an idea of the deep retirement of my situation, I
am only in possession of the news of Tuesday last—a most interesting period. The frost here is the most intense I ever recollect. It will be as severe in France, in spite of its southern
situation, as forming part of a great continent—in which case, if
the allies do not find good quarters, they will be ill enough off.

My wife joins me in kindest remembrances to yourself, Mrs. and Miss Jones. My best compliments to the young gentlemen. I trust that Mr. Thomas's cold has left him.—Yours most truly, THOMAS CHALMERS.

No. XL.

Kilmardinny, 3d January 1816.

MY DEAR SIR,—I am here spending a few days, as I do not find the Glasgow frosts to be altogether so congenial to my feelings as the same kind of weather in the country.

I had not got over a single paragraph of your manuscript* without a very warm and pleasurable impression of the friendship which dictated it. I trust I shall never forget the proof it exhibits of a very cordial, open, and generous attachment to myself; and I do feel the very sincerest gratitude for your spirited and able vindication.

I was particularly pleased with your bold assertion as to your own experience of ministers who reprobated as unscriptural a ministerial address to sinners, and who even found fault with yourself for so doing. This put me in mind of the great comfort and direction I derived from your conversation, some years ago, when I was greatly oppressed with anxiety about being more formally orthodox in my sermons. I saw that you were not at all so fettered, and I liked the boldness, and freeness, and urgency with which you entered immediately on every one truth, for which the Bible gives its plain and authoritative warrant. You told me at that time, that as I got older I should get more confident; and I trust that any confidence I have may not be confidence on any other ground than on the ground of Scripture, and on the revelation of Him who bids us call no man master but Himself only.

* A critique on some of the Reviews of Dr. Chalmers's "Address to the Inhabitants of Kilmany."—See Memoirs, vol. ii. pp. 16, 17, and Appendix A, 491-494.

You have well answered that very strange charge of the reviewer, that a mourning for sin, and an easiness about particular sins, is a contradiction in terms. A mourning for one particular sin, and a being at ease about that particular sin, is doubtless a contradiction ; but it is really in the face of all experience to say, that a man may not contract a listless habit of indulgence in certain offences with a general habit of anxiety about himself, on the score of sin and his salvation from it. I think it one of the most frequent and familiar exhibitions of human character.

Will you accept of my gratitude for the whole argument ? It is a very complete and impressive one. You have very dexterously alluded to the favourable review of the *Observer*. It was really wrong to pit me in the way they did against a whole description of clergymen. The review in the *Herald* is much kinder, and in a better spirit. I got it sent me by Greville Ewing, with an intimation that he was the author of it. I had a closet conversation, on the subject of the Address, lately, with our friend Dr. Balfour, who dissents from several of its positions ; but I have found in him an unquelled kindness of temperament, which no differences, either in opinion or practice, can possibly extinguish. We see wonderfully little of one another, owing to his not walking, and to my not visiting. Dr. Lockhart is more in my way. I do not find the preaching easier yet ; and the winter of Glasgow has turned out differently from what I expected. The frost, which I formerly found so bracing, condenses the smoke of our public works, and fills all our streets with a darkness that may be felt ; but the goodness of my friends is unbounded ; and should I be enabled, through an occasional change of air, to weather this one season, I trust that I shall be enough seasoned and smoke-dried for the same kind of durability with a stock-fish.

My kindest love to Mrs. and Miss Jones, in which Mrs.

Chalmers joins me. We are concerned to hear of poor Mrs. Pitcairn. I am glad to observe that David is picking up his spirits a little. My prayers are for your personal and ministerial comfort.—Believe me to be, my dear Sir, yours with great esteem and regard, THOMAS CHALMERS.

No. XLI.

Glasgow, 26th March 1816.

MY DEAR SIR,—I have seen the *Instructor* of this month, and recognise in your article all the spirit and ardour of honest conviction, along with the evidence of a friendship to myself, for which I cannot be too grateful. I think it pretty discernible in the reply, that there is the blinking and the evasion of a worse cause. It is ridiculous to deny a prototype to the character of which you assert the reality. They are met with on my daily path in dozens ; and I do think it a pity that, in these argumentations, they cannot refrain from the invidiousness of petulant and personal observation.—I remain, my dear Sir, yours, &c., THOMAS CHALMERS.

LETTERS TO MRS. COUTTS.

[Mrs. Coutts was daughter of the Rev. Dr. M'Culloch of Dairsie, and widow of the Rev. Robert Coutts of Brechin. After her husband's death, she resided with her father, whose parish was situated a few miles from Kilmany. Dr. Chalmers's removal from that neighbourhood suspended an intercourse, afterwards resumed at Edinburgh, to which place Mrs. Coutts removed after her father's decease. Her singular vivacity of temper and intellect especially endeared her to Dr. Chalmers ; and it was at her house that his last visit was paid on the day preceding his death. See Memoirs, vol. iv. p. 513.]

No. XLII.

Kilmany Manse, 24th October 1811.

MY DEAR MRS. COUTTS,—My sister Jane left this for Anster about three weeks ago. She regretted the necessity which

F

took her away before making you a visit, from which she promised herself much enjoyment. I follow her about the middle of next month, and, though I will not promise, I have the firm purpose of seeing Dr. M'Culloch at Dairsie before taking my departure. I would be very glad to understand that Mrs. M'Culloch's health admitted of my spending a day with him. I shall bring "Hannah More" with me if I do come, and nothing but the want of a right opportunity has prevented me from sending it. I have also to return " Henry's Life," from the perusal of which I have derived great pleasure. The pigmies of the present age, when they think of his zeal and his prodigious industry in the good way, may well feel humbled at the comparison. Have you read Foster's " Essays ?" They are written in a strain of very profound and original sentiment. The only essay professedly religious is, " On the aversion of Men of taste to Evangelical Religion,"—a most masterly performance, in which he stands forth the sturdy champion of all that is peculiar in the doctrines of the New Testament, but pleads the importance of delivering them in a phraseology and style of expression more congenial to the literary habits of the age. He, of course, does not surrender a single fraction of the sentiment, and even annexes the most pointed reprobation to the mind that can suffer itself to be seduced by the associations of taste from the truth as it is in Jesus. Yet on the principle of being all things to all men that we may gain some, it is right that the fishers of men should accommodate their bait to the prize which they are attempting to secure. He exposes the antichristian tendency of those sentiments which issue every day from the schools of polite literature. And on the principle that Christianity should be made to extend her triumphs in every quarter, he is for arraying her in the same academic elegance of style that has hitherto been too exclusively appropriated to subjects of general literature. You will of course perceive that it would be wrong in a country clergyman to be so far seduced by the splendour of this elegant speculation as to refine himself from the humble and untutored people among whom Providence has appointed him to labour. I may add, (and it is a sentiment in which Foster most cordially acquiesces,) that in every mind seasoned with that taste which is from heaven, the native weight and importance of Scripture truth will be always seen to carry it over all the repulsions of a homely or obsolete style of expression.—With best compliments to all at Dairsie, I am, yours with much esteem,

THOMAS CHALMERS.

No. XLIII.

Kilmany Manse, 19th *December* 1814.

MY DEAR MRS. COUTTS,—I, some days ago, sent my concurrence in the Glasgow appointment, finally decided thereto by a long letter from Dr. Balfour, in which, among many other things, he says that the consequences of my refusal would be *dreadful.*

I am most desirous to remain here till September, and it is in the power of the Presbytery at Glasgow to grant me that accommodation. May I request you to join your influence with Dr. Balfour to my request for that object, that he may enable me to stem that rapacious spirit of impatience and monopoly which looketh only to its own things, and not to the things of others, and conceiveth that everything here must be given up for the devouring and clamorous demands of the people of Glasgow.

I am not insensible to the violent separation from a people whom I love, and if I never had the lesson of sitting loose to the world brought home to my feelings, I feel the greatness and necessity of the duty now.

I have been thinking a good deal of the part which people

might take, separately from their minister, in the great business of promoting the growth and preservation of religion in the neighbourhood. And I have much to talk with you about those fellowship meetings, &c., which private Christians may form, and so obtain an interest in the unfailing promise of Christ, that where two or three are met together in His name, there He will be in the midst of them.

My prayer is, that you may be long preserved a blessing to this neighbourhood, and be enabled to exercise among your acquaintances that most precious of all wisdom, the wisdom of winning souls. . . .

O that God would put it into the hearts of the people to be in earnest about His favour! that the natural tenderness that they now feel may turn into a deep and serious concern about the things of eternity, and that a spirit of united prayer poured upon them for the object they profess to have so much at heart, may be the blessed means of securing to them a pastor according to God's own heart, who will feed them with knowledge and understanding.

May I request your prayers for the last object in behalf of my much loved and much regretted parish.—Accept the assurance of my warmest and most affectionate regards, and believe me to be, my dear Madam, yours very sincerely,

THOMAS CHALMERS.

No. XLIV.

Kilmany Manse, 27th January 1815.

MY DEAR MRS. COUTTS,—I send you Alleine's " Alarm," of which I was happy to find that I had a copy additional to the one I have recently parted with. You may take your own time to it, and it is my prayer that it may be the instrument of a blessed and enduring change upon those whose good you have immediately in view by it. I am afraid there is a diseased touchiness upon the subject of good works, and an unscriptural alarm about the danger of pressing the plain and obvious work of repentance on sinners at the very outset of their seeking after God. Let me take for an example the case of a young female inquirer addicted to the obviously wrong thing of carrying it with petulance and disrespect to her parents. I do not think it possible that I can at too early a stage press upon her the obligation of the Fifth Commandment. To the question, What shall I do ? I would give Paul's answer to the jailor; but is there anything in his answer so fitted to engross the mind and monopolize the whole of its attention, as to leave no room for the answer of John to similar questions in the third chapter of Luke? Give up this wrong thing, cease your petulance to your father or mother. Their doing so may induce in it the risk of their resting in a performance of their own, and so turning their attention from Christ as their alone resting-place. But the scriptural way of protecting them from their danger is not to remit the practical urgency with which you exhort them to cast off their transgression, for this would be in opposition to scriptural example ; but, along with the practical urgency, to give them the information which the Bible gives respecting the ground of acceptance—faith in the Saviour, the necessity of the new birth, the alienated state of the heart by nature from God, which may consist with many acts of outward reformation ; and the only way in which this alienation can be overcome, even by a sense of God's love shed abroad in it by the Holy Ghost. In the meantime, their giving up what is plainly wrong is a proof of earnestness. It is a putting of themselves into the attitude of seekers. Nay, what is more, it may be the expression of faith in its infancy—the beginning of the good way ; the day of small things ; the smoking of the flax ; the first evidence of a regard to the Saviour, and such an evidence as He may reward with His promised manifestations. (John

xiv. 21.) All this may be going on without subjecting ourselves to the necessity of waiting till a certain progress be made
ere we preach Christ in all His fulness and in all His freeness.
Both may be brought forward from the very outset. The effect
of the one is to throw the learner into the attitude of service ;
the effect of the other is to throw him into the attitude of faith
or dependence, or perhaps, most frequently, of dim and confused
expectation of some great privileges which as yet he sees not
in all their extent and in all their preciousness. Now, this
compound attitude of service on the one hand, and expectation
on the other, is what I think I see clearly exemplified in the
New Testament, as by the disciples of John the Baptist, Na-
thaniel, Zaccheus, Cornelius, Anna, and the twelve tribes.
(Acts xxvi. 7.) There has been a sad deal of puzzling with
these examples by the *orthodox*, who, instead of quietly submitting to them, have laboured to dispose of them. This I
conceive to be wrong ; and on the other hand, these *modérés*
are still more so who shelter themselves under these examples
in their opinion about the sufficiency of works. Whereas
in every one of them there was no resting in present services
whatever, but a carrying forward to Jesus Christ and Him
crucified.

Do forgive this presumption in one who is so far behind
you in the school of Christ, and who feels himself at the mere
threshold of the subject.—Believe me to be, my dear Madam,
yours with great regard,   THOMAS CHALMERS.

No. XLV.

Glasgow.

MY DEAR MRS. COUTTS,—I have many apologies to owe you
for delaying my answer so long to your most interesting letter.
It came to me at a time when I was highly excitable, and
touched upon the most excitable topics ; and be assured that

the gratifying intelligence it contained of something like a good impression on the minds of my much loved and much regretted people, was not less calculated to move me to the tenderness of tears, than all the painfulness of a removal which in actual feeling was greatly more severe than anything I ever anticipated. I could not but feel how pure and how soothing is the affection of Christians when I read your kind and interesting epistle ; and surely if in this dead and darkened world it is found that the sympathy of our common Lord can draw so powerfully and unite so closely, what must be the transports of cordiality which await us in the great family of heaven, when that Lord who is now the object of faith so dull and so languid, and so oppressed with the burden of sin and of sense, as I feel it to be, shall become the object of beatific vision, and all hearts shall join in one unceasing song to Him who sitteth on the throne and to the Lamb for ever and ever ?

I thank you for your kind notice of Alexander Paterson. Will you deliver to him my assurance of the deep interest I take in his progress and stability as a Christian ? Tell him from me that he must look to the things of others as well as to his own things, and that, by mixing discretion with zeal, I trust that he may do much through the private channels of his acquaintance. Both you and he will be interested to know that two of my inquiring communicants at present have assigned the reading of Alleine's "Alarm" as the first cause of their earnestness in the matter of salvation ; and I trust that this will encourage him to persevere in a method which he found to be successful on a former occasion, of directing the attention of others to such books as, by the influence of the all-essential Spirit, may set a-going in the souls of others such a good work of seeking as may find its accomplishment in their finding those things which belong to their peace.

Speaking of my communicants, do you know I have been

much interested in the young who have come forward? They are twenty-three in number, and upon the whole I am much satisfied. In the country, the principle of accommodation to custom is much stronger than in the town, and accordingly I have found more of genuine conviction, and more of real and inquiring earnestness, at present, than I ever recollect on any similar occasion. But how liable to delusion we all are upon this subject! It is by their fruits only that we can know them; and I think that in my attendance on the unhappy men now under sentence of death, one of the most heartless circumstances in the matter is the total uncertainty we are under of the actual state of their hearts. One of them is a Roman Catholic, and I was much struck at the outset with his fluency and doctrinal knowledge, and, above all, his intrepid composure in the dreary prospect before him. I thought at the same time that there was a want of softness and contrition in his tone, different from what I would have expected of one who felt his own demerits and obligations to a Saviour; and now I am strongly inclined to suspect that his priest has been ministering a peace to him which I fear is no peace. He is to suffer to-morrow, and I, this night, got a message from him, through the medium of his own clergyman, that he wishes to be attended by him exclusively.

We have great reason to be thankful that we have got comfortable lodgings, and all enjoy an average share of health. My dear wife is taking well with her new situation, and Anne is making rapid progress. Miss Pratt and my brother Charles are also with us. I limit myself to a given number of visits, and have had a pretty severe contest to maintain with my friends upon the subject. We dined last week at Mrs. Dinwiddie's with Dr. Balfour's people: her kindness is unbounded. There is one circumstance I cannot but admire in Dr. Balfour. I have found it necessary to take my own way in several things which went

Christian maturity / humility

contrary to his wish and to his opinion, and I am sure that my conduct in reference to him has been such as would have impressed an ordinary man with the idea of my being a captious, cross-grained, and truly cappernouted personage. Yet there is a Christian kindness about him which survives all this—which remains unquelled in the midst of all annoyance, and which has compelled such a reverence for him on my part, as I trust will last during all the remainder of our earthly pilgrimage. . . .

O write us soon, for a letter from you is indeed a very great refreshment. Tell me of any good you know to be doing in your neighbourhood. I will not say much of the state of things here till I know more about it. I have heard some sermons from others since I came here. Dr. Balfour I think the most useful and impressive of them all. Mr. Love preaches in a line which to me is highly interesting. It must be unacceptable to the Independents, those men of *simple assent,* who make it so very simple that it appears to me to take in only one truth, when in fact the Bible takes in many, and furthermore tells us that he is instructed in the mysteries of the kingdom of heaven who lays up in the treasure of his understanding things new and old. It is true in the most absolute and unconditional sense of the word, that by faith we are saved ; but it is a faith in the whole of God's testimony, and if you give me this, you give me a Christian who feels as much peace as the doctrine of Christ's sufficiency warrants him to do, and aspires after as much repentance as the teaching of Christ lays upon him, and prays for as much aid from the Spirit as Christ is commissioned to bestow, and aims at all that variety of grace and accomplishments which the Law and the example of Christ oblige him to. There is a way of dividing Christ so as to make some part of it stand on the foreground, and some in the distant and almost unperceived background of our contemplation ; but

I fear that many a zealot of orthodoxy will have been found in this way to have in fact rejected Scripture by rejecting the profit which all Scripture is fitted to confer upon the entire believer.—Yours very affectionately,

THOMAS CHALMERS.

No. XLVI.

Glasgow, 28th February.

MY DEAR MRS. COUTTS,—Your most refreshing letter I got a few days ago, and what I shall first reply to is your inquiry after my health, which I can assure you never was better than I now feel it to be. I take my own way as to invitations and parties, and when I do go from home, it is generally to some mercantile villa in the neighbourhood, where I spend a few days and am let alone, and am suffered to eat and study and take exercise just as pleases me. I am surrounded with kindness, and the only thing I regret is, that I am sure the aspect of determination by which I hold out against its numerous and ever-plying proposals, must carry in it the expression of gruffness to the natives of this dinner-giving city. There is no help for it however ; and I please myself with thinking that, under God, I am indebted to all this regularity for the degree of strength and freedom from all that is physically unpleasant which I now so happily enjoy. . . .

The weather has got fine and agreeable, and could we only realize more of the presence of God in our souls ; could we carry about with us a more affecting sense of eternity ; could we live in a more simple reliance on the promises of Christ, and glory more in His cross, and, renouncing every dependence, admit the record of God about His Son as the exclusive and unmingled ground of all our securities and all our hopes ; could, I say, our spiritual interests be in a state of prosperity, we, in every other respect as to health, and circumstances, and kind friends, and agreeable family tempers and affections amongst us, have great reason to bless God the giver of all comfort, and the God of all consolation. . . .

I have very much of what I could call a picturesque memory—that is, I retain a vivid impression of all the visible scenery which is spread around a much loved and much regretted neighbourhood. I have at this moment a panorama of Dairsie before the eye of my fancy : and the Manse, and Osnaburgh, and the front of your father's house, and Craigfoodie, with the whole mountainous line which defines your northern boundary, pass in bright succession before me. I should not have mentioned this, but to assure you that as the places have taken a rivetted hold on my memory, so the persons have taken an equally firm and obstinate hold of my affections. I bear on my heart a great degree of tenderness for you all. I think I see a strong mark of nature now in the names that crowd so many of Paul's Epistles. His affection for the people drew him out to name them, and he had a pleasure in so doing. I feel the same pleasure in desiring you to remember me to Dr. M'Culloch and Miss Collier,* whom I love in the Lord ; Misses M'Culloch, Nancy, and Robina ; Mr. Swan, whose spiritual progress I rejoice in ; and last, though not least, Alexander Paterson. Do you know if he received a letter I sent him some weeks ago ? I should have written Miss Collier and Mr. Swan before this, but they shall come next in turn. Will you tell Miss Collier that I met her brother once, and only once, since I came to Glasgow ? I have had a good deal of debate with the ladies about their female societies of late, and they have turned a good deal quieter upon my hand. My business is also simplifying, as I refuse every work that is not strictly ministerial. The load is enough to crush the shoulders of twenty clergymen ; but I think it is their own fault to submit to it. May God

---

* Who frequently resided at Dairsie, with her friend Mrs. Coutts.

prosper your soul. Do let me have a letter soon from your quarter. Mrs. Chalmers joins in compliments.—I am, my dear Mrs. Coutts, yours most truly,   THOMAS CHALMERS.

No. XLVII.

Burntisland, 18th December 1817.

MY DEAR MRS. COUTTS,—I received yours while at Anster. One of the ingredients in the mortification I felt at the very unexpected recall I got at Kilmany* was, that it completely put an end to my hope of seeing your much loved neighbourhood during this excursion. I left Anster last week with the purpose of preaching at Dunfermline, but have been arrested in my progress by a cold which has hung about me for some weeks, but which I am hopeful is now getting away.

I never do leave Glasgow without returning to it with a new experimental lesson on the positive hazard and criminality of involving myself in too many preaching engagements, and I very much fear that, unless an invariable rule be laid down and acted up to, the urgency of people who, in the shape of kind friends, and zealous lovers of that which is good, and most confident advisers of that which it is duty for me to attempt, will at length compel me to retire, either by death or by resignation, from the work of preaching altogether.

Your letter refreshed me greatly ; and I never do get a favour of that kind, either from you or from Miss Collier, without the feeling that it is altogether suited to me. For in truth, my dear Madam, I feel that I have got no farther than to the threshold of those great topics which constitute the life and the aliment of a believer. I long to realize the joys and the exercises and the habits of experimental religion, to love Christ as fervently as good Samuel Rutherford—whose letters I am now reading—seems to have done, to have more devotedness, and more

* See Memoirs, vol. ii. p. 137.

spirituality, and more of the real feeling and desire of one who is crucified to the world, and alive only unto God. But all this I am most wofully short of. It comes to me all in word and not in power; and little do you know what a barren and in every way heartless subject you have to deal with. But the error lies in thinking that I can work my own way to my own enlargement; in not practically clinging to Christ as my alone sufficiency; in not simply leaning upon the promises which are yea and amen, and praying in faith to Him from whom every good and perfect gift cometh. I entreat your prayers, and those of your respected father and Miss Collier. I wish you had told me more particularly about her. The wheeling variety of my present situation may diminish my intercourse with my old acquaintances, but sure I am that it has not abated the regard I feel for the Christian society of your neighbourhood. Will you give my kindest remembrances to your father, Misses Collier, Coutts, and M'Culloch? Tell Alexander Paterson how much I regretted the shortness of my interview with him, and what a pleasant thing it would have been to me to have gone over to Dairsie from Kilmany with him on the Sunday evening that I preached there.—Believe me to be, my dear Mrs. Coutts, yours most affectionately, THOMAS CHALMERS.

No. XLVIII.

Trackboat, 26th September 1818.

MY DEAR MADAM,—I am thus far on my way to Glasgow— looking behind me with most affectionate regret, and before me with a desolate feeling of coldness and apprehension. God has not been pleased to turn my taste and my liking towards my present situation. I am sure I do the people of Glasgow great injustice; but I have never yet had any homeward associations with that town. Still there is in it a great quantity of Christian worth; and it is, in truth, a most unseemly exhibition, that I should receive so much in the way of affection, and render so little back again. But it is the glare, and the publicity, and the continual controversy, and the jarring of human faction, and the total want of that kind and familiar intimacy which gave such a charm to all my intercourse with Dairsie and Kilmany, that have withered up the scene of my present duties, and spread something like the aspect of wilderness over the whole extent of it. I have great need of your prayers that I may be more submissive to the will of God —that I may give myself entirely over into His hands, that I may be enabled to do His work, and look not anywhere on this side of time for my pleasant resting-place. Oh, that I could find a readier access to the conscience—that I could manifest the truth more powerfully and more permanently—that I could keep by the simplicity that is in Christ, and beware of making His cross of none effect by the words of man's wisdom !

I think more favourably of Fife, in the Christian sense of the word, than I did on any former excursion. There is more seeking than I ever observed before ; but such is the delusion of the human heart, that one may find rest in the consciousness of being a seeker. One may please himself with his earnestness, and, going no farther, may cease to be earnest any longer. One may receive an impulse, and yet stop short of salvation. One may, in fact, be establishing a righteousness of his own, when, like Paul, it should be his supreme desire to win Christ, and to be found in Him, and so submit himself unto the righteousness of God.—Believe me, my dear Mrs. Coutts, yours most truly, THOMAS CHALMERS.

No. XLIX.

January 1817.

MY DEAR MRS. COUTTS,—I received your kind letter some time ago, and never receive any letter from you without recognising the style and character of one of the great spiritual family. It is a family composed, I believe, of the professing of many different creeds, and the members of many different denominations; and yet the difference cannot be such as to impair that oneness which the Great Head of the Church ascribes to all his followers. But I have seen so many examples of late of satisfying evidence, that the root of the matter might be in the mind of a Presbyterian, and an Independent, and a Baptist, and an Episcopalian, and an Arminian Methodist, and even a Roman Catholic, as disposes me very much to withdraw my attention from the distinctions of man, and fix it on the message of God, as it comes to us in its direct and original form in the book of His own counsel. There is danger of resting in the face of such grounds, of being satisfied with names without ideas, of the kingdom of God coming to us in language only, and not in power, of holding converse with an argumentative theologian, while an utter stranger to converse with the Author and the Finisher of Faith. And, therefore, it is that, when satiated and bewildered among human illustrations of the truth, I think it a good escape for the mind to look to the truth as it is in the Bible—to sit down to it just as I was reading it for the first time, with the conscious ignorance and docility of a child—to stir myself there, that I may lay hold of God, and lay hold of Christ, just as God has set Him forth to me.

I have been greatly refreshed by a visit from a truly spiritual man, Mr. Erskine of Linlathen. His whole soul is in Christianity—resting all his hope on the basis of Christ's death —and dissolved in tenderness and admiration at the blended love and holiness of God as manifested in that transaction. I know nothing that more realizes Christ to us than when we read Him in one of His own living epistles, than when we see His workmanship before us in the heart and habits of a fellow Christian.

Mrs. Chalmers was complaining, and so seriously, some weeks ago, that I was much alarmed for her. Appearances, however, are again more favourable, and I desire, from this lesson, to learn the precariousness of all earthly blessings—to build my foundation somewhere else than in this vale of suffer-ing and of change—to cast it deep on the faith of the Gospel, that I may have the Giver of eternal life for my friend, and eternal life itself for my inheritance.

I saw lately the observation, that justification was only the means to an end—that the great and ultimate object of Christ's undertaking was to redeem us from all iniquity, and purify us unto Himself a peculiar people, zealous of good works. Is there no danger of an inquirer being satisfied with justification as the object in which he terminates? It certainly is not the object in which Christ terminates, nor will the accomplishment of it be enough to make out that travail of His soul upon us by which He is satisfied. Let us, therefore, while we lodge all our security for acceptance on His propitiation, go zealously on in co-operation with Him, as the Lord our strength and our purifier—that He may be magnified in our bodies—and that, by growing in holiness, we may be fit for the only happiness which Heaven has to offer.—I remain, my dear Madam, yours very truly,   THOMAS CHALMERS.

No. L.

Glasgow, 8th February 1822.

MY DEAR MADAM,—It grieves me to have deferred writing you so long. I had a very heavy arrear of correspondence upon me, which I have not yet liquidated wholly. I sympathize most deeply with you all in the result of your application to Lord Elgin.* I am not at all clear that it is right to urge his Lordship in the face of a private engagement. I see nothing

---

* An application to Lord Elgin, as Patron, relative to a ministerial appointment.

for it but quietly to wait that counsel of the Lord, which alone shall stand, after all human desires have been tried and found ineffectual. There is one very open and distinct line of duty for all who feel concerned in the religious prosperity of your most interesting parish, and that is, to multiply as much as in you lies the lay securities for the growth and transmission of a Christian spirit among the families. In this view I hold all your schools to be of capital importance, and I would not have you to underrate the capabilities even of the humblest labourers in the cause. I should not be surprised if Alexander Paterson, in his day and generation, shall be found to have turned more unto righteousness than many of the most esteemed and evangelical clergy of our Church.* At the same time it is of prime importance to a parish that there be in it a sound, and scriptural, and, withal, an exemplary clergyman. I am delighted with your account of Mr. Simpson, and also with the testimony that Alexander Paterson has borne of Mr. Cook in Kilmany.

I have been reading Thomas à Kempis lately, on the "Imitation of Jesus Christ,"—a very impressive performance. Some would say of it, that it was not enough evangelical. He certainly does not often affirm, in a direct and ostensible manner, the righteousness that is by faith. But he proceeds on this doctrine, and many an incidental recognition does he bestow upon it ; and I am not sure but that this implies a stronger and more habitual settlement of mind respecting it, than when it is thrust forward and repeated, and re-repeated, with a kind of ultra-orthodoxy, as if anxious to vindicate one's soundness, and to acquit oneself of a kind of exacted homage to the form of sound words. I think it of mighty importance to lay down the extent of the required sanctification, and strenuously to

* See a very interesting Memoir of Alexander Paterson, entitled " The Missionary of Kilmany, by the Rev. John Baillie." Edinburgh, 1853.

urge it. I have been thinking of the Saviour's expostulation with Nicodemus in this view—" If thou believest not when I tell you of earthly things, how can ye believe when I tell you of heavenly things?" If we believe not in the change that must take place upon the earthly subject, even man, ere he can be admitted to the Kingdom, we may feign, but we do not really put any belief in the change, from wrath to complacency, that has taken place in the mind of the Heavenly Lawgiver towards those who flee for refuge to the great propitiation. The earthly thing which Christ had spoken of was regeneration ; the heavenly thing which He proceeded to speak of was the atonement. If we believe not the one, we have no real belief of the other.

But nothing can be more precious than Romaine. His three treatises on " Faith" are all overrun with the flavour of the very essence of the Gospel.

I have no news. A perpetual bustle, and, at the same time, a stir and an activity in Christian things, which I regard as hopeful in this place. May God bless you and yours. I always rejoice in a letter from Dairsie. I offer my most affectionate regards to the venerable Doctor, Miss Collier, Miss Coutts, Miss Nancy, Mr. Simpson, and last, though not least, Alexander Paterson. Mrs. Chalmers joins me in best compliments.—I am, my dear Madam, yours very affectionately,

THOMAS CHALMERS.

No. LI.

St. Andrews, 23d April 1827.

MY DEAR MADAM,—I had very great pleasure in the receipt and perusal of your much esteemed letter. But why, my dear Mrs. Coutts, do you talk of *intruding* upon me? Our intercourse has of late been rare, and our correspondence far less frequent than it ought to have been. But I never can forget the Christian kindness and encouragement which I enjoyed under the roof of your excellent father, and all the friendly converse that I have had both with yourself and Miss Collier. Dairsie is one of the most memorable portions in my retrospect of the past; and all the feelings which I had then are undiminished by change of scene or distance of time.

My mother's was indeed a most triumphant death. Her peace and joy were altogether in *believing*. Her Christianity was objective, and that of one who looked outwards. She read Owen's "Spiritual-Mindedness" some months ago; but she remarked that when she looked only to herself, she found that all was corruption, but that all her trust was in the Saviour. She expressed an abundance of peace which flowed through her heart like a mighty river.

Mrs. Chalmers and our children are well. Do give my kindest regards to Miss Collier and Mr. Simpson, in which Mrs. Chalmers joins.—Believe me, my dear Madam, yours most affectionately, THOMAS CHALMERS.

No. LII.

Colinswell, by Burntisland, 2d April 1834.

MY DEAR MRS. COUTTS,—Miss Young is just leaving us; but I cannot let her go without assuring you both of the gratification and the gratitude which I felt in consequence of your kind and liberal offer of Thursday last. It is true that the means for my first enterprise are already provided;* but, should I succeed, I have still a second in reserve—respecting which I may, in the course of months, communicate with my friends, and you among the number—my only anxiety being that you do not make an inconvenient sacrifice.

I observe, that in spite of my explanatory letter, there is

* See Memoirs, vol. iii. pp. 445, 446.

still great misrepresentation of our objects. It is a marvellous time ; and though I feel it my duty to labour while it is day, yet I cannot help the presentiment of a dark midway passage that must be described ere the world shall emerge into the peace and righteousness of its latter-day glory.

Meanwhile, I cannot describe how inexpressibly soothing it is to be sustained by the countenance and affection of one's oldest and best-tried Christian friends. You have had much to exercise you ; and it is my earnest prayer, that in the light of God's reconciled countenance, ever growing into brighter and more cheering manifestations, you may increase day by day in that peace and joy which passeth all understanding.— Ever, believe me, my dear Mrs. Coutts, your most attached and grateful friend,   THOMAS CHALMERS.

No. LIII.

Penicuik, 12th July 1834.

MY DEAR MRS. COUTTS,—May God grant the fulfilment of your wishes in regard to the effect of my own solitude upon my heart and principles. It gives me a fresh view of my native ungodliness, that even in this deep retreat I cleave so much to the things of sense and of time. I am never better than when I take a simple and objective view of the great propitiation, and look on the sunshine of God's reconciled countenance to be an element I am as free to rejoice in as I am to breathe the air that is around me, or to open my eyes on the light of Nature.

I beg you will excuse the brevity of this letter—a poor return for your deeply interesting communication. But the truth is, I am ordered to work as little as possible. The most prominent of my symptoms is an almost perpetual noise in my head, which is aggravated always by exertion.*

* See Memoirs, vol. iii. pp. 433-444.

Give me a place and an interest in your prayers.—Ever believe me, my dear Mrs. Coutts, yours very affectionately,

THOMAS CHALMERS.

No. LIV.

Burntisland, 9th July 1841.

MY VERY DEAR MRS. COUTTS,—Be assured that I feel very calm and confident on the Church question—not on the ground of the Parliamentary Returns, or in the assured prospect of any thing being done in our favour by the present or any future Government, but on the ground that our way of duty is clear, and that if our ways please God, He will make our enemies to be at peace with us.

Should the Establishment be broken up, I think, that if true to our principles, there is a very great field of usefulness before us ; and that we need be at no loss for turning ourselves to such openings for the Christian good of the people, as will amply compensate for all the hardships to which we might in consequence be exposed.—Ever believe me, my dear Mrs. Coutts, yours with the greatest esteem and regard,

THOMAS CHALMERS.

No. LV.

Morningside, 13th December 1842.

MY DEAR MRS. COUTTS,—It gives me great pain to decline your application for myself, though I shall transmit your request to Mr. Hanna ; and it will afford me great pleasure if he can comply with it.

I never do preach but with a serious invasion on my press of study, and so a very hurtful encroachment on an object to which I should like, if I were permitted it, to devote all my strength for the remainder of my days, and that is, the completion of my theological lectures for the benefit of my students, and as an offering to the cause of theological education. The troubles of the Church, and my implication therewith, have deprived me of years of preparation ; and one of the cruellest effects of any public appearance I make is, that it is followed up by a host of applications—some of them from my best and dearest friends, which I feel it most difficult, but, withal, most necessary and incumbent upon me to reject. This distresses, but it must not influence me. I may not be able to justify these refusals to others ; but the constant feeling of exhaustion, wherewith I am at all times haunted and well-nigh overborne, forms to my own mind and conscience a sufficient exoneration. —I ever am, my dear Mrs. Coutts, yours very truly,

THOMAS CHALMERS.

LETTERS TO MISS COLLIER.

No. LVI.

Kilmany, 17th December 1814.

MY DEAR MISS COLLIER,—I some days ago sent my letter of acceptance to Glasgow. I know well that there is a disposition to withhold sympathy from that suffering which a man entails upon himself by his own voluntary act. In cases like the present, however, I am not sure that this is altogether fair ; for, independently of my not being my own master, but the servant of another in the determination of this matter, I could not have escaped suffering by the adoption of either side of the alternative ; for by accepting, I bring down upon myself all the bitterness of regret at being torn away from a much-loved parish and neighbourhood ; and, by refusing, I would have brought down upon myself the severest remonstrances from the most eminent Christian friends I have in this world. As it is, I feel myself in a situation altogether unlike any former experience I ever had. And if, to alleviate the pain of my approaching separation, I must sit as loosely as possible to the things and the people around me, I trust I may learn from it the still greater and more salutary lesson of sitting loose to all the interests and concerns of that world which the likeliest of us all must soon take our departure from. This tenderness about leaving my people is one thing, and may exist in a breast where there is no serious concern for their souls, which is another thing. And O that the same God who sent forth His mighty Spirit to convert three thousand souls at the utterance of one sermon, would so arm me with arguments, and so press them home with efficiency upon the hearts of a people made willing and obedient in the day of His power, that the few remaining months of my residence amongst them might witness the accession of many sons and daughters to righteousness. We would have been much the better of a visit from you had your engagements permitted it. My wife regrets your absence on this occasion. Will you let us know when we may have the pleasure of seeing you ?

Never forget that a private individual is invested with the care and the keepership of others, as well as a minister of the Gospel ; and it is my prayer, that wherever you are, you may be a leaven for good by your example, and conversation, and prayers. I earnestly crave the benefit of your intercessions in behalf of myself and of my parish. My wife joins in most cordial compliments and wishes.—I am, my dear Madam, yours most truly, THOMAS CHALMERS.

No. LVII.

Kilmany Manse, 20th April 1815.

MY DEAR MISS COLLIER,—I was greatly concerned to see Mrs. Coutts so poorly on Tuesday, and I send this messenger to you asking to know particularly about her.

May her spirit be upheld in this the day of her extremity; may she be enabled to throw herself upon the Saviour. The Bible has taken many ways of stating to us His sufficiency, as if, lest one way of it should not be apprehended, another way may send home the truth with demonstration and power. Thus it sometimes sets Christ before us in the light of the second Adam, and tells us that He is more than able to repair all the mischief done by the first Adam. Well then, all this guilt, all this misery, all this helplessness, by which I feel myself burdened and overdone, was entailed upon me by the Fall; and the very errand on which Christ came was to sweep the whole calamity, in all its extent and in all its soreness, away from me. Let us cling to Him. Let us do Him the honour to believe that what He came to do, He is able to do. Let us be ready to say "Yea" to His question, "Believest thou that I am able to do this?"—and according to our faith, so shall it be done. It is my prayer, amid the trying circumstances in which our friend now is, she may feel the richness of this truth, that the Great Intercessor liveth; that He is full of tenderness; that He is, indeed, a merciful High Priest; and that He knows well how to succour her, for there is not one of her temptations which He Himself has not struggled with. There is no want of willingness in God; it is in our own heart that the straitening lies. He calls upon us to lay hold of His strength that we may make peace with Him; and adds, that in so doing, we shall make peace with Him. Wonderful assurance! It is just saying—lean, and you shall be supported; throw yourself upon me, and I will bear you up; cast your burden to me, and I will sustain it. Oh that this faith were wrought in us with power, and the precious fruits of faith were getting more discernible every day upon our hearts; that we were dying unto the world, and unto all its distinctions and pleasures; that the realities of the spiritual and unseen world were taking a more effectual hold of us ; that we were walking by faith and not by sight ; and knowing our insufficiency for these things, were drawing by prayer out of the fulness that is in Christ Jesus, all our light, and help, and direction.

Do write me by the bearer.—Yours most truly,

THOMAS CHALMERS.

No. LVIII.

Glasgow, 1815.

MY DEAR MISS COLLIER,—I received your letter with much joy, and felt greatly refreshed by the perusal of it. Be assured that you cannot derive a greater satisfaction from our correspondence with each other than I do myself ; and I look back to our many walks and many conversations as those seasons which memory loves to dwell upon, when I took sweet counsel together with a Christian friend. I have not yet met with anything here that can replace what I feel the want of, though at the same time I feel my heart slowly opening itself to the impression of that kindness, and worth, and sterling Christianity which surrounds me. But I am as yet too much lost, and my attention too much divided among the general society of the place, to have many strong drawings in the way of individual friendship. This general intercourse, indeed, has the effect of keeping me asunder for some time from my best friends. I cannot see much of Dr. Balfour. Mrs. Dinwiddie arrived a week ago, and I had to resist her kindness, which I the more regret because I know it to be genuine and sincere ; but I shall spend a day with her in about a fortnight. There are some very interesting people among my own hearers, whose acquaintance I mean to cultivate ; but at present the invitations come so thick upon me, that I, who have restricted myself to a limited number of teas and dinners, have nothing for it but to put many of these away from me. The following are

H

the texts I have preached upon since I came to Glasgow:—
1 Thess. v. 25 ; 2 Cor. x. 12 ; Mark xii. 37 ; Romans viii. 7 ;
Acts xxvi. 25 ; Phil. iv. 13 ; Matt. iii. 2 ; Job ix. 30-33 ; Psalm
lxxxv. 10 ; Luke i. 74, 75 ; 1 Cor. iii. 1 ; Luke ii. 14.

I do find in myself a tendency to speak beyond my strength,
but I have great reason to be thankful that I am pretty well
in health. Grace and Anne are both well. Miss M. Balfour
is with us at present ; Charles came a few days ago, and we
have two boarders ; so that with Miss Pratt, our home establishment is pretty extensive at present ; and as I refuse callers
before twelve, and go out only a certain number of times, I
trust I shall have a sufficiency of time for the preparations of
the pulpit. I have only been visiting sick persons since I
came, but I trust that I shall extend this part of my duty. I
have been twice with two men under sentence of death, and
mean to visit them occasionally till the day of their execution.
One, a Roman Catholic, is very much impressed, and seems to
be mainly right in his doctrinal notions. The other is very
ignorant, and I thought very hard at my first visit. I think,
however, that I have made progress with him since ; but, alas !
appearances are most fallacious, and it is, indeed, a work of
great seriousness, and demanding a feeling of dependence on
God for wisdom to divide the word of truth rightly on such an
occasion.

Tell Mrs. Coutts that I mean to write her shortly. I should
have written her before I wrote you ; but the truth is, I sat
down to this letter under a general impression of debt to your
neighbourhood, and as you are my most recent creditor, you
were most in my mind at the time of my beginning to write.
I cannot describe the soft but mournful tenderness I feel when
I think of your neighbourhood, nor will I disguise the very
warm affection I have both for yourself and Mrs. Coutts, and
the friendship and veneration I feel for Dr. M'Culloch ; along

with these, will you remember me to Mr. Ewan and Miss Robina? Your sister, Miss Mary, I desire to be remembered to. Tell Alexander Paterson how much I am interested in him, and that I trust he will never let go the beginning of his confidence. Give my kindest regards to him; and let him send me by you, if he does not incline to write himself, all the Christian news of his neighbourhood. Give my best and my friendliest greetings to Mr. and Mrs. Walker, and assure them of my good-will for themselves and family. Oh, how it melts and subdues me when I write all these names, and think of the dear neighbourhood with which they are associated.—May power from on high ever rest on many of its families; and may the grace of the Lord Jesus be poured in rich effusion over your much-loved land.

My wife and I both were greatly moved and interested by your kind letter. I hope you will soon see us in Glasgow. Let me know of your movements; and may the Lord guide and protect them.

We live in Charlotte Street, have a garden, and are most eligibly situated. May God prosper you, and give you His peace to rule in your heart.—Yours most affectionately,

THOMAS CHALMERS.

No. LIX.

MY VERY DEAR MISS COLLIER,—I received your highly acceptable communication; and you know how much the kind and Christian remembrance of an old and valued friend acts as a sweetening infusion in that compound of many ingredients which make up the life and history of a city minister. I have much reason, however, for thankfulness, and trust that I am finding my way, through the leadings of a good and a free Spirit, to the habits of a more even and simple reliance upon Him in

whom I desire to find all my completeness and all my rest.
How precious to know, that it is by keeping in memory the
truths which we received at the first—that it is by holding fast
the beginning of our confidence, and not casting it away—that
it is by cleaving unto Him in whom we ought always to abide,
with an utter sense of our emptiness and of His fulness—that it
is this attitude of quietness which, after all, is our only attitude
of strength, and by persevering in which we are made more
than conquerors.—My dear Madam, yours very truly,

THOMAS CHALMERS.

No. LX.

Glasgow, 3d June 1816.

MY DEAR MISS COLLIER,—I mean, if God will, to go from
this in the middle of July, and stay away six weeks. I shall
be much of that time in the neighbourhood of Kilmany, and,
of course, some days in Dairsie. All this, however, is only expressive of my intentions, and not of my promises, of which I
am most fearful ; and as my object is to rest, I trust I shall
not have the fatigue of urgency to undergo on the subject of
preaching, as I must be very sparing of myself during my absence from Glasgow. I still feel the overdoing of too much
exertion in the business of Glasgow. The preaching is heavy
for me ; and the teasing invitations, pressed with a degree of
rudeness that is very provoking, I find it difficult to ward off
from me. I am sorry to say that Dr. —— is most egregiously
culpable in this respect ; and I have learned from him of how
little avail the mere feeling of kindness is towards the happiness
of others, unless a consideration and a respect for convenience
and liberty go along with it. I wish I could report favourably,
either of myself or others, as to the most substantial of our interests. I hear sometimes of good done, and I am convinced
that to a certain degree there is a reality in the matter. Of

one thing I am getting every day surer—that no human power, either of argument or of address, can work the progress of a single inch towards the conversion of a human soul. It is of my might and my wisdom, saith the Lord ; and till we feel our dependence upon this I am convinced that He will humble and mortify all our sufficiency. I feel my need of your prayers, both for my personal and ministerial welfare. This is Monday, when I am sadly liable to be driven out of the mildness and endurance of the Gospel, by the feebleness of yesterday's fatigue, and the annoyances with which a selfish and inconsiderate public beset me. I have this day had to ward off four dinner invitations, and to fight a stout battle about two of them. I trust that this matter will at length find an adjustment in the people's letting me alone. But I must give up this querulous strain.

Give my kindest compliments to Dr. M'Culloch, Mrs. Coutts, Miss Coutts, Mr. Ewan, and the two Misses M'Culloch. I sigh for the repose and pure air of your charming neighbourhood.— I ever am, my dear Miss Collier, yours most affectionately,

THOMAS CHALMERS.

LETTERS TO WILLIAM WILBERFORCE, ESQ., M.P.

No. LXI.

Glasgow, 9th February 1818.

MY DEAR SIR,—The concluding paragraph of the Prince Regent's speech* has given great satisfaction to the friends of

------

* Recommending to the attention of Parliament the deficiency in the number of places of worship connected with the Established Church, as compared with the increased and increasing population.

religion in this quarter. It, at the same time, by suspending measures till the specific proposal of Government be known, has given a temporary check to their operations for adding new churches to the Establishment in Glasgow. My own apprehension is, that if Government shall offer to carry this into effect by a pecuniary grant *merely*, it will do but little for us here in proportion to the needs of our population, and at the same time will do as much as will satisfy and set at rest the lukewarm friends of the cause.

What I think would be most desirable in any legal enactments on this subject, would be to afford facilities to the enterprise of individuals who, on their own risk, might combine to build churches in connexion with the Establishment, and thus extend the object of Government, and that without any expense to Government. You know what Mr. Gladstone of Liverpool has done in this way, having added two churches to that town at his own risk. Now, it is my conviction, that a proper encouragement being held out to individuals, much may be done in the same way in the larger towns of Scotland.

For instance, if Government were so far to countenance such speculations, as to vest the individuals who came forward with funds for the erection of churches and the maintenance of their clergy with the right of nomination for a hundred years, after which the patronage might fall either to the Crown or to the Magistrates and Council, I have no doubt that in a very few years indeed we should see at least half a dozen of additional churches in this place, and that without any expense to Government at all. A great collateral advantage that I could anticipate for such an arrangement is this—a purer exercise of patronage. It is a great security for our getting a good evangelical clergyman when the patron is strongly interested in the popularity of his choice ; and we cannot be too grateful when we think how wisely and mercifully God can bring

about the extension of His kingdom among men even out of
the sordid elements of human interest and human passion.

May I submit to you another observation on this point. A
church without a local district annexed to it in the shape of a
corresponding parish, is not the best arrangement for getting
it filled with hearers. Give the preacher a superintendence
over a certain range of population, and his week-day attentions
amongst them will at length bring them to his Sabbath ministrations. The habit of church-going has got most wofully
into desuetude, and nothing should be overlooked which can
help to restore it. I think that I speak what is practically
and experimentally true, when I affirm the mighty operation
which lies in the mere attaching of a certain portion of town
over which the minister has the official right of expatiating
through the week to the church where he preaches on the
Sabbath.

You may remember my former communications on the
subject of the Edinburgh Professorship. I wish that no further application should be made to Government on this subject. I feel as formerly on the suitableness of such an office
to my taste ; but I know of nothing which more effectually
neutralizes a man's usefulness in this age of party violence and
imputations, than the appearance of receiving anything from
Government. Even for the sake of the interests of loyalty
and good order, I would rather decline any benefit from the
patronage of the State, knowing well that the only way in
which a man's testimony can have weight amongst his citizens
on the side of loyalty, is that they be thoroughly convinced of
its being a disinterested testimony. Permit me to say, that
this conviction of mine stands most intimately associated with
all that I have observed of the conduct of you and your friends
in Parliament.

From a letter I received some time ago from Lady Grey,

I was glad to observe that you approve generally of my views on Pauperism. I have another article on the same subject in the next number of the "Edinburgh Review."

I cannot conclude without expressing the very warm affection that I entertain for you. It is my earnest prayer that your life and your labours may long be preserved to us. I beg my most respectful compliments to Mrs. Wilberforce.—Believe me, my dear Sir, yours with most cordial esteem,

THOMAS CHALMERS.

No. LXII.

Glasgow, 28th December 1818.

MY DEAR SIR,—I have no one topic connected with business about which to write to you; and indeed I always grieve for any necessity of this kind, thinking, as I do, that there ought to be a general combination on the part of all your friends to let you, as much as possible, alone. There is positively nothing which they ought more to study than to abridge the numerous exactions which are perpetually made upon your attention and your time, and to suffer you that undisturbed repose which it would be desirable that you could be permitted to enjoy.

The chief impulse under which I write is that produced by your last letter—on my review of the various letters I have received during the currency of the year that is departing away from us, and which breathes so kindly and so affectionately towards me, that I cannot but send you the warmest acknowledgments of my gratitude and regard.

I further take the opportunity of stating, in reference to a certain confidential subject on which you did me the honour of addressing me some months ago, that I have introduced the matter into several companies, and in general found that the task of vindication was altogether superfluous. I in particular recollect having started the topic in one of the highest of our circles here, when our then member, Mr. Finlay, was present ; and I had the utmost satisfaction in hearing the cordial testimony he bore to the entire consistency and integrity of your Parliamentary conduct. Such is the worthlessness of mere partisanship, that none can stand out with any degree of conspicuousness to the public eye without becoming the subject of vile and calumnious aspersions. But it is a satisfaction to know, that even in this alienated and accursed world there is often so willing a tribute rendered to principle, even in quarters where the natural enmity of the human heart is most apt to be provoked with the exhibition of it.

I beg to offer my affectionate regards to Mrs. Wilberforce. She will perhaps be interested to know that Mrs. Parker is in my immediate neighbourhood, and that I have the felicity of occasional intercourse with her.—Believe me, my dear Sir, yours with the most cordial esteem,

THOMAS CHALMERS.

No. LXIII.

Glasgow, 25th June 1822.

MY DEAR SIR,—I promised to write you on a subject, the interest of which for the time has gone by. I have long looked with a most approving eye to the part you take respecting the Catholics of Ireland ; and I simply wanted to let you know, that the evangelical party in our Church are fast hastening towards the same enlightened spirit of Christian and liberal policy in regard to them. There are still a few sturdy old clergymen amongst us who have not yet got the better, and never will, of the sore recollections of their covenanting forefathers. But with the exception of these, and of some others who take the opposite side of the question from political motives, I do think that the Church of Scotland would like

I

the removal of the existing disabilities.   What a piece of kingly
munificence would it have been had his Majesty been enabled
to carry the deed of emancipation to Ireland along with him.

I have not forgotten the very great exertions you made
in behalf of three Canada emigrants about two years ago ;
and I really think that it ought to be a principle with all
your friends to form themselves into a cordon of defence,
for the purpose of protecting you from all manner of intrusion.
I hope that you received my last, written about a fortnight
ago.   You honoured me by asking my sentiments on the subject of public affairs, and I ventured a few affirmations on a
matter that I am far from being qualified to pronounce on.   I
see that the public funds are to be held inviolable, and there
is assuredly something noble in the principle of it.   I cannot,
however, get the better of a principle that I have long held on
the subject of taxation, and that is, that all taxes fall ultimately on land, the capitalist finding an indemnification for
his taxes always in an increase of profit, and the labourer in
an increase of wages.   I should like to see the whole revenue
of the Government raised by a land-tax, equally including
stock-holders as the mortgagees or co-proprietors of the soil.
The burden would thus *appear* to fall exclusively upon one
class.   But in truth they pay all at present directly or indi-
rectly ; and were they made to pay all by a direct levy, they
would find almost instant indemnification for a measure that
would look very formidable at the outset by a fall of price in
all the comforts of human life.

We had a visit from Mr. Gray of Sunderland lately, one of
the good men of the Church of England.   It is truly refreshing to have a visit from such ; it always puts me in mind of
a saying of Brainerd's, that he has heard hundreds speak
about religion, but not above one or two speak religion.   We
Scotch speak about it—look at the matter intellectually—come

forth with our didactic and metaphysical speculations about the thing; but the evangelical English, as far as I can observe, possess the thing; and possessing it, they have by far the most effective ingredient of good preaching, which is the personal piety of the preacher himself.

It is my prayer that you may long be preserved amongst us. May you taste the comforts of retirement; and may a foretaste of Heaven mingle with them. It is a sad world surely, when one cannot bustle his way through it even in pursuit of what is good, without the danger of being bustled out of all his spirituality. This I feel every day. But Christ did not pray that His disciples should be taken out of the world, but that they should be kept from the evil of it.—With most affectionate regards to Mrs. Wilberforce, believe me, my dear Sir, yours very truly, THOMAS CHALMERS.

No. LXIV.

Glasgow, 8th July 1823.

MY DEAR SIR,—I feel obliged by your kind inquiries respecting myself. I at one time thought of writing you an explanatory letter on the subject of my departure from Glasgow; but I was assailed with such a torrent of unexpected abuse because of it on the part of my best friends, that I resolved to wait their attentions ere I should write one word upon the subject. I believe it is now pretty obvious to them all, that a University where young men are reared for the public offices of the Church, is a higher station in the field of Christian usefulness than any one of these offices. I was not unmindful of this consideration when I made my choice; and it was a choice that I embraced more readily, as I had long found that the fatigues of action were encroaching too far on the tastes and habits of a studious life; and more particularly as the pressure of my fatigue was greatly aggravated by the various and to all appearance interminable controversies that had been raised against me.

Meanwhile I am much engrossed with the concluding duties of my present office, and preparation for the duties of my new one ; and this engrossment must last till the summer of 1824. I expect ere I leave Glasgow to have perfected my parochial arrangements, and to leave them on such a footing as to make it obvious to all, that it is not I who have resolved the problem of pauperism for St. John's, but that the human nature of the people has done it for me, and will do it for any other that simply lets the arrangement alone. The difficulty of the problem does not lie with the poor—it lies with the rulers and managers of the poor. The barrier is not in the necessities of the lower orders—it is in the obstinate prejudices of the higher orders ; and I lay my account with a far more formidable obstacle to the abolition of this great moral evil in the Parliament of England than in the people of England.

May I be permitted to say, that I have long regretted the very inconsiderate encroachments which even your friends make upon your time and ease. I should rejoice in a calm and tranquil evening of life for you ; and my prayer is, that you may have many happy days on earth brightened with the hopes and the foretaste of Heaven in the bosom of your family. I feel the utmost gratitude for all your attentions to myself ; and shall ever reflect with a pleasure, not perhaps unmixed with some pride, on the intercourse that I have had with yourself and the other distinguished philanthropists of England.

We expect Mr. Clarkson in Glasgow next month. There has been a Committee formed for promoting the abolition of slavery.—With most respectful compliments to Mrs. and Miss Wilberforce, I am, my dear Sir, yours with great regard,

THOMAS CHALMERS.

No. LXV.

St. Andrews, 28th October 1825.

MY DEAR SIR,—Mr. Collins shewed me a letter from you, wherein you made a reference to me on the subject of the London University. I was then in Glasgow, and in the midst of many engrossments. I now avail myself of a moment's leisure for a few slight remarks on the way in which a Christian education may be made to keep pace with the general education which such an institution is so fitted to advance. I have no leisure for any publication on the topic, however short.

There are many difficulties attendant on the introduction of Theology among the other professorships, and most of which have been already adverted to in the deliberations which have taken place on the subject. And I am not sure that you got rid of these difficulties by generalizing the course into a mere series of lectures, on Natural Theology and the Evidences of Christianity. For my own part, I have now long thought that the most powerful of all those evidences is founded on the adaptation of the gospel to the moral wants and condition of our nature—a subject which might be treated in a way that is quite philosophical, and that would harmonize with the tone and habits of speculation which may have been acquired by the students at the other classes ; but still a subject which cannot be fully expounded without a reference to the peculiarities of the evangelical system. And if to keep clear of these peculiarities you restricted the professor to certain text-books, as those of Paley and Butler, and others that were specified, this were laying a fetter upon the business of the professorship, which no man of genius or of vigorous and excursive powers could with any comfort submit to.

How would it do instead of making a regular professorship for this subject, to make a lectureship of it, consisting of a

course of three months, and in which, if the teacher gave satisfaction, he could be invited indefinitely to repeat his course in
future years—and whom you get quit of, should he go astray
or give offence, by simply ceasing to invite him any more. By
such an appendage to the University, you might perhaps
secure a theological infusion without the hazards to which a
regular professorship of Theology might expose you. You
might at all events, by such a device, feel your way to a right
and permanent arrangement of this difficult question.

On the whole, I should think it best of all that a separate
institution were formed, neither connected with the London
University, nor even recognising it, but whose real design was
to accommodate the defence and illustration of religion to that
higher intellectual state of the public which must be the result
of such an institution.   You are aware that some of our ablest
authorship has proceeded from endowments of this sort, as the
Boyle Lectureship, and many others.   But I would not give
it a preaching, but rather a professorial aspect.   The whole
expense of it might be limited to the erection of a fabric having, at least, one ample hall, where a general course on Natural
Theology and the Evidences could be delivered once a year, by
a lecturer who might be changed or continued at the pleasure
of the directors.   He should be remunerated chiefly, if not
solely, by the fees of attendance, which ought not to be higher
than those in the University.   In this way you might neutralize
the whole apprehended mischief, and even convert the higher
scholarship of the Metropolis into a positive good; for, be
assured, that in like manner as a reading Catholic population,
though taught in schools whence the Bible has been excluded, is
a better subject for a Christianizing process than a non-reading
population; so a highly educated public, even though formed
in academies whence Christianity is kept out, is still a more
hopeful subject for the formation of Christian philanthropists

than a rudely ignorant and unlettered public. In every possible stage of mental cultivation, Christianity may be exposed to an incidental bane; but she possesses an inherent antidote wherewith to counteract and to prevail over it, so that, in the long run, I anticipate the greatest good from all those leanings of the public and popular mind towards a higher scholarship. Only let them be followed up by Christians with such expedients as might suit the spirit and philosophy of the times, and more especially in London.

I shall be most happy of a further correspondence with you upon this subject. I offer my respectful compliments to Mrs. Wilberforce, and I have the honour to be, my dear Sir, yours with greatest esteem, THOMAS CHALMERS.

No. LXVI.

St. Andrews, 22*d January* 1828.

MY DEAR SIR,—I have been much gratified by the receipt and perusal of your letter, and more especially by your congratulations upon the subject of my recent appointment. I do not commence the duties of my new charge till November next; and, along with the labours of my Professorship here, I fill up the intermediate time with the still higher labours of a very arduous preparation.

I am very glad to observe that this new arrangement has at length reconciled you to my movement from Glasgow; though independently of any such ulterior view, I felt the obligation, in point of Christian usefulness, to accept of my present office— and should have continued so to feel, though I had remained here to the end of my days. I am sensible that in this feeling there are some of my best friends who do not sympathize with me—overlooking, I think, two considerations which had decisive effect with myself. The first is, that a University stands to a single church in the relation that a fountain-head, whence many streams issue, does to one only of these streams. The second is, that Moral Philosophy stands to Christianity in the relation that Law does to Gospel; that the preaching of John the Baptist did to the preaching of the Saviour.

In reply to your kind inquiries regarding my children, I have to inform you that I am the father of six daughters—the eldest fourteen years, and the youngest one month, and of nearly equi-distant ages. I have lost none of my children, and have much reason to be thankful that Mrs. Chalmers (who begs her most respectful compliments to you) though delicate, on the whole, is remarkably well at present.

It is the cordial wish of myself, and, I am sure, the wish and the prayer of all your Christian friends, that you may be spared to spend amongst us a long old age of piety and peace. May you still have many days of rest and of rejoicing on the borders of Heaven; and may that Book, which spoke power-fully to myself, and has spoken powerfully to thousands, repre-sent you to future generations, and be the instrument of con-verting many who are yet unborn.

With my respectful regards to Mrs. and Miss Wilberforce, I have the honour to be, my dear Sir, yours, with greatest esteem,   THOMAS CHALMERS.

No. LXVII.

St. Andrews, 17*th June* 1828.

MY DEAR SIR,—I should have replied sooner to your most welcome communication; but I have been from home, and I did not receive it till yesterday, when it was too late to reply to it by the post.

Mrs. Chalmers and I are both delighted with the prospect of having you for a guest. We remain here till late in October, it being far the best place for the prosecution of those studies

which are so indispensable to the arduous office upon which I
am so soon to enter

We shall have two rooms at your service, and promise you
all the gratification which a most thorough retirement and the
most cordial welcome can afford. We both are quite alive to
the honour and the enjoyment of such a visit.

It is not necessary to write at present on the subject of a
Scottish tour, seeing that the movement should be a circular
one, and that your coming to St. Andrews, by Edinburgh, is just
taking our side of the circle first. Your return should be by
the North of Scotland and the West Coast; but the details of
the ulterior journey had far better be discussed in conversation.

We trust that Mrs. Wilberforce and your daughter will
accompany you.—I have the honour to be, my dear Sir, yours
with greatest esteem and regard,   Thomas Chalmers

No. LXVIII.

St. Andrews, 15th July 1828.

My dear Sir,—Mrs. Chalmers and I have been made quite
happy by your last. It will give us great pleasure to see your
son. We can accommodate him as well as the ladies, who, I
think, will enjoy Scotland ; and I fondly trust that you will be
much the better of the journey. The house we at present
occupy is very commodious, and has some pretensions to the
name of classical—it not only having in it the study of George
Buchanan, but having lodged Dr. Samuel Johnson when he
visited St. Andrews.

Our autumns are generally drier than our summers, but
there is no such great or regular difference as would lead me
to fix on any particular month in the way of preference. On
the whole, I would not think it advisable to travel in Scotland
after the end of September.

We have the greater and the smaller Highland tour—the

former taking you as far north as Inverness, and farther if you choose ; the latter a smaller sweep by Perth, Dunkeld, Blair, Killin, Argyleshire. The former would also comprehend Argyle-shire. You commence either from St. Andrews, and terminate what is purely Highland in the journey at Glasgow, whence you could make smaller excursions to Stirling and the Trosachs.

Abstracting from all detentions on the score of society, you could make the larger sweep from St. Andrews to Glasgow by moderate journeys in a fortnight, and the smaller sweep in nine or ten days. I make allowance for the remarkable scenes on the journey.

In fixing your itinerancy my only difficulty relates to the larger tour, because there are three great northern roads, and I know not which of these should be surrendered. I am anxious to secure the middle road, as being the more characteristic across the Grampians. But I would be unwilling to sacrifice the eastern, which takes you by Aberdeen, and carries you to some remarkable objects on the coast. I would very much defer to Mr. Charles Grant's opinion, who, by the way, is extensively acquainted in Inverness-shire. My letters of intro-duction will be a few to the aristocracy, but chiefly to the more meritorious clergy along the line of your journey, who will be delighted to show you every attention, and whom you will find to be at once intelligent and congenial.

May I request to know your movements when you have fixed them.—With most respectful compliments to Mrs. and Miss Wilberforce, in which Mrs. Chalmers joins, I have the honour to be, my dear Sir, yours with greatest esteem,

Thomas Chalmers.

No. LXIX.

St. Andrews, 31st July 1828.

My dear Sir,—Your final determination for this season, on the subject of a Scottish tour, could not fail to disappoint us, though it is impossible not to acquiesce in the reasons of it. The expectation of seeing you had begun to awaken a great competition for the pleasure of your society ; and, among others, Lord Leven, who, with his friend Captain Thornton, honoured me lately with a short visit, was confidently looking forward to a visit from you. We shall be exceeding glad of meeting with you anywhere, though the seclusion of St. Andrews would certainly have afforded greater advantages for intercourse than I can hope to have in Edinburgh. But there, too, we should feel it a gratification and an honour to have you under our roof.

I have just returned from Glasgow, where I have been visiting the afflicted family of my friend Mr. Parker, who died suddenly within these twelve days.

I observe the struggle and opposition that you have had to encounter in the erection of your chapel. Such is the identity of the anti-evangelical spirit all over the world, that I recognise the perfect identity of your experience with all that we have had to contend against among ourselves. Our General Assembly, however, is now far better disposed to these erections, and the chapel cause has been making great progress of late in Scotland.

Mrs. Chalmers joins in kindest regards to yourself, and with our united respects to Mrs. and Miss Wilberforce, I have the honour to be, my dear Sir, yours with greatest esteem,

THOMAS CHALMERS.

No. LXX.

Edinburgh, 24th *November* 1832.

MY DEAR SIR,—I received your letter of the 3d of October, by the hands of Mrs. Wellman, only two or three days ago ; and it was read, both by myself and Mrs. Chalmers, with great interest and emotion. I receive it as the most unequivocal expression of your friendship which could possibly be given, that you have thus laid open to me the personal and family trials wherewith a mysterious but merciful Providence hath exercised you ; and we particularly rejoice in your own distinct and declared experience, that though clouds and darkness are round about Him, and there is much of the inscrutable in His dealings with the children of men, yet is there wisdom in all His ways, and kindness in all His visitations.

We felt deeply the death of your daughter, whom we saw last in June 1830. May we all grow in a well-founded hope of that inheritance above, where sorrow and separation are unknown.

With our united and respectful compliments to Mrs. Wilberforce, I have the honour to be, my dear Sir, yours with greatest esteem and regard,   THOMAS CHALMERS.

LETTERS TO MRS. GLASGOW OF MOUNTGREENAN.

No. LXXI.

Glasgow, 24th April 1819.

DEAR MADAM,—Your interesting and kind letter reached me at least three weeks after it was written, and when I was in the midst of all that heat and hurry which are unfortunately too much associated with the business of the Sacrament in our large towns. I have since had a small excursion into the country, and this is the first day of my return home. I think it necessary to state all this, for it does require explanation that a letter so replete with valuable and friendly observations should have remained for such a length of time unanswered.

The notice that has been excited by my publications is certainly beyond all that I could have ventured to anticipate ; and my attention has been a good deal exercised on the question

—in how far this was due to the pure and single ingredient of Christianity, or to certain adventitious ingredients which entered into my exposition of it? and I trust that I speak the genuine desire of my heart, when I affirm the feeling of a much truer satisfaction in being made to understand that any hearer has become more reconciled than before to the preaching of those who hold fast the simple and unaccompanied Gospel, or that any reader has acquired either a juster perception or a more approving taste for the doctrine of the Bible.

In these circumstances I could not fail perusing your letter with much interest and gratification; and happy shall I be that, by entering upon the fellowship of confidence and affection with Christ, you experience in your person the fulfilment of all His promises, receiving from Him power to become one of the children of God, created anew unto good works, and rendered a new creature in Him who died for you.

Be assured, dear Madam, that you cannot think too extravagantly either of your own native guilt or native helplessness, and that on such a feeling as this you need lay no limitation whatever. And on the other hand, you cannot think too confidently either of Christ's power or of Christ's willingness to expiate the one and to perfect His own strength in the other. It is my earnest prayer that neither of us be permitted to stop short with approving of this process intellectually, but that we shall be led by the good Spirit of God to enter upon the process actually and experimentally. I have just room to add, that I do not know a more stimulating kind of reading than the lives of religious persons—Philip Henry, Matthew Henry, Doddridge, Halyburton, Newton, are among the most useful subjects of religious biography that at present occur to me; but let all our reading be subordinate to the Bible.

After the many kind encouragements which you have had the goodness to afford me, I assure you of my hearty inclination to

visit Mountgreenan, and will certainly never be in your neighbourhood, with health and any degree of leisure at all, without
offering my respects to you. I am greatly engrossed at present
however, and from the circumstance of my relations being all
situated on the east side of the island, I have it rarely in my
power to be in your neighbourhood.—Believe me to be, Madam,
yours with great regard and esteem,   THOMAS CHALMERS.

No. LXXII.

Anstruther, 13th August 1819.

MY DEAR MADAM,—I am here upon sea-bathing. You were
from home when I was last in your neighbourhood, and I fear
that I shall not be able to make out my meditated visit to
Mountgreenan for some time. Your last letter interested me
greatly, and the question about sin I trust proceeded from a
mind more enlightened, both as to its existence and its enormity,
than before, and therefore having more of its magnitude in view
as residing in her own character, while in respect of its absolute
magnitude it is actually becoming less.

The topic to which you adverted has puzzled and mortified
many an aspiring disciple of Christ. He becomes the sanctification as well as the redemption of those who believe in Him,
and why, then, is He not now my complete sanctification?
Just because we do not yet completely believe in Him. In
proportion to the strength and consistency of our faith is our
experience of His faithfulness. He gives power to become the
children of God to as many as receive Him. (John i. 12.) But
not to keep Him, just brings us back to the condition in which
we were when we had not received Him; and so is it worthy
of remark, that unless we keep in memory the truth which we
have learned, we have believed in vain, and are not saved.
(1 Cor. xv. 2.) The great excellence of the Gospel is, that the
same principle which stands connected with our acceptance in

the sight of God, (Acts xiii. 39,) will also, if admitted and *kept* in the heart, maintain within it the principle of all holy and affectionate obedience. (Gal. v. 6 ; 1 John v. 4.) But faith is a progressive principle. In its infancy it often fluctuates into feebleness, and appears to fade away altogether. It says nothing against but for the supremacy of its influence that, when away from the mind of man, he relapses into the sin and the vanities of nature, and that it is only when present in the mind that this new and implanted principle ensures the ascendency of the Spirit, and subordinates the flesh to its pure and prevailing influence. It is of importance to know, that the privilege of a Christian in the world consists not in an exemption from the motions of the flesh, but in a power of control over them. There is a conflict between nature and grace, even unto the end. (Gal. v. 17.) Paul describes this conflict in his own person. (Rom. vii. 9-25.) Sin was present, but it had not the dominion, when he recurred by faith to Christ as his helper. To feel the instigations of sin is one thing, to walk after these instigations is another. Commit yourself to Jesus as the Lord your sanctifier, and you will experience the same reason of gratitude that Paul did when he uttered the exclamation, Rom. vii. 24, 25 ; and in Rom. viii. 4, you find that through Christ strengthening him, he, and every true believer after him, walks after the Spirit.

I have often thought that " *whosoever* is born of God committeth not sin" would be more intelligible, and apparently more consistent with experience, were the first word rendered, which I think it might be, " whatsoever," viz., the new principle of regeneration—the love which faith worketh—the radical element of the new man, out of which no sin can possibly emerge, and which, in proportion to its growth in the Christian, will more and more prevail over the old man, and expel sin from the whole man, compound as he is in his present state of the two put together.

Out of all this observation I would say, in the first place, that the best practical attitude for obedience from one hour to another, is to live in faith on the Son of God from one hour to another—is to feed the flame of gratitude all the day long, by trusting all the day long—is to commit yourself in good earnest to Him under this one and that other temptation, and then see whether He will not keep that which is so committed—see whether, when the Lord is besought earnestly, He does not indeed and in truth return the answer, "I will make my grace sufficient for you; I will perfect my strength in weakness."

Let me say, in the second place, that though the existence of sin be compatible with a state of safety, (1 John i. 8,) I know not a worse symptom than when a professing disciple is willing, on this account, to lay down the armour of hostility against it. It is a war in which no quarter must be given—a war of extermination—a war with self, and with temper, and with wilfulness—a war which is never slackened by the offers of pardon or the hopes of impunity. It is remarkable that after John has brought forward the things stated in chapter i. of his first Epistle and verses 7 and 9, he should say, in chapter ii. verse 1, he wrote these things not that they might securely sin, but that they might *sin not*, and follows up this with another ample declaration of the grace and forgiveness by which the Gospel is characterized.

Did I think that natural talents were enough for an intelligent perusal of the Epistle to the Romans, I would recommend this epistle to none more readily than to yourself. But in the actual truth of the case, let me recommend the perusal of this admirable compendium of Christianity with earnest prayer—with sustained and persevering attention—with a constant feeling of dependence on that Spirit who, by the Word as His instrument, can alone effectually teach you, by taking of the things of Christ and shewing them unto you.

I have read with impression lately Alleine's "Alarm to the Unconverted," and I am now reading Doddridge's "Rise and Progress of Religion." The former is a very close and vigorous performance. Its occasional coarsenesses of imagery and expression I feel persuaded that you will now overlook; nor do I know a more pleasing collateral transformation that takes place on an inquirer than when, in spite of accompaniments which at one time would have utterly repelled him, his taste becomes reconciled to the phraseology of evangelical writers from the weight and preciousness of the matter which it conveys.— Believe me, my dear Madam, yours with great esteem and regard, THOMAS CHALMERS.

No. LXXIII.

Glasgow, 30th April 1821.

MY DEAR MADAM,—I send you my book on National Resources. I should like your frank and explicit avowal respecting the merits of my theory, which to me is still as convincing as when I first conceived it.

I look back with no common emotions of interest and delight to the hours of enjoyment I had while under your hospitable roof; and it is indeed my earnest wish and solicitude that your decided tendencies to the best of subjects may end in a blessed consummation. There is no possibility of coming forth with any prescription as to the time that might allowably be given to literature, and elegance, and society; and it would obliterate the character of Christianity altogether were she made so to deal out her allowances by hours and by quantities. The great object is to keep the heart with all diligence, and if it were right, everything else would find its right and natural adjustment in the system of one's concerns, and from a code of restraint the law of the Gospel would rise to the high distinction of being a law of liberty. For the right keeping of the heart,

K

I know not a more summary and thoroughly evangelical expedient than we find in Jude 20, 21.

It may however be affirmed, that it is a good discipline to maintain self-denial in reference to all our natural indulgences, and we cannot be too thoroughly aware, that just as it constitutes the crime of idolatry, whether the image we fall down to worship be of gold or of baser materials, so it is quite a possible thing to feed the defection of the heart from God by a refined, as effectually as by a coarser species of worldliness.

I crave my most respectful regards to Mr. Glasgow, whose kind reception of me I felt to be truly gratifying.—I am, my dear Madam, yours very affectionately,

THOMAS CHALMERS.

No. LXXIV.

MY DEAR MADAM,—I have at length perused your paper, and though to me there is no task more fatiguing and more formidable than that of transferring my mind to a new subject, with the view of critically appreciating the argument that has been raised upon it, yet I trust I have been enabled to seize upon the principle of your composition, and on rational and deliberate grounds to acquiesce in it. I have neither Alison nor Jeffrey by me, and am unable to estimate the whole amount of the difference between your theory and theirs; yet I can perceive a very important novelty in the compromise that you have struck between Socrates and Plato; in conceding to the former his principle of utility, as indeed the inherent or pervading principle of all beauty; and to the latter, that as our impressions of utility vary in different individuals with the accidental circumstances or affections, the character of beautiful which we assign to visible objects will depend on the character of our own emotions. I felt myself on more familiar ground, and where I was perhaps better able to estimate the value of your argument when I approached towards the conclusion of your essay. It is indeed a most important truth, that in morals and theology the soundness of the affections stands most intimately linked with the soundness of the understanding; and I can perceive how this very principle does indeed shed a most beautiful light on the department of Taste, the correctness of which will, according to the views that you have so ably unfolded, depend on the correctness of the heart and feelings.

You still, I apprehend, leave as wide though not so extensive an empire as does Alison to the law of association. The physical pleasure that certain sounds or sights confer, from their suitableness to the bodily organ, is no doubt an ingredient of beauty which has its primary and immediate residence in the object itself, though the remembrance of this in time past will influence to a certain degree, too, the present emotion wherewith the object is regarded. But saving on this ground the principle of utility seems to have no other instrument than association for working its influences upon taste.

Mrs. Chalmers and our family are still at Ardincaple, and I do feel the sea-bathing to be of great benefit, and retirement a very great luxury. I took the liberty of recommending a few Christian duodecimos to you when we last met. May I add to the list Romaine's "Life of Faith," and Romaine's "Walk of Faith." I think he unfolds the most peaceful, and, at the same time, the most powerful way of prosecuting the good work of sanctification.

I again beg my most respectful compliments to Mr. Glasgow, and with every assurance of esteem and attachment to yourself, I entreat you to believe me, my dear Madam, yours very truly, THOMAS CHALMERS.

No. LXXV.

Glasgow, 15th November 1821.

MY DEAR MADAM,—I am glad you have looked into Edwards ; I think that the great strength of his argument for the agreement of his doctrines with moral distinctions, lies in an Appendix that is subjoined to all the later editions of his works. I am quite aware, however, that he has failed to convince some of the ablest and most accomplished understandings. I feel both amused and interested by the lucubrations of Mr. Stewart on this subject in his Preliminary Dissertation.

Edwards, though the profoundest of all writers on the more deep and hidden tracks of speculation, is also the plainest and most practical on the more popular topics of Christianity ; nor have I read anything more urgently, and even appallingly impressive, than are some of his sermons. His works are now formed into a complete edition ; and I think of them that they should hold a place of supereminence in every theological library.

We must have more conversation on the subject of Alison and Jeffrey on Taste. I have still the haunting impression that Alison would concede to you the opinion that you have formed, and at the same time affirm it to be in entire unison with his own theory. If I recollect him right he denies the power of calling forth the emotions of taste to any qualities strictly material, independent of their association with something else, or that there is nothing either in colour or form to awaken these emotions. There are at the same time *inherent* qualities in external and visible objects which may be conceived as disjoined from either their colour or shape, as the usefulness of a horse. This usefulness might enter into our impression of the beauty of the animal, or in other words, it may be something inherent in the horse that constitutes part of its beauty; and yet a something

reducible into the principle of association, because that something is not addressed immediately either to the eye or the
ear, or any of the senses. The sight of him suggests his usefulness, and it is not what is immediately before you, but what
the mind is led to conceive from it that is the cause of the
emotion in question. I speak rather in the obscure and
floundering style of one whose mind is not made up on the subject ; and I am sure you must think me provokingly stupid in
regard to it.

It delights me to witness the approximations of one who has
so much both of literary accomplishment and intellectual vigour,
to a doctrine that is still an offence and a derision among the
philosophers of our existing generation ; and when I think of
the great moral distance that there is between an appreciating
taste either for Alison or Stewart upon the one hand, and a
relish for the writings of Guthrie or Romaine, or Owen, or John
Newton, upon the other, I cannot but rejoice in the infusion of
the latter into a mind before strongly impregnated with the
former, as the hopeful evidence of one who is under the workings of a high and heavenly influence ; and it is indeed my
earnest prayer that, through the Word and Spirit of God,
you may become every day wiser unto salvation.—With most
respectful compliments to Mr. Glasgow, believe me, my dear
Madam, yours with great esteem and regard,

THOMAS CHALMERS.

No. LXXVI.

Friday, 11*th July* 1822.
MY DEAR MADAM,—In the publishing of your Essay there are
two things that must be taken into account:—First, the taste
of the public has declined prodigiously of late years for all the
topics of pure and abstract speculation. The talent of our land
has now forced its way into the channel of periodical litera-

ture ; and there is certainly a force and spirit in our magazines, and reviews, and even newspapers, which might have done credit to the best of our British classics. But certain it is, that a separate and independent essay on such a topic as you have chosen, is not fitted to meet the present direction which the demand for reading has taken. No merit or power of argument, or of matter, that is of so scientific a character, will countervail the present tendencies of the popular tastes,—and the slow sale of Brown's "Lectures" is a very striking instance of it. The same remark applies, I believe, to Stewart's works ; so that both he and Playfair, to widen the circulation of their views, have thrown them into Encyclopædias, these great periodical eddies of literature in our day.

But, secondly, to make a work of abstract speculation noticeable and an object of demand, it should be brought out in the permanent form of a book. It is a heavy additional drawback on the circulation of an argument that is purely philosophical when it is offered to the public in a pamphlet. Brown's Essay on " Cause and Effect" appeared at first in this ephemeral form, for it had a temporary importance from the Leslie controversy ; but to stamp endurance upon it, it had to be dilated into a volume. The same is true of a most profound metaphysical pamphlet of Edwards, which might have come out still-born, or speedily died away from all general observation, had it not been incorporated with his " Essay on the Will" in an Appendix.

The suggestion that I would found upon all this—but with the utmost deference, and in the hope that you will give it no further place than you really think it entitled to—is, that the Essay should appear, in the first instance, in one of our most distinguished periodicals, (say the " Christian Observer,") where it might call forth a world of observation and argument, and give a direction, perhaps, to other illustrations of the principle on your part ; and when enough of materials have been thus digested and accumulated for a volume, let it pass into this state, as Cunninghame's last work did, which, in fact, was brought out by a gradual preparation of this very kind.—With most respectful compliments to Mr. Glasgow and Miss Dunlop, I entreat you to believe me, my dear Madam, yours most truly, THOMAS CHALMERS.

No. LXXVII.

Glasgow, 15th November 1822.

MY DEAR MADAM,—I do not know whether Mr. Collins has written you in regard to the dedication; but you must really permit us both to say that there are many serious and weighty objections against the appearance of it. I have already been made the subject in print of most gross and ungenerous imputations, on the score of the interested connexion which is alleged to subsist between myself and that house; and anything so very eulogistical printed by them would, I am sure, give a colour to these imputations, and altogether form such an exhibition as might revolt even many who at present entertain no suspicion of that kind.

I fear that this would be an insuperable barrier to the publication of your work *by that house*, if the dedication be persisted in; and I farther entreat your forgiveness when I say, that though published in any circumstances I should be distressed by the appearance of it. It is no doubt most flattering to myself that I should stand so high in the estimation of one whom I myself so highly and so sincerely esteem. But I would infinitely rather that the world was not admitted as a spectator upon this gratification, which to me were far more precious and satisfying if, undisturbed by the public gaze, it were left in the state of a friendship that none but the parties themselves should know, and which none else could appreciate.

I look earnestly forward to a favourable deliverance from

you upon this point; after which I shall have occasion to advert to other particulars connected with the publication.

With most respectful compliments to Mr. Glasgow, and most affectionate prayers for your own advancement in all that is good, and gracious, and heavenly, I entreat you to believe me, my dear Madam, yours most truly,   THOMAS CHALMERS.

No. LXXVIII.

2d April 1823.

MY DEAR MADAM,—I felt exceedingly grateful for your letter, and much interested by all that you mention on the subject of the Essay. I have read it deliberately since I saw you, and I do think that it will most assuredly work its way. I left a copy with Dr. Charteris of Wilton, in Roxburghshire, about a month ago, who is much pleased and interested; and it has been read with very intelligent approbation by some cultivated ladies in that neighbourhood. I expect, however, soon a still more solid and profound testimony from Mr. Douglas of Cavers, author of the " Hints on Missions," who has much exercised his talents on the philosophy both of taste and metaphysics. The subject is such that I should look for a very gradual sale. Mr. Alison's first edition lingered for many years in the market, but I trust that yours will obtain an earlier impulse than his did from the reviews and journals of the day.

It grieves me to say that some recent accessions of labour and employment make it quite imperative upon me to husband my time to the uttermost, and more particularly to abridge all my excursions from home. I have on this account declined Mr. Wilson's invitation, and I really can perceive no outlet from my accumulated urgencies till the summer of 1824.

I beg my most respectful compliments to Miss Dunlop and Mr. Glasgow.—I am, my dear Madam, yours with great esteem and regard,   THOMAS CHALMERS.

No. LXXIX.

Glasgow, 21st August 1823.

MY DEAR MADAM,—I have to apologize for delaying to acknowledge your kind attentions to me. However much I am
gratified by your opinion of what you have seen of my coming
volume, I cannot but feel assured that your partialities in
behalf of its unworthy author have enhanced your estimation
of it. I cannot feel too grateful for your expression of friendship towards me.

You are kind enough to interest yourself in my preparation
for the Moral Philosophy. I am far from satisfied, and must
just flounder my way through the new materials of the subject
next winter in the best manner that I can.

I can, however, see it to be replete with interest; and that
so far from detaching one's regards from the first and greatest
of causes, I do not know how one can labour more directly or
more importantly in its service than by a right elucidation of
all the topics connected with moral science. I trust that I
may at length be enabled to find my way to your favourite
subject—the action and re-action that taste and principle have
on each other. I was glad to understand from Mr. Collins that
Foster appreciated your views. I hope that you have seen the
last " Edinburgh" on newspapers. It gives us a singular view
of the present state of the reading public; and I am more persuaded than ever, that the readiest way of obtaining public
attention to almost any subject is through the medium of
periodicals. I would strongly advise extracts from your work
in some of our monthly publications; as to them the whole
talent of our writers, and the whole attention of our readers,
seem to have taken, what I think, a very unfortunate direction.
I trust that the good old fashion of entire, and independent,
and systematic treatises will again be restored, as there is

L

really nothing more fitted to superficialize an age than the sketches, however forcible, and the sallies, however lively, that have given such currency to our ephemeral literature.

I beg my most respectful compliments to Mr. Glasgow and Miss Dunlop ; and I entreat you to believe me, my dear Madam, yours with much esteem and regard, THOMAS CHALMERS.

No. LXXX.

St. Andrews, 24*th August* 1824.

MY DEAR MADAM,—I have never lost sight of my promise to send you a sermon on Colossians iv. 5. I find that it does not by any means exhaust the subject, and, indeed, forms only the part of a projected treatise on the kindred subjects to that of which it treats. It is on this account that I would take the liberty of requesting you to send it back when you are done with it ; at the same time you are most welcome to take a copy, and make any use of that copy which you please. But I shall require it, both for the preparation of my treatise, and also, perhaps, for preaching occasionally.

After the bustle of Glasgow, there is a peculiar charm in the calmness and tranquillity of St. Andrews.

With most respectful compliments to Mr. Glasgow, I have the honour to be, my dear Madam, yours with great esteem,

THOMAS CHALMERS.

No. LXXXI.

St. Andrews, 26*th October* 1824.

MY DEAR MADAM,—I received your kind letter of the 7th of October, by the hands of Miss Dunlop, whom I had very great pleasure in meeting when last in Edinburgh.

I feel the exceeding justness of your remarks on the subject of my sermon. There is a great want of specification in its advices, and I fairly confess that I should feel it very difficult to condescend upon the details of our conversation, as becometh Christians, with the people of the world, and as yet am really not qualified for more than the very general bearings and landmarks of the subject.

But what interested me far more, though very painfully and with deep sympathy for yourself, was, the account that Miss Dunlop gave me of Mr. Glasgow. His illness was subsequent, I observe, to the date of your letter, and I cannot think without emotion of the exercise that your mind and feelings must undergo. We have had experimental proof, on such trying occasions, of the efficacy of prayer; and sure I am, that however general this direction may be, it is pertinent and particular enough to have been often followed up by a special blessing even in those cases that looked most hopeless.

My syllabus of lectures is, indeed, a very imperfect exhibition of the great subject to which I should like to devote much of my future attention. I must model and remodel many times over ere I can bring it to that state in which I would like to leave it conclusively. Mrs. Chalmers and our children, I have reason to bless God, are in very good health. She feels deeply with myself for the situation of Mr. Glasgow, and desires, along with me, her best and kindest regards.—I entreat you to believe me, my dear Madam, yours with the greatest esteem and regard,   THOMAS CHALMERS.

No. LXXXII.

St. Andrews, 26th February 1825.

MY DEAR MADAM,—Your kind letter of 11th December I should have replied to long ago. I enter fully into the difficulties of your situation, and am grieved to hear from most recent accounts that Mr. Glasgow's health is not improved; but surely, if aught should reconcile us to these adverse visitations, it must be their undoubted efficacy as the instruments often of a great revival to the soul that is exercised by them. There is nothing of which I am more thoroughly aware than the utter difference which there is between a speculative and an experimental conviction of the same truth. I may know that there is peace with God through Christ, without that peace being actually mine : I may have the most orthodox notion of the ground of acceptance, without personally resting on that ground and having the sense of my own acceptance : I may have a just perception of the truth as it is in Jesus, without any real part in it; and this appears to me to be the use of affliction. It loosens us from the earthly dependence, and forces us to feel and to sound as it were for a heavenly one. Instead of merely looking to the solidity of that foundation which God hath laid in Zion, we are led actually to lean upon it. That which was formerly a thing of contemplation comes to be a thing of personal interest ; and whereas the understanding alone was formerly concerned with the doctrine, the heart and the hopes and all the feelings of our nature come into busy engagement with the truths of revelation which the mind now gladly seeks to in the absence of those worldly blessings that wont to be enough for it.

It was therefore with no common interest that I read of your spirit of adoption, and your sense of peace in Christ Jesus— most precious experiences which I pray you may ever be enabled to retain, and which I can assure you are worthy of whole worlds to be realized.

There has left us for Glasgow a very particular friend of mine, Mr. Craik, a student of St. Andrews, and of most extraordinary eloquence and power. He has just delivered a course of lectures here upon English Poetry, and with very great force and felicity, both of imagination and language. He is to deliver the same lectures in Glasgow, and, though I fear it is out of the question that you should be in Glasgow during any part of his stay, yet acquainted as you are with the most literary and cultivated of the mercantile class in that city, I should deem it a kindness if you would simply state to any of them the kind of entertainment which they may expect by attending Mr. Craik. They will find in every one of his lectures a very rich feast, both of intellect and fancy.

Mrs. Chalmers and our family are all in good health.—With best wishes and prayers, both in behalf of yourself and Mr. Glasgow, I have the honour to be, my dear Madam, yours most respectfully,   THOMAS CHALMERS.

No. LXXXIII.

Glasgow, 22d September 1825.

MY DEAR MADAM,—I have the utmost desire to meet with you, and contemplated writing you, when I should be at Fairley next week, upon the subject. I am glad to understand that Mrs. Parker has asked you to be there along with our family. I shall yet be other four Sundays in Glasgow, and have therefore time enough for postponing the consideration of any ulterior arrangement till next week.

I am much gratified by being made to understand from you that Mr. Glasgow is in a more comfortable state of health. May the Giver of all grace sanctify the various trials and appre-hensions to which we are exposed in this our earthly pilgrimage. This is the day on which I preach a sermon at laying the foundation of Knox's Monument, a subject not at all points congenial to me, but which was put upon me by the excessive urgency of some of my friends.—I am, my dear Madam, yours with great esteem and regard,   THOMAS CHALMERS.

No. LXXXIV.

Glasgow, 12th October 1825.

MY DEAR MADAM,—I spent all last week with my friend Mr. Wood, and got quit of my sore eyes in a few days. Will you have the goodness to say to Dr. Allan that I made use of his prescription with great effect.

I found it a very tough and arduous undertaking to deliver myself on the subject of Predestination in one day. However, I am now done with the subject; and while quite assured of the doctrine, I feel equally assured that it leaves all the incitements, and all the obligations, and the whole work of practical Christianity, from its commencement to its consummation, precisely where it found them. It is worthy of all observation, that while the Gentiles are represented as the objects of a previous Predestination, we are made to understand at the conclusion of the chapter, that this was made good by their acceptance of the free offer of the Gospel; and that those decreed reprobates the Jews, only became so through their rejection of that offer; and that the whole argument closes with a " whosoever," a wide and a welcome proclamation to all who will. Our business surely is not with the decrees, whereof we know nothing, but with the instant declarations which are sounding in our ears, with the word that is nigh unto us, with God not in the act of ordination millions of centuries back, but with God in the act of urgent, and kind, and honest entreaty at this moment. Let us therefore leave the secret things which belong unto God, where they ought to be left, and proceed on those revealed things which belong to ourselves and to our children.

May I be permitted to say, that if I may judge from my own feelings, the trials wherewith you have been exercised must greatly enhance the regard and the interest of all your friends. It is a difficult, but to a Christian not an impracticable achievement, to count it all joy when he falls into divers tribulations. A believing view of eternity would absorb all our griefs and all our provocations. May the God and the Giver of all comfort prove a resting-place to your spirit, and may you be enabled to hide yourself in the pavilion of His residence till all calamities be overpast.—I am, my dear Madam, yours with the greatest esteem and regard,   THOMAS CHALMERS.

No. LXXXV.

St. Andrews, 13*th December* 1825.

MY DEAR MADAM,—I feel myself a good deal goaded at present with the necessity of having my third volume on the Christian and Civic Economy of Great Towns in readiness for the press by January. It has been got up in a sad hurry, and with none of that leisure and care which I should like to bestow on all my future literary preparations. But it is my last engagement, and I am glad, by getting quit of it, to be wholly emancipated for the pursuits of my new profession, which are only commencing now in good earnest.

I observe by your last, that you have been exercised afresh by the death of relatives. May these visitations lead us to a truer estimate of the worth of things, that we may neither be elated by this world's abundance, nor cast down by its adversities and its crosses. It is remarkable that in the parable of the sower, the cares of this life are enumerated along with its pleasures among the thorns which overbear the good seed of the word of God. I have often thought, too, of the sorrow of this world being adverted to as a counterpart to godly sorrow, and of the property which is ascribed to it—"that it worketh death."

I am delighted with the justness of your views on the subject of Predestination. In regard to the union of fear and love, I feel the importance of what you say in regard to the former affection as an instrument for the conversion of sinners. It is exceedingly good to mark the gradual operation of this feeling in bringing the inquirer onward from the beginning of wisdom to the state of being perfect in love. I did touch upon this matter in a sermon on the text, " Some save with fear, and others with compassion, making a difference." But it would require to be much more fully illustrated.

I do not know if you have seen " Leighton on Peter." I am sure that you would rejoice in that book as a very high Christian feast.—I am, my dear Madam, yours with the greatest regard, THOMAS CHALMERS.

No. LXXXVI.

St. Andrews, 7th June 1826.

MY DEAR MADAM,—I fear that my first Sunday at Glasgow must be so late as the first Sunday of August, or August the 6th. I mean to approach it by a very unusual route by East Lothian, Berwickshire, Roxburghshire, Dumfriesshire, Galloway, and Ayrshire. On this line I visit several of my acquaintances, and more especially a sister, married only yesterday to a clergyman in Kirkcudbrightshire. If perfectly convenient for you, I would come from Irvine to Mountgreenan on Saturday the 5th of August, and return from Glasgow on the evening of Sunday the 6th, to spend a week there. I trust, however, that you will decline receiving me if either the state of Mr. Glasgow's health or any other circumstance should render it unsuitable.

I will not disguise it, that next to the happiness of your own society, I value the quietness and retirement of Mountgreenan, and would gladly avail myself of these advantages for a more intense work of Sabbath preparation than I have yet been able to fulfil. The truth is, that I have found the study and society together greatly too much for me on my recent visits to the west; and I should vastly desiderate that entire command of the forenoon which you have ever had the goodness to allow me, and which, intermingled as it was with recreation and converse of the highest order, has inspired me with the pleasantest recollections of your place and neighbourhood.—I am, my dear Madam, yours with the greatest esteem and regard,

THOMAS CHALMERS.

No. LXXXVII.

St. Andrews, 4th December 1826.

MY DEAR MADAM,—I am much interested by what you say of Mr. Cunninghame. When I had the pleasure of meeting him at Mountgreenan, he interested me much more than I had ever before been in the study of prophecy, by the assertion that he made, both upon his own experience and upon that of others, of its spiritualizing tendency. I have resolved to make a deliberate effort upon that subject, but have scarcely had time to begin. I have, however, been reading some proof-sheets of a new publication by Mr. Irving—that is, the translation of a prophetic work from the Spanish. It seems very able. I believe it will make me a millenarian ; and I can certainly conceive from it that the study of prophecy should have a very powerful effect in strengthening one's practical Christianity. I am glad that your work is speedily to be made the subject of a review, which I sincerely hope will do justice to it. That my mind is not absolutely established on the side of its theory does not affect the question of whether or not I think it should have been published. Both Alison's and Jeffrey's books on the same subject are valuable accessions to English Literature, even though their theories do diverge somewhat from each other, and though I cannot say that either has made me a decided proselyte. The same applies to what Brown has written upon this subject. Successive authors might make successive approximations to the truth, and though one is doubtful as to the truth of any of their promulgated systems, yet he may not be at all doubtful of its worth as a contribution to the mass of literature on that subject. I must repeat, however, that I should have preferred your work to have come out, in the first instance, through the medium of some of our best journals, as being far the most noticeable way in the present direction which the public have taken towards periodical literature. I experience this in the dull sale of my own works on Political Economy.—I am, my dear Madam, yours very respectfully, THOMAS CHALMERS.

No. LXXXVIII.

St. Andrews, 21st February 1828.

MY DEAR MADAM,—Accept of my best thanks for your friendly congratulations on the subject of my recent appointment to Edinburgh. The preparation is a work of great labour, and indeed I may say that it is now my main though not my only employment, as I have at present the teaching of two classes besides. In the course of my reading for the Theological Chair, I have fallen in with a French work of Leibnitz's, entitled " Essais de Théodicée sur la bonté de Dieu, la liberté de l'homme, et l'origine du mal." I am sure it would interest you. He is a Necessitarian ; but though not so close in argument, is far more illustrative and philosophical than Edwards. He has besides a richness and an elegance which the other has no pretensions to. He gives much information about the state of moral and metaphysical science in the Continent at that period ; and though he has not just resolved the question of the origin of evil, yet he has advanced such plausibilities upon the subject as serve to reconcile us in the meantime to a suspension of our judgment till " the day shall declare it," even the " day of the revelation of the mystery of God." I do not recommend this work for its practical piety, but rather for what may be called its philosophical orthodoxy ; and it is most interesting to follow the speculations of one so illustrious in science, on the sublime doctrines and mysteries of our faith.

My work of practical piety at present is Boston, one of our

Scottish authors. I am now reading his " Fourfold State," and I think his little treatise entitled " The Crook in the Lot" is very precious.

I fear that my engagements are such that the composition of a sermon on any special topic at present is out of the question. The subject that you advert to, however, is one on which there must be some impressive treatises ; and it occurs to me to say that if I remember right there are French tracts which have been published by the Continental Society, and some of which I am confident must bear upon Scriptural reading. I know not a cheaper and more productive benevolence than the distribution of such pamphlets when well chosen.

We are all pretty well. May the God of all mercy ever be with you, and in His precious Bible may you never want for refreshment and consolation.—Believe me, my dear Madam, yours with greatest affection and esteem,

THOMAS CHALMERS.

No. LXXXIX.—LETTER TO MRS. DUNLOP.

Skirling Manse, Biggar, 8th June 1842.

MY DEAR MRS. DUNLOP,—I was much impressed by your farewell sentence at our parting in the Meadows on Saturday afternoon, and have felt ever since that I could not do adequate justice to the common sentiment which I believe actuated us both, without addressing you a few lines upon the subject.

In one respect our experience is very much at one. In early life my fellowships, and of course my preferences, were all on the side of that cold and moderate system of Christianity which is sometimes dignified by the appellation of rational. I have heard you complain that you almost never heard any exposition of the evangelical system from the pulpit ; and that when that mode of preaching became more frequent and fashionable, it came upon you with a sense of novelty. With me, again—and here perhaps we differ in our histories—that system was not unknown, but then it was the object of antipathy and distaste ; and nothing can be more distinct than my two mental states in reference to Christianity before and after the age of thirty, since which time the peculiar doctrines of the gospel have risen every year in my estimation ; and I have long been persuaded that the only way of salvation is through the knowledge of Christ and of Him crucified.

To me the most precious verses in the Bible are those which give a specific and pointed direction to the overtures of reconciliation in such terms as warrant the reader to apply them to himself individually. For example, " The blood of Christ cleanseth from *all* sin." Why not from my sin ?—" Come unto me *all*." Why not I ?—" *Whosoever* cometh shall in no wise be cast out." Let me come then, sure of Heaven's welcome and of Heaven's good-will.—" If *any* man open the door of his heart, I will enter and be at peace with him." Let me take to myself the encouragement of this blessed saying, " *Every one* that asketh receiveth." Let me ask till I receive, seek till I find, knock till the door be opened. I have often said that there is not a greater help to the way of peace than a prayerful reading of the Bible. The profitable way of reading is to read it with application, and as if God through His word were holding individual converse with me.

I was much gratified by your favourable opinion of my daughter Grace. Though I say it myself she is no ordinary person ; and therefore it is, that she has lived beyond the sight and sympathy of ordinary minds. She is with me here at Skirling, as well as Mrs. Chalmers, and I hope that both of them will benefit by the change of air. Mrs. Glasgow* I always regarded as a very intellectual person, and she blended the

* Mrs. Dunlop's sister.

spiritual with it during the last years of her life ; and I remember well the pleasure I felt in observing how she congenialized with the homely but substantial writings of the good old puritans, and that notwithstanding her refined literary taste. It is this union of the literary with the evangelical which makes Grace so interesting to me.

It is my earnest prayer, my dear Mrs. Dunlop, that the evening of your life may be more and more irradiated with the hopes of the gospel ; and that you may have great peace and great joy in placing your full reliance on that mercy which in the economy of our redemption stands associated with a truth which never fails.—I am, my dear Madam, yours very truly,

THOMAS CHALMERS.

LETTERS TO MRS. PARKER.

No. XC.

Glasgow, 7th May 1823.

MY DEAR MADAM,—Mrs. Chalmers desires me to say, that as soon as Dr. Rainy authorizes the movement, she will most gratefully avail herself of your kind invitation.* Blochairn has often been a most precious and important asylum to me, and it is there that I have been always most protected from all that could interfere with mental exercises. With kindest compliments to Mr. and the Misses Parker, I entreat you to believe me, my dear Madam, yours most gratefully,

THOMAS CHALMERS.

No. XCI.

Blochairn, 1st July 1823.

MY DEAR MADAM,—I feel the utmost gratitude for the very perfect accommodation that I here enjoy, and shall never for-

* See Memoirs, vol. ii. p. 472.

get the lasting obligations under which you have laid both myself and my family. We have a few callers, but nothing oppressive in this way. Dr. Lockhart and his lady have paid us a short visit : we feel exceedingly comfortable ; and, I am sure, are greatly better off than we could possibly have been in any situation that had been selected by ourselves. Grace has been thrown somewhat aback by cold, but has certainly made progress upon the whole since she came out to Blochairn.

I cannot adequately express the thankfulness I feel for that kind Providence which has conducted me to the arrangement that I now enjoy. I would have sunk under the accumulated weight of my prospects and preparations had it not been for this precious season of tranquillity. I have now the likely anticipation of such a readiness for my new office as may warrant the hope of getting over the approaching winter with some degree of comfort.—With kindest compliments to the Misses Parker and Mr. James, I entreat you to believe me, my dear Madam, yours with gratitude and esteem,

THOMAS CHALMERS.

No. XCII.

Blochairn, 11th July 1823.

MY DEAR MADAM,—Mrs. Chalmers was interrupted in her purpose to write this letter, and as she is still in bed, and our messenger with us at present, I have to state from her, that she knows you will be gratified to hear that Grace, in spite of short and temporary fluctuations, from one day to another, is making steady and general progress, and is certainly much stronger and better than when she first came out. I have great satisfaction in adding, that Mrs. Chalmers herself is evidently improved by her country residence ; and there are additional grounds of thankfulness for all the convenience and pleasure enjoyed by myself in this most retired and romantic spot.—
Yours most affectionately,   THOMAS CHALMERS.

No. XCIII.

9th October 1823.

My dear Madam,—Mrs. Chalmers fixes on Friday week, being the 17th of this month, as the one that would suit her intended movement, for your servant being at Blochairn. We had proposed to move on the Saturday, being the 18th, and we think it well that the turmoil of the Synod is over before we enter into Glasgow. The remaining few weeks will no more than suffice for our preparations previous to our departure.

There is one point of negligence on which I cannot reflect without compunction. I have not visited those humble neighbours whom I should have plied with ministerial advice and attention. I have only seen Mrs. Sibbald once, and Mrs. Smith but for a single moment, when I left a promise that I have not, from bad health, been able to fulfil. Walter's wife I have never visited, and on looking back, I can offer no other explanation than that I have allowed my prospective labours to encroach a great deal too much on my present duties.

We shall always look back on Blochairn with feelings of peculiar interest and delight, and will never fail to join with the recollection that kindness from which our family have derived such inestimable benefits.—Yours very affectionately,

THOMAS CHALMERS.

No. XCIV.

Blochairn, 20th October 1823.

My dear Madam,—We have delayed leaving this delightful neighbourhood for two days longer than we originally purposed, and only take our final departure this morning. We fear that this may have somewhat disturbed and deranged the operations of your servants. Our little Grace, in virtue of a severe toothache, had become quite feverish on Saturday, and we were apprehensive of the consequences of a removal. I myself had been laid up, and am now greatly the better of the repose and retirement of one rural Sabbath. We are now in full equipment for moving. There is, indeed, an impressive necessity now for beginning our operations at Windsor Place as soon as possible. But we do leave this interesting mansion with deep emotions of regret. My walks have supplied me with many local associations that will serve to impress with vivacity upon my remembrance an abode wherewith I shall ever connect the most inestimable blessings to my family.

I shall not trouble you any further with the expression of a gratitude that I am sure, both with Mrs. Chalmers and myself, will never be effaced, but remain indelible under all the varieties of our future history in the world.—Yours most affectionately,   THOMAS CHALMERS.

No. XCV.

St. Andrews, 5th January 1824.

MY DEAR MADAM,—I should have written long ere now of Mrs. Chalmers's arrival, and of her excellent health. I have the utmost reason to bless God for the state of my family.

We have greatly humanized the appearance of our house since Mr. Parker saw it, and I beg that he will give up his benevolent alarms upon that account. The public rooms are both most comfortable, and, with the exception of our bedroom, they are all in a very fair and habitable state. The truth is, that my Glasgow friends were not in fair circumstances for a right judgment upon the matter, as they saw the house in a wholly dismantled state, and without furniture. I have Mrs. Chalmers's authority for saying, that it is a much better habitation than she had been led to apprehend it.

It will, I am sure, give you much pleasure to know, that hitherto I have had great peace and comfort in St. Andrews.

The weather has, upon the whole, been uncommonly fine, and the walks are delightful. It is not that I have little sensibility towards Glasgow, the place I have left, but that the air, and the tranquillity, and the style of occupation of the place I am in, are all so very congenial to my habits, that I have so much of enjoyment in St. Andrews; and it gives me the utmost pleasure to connect the facilities of my present condition with my residence in Blochairn. It is to that arrangement that I owe such an amount of preparation for my class as has made an undertaking practicable that otherwise would have been most oppressive.

I feel that I have been wanting in my duty not to have written you sooner, and greatly wanting in it not to have written Dr. Rainy,* whose unwearied friendship and assiduous offices of kindness to my family have given him as high a place in my gratitude as he before had in my esteem and regard.

Mrs. Chalmers joins in kindest regards to the whole family, and our children—who by the way attend a most excellent school at our very door—send their best wishes to Miss Anne Parker. May the protection of heaven ever be over you; and may the sense of God, as God in Christ, be ever present, both to cheer and to sanctify the hearts of all in whom you are interested.—I am, my dear Madam, yours with the utmost gratitude and esteem,   THOMAS CHALMERS.

No. XCVI.—LETTER TO MR. PARKER.

St. Andrews, 25th February 1825.

MY DEAR SIR,—It gave me the utmost satisfaction to hear from Mrs. Parker of Mr. James's† academic honours: I had before been apprized of them by the London newspapers.

The letter I received some time ago from Mr. Charles took

* Mrs. Parker's brother.
† The late Vice-Chancellor, Sir James Parker.

M

no notice of his providential escape at Guadaloupe. I was much impressed by Mrs. Parker's description of it, and I do sincerely hope that a circumstance so awakening will not be lost on your son who has been delivered in a way that so strikingly announces the hand of an unseen Preserver.

Mrs. Chalmers and the family are all in remarkable health. The weather here is quite marvellous for the season. We have had a succession of the finest vernal days—or I might say, weeks—that I ever recollect, though we cannot but have an overcast before the winter has altogether passed away.

With kindest and most respectful compliments to Mrs. and the Misses Parker, in which Mrs. Chalmers joins, I am, my dear Sir, yours most truly,   THOMAS CHALMERS.

No. XCVII.

St. Andrews, 25th June 1825.

MY DEAR MADAM,—As Mrs. Chalmers is somewhat taken up with the children, she has requested me to answer your very kind letter to her. We are both very sensible, and have had much experience of the charms of Blochairn ; and have resolved, with much gratitude, to avail ourselves of your kind offer of its accommodations. The only condition is, that Mrs. Rainy shall not in the least be put out of her way by our intrusion, which cannot, however, with the arrangements which are before us, last longer than a fortnight, as our various excursions to Fairley, Mosshouse, &c., will take up the great majority of our time in the west.

We had very great pleasure in the visit of Mr. and Mrs. with Miss Babington. There is a life and a refreshment in the converse of religious people, of which we here stand eminently in need. Since they left us we have been much gratified with a visit from Mr. Thomas Erskine, author of some most valuable treatises, and a truly spiritual as well as richly-gifted intellectual man. He regretted having missed the society of the venerable Mr. Babington, to whom, by the way, I have written to the care of Mr. Parker.

Mr. Erskine sends the kindest inquiries after Dr. Rainy and Mr. R. Brown, whom he had formerly met with in Glasgow.—Yours with great esteem and regard,

THOMAS CHALMERS.

No. XCVIII.

Blochairn, 13th September 1825.

MY DEAR MADAM,—We have been very happy here in the midst of great quiet and of the most unbounded kindness. The scheme of our future movements is somewhat embarrassed by a public sermon which I have to preach in the middle of next week ; and I find in consequence that it will answer best for us to come down to Fairley on Monday the 3d of October, being Monday fortnight. But should any other week be more convenient for you, I beg that you will mention it.

I am glad to understand that Mr. Parker is so much better, and that Mr. James purposes to stay with you till the 10th of October. I am very desirous of some conversation with him, and more especially since I understand that his studies have been directed to Political Economy.

Mrs. Chalmers joins me in kindest compliments to you and the Misses Parker. Both the families here are in great health and enjoyment.—I am, my dear Madam, yours very truly,

THOMAS CHALMERS.

No. XCIX.

Glasgow, 3d August 1826.

MY DEAR MADAM,—Your very kind letter I received yesterday.

I can assure you that it is with no ordinary regret that I

bereave myself of your society during this excursion. It was my firm purpose to have been a week at Fairley ; but the composition of a preface for Mr. Russel's "Sermons," rendered it, in the first instance, necessary that I should be in the immediate neighbourhood of Glasgow, and, in the second instance, desirable that I should have the command of six entire days for study in the week—an advantage which I behoved to forfeit by the steamboat passages to and from Fairley. This last advantage I secure at Mountgreenan, for I drive there on Tuesday evening, and back again on the morning of the Monday after.

What I desiderate is, a visit to the west, without the encumbrance of any duty or task work, when I should enjoy the society of my friends ; and I do sincerely hope that, in a future summer, I shall be able to avail myself of your great kindness, and make Fairley the head-quarters of a little tour along the Firth of Clyde, which I have not yet explored, along its coasts and through its islands.

I beg my kindest regards to Mr. Parker, who, I trust, will get fast well ; and to Miss Parker. I go to Blochairn to-morrow.—I am, my dear Madam, yours most truly,

THOMAS CHALMERS.

No. C.

St. Andrews, 19*th January* 1827.

MY DEAR MADAM,—It at all times gives both to me and to Mrs. Chalmers the utmost refreshment and real pleasure to hear from yourself and your family. I hope that the imagination of my time being too much engrossed for a correspondence that we feel so desirable, will not diminish either the regularity or the frequency of it. The truth is, that my time is not so engrossed here as it was in Glasgow ; and besides, the habit into which I have got of setting apart an hour a day to letter-writing, enables me to overtake all the duties which in this way are laid upon me.

I am much interested by your information regarding Mr. James. I saw an advertisement the other day of a work on "Political Economy," by a member of the University of Cambridge. Its specific subjects were those that we had very fully discussed on my last interview with him at Blochairn; and which is not always the case, we agreed in our sentiments. I was tempted by this circumstance to conceive that he might have been the author. I am sure that his decided Christianity would prove a far higher gratification to you than his first-rate talent; and I pray that your anxieties and supplications for the souls of your relatives might bring down that influence which alone can convert and sanctify. I would answer every letter, if James would but write me.—I am, my dear Madam, yours with greatest esteem and regard, THOMAS CHALMERS.

No. CI.

St. Andrews, 18th August 1828.

MY DEAR MADAM,—As I leave Mrs. Chalmers to fill up this letter, I have just room to say, that I received your son's valuable present of Schleusner's "Lexicon." I am quite sensible that the best ingredient of a gift is the disposition which it indicates in the giver; and I prize very highly indeed the friendly regards of your family towards me. At the same time I cannot but further remark on the great worth to me of the particular book which he has selected, fitting in so exactly as it does with my present professional studies, that, from the moment of its arrival, I have made, and will continue for some time to make, daily use of it.

I beg my kindest regards to the Misses Parker, and Mr. James and Mr. George. May you have great comfort in them; and may the afflictions and trials of earth ripen you and yours for Heaven.—Believe me, my dear Madam, yours most truly, THOMAS CHALMERS.

No. CII.

Edinburgh, 17*th November* 1828.

MY DEAR MADAM,—We were both much gratified by your letter. A notice from an old and tried friend is peculiarly welcome to those who have the feeling of being strangers in a strange land. In many respects I have made a great personal sacrifice by renouncing the comfort and ease of St. Andrews ; but the call of duty appeared quite clear and imperative. Mrs. Chalmers has left our old and beautiful house with very great reluctance ; and we have not altogether met with very re-conciling circumstances since our arrival. But we are in the best hands, and all, we trust, will end well.

I cannot express the tenderness that is felt by us all, and more especially by myself, for the various members of your much-loved family. We feel it a great alleviation to the sorrow of our removal from St. Andrews that we are so much nearer to you. May the God of all comfort and grace uphold you in the midst of your trials. Anne says that she will write to your Anne soon. Our address is 11, Argyle Square.—I am, my dear Mrs. Parker, yours most truly,   THOMAS CHALMERS.

No. CIII.

Edinburgh, 30*th January* 1829.

MY DEAR MADAM,—I gladly avail myself of the opportunity by Mr. Smyth to offer you a few lines. We are all in a con-valescent state now, though Mrs. Chalmers perhaps feels more overdone than she did when her labours in the sick-room were more abundant.

You have really rendered us a substantial accommodation by taking Anne from us in our state of danger and infection. It was a great relief both to myself and Mrs. Chalmers her being taken out of the way ; and it was made all the more complete that you kindly assured us of her presence being no inconvenience to yourself. We both think that the time of her return to us should be now drawing near; and Mrs. C. calculates from the number of her music ticket that she should be with us by the 12th of February.

I received a letter full of cordiality and of most gratifying friendship from Mr. Charles, to which I shall reply in a few days. He little knows the value that I set upon his attachment; and never, in fact, did I feel myself so blended by all the ties of memory and of the heart with any family.

I sincerely hope and pray that the impression on Grace's mind may prove a lasting one, and form the anointing that remaineth. We feel not enough our responsibility for the souls of our children, and how much it is our duty to pray, and to labour, and to watch for them. May the Giver of all grace prepare all the members of both our families for Heaven. He willeth all men to be saved; and what an encouragement to us that He makes this the express ground of our duty to intercede for all.

I beg my kindest regards to the Misses Parker, Mr. George, and the two Annes, in which all here join; and I entreat you to believe me, my dear Mrs. Parker, yours most truly,

THOMAS CHALMERS.

No. CIV.

Kirkaldy, 24th April 1829.

Dr. Alexander Chalmers of Kirkaldy died on the 22d, at half-past one in the morning.

MY DEAR MADAM,—The interest you take in our family has determined me to send the above intimation, though I believe you did not know my brother. He was a mighty favourite with us all; and, meanwhile, we are greatly solemnized by the

warning. But this is so very different from being spiritualized by it, that there is a loud call for prayer and persevering
energy, in order that instead of a transient emotion, it may
ripen into a practical and an enduring principle. The anointing which remaineth can alone accomplish this.—I entreat you
to believe me, yours with greatest affection and esteem,

                                        THOMAS CHALMERS.

                           No. CV.

                                 Burntisland, 28th September 1830.

MY DEAR MADAM,—I received your kind letter only to-day,
I having come here for a little retirement, and that I might
prosecute the work of my preparations at leisure. We have
long heard of your illness ; and I heartily reproach myself for
not having written sooner. I can truly say that there is no
individual out of my family whose acquaintance I am so glad
to retain and so anxious to improve with the closest possible
intimacy. I know that I will annoy you if I speak of gratitude, though that is a feeling which does and which ought to
burn strongly in our hearts. But you will at least permit me
to speak of friendship, and under its impulse it is my fervent hope and prayer that you may be speedily restored to
health, and be long spared a comfort to us all and a blessing
to your family.

Health may fail; but the hope of the gospel will not fail
you. The more firmly you cherish it, the more surely will all
its objects be realized.

I go to London myself in about a fortnight. It is a great
annoyance to me, but I am under a kind of moral compulsion
to take the journey.

In reference to your application for a sermon in behalf of
our colonies, it would be quite unfair in me not to let you
know how the matter stands. I am overborne with the work

of my own proper vocation ; and I really cannot engage for any other work but at the expense of what I esteem a higher duty, and therefore with as great pain to my conscience as to my convenience.—I am, my dear Mrs. Parker, yours most affectionately, THOMAS CHALMERS.

No. CVI.

Edinburgh, 1st February 1831.

MY DEAR MRS. PARKER,—I have always the utmost pleasure in hearing from you, and should be sorry to let any other beside myself reply to communications that I so highly value. Your letter of the 25th of January has greatly relieved us; for when I was in Glasgow a month ago, I had not so favourable a report of your health as you have yourself sent me. May the God and Giver of all mercies perfect your recovery, and enable you to bear up under the inclemencies of this severe winter. To-day we have a perfect tempest of drifting snow; and the winter may be said to have fully and fairly set in.

Mrs. Chalmers has relapsed this winter to a considerable degree into her wonted delicacy ; and when I think of her present family duties, I am not without uneasiness. But let us roll over all our anxieties upon God, casting our burden on Him and He will sustain it.—With kindest regards to both the Misses Parker, in which all here join, I am, my dear Mrs. Parker, yours most affectionately, THOMAS CHALMERS.

No. CVII.

Penicuick, near Edinburgh, 19*th July* 1834.

MY DEAR MRS. PARKER,—I write by my children who I expect will be with you in about a week. I am much interested in Grace, who, I think, is somewhat more impressed at present than usual ; and I should rejoice in any opportunity you had of keeping the minds of either of them alive to the

N

great matters of their everlasting concernment. I earnestly wish, in behalf of us both, that we might be blest with the high privilege of a thoroughly Christianized family.

I am to write Mr. Dow. I take the greatest interest in his parochial operations. What has been done for Fairley is quite beautiful, and will tell I think most beneficially in the way of example. I hope you continue to have great comfort in the services of your new church.

I live in great repose here, and have been ordered an entire cessation from study, which I am strictly observing. I think that this summer will determine whether or not my constitution has received a permanent shock.

Give my kindest regards to Miss Parker and to Captain and Mrs. Darroch when you see them.—I ever am, my dear Mrs. Parker, yours most gratefully and truly,   THOMAS CHALMERS.

No. CVIII.

Burntisland, 14th September 1836.

MY DEAR MRS. PARKER,—Nothing but circumstances prevents me from availing myself of your kind invitation ; the days I spend at Fairley being always the sunniest and most delightful I spend anywhere.

I beg my kindest regards to Miss Parker, and also to Mr. and Mrs. James, if still with you, and to Captain and Mrs. Darroch. It is truly refreshing amid the storms of a world that lowers hostility and menace against all who offend it, to turn one's thoughts to those in whose friendship and kind affections they feel the most perfect confidence.—I ever am, my dear Mrs. Parker, yours most truly,   THOMAS CHALMERS.

CIX.

Ardgowan, 27th October 1836.

MY DEAR MRS. PARKER,—I cannot say it was officious, but I must say it was greatly overkind of you to pay the noddy. I am never happier than when enjoying your hospitality ; but you must ever allow me to pay my way to and from your much loved abode.

I find that Sir Michael had after all sent a carriage for me to your house, which I regret we left before it had arrived.

We have just lunched—Mr. Patrick Stewart is one of the party. I like the Duke of Somerset exceedingly—plain, un-affected, and very intelligent. Lord James Stewart and his lady are here, whom I had met before in England. These, with the Duchess and Dowager Lady Stewart, make up all the strangers ; so that I do not feel the visit to be so cold or for-midable as I had apprehended it to be.

I am not to annoy you with my expressions of gratitude ; but I must be permitted to say, that every visit to Fairley rivets more closely the deep affection which I feel for you and yours.

May the providence and grace of our All-kind Father be richly experienced by you all, that after a life of discipline and preparation here we may all meet again in the blissful realms of light and life above.

With kindest regards to Captain and Mrs. Darroch, I ever am, my dear Madam, yours most affectionately,

THOMAS CHALMERS.

No. CX.

East Kilbride, 2d November 1836.

MY DEAR MRS. PARKER,—I received this day your most wel-come letter ; and though I leave the greater part of this sheet to be filled up by Margaret, (who owes you much for your great goodness to her,) I cannot give it over to her without letting you know how much I felt interested at Ardgowan by the de-cided piety of Lady Stewart, and the promising dispositions of Sir Michael. Here, too, there is much that claims my gratitude in the palpable usefulness of Mr. H., in the acceptance he meets with among all classes—the kindness of the higher ranks, and honest heartfelt cordiality of the general population.

In point of beauty and fertility it is a far better parish than I expected it to be ; and the manse, now building, seems a very perfect one.—Ever believe me, my dear Mrs. Parker, yours most affectionately,   THOMAS CHALMERS.

No. CXI.

Burntisland, 5th September 1837.

MY DEAR MRS. PARKER,—It is very much to the regret, both of Mrs. Chalmers and myself, that our engagements have so multiplied upon us as to make it impossible that we should visit Fairley this season—the place of all others in which it is my delight to live and to luxuriate, for nowhere do we enjoy more of kindness within-doors, and more of beauty all around us.

I have great reason to be thankful that Mrs. Chalmers enjoys so much better health this season than she has done for several years. It is of mighty advantage to her that we now live out of Edinburgh, and between Morningside and Burntisland I trust that, through the blessing of God, she may be long spared to me.

May He, who is the Giver of all that is necessary both to life and to godliness, shed all blessings, spiritual and temporal, on yourself and all the members of your family.—Ever believe me, my dear Mrs. Parker, yours with greatest esteem and regard,   THOMAS CHALMERS.

No. CXII.

London, 15th July 1838.

MY DEAR MRS. PARKER,—I should have written you long ago ; but Mrs. Chalmers's repeated illnesses have protracted our stay in France, and so prolonged our journey homewards, that I have waited till now in vain ere I could state, with any degree of certainty, the likelihood of our future movements. We are now thus far on our way to Edinburgh, and should have been in the steamer which went off last night, but for another relapse, which we are hopeful, however, will, through God's blessing, allow of our taking the next opportunity by sea, which is on Wednesday evening, taking us home on Friday the 20th, from which day I am quite at your disposal.

May I therefore beg that you will write me at Edinburgh, on receipt of this, and tell me the day that you have fixed upon, when I shall hold myself in readiness to leave home two days before it. I quite lay my account with the possibility that in consequence of my delay you may have made another arrangement. This would deprive me of the gratification of seeing Miss Parker, before her change of state, but not of visiting Fairley, as I am engaged to visit Sir Andrew Agnew as soon as possible after the 1st of August, and I could not do better than take Fairley in my way. I do hope that these unlooked for postponements on my part have not embarrassed you. A few days at home would certainly be convenient; but to make it possible for me to move any day you may choose to name, I have sent some commissions forward to Edinburgh by post.

I feel the greatest possible interest in you and yours; though I have not had the opportunity of expressing all my sympathies on the late melancholy event in the history of your bereaved household.* May these affecting changes teach us to sit loose to a world that will soon pass away from us, and to seek our portion in Him who is the same to-day, yesterday, and for ever.—Ever believe me, my dear Mrs. Parker, yours most affectionately,   THOMAS CHALMERS.

No. CXIII.

Edinburgh, 5th November 1838.

MY VERY DEAR MRS. PARKER,—I cannot, now that Margaret is on the eve of returning to us, refrain from pouring forth the

---

* The death of Mrs. Parker's youngest son.

feelings of a most cordial and affectionate gratitude for all the goodness that we have received at your hands ; and it is my prayer and my trust that the friendship begun here, and the fruits of which we have so richly experienced, may at length be transplanted and take root in Heaven, where, may it be God's blessed will, that the two families shall meet in full company together, and partake in the services and the joys of a blissful eternity.

Anne and the baby are with us. He, I do fear, is in a very precarious state, though somewhat better to-day. Mr. Hanna is at Belfast ; and we have just heard from him of the death of his younger brother, John—the last son but himself, and a sad blow, in which you, my dear Madam, will know fully to sympathize with both the parents.—I ever am, my dear Madam, yours most affectionately,   THOMAS CHALMERS.

No. CXIV.

Edinburgh, 1st June 1839.

My DEAR MRS. PARKER,—I should long ere now have communicated the intended marriage of Eliza with Mr. M'Kenzie, the minister of Dunkeld. I have long felt that ours is more a family relationship than an ordinary friendship ; and nothing but the extreme pressure of employment would have prevented an earlier notice of this arrangement. It is proposed that the marriage shall take place in August.

I feel somewhat languid and overdone after the fatigues of the Assembly. If God be pleased to spare me, there are few things which I should like better on this side of death, than an evening of life spent in complete retirement from all public business, and devoted to the enjoyment and converse of those Christian friends who are looking heavenward. Let us hope and pray that all our present divisions may be overruled for the good of the Church, and the glory of the Redeemer.

Mrs. Chalmers is at present in tolerable health, and all unite in most affectionate remembrances and wishes to you and yours.—I am, my dear Madam, yours very truly,

THOMAS CHALMERS.

No. CXV.

Balblair Cottage, 23d August 1839.

MY DEAR MRS. PARKER,—I cannot resist my inclination to tell you how much I have been gratified by my visit to the land of your nativity. I have been two nights here in a summer cottage of Mr. Dempster's of Skibo, now looking on the scenes of your infancy, and greatly delighted with the beauties of the neighbourhood. Yesterday I went down to Dornoch, and on my way visited the Manse of Criech, determined to make myself personally acquainted with the localities of your birthplace. The old gentleman was at family-worship; but we were conducted to the west room up stairs, whence I looked down upon the church with the old burial-place to the east of it, and from the gable window on the church of Kincardine, and the mountain barrier with Ducairn Brae and the hills of Strathcairn beyond it. We took a hurried leave of the old gentleman. I was delighted with the beauty of the ride all the way to Dornoch, which looked in its greatest perfection on a glorious sunshine day with its tide full. I cannot imagine a finer feature than the Dun of Criech, and the exquisite little bay behind, and on the east side of it. Nothing could exceed the blandness and cordiality of our reception by Mr. and Mrs. Kennedy; when beside his son George, we found Mr. and Mrs. M'Pherson of Golspie with their two daughters, Mr. M'Kenzie of Rogart, Mr. Campbell of Kildrum, and Mr. M'Kay of Clyne. I had a meeting in the Cathedral of about 300, and was honoured by the presence of Mr. Gunn and other grandees of the district. Mr. Dempster of Skibo was along with us; and we had a very pleasant dinner-party of twenty-two in the inn afterwards. The Cathedral is a very interesting relic, now completely renovated and restored, of the olden time.

Will you tell Dr. Rainy that far the most interesting geographical acquisition I have made was from a hill behind Balblair Cottage, whence I could see in greatest possible beauty, and through a clear atmosphere, the abrupt and precipitous outline of the hills in Lochbroom, Benmore, Assynt; the hills of Edderachillis; Benhope, which sends its waters to the Pentland Firth; Benklibreck, in the very centre of Sutherland; and the end of Loch Shin; and the beautiful Vale of the Oykel.

Since beginning this letter I have been with General Munro of Teaninich, to Cromarty, Fortrose, Avoch-house, and Roxhaugh, in which places I renewed my acquaintance with the two Ladies Mackenzie, the latter of whom I had not seen for thirty-eight years. I am now at Rosskeen with Mr. Carment, and am going forward to Dingwall and Inverness.

May the God of all grace bless and sanctify us and ours; and with my best regards to Mrs. Cardwell, who I rejoice to hear from Mr. George is better, I ever am, my dear Mrs. Parker, yours most affectionately,　　　THOMAS CHALMERS.

No. CXVI.

Edinburgh, 31*st January* 1840.

MY DEAR MRS. PARKER,—I am always delighted to hear from you, and only regret that the amount of other correspondence not so welcome or agreeable should preclude my writing you so frequently as I could wish. Mr. Cochrane, our secretary, would reply to your letter in behalf of a new extension church, for which we shall most cheerfully do all we can. It is altogether a fit object for our largest possible aid; and I only regret that the unfortunate juxtaposition of another question now agitating the country, and menacing the Church, is for the present keeping our cause at abeyance, insomuch that our Supplementary Fund which should by this time have reached £100,000, does not exceed £40,000—enabling us to allow, as yet, only £400 for each of the next hundred churches; I trust, however, that times will improve.

With best regards to Mr. and Mrs. James Parker, and Mr. and Mrs. Cardwell, and earnest prayers for the spiritual well-being of all who are near and dear to us, ever believe me, my dear Mrs. Parker, yours most affectionately,

THOMAS CHALMERS.

No. CXVII.

28th April 1840.

MY DEAR MRS. PARKER,—I most sincerely hope that you will accede to our joint request. There is nothing I would more enjoy than a few quiet weeks in secluded intercourse with yourself, an opportunity we may never else have on this side of that death which is coming nearer to us every day, and which I pray may not find us unprepared for the great and solemn change.—I ever am, my dear Madam, yours most affectionately, THOMAS CHALMERS.

No. CXVIII.

Burntisland, 29th September 1841.

MY DEAR MRS. PARKER,—We have heard with great interest of your brief visit to Dunkeld, and are delighted when circumstances prevent that more direct and personal intercourse in which I always have the greatest pleasure, if I can even hold converse with you through the medium of any of my family. But this is not enough to satisfy the demands of my heart for a more frequent association with the best and truest of my friends; and as I am really not able to come west this season, I have most earnestly to beg—and in this I am joined with equal earnestness by Mrs. Chalmers—that you will manage to spend as much time with us as you can this winter. We leave this for Edinburgh on the 9th of October, and have no other prospect than that of being constantly at our home there till April. You will find us very domestic and very quiet, as your nieces, the Misses Brown, can attest, whose visit, last winter, gave us so much pleasure. We do hope therefore that no obstacle will stand in the way of an arrangement which would afford so much real delight to our family. We can promise you all the repose and independence that you require; and feel assured that, with the blessing of God upon our intercourse, your visit might be productive of great profit as well as comfort to us all. Let me entreat therefore that you will entertain the proposal. We shall leave you to name your own time, our only desire being, that you will not make your visit a short one.

With the kindest regards of us all, ever believe me, my very dear Madam, yours most affectionately, THOMAS CHALMERS.

No. CXIX.

Edinburgh, 7th January 1842.

MY DEAR MRS. PARKER,—It is a great disappointment to us all that we are not to have the pleasure of a visit from you this winter, and we very much regret the cause of it.

It is my earnest prayer, that the same Providence which has hitherto watched over you, may still preserve and prolong your days in the midst of us, and that, under God's blessed will, we may still have much intercourse in this world.

The state and prospects of the Church are well fitted to loosen our attachment to all that is earthly. The issues of our present contest are as uncertain as ever; and I can well see a fixed purpose on the part both of Government and of the higher classes to flood our Church with Moderatism.　It is difficult as yet to say what the friends of a pure and scriptural Christianity ought to do ; but I trust and pray that they might be ready for a sacrifice rather than give up their principles, or surrender the religious good of the people of these lands.　Let us hope that our way will be made clear before us ; and meanwhile it is well to be still and know that the Lord reigneth.　.　.　.

With best regards to Captain and Mrs. Darroch, General Darroch, and Mr. Rainy, I ever am, my dear Madam, yours very truly,　　　　　　　THOMAS CHALMERS.

No. CXX.

Edinburgh, 30*th December* 1842.

MY DEAR MRS. PARKER,—I expect very shortly to present you with my views on the subject of your much esteemed letter.　Meanwhile I enclose a specimen of what we are doing,* and what I believe might be done in every parish were it not for the indolence or the fears of those who have the natural influence over its people, and whose part it is to take the charge of them.　With but a zealous and intelligent agency I never found any failure on the part of the humbler classes.

Our collectors met yesternight for the first time, and the united contributions amount to the rate of more than £300 in the year—a proportion to the number of our people which, if carried over the whole of Scotland, would yield half a million annually.

May I beg that you will let our friend at Gourock know that the Sabbatical question of which she wrote you I have treated in a sermon to be found in vol. ix. of the series of my Works.

I have a most delightful recollection of my last visit to you. May the Giver of all grace pour His best blessings on you and

---

* Enclosed was a tract, " What should the People do?"

yours. Our family are at present in their usual health, and
unite with me in warmest regards. I beg to be cordially remembered to Miss Hutchison, Captain and Mrs. Hay, and Miss
M'Call.—I ever am, my dear Mrs. Parker, yours with the
greatest affection,   THOMAS CHALMERS.

No. CXXI.

Edinburgh, 14th January 1843.

MY DEAR MRS. PARKER,—I received your truly munificent
proposal some days ago, but I have not yet reported it to the
treasurer of the Provisional Fund, as I think it possible that
you may perhaps, on reflection, prefer sending what you have
to give through the medium of a Fairley Association, should
such be formed. My reason for, at least, offering this suggestion
is, that here in Morningside the large and small subscribers
have joined their contributions in this way, and with great good
effect in the way of example on our little parochial community
here. But though I submit this alternative to you, I, of course,
will most gladly abide by whatever decision you may think it
right to adopt.

I enclose an address which I am now distributing amongst
my friends. Sir James Graham's letter is convincing many
that instant efforts must now be made to raise funds—that, in
fact, the crisis has already arrived, or, at least, that all should
now act as if it had.

May the wisdom that is from above animate and direct our
Church on the present eventful occasion.—Ever believe me, my
very dear Madam, yours most affectionately,

THOMAS CHALMERS.

LETTERS TO MRS. DARROCH.*

No. CXXII.

Edinburgh, 4th February 1844.

MY DEAR MRS. DARROCH,—I wrote Mrs. Cardwell last Sabbath, and imagine that she must now have left for England. A week has since intervened, but it makes no difference in the feeling, which will long remain with me, of the great and yet recent calamity wherewith we have all been visited. The sense of recency will subside, but never on this side of death the sense of a very great and mournful bereavement. Such a friendship, so steadfast and so exuberant of all that was kind, and beneficent, and generous to me and mine, I never expect to be replaced in this world.

I wonder that people should make a question of our knowing each other, and having the Christian attachments of the present life renewed and perpetuated in a future state. The passage in 1 Thess. iv. 13-18, leaves no doubt in my mind on this subject—a passage given to us for the express purpose of mitigating our sorrow because of those who, like your dear and sainted mother, have fallen asleep in Jesus. The proper and the obviously intended comfort here presented to us is, that we, their followers in the same faith and hope, shall be ever with the Lord, and therefore ever with them also. And then as to the idea that all special affections will be lost in a general and equal charity for all alike, we should ever recollect that our Saviour on earth exemplified a more intense friendship for some than for others, as in the case of John, who is signalized among all the other disciples as the one whom Jesus loved. Now, the very character He had on earth He has borne up with Him to heaven, and we, if like unto Him, may indulge the very pre-

* Mrs. Parker's eldest daughter.

ferences and special likings which He did. And on these
grounds I do cherish the hope, that not only will I know and
recognise and renew my acquaintance with her in heaven, but
that I will continue there to be on the same cordial, and intimate, and affectionate footing with her which has subsisted
here for the long period of nearly thirty years, and that without
a flaw.

The comforts of religion are the only comforts which should
be urged on such occasions ; for they are, indeed, the only
comforts which avail us.   Could we have but a realizing sense
of that secure and blissful place where are the spirits of the
just made perfect, it would greatly soften and alleviate the trial
which now lies upon you.   And it would do more than console :
it would help to transfer and to elevate our affections from
earth to heaven.   Never, I believe, had a family greater cause
for rejoicing, even under the weight of this heavy bereavement,
than the children, and relatives, and friends of her who has
now left us for a season, but whom we shall meet again, if but
followers of them who through faith and patience are now inheriting the promises.

Every such dispensation should have the effect of keeping us
closer by the Saviour.   What a privilege it is, that we have free
access to God through Him ; and to God in the endearing
character of a Father reconciled to His strayed children, and
rejoicing over them to do them good.   He founds an argument
on the kindness of our earthly parents which I think should
tell with immense power upon you in your present circumstances.
You cannot fail to recollect—they will come to your memory
with a touching and tender impression that might well-nigh
overwhelm your feelings—all the goodness you have experienced
at the hands of your earthly parents, their longing earnestness
for your wellbeing, their efforts, and attentions, and sacrifices
to make you happy.   It is on these sure premises that the

argument of our blessed Saviour must come to your heart with resistless demonstration,—" If ye that are earthly parents know how to give good gifts unto your children, how much more shall your Father in heaven give good things to those who ask Him ? Ask, and ye shall receive ; seek, and ye shall find ; knock, and the door shall be opened to you."

My kindest sympathies and regards to Major Darroch and to the General, whom I love ; and ever believe me, my very dear Mrs. Darroch, yours with sincerest affection,

THOMAS CHALMERS.

No. CXXIII.

Edinburgh, Morningside, 2d February 1845.

MY DEAR MRS. DARROCH,—How the visions of the past flit on my remembrance while writing to you. It is a matter of very great thankfulness in regard to your brother that an outgoing has at length been opened for him. But when one thinks of the shortlivedness of all that is earthly, and looks back on the days both of Blochairn and Fairley, as now to be numbered with the times before the Flood, it makes us sit loose to the prospects of this world, and to acquiesce in the sentiment of the poet, that there is nothing bright but Heaven ; or rather to present it in a more authentic form, that the fashion of this world passeth away, but that He who made the world endureth for ever.

I most thoroughly sympathize with feelings so naturally awakened, and so touchingly expressed on the occasion of this sorrowful yet sacred anniversary. It is good to recall the memory of the righteous, for it is a memory which is blessed.

I have not seen Winslow's work ; but I am reading with the greatest interest our old friend E. B. Elliott's work on the Revelation. I will do him the justice to say that I think it far the completest and most satisfactory exposition of the prophecy which I have read, though he does our Free Church the very grossest injustice by his rash and most ignorant deliverance upon our question.

Do give my best regards to Mrs. Cardwell when you write to her.—Ever believe me, my dear Mrs. Darroch, yours most affectionately,　　　　　　　　　　　Thomas Chalmers.

No. CXXIV.

Fairley, 15th June 1845.

My very dear Mrs. Darroch,—I have been here for several days, and much both in the house and grounds, which are so familiar to me. I never felt such an experimental impression of the precariousness of all things here below as now, when the scene of my brightest recollections is so transformed by the disappearance of her who gave its chief interest to the village and neighbourhood, and to all their society. Yet I cannot say how thankful I am that I am so kindly, nay, urgently entreated to make as much a home of the house as possible. Our headquarters are with Miss M'Call, but my forenoon study is your dear mother's bedroom ; and I can evidently see that both Mr. and Mrs. George are disappointed if I do not follow it up by dining with them, which I am all the more inclined to do, that it gives me the opportunity of talking and taking an afternoon round with him. I rejoice to find that he is obviously progressing in health and strength, though I think he is perhaps inclined to exert himself too much, and not to make a sufficient use of his sofa. You may well believe that the well-known relics and memorials of other days inspire a pensiveness which is melancholy no doubt, but still which I love to indulge in. Let me die her death that I may share in her blessed resurrection.

We remain here till Wednesday the 25th, or other ten days. We thence go in a body to Arran, and are besides engaged to spend some time at Tillichewan. I think it better to transport my family by one movement from Arran to Tillichewan; but either during my visit there, or at the termination of it, I must spend some time, though it should only be one day, at Gourock. I know not how it is with younger people, but I confess that the twenty-eight years of converse and correspondence with you and yours have established in my heart a most intense and steadfast feeling of relationship to you all. Give my best regards to Major Darroch, and to the General, whom I love. I am reading to-day a book which I am sure would have been rich and precious as marrow to the dear and departed saint who is now in Heaven, " Owen on the Glory of Christ." He died at sixty-seven,* and it is his last work—the work of one who writes as on the borders of eternity. I am only two years behind him, and four years behind what her age was when, seventeen months ago, she entered into rest.—I am, my dearest Mrs. Darroch, yours very affectionately and truly,

THOMAS CHALMERS.

Monday Morning.

Since writing the three last pages, I called on your brother yesterday evening (Sunday). He asked me to conduct family worship, which brought to me the vivid and affecting recollection of similar occasions. The identical form was brought in, and the identical man-servant sat on it, along with four maid-servants. These things tell powerfully on my memory, as do the pictures in the dining-room, and the paper in the drawing-room. I am glad I have come here; and what makes it all the more satisfactory is, that I am on such pleasant and kind terms with your brother, who begs, that over and above my study and my dinner, I should also take my siesta in his house.

* The age at which Dr. Chalmers also died.

O

I have not yet thanked you for the great enjoyments which my family had in Gourock House, and more especially my little grandson.—T. C.

No. CXXV.

Wishaw, 29th July 1845.

MY VERY DEAR MRS. DARROCH,—We arrived here to-day at twelve, by the railway. Nothing could exceed the kindness of Mr. and Mrs. Tennant, with whom we spent a very pleasant evening, and had a very delightful, and to me all the more so, that it was a small party—consisting of themselves along with Drs. Forbes and Rainy, both of whom I hold in high estimation.

I am at present with my brother here, and expect, if God will, to reach home on Thursday.

This excursion to the west has given me a higher opinion than I ever had before of the Christian worth and friendship which we have so abundantly experienced in the various quarters that we have visited. And certainly there is no place which stands dearer to all my recollections and regards than Gourock. I love the General, and my next letter will be addressed to himself some time next week I hope. May the Spirit work effectually in him and in all of us. I shall never forget those words of death-bed experience and manifestation uttered by her who has gone before him, and which read so impressively upon her tombstone,—" Let me die the death of the righteous, let my latter end be like theirs."

It was proposing a great deal too much that I should take east with me the precious MS. which you had entrusted to my keeping for a few weeks. I had looked it all over, but had not read it all thoroughly. I hope, however, that my next visit will be one of greater quietness than I was permitted to enjoy in any other house than your own. It were altogether delicious to read with you within doors the sentences that flowed from the pen and were dictated from the earnest heart of her who is

now enshrined in blessedness and glory among the spirits of the
just made perfect.   Oh that, like her, I could live a life of faith
on the Son of God, and then should I live a life both of love
and of holiness.   May the Giver of all grace sanctify and elevate
my affections, and save me from all those evil influences which
war against the soul.—I ever am, my dearest Madam, yours
with the greatest affection,   THOMAS CHALMERS.

No. CXXVI.

Monzie, 13th August 1845.

MY VERY DEAR MRS. DARROCH,—You must not forbid my
writing to you ; for I have great pleasure in keeping up a correspondence that originated in the most precious recollections
of other days, and is fitted to perpetuate and to foster them.

I omitted to leave the enclosed with you, (copy of a marriage service,) having reserved to myself a short-hand copy of
it, which I shall put in the portfolio of dear Mrs. Parker, along
with the precious death-bed sayings of Mrs. General Darroch.
The blank paper which you have left me of that truly valuable record can just accommodate in short-hand the other
record which I have only read this day for the first time since
I uttered it in the drawing-room at Fairley.   I am glad to
observe that there is no want of keeping between them ; and
that on that occasion I spoke in the degree I did of the coming
death and the coming eternity.

Have the goodness to tell Mr. East* how thankful I am for
his work, with which I hope to make myself acquainted soon.
It will give me the greatest pleasure to see him on his way
through Edinburgh.   When I am at home his best chance for
seeing me is at nine to breakfast.   I fear, however, that I shall
be a good deal from home all this month, and also part of the
next.   I am to make a point, however, of remaining at home

* The Rev. Timothy East of Birmingham.

afterwards for many months.—Believe me, my very dear Mrs. Darroch, yours most sincerely,   THOMAS CHALMERS.

No. CXXVII.

Edinburgh, 5th February 1847.

MY VERY DEAR MRS. DARROCH,—This is very very sad. I like the General, and always liked him ; nor am I at all surprised when you tell me of the manner in which he is affected by your utterance of Bible texts. It is quite in keeping with the way in which he was moved at family-worship on my last visit to Gourock House. May God by His Spirit, though in His own mysterious way, bring home that truth to his mind, the knowledge of which is life everlasting.

Perhaps he will recollect my name, and if he do, I should like my message to him to consist of the following verses, which might be read to my dear old friend as he is able to bear it :—John xiv. 1 ; 1 John iv. 8, last clause ; 1 John iv. 10 ; 1 John i. 7, last clause ; Isaiah xliii. 2, first clause ; Isaiah xlv. 22 ; Isaiah xlv. 21, last clause ; Luke ix. 56 ; John iii. 14-17 ; 2 Cor. v. 19.

May He who is a very present help in the time of trouble, be present with you all on this solemn occasion. What a world of change and utter vanity we live in ! May we die unto it daily, and live unto Him who liveth for ever.

God bless and sustain you all, my very dear Mrs. Darroch, yours most affectionately,   THOMAS CHALMERS.

No. CXXVIII.

Morningside, 14th February 1847.

MY DEAR MRS. DARROCH,—Having not heard from you since your note of Monday, I flatter myself that there has been no change for the worse.

Meanwhile let us humbly hope and earnestly pray for the merciful dealings of God's free and willing Spirit with his soul.

What an encouragement and what a liberal warrant for those intercessions which God wills us to make in behalf of all men, and on the express ground too that He wills all men to be saved and to come to the knowledge of the truth. Couple this with the declaration that whatsoever we ask for, which is agreeable to the will of God, that we shall receive ; and I can imagine nothing more complete in the way of authorizing us to ask till we receive, to seek till we find, to knock till the door of salvation be opened, that we and those who are near and dear to us may enter in.—Yours with great affection,

THOMAS CHALMERS.

No. CXXIX.

Edinburgh, Morningside, 21*st February* 1847.

MY VERY DEAR MRS. DARROCH,—I was prepared to receive your affecting intelligence ; but however much looked for, the event itself never fails to strike and to solemnize us. This is as it ought to be ; but how little, alas ! does the mere pathos or tenderness of natural feeling avail of itself to make us wisely and practically, and to good or saving purpose, considerate of our latter end.

I always liked the General, and ever felt as if there was the force of a natural affinity betwixt us. I am much interested by what you tell me of his latter end. " God is love," and that is a consideration which ought always to keep us from despair, either for ourselves or others, though without prejudice to the moral influences of another lesson, no less emphatically true, that " God is holiness."

What a blessed economy, what an exquisite skilfulness in it, how unsearchable are its riches, in that by virtue of its provisions, these two attributes of the Divinity are so fully harmonized ; mercy and truth have met together, righteousness and peace have entered into fellowship. May yours, my

dearest Mrs. Darroch, be all the comfort and all the sanctifying influence which this contemplation is fitted to administer,
as in the glass of the Gospel you look at the blended love and
holiness of the Godhead.

I beg that you will offer to the Major my most affectionate
condolence, and to all your family; and when you write dear
Mrs. Cardwell, tell her of my heart-felt regards. What a retrospect of other years is now present to my memory; and in
vivid picture there is also that family burial-place to the south
of your house where the General is now lying. May your
children learn wisdom at his grave.—My dearest Madam, yours
most affectionately,   THOMAS CHALMERS.

LETTERS TO GENERAL DARROCH.

No. CXXX.

Burntisland, 23d June 1841.

MY DEAR GENERAL,—Before making a specific reply to your
question, I would first premise, that it conveys to my mind no
assurance of Parliamentary support to our Church from any
individual, of whom I am told no more than that he belongs to
a certain party in the State, on whatever side he may happen
to be.

Having made this general statement alike applicable, either
to Conservatives merely as such, or to Liberals merely as such,
let me now state what appears to me at present the great
difference between them.

Should the Conservatives prove the dominant party, and if
their collective mind is to be interpreted by the recent declaration, (too authentic, I fear, of Sir Robert Peel's,) then the
dissolution of our Church, as a National Establishment, must

be the inevitable result. Should, on the other hand, the Liberals be the dominant party, and if their collective mind is to be interpreted by the various sayings of Lord Melbourne, which, all taken together, indicate a downright indifferency to the whole matter, then, without one scintilla of affirmative confidence in them as a body, there is still the possibility that under them we may at least be let alone by the Legislature— so let alone as we have been during the last two years. In this view of the matter, the two terms of the alternative, on which you have to balance your decision, are the certainty of destruction or the chance of safety.

I have only to add, that the declaration of Mr. Stewart contrasts favourably with the acts of Colonel Mure, by which I mean his late votes in the General Assembly. And furthermore, that whereas nothing can be more annoying than the lame and impotent defences made of the Church, even by the best of her lay friends, whether in or out of Parliament, due of course to the want of a distinct understanding on the question, I must say, that I have not read a more clear, distinct, and able statement for the Church, by any of our merely secular and political supporters, than the one I read to-day from a reported speech of Mr. Stewart's in the town of Greenock.

I am sensible that, instead of presenting you with any decision of mine, I am only presenting you with the data, in which, perhaps, you may find some help in coming to your own decision on this subject.

You will perceive from the above that the declaration of Sir Robert Peel necessarily influences and affects my views upon this question, and makes me look on the Conservatives as now standing in a different relation to the Church from that in which I at one time regarded them both with confidence and pleasure. How I long for a Wilberforce party in Parliament, consisting of men who would make it the polar star of their public and Parliamentary conduct, to adopt such measures as were best for the moral and religious wellbeing of the population.—I ever am, my dear General, yours most respectfully, and with the utmost regard,   THOMAS CHALMERS.

P.S.—Since writing the above I have seen a gentleman who has been strenuously insisting that the policy of Scottish Churchmen is to send as many Conservative members, pledged to Non-intrusion, as possible, so as that they might favourably influence Sir Robert in the cause of our spiritual independence. I am not able to decide among these conflicting elements what our best policy is in the matter of these elections ; but in the matters which properly belong to us, I believe that our true policy is a fearless course of principle, and thorough determination rather to separate from the State than give up by ever so little our own final jurisdiction in things ecclesiastical.

No. CXXXI.

Morningside, Edinburgh, 10th August 1845.

MY DEAR GENERAL DARROCH,—I have long meditated a letter to you, and I am greatly encouraged to use this freedom by the uniform urbanity and kindness which I have ever experienced at your hands. Nothing can exceed my grateful recollection of our last interviews ; and I fondly hope that the lessons which I read in the affecting memorials of the departed upon the tablets behind your house will make an indelible impression upon me. " I see it all now," and " this is real life," carry more of an experimental demonstration for the truth of religion and the reality of eternal things than any dying testimony that I remember to have met with in the biographies of the good and the faithful. It is well that you have recorded these precious and inestimable sayings on the tombstone of her who poured them forth in her last and closing accents upon earth. May they tell effectually upon us all, and lead us to be followers of them who through faith and patience are now inheriting the promises.

I begin to feel more than ever the rapidity of time, and the urgency of the call for readiness against the day of our great and coming change. And I should say, that the first and greatest step towards this condition of readiness is, just to accept of the forgiveness which God holds out to all on the footing that Christ hath died for us. This forgiveness is ours if we trust in Him who hath set forth His own Son as a propitiation for the sins of the world. On this foundation, on this foundation only, do we stand in secure reconciliation with God; and so standing, might we plead with all confidence for the fulfilment of His own promise, that He would pour forth His Spirit upon us, and shed abroad His love in our hearts, and make us new creatures, and prepare us for the everlasting enjoyment of Himself in heaven, where there is fulness of pleasures at His own right hand.

It is truly my earnest prayer, dearest Sir, that such might be your blessed experience in time, and such the portion of your eternity. The world is fast receding from us both. These days and years are flying over our heads with a speed which seems to increase with every new revolution of the seasons. And it is a world, too, in which, by our Saviour's own statement, (John xvi. 33,) we should be ever laying our account to meet with tribulation. But what a delightful counterpart to this is the other statement, that in Him we shall have peace; may this peace, my dearest General, be yours; may you have great peace, great joy in believing. I can truly say of this world, that in it I would not live alway. One's path here—and I have the frequent experience of it—is beset with vexations and discomforts on every side. But what a deliverance to take refuge from all these in the love of a pitying Saviour, and in

P

the firm prospect of that eternal life which is the gift of God through Jesus Christ our Lord.

I have been pondering some of the other death-bed sayings of dear Mrs. Darroch. They have been furnished to me by your daughter-in-law, one of my best-loved friends. I have been greatly affected by the perusal of them. They form altogether a most precious and animating record of her who has gone before us. Let us die the death of the righteous, let our latter end be like theirs. Truly hers was a latter end of peace, clothed upon with the righteousness of Christ, and looking confidently forward to its rewards, she died, as did my own mother about eighteen years ago, in the triumphs of the faith.—I ever am, my dear General, yours with the greatest regard,

THOMAS CHALMERS.

LETTERS TO DR. RAINY OF GLASGOW.

No. CXXXII.

Edinburgh, 11*th February* 1844.

MY DEAR SIR,—I have not been more moved for a long time than by the replies of Mrs. Darroch and Mrs. Cardwell to my letters, which both arrived by the same post—the one from London and the other from Gourock—and the perusal of which at the same time I felt to be peculiarly impressive. The powerful reaction of their mother's death upon each of their minds will, I trust and pray, be signally blest to them both. I know not a death, indeed, within the whole compass of my recollection, more fitted to be spiritually fruitful than hers. Verily though dead she yet speaketh, and her memory is blest.

I think it was you who gave me Fisher's "Catechism," the doctrine of which (the Marrow doctrine) is very congenial to me. Let me recommend three recently republished Essays on the Assurance of Faith, by Anderson, Erskine, and Cudworth, which I think you would like. I shall be glad when you have read it that you tell me what you think of Anderson, who is new to me, but whose views I think are very clearly given and very precious. They are quite at one with those of Fisher, whose Catechism you gave me. Had I lived a hundred years ago, I would have joined the Marrow men.

I do hope that dear Mrs. Parker's death will tell beneficially upon all her children. I cannot rid myself (and most assuredly I have no wish to do it) of the feeling of a very strong and special affinity—as strong as that of blood or kindred—to them all. By this death I feel as if I had one tie less to earth and one tie more to heaven.

Give my very kindest regards to Mrs. Rainy; and with earnest prayer for God's best blessings upon you and yours, ever believe me, my very dear Sir, yours most truly,

THOMAS CHALMERS.

N.B.—The three Essays I mention are bound up in one small volume, entitled "Essays on the Assurance of Faith." Johnstone here is publisher.—T. C.

No. CXXXIII.

Edinburgh, 6th March 1847.

MY DEAR SIR,—I am anxious to know if you think that larger sacrifices and exertions are necessary to keep our countrymen from dying of hunger. I have a very strong persuasion that we greatly underrate the magnitude of the distress, and I should have the greatest value for your testimony upon the subject.

I send you one or two documents that have at least some relation to the matter in question.

I have the utmost liking and respect for your son, as one of the most intellectual, and, I hope, pious, and altogether among the best conditioned of my students. Kindest regards to Mrs. and Miss Rainy.—I ever am, my dear Sir, yours very truly,

THOMAS CHALMERS.

How I rejoice to observe the notice which is taken of your brother's patriotic efforts in the Government volume of Correspondence on the Highland Destitution.—T. C.

No. CXXXIV.—LETTER TO MRS. BROWN.

Kensington Place, 3d May 1818.

MY DEAR MADAM,—In this season of very painful interest and anxiety to us all, I feel inclined to write a few things, knowing well, at the same time, how powerless the words or the wisdom of man are in such an hour of heavy trial as that which has come upon you, and that it is God alone, who hath sent the trial, that can send out of His sanctuary the needful help and consolation. He alone can prepare you for the whole of His will, and bring you out of this arduous struggle between the feeling of nature and the faith of His own Gospel, and teach you to suffer as well as to do, and gently calm your heart into a settled acquiescence in that order which, for wise and righteous reasons, He hath been pleased to institute, and by which we are made to understand that it is through much tribulation we shall enter into the kingdom of God.

Our first prayer in the matter of trials should be, " Lay not upon us trials beyond what we have strength to bear." But if we see the likelihood of a trial approaching ; if the progress of the event looks threatening ; if explaining the will of God by what has happened, or is like to happen, we have reason to fear or to conclude that such is His appointment—then our next prayer should be, " Give us strength to bear this trial." It has been well said, that duties are ours and events are God's. We are sure that He does not afflict willingly. We are sure that there is mercy in all His visitations, and that His chastening hand yieldeth the fruit of righteousness. It is said of God by His own Son, who was meek and gentle, and wept over the sufferings of nature, and had compassion on the widow of Nain —it is said by Him, that if a tree bring not forth fruit, He purgeth it or pruneth it, that it may bring forth more fruit. The desire of our heart runs too much to the creature, and He, in kindness, taketh away from us the dearest and best-loved object, that this desire may be checked and restrained, and turned in the right and salutary direction towards Himself. It looks very dark and overwhelming to us in the meantime ; but that is because we are ever regarding the world as our all. It would not look dark did we thoroughly feel ourselves to be strangers and pilgrims in the world—did our eye carry our mind forward to eternity—did we see time in its true character as a rapid journey to our stable and ultimate home—did we contemplate death as a removal, and think believingly of that city which hath foundations, and whose builder and maker is God.

It is a cruel flattery of human wishes to disguise the uttermost extent of the possibility to which we are liable. Your excellent son may recover, but he may not ; and your mind should be familiarized to both terms of this alternative, and you should be feeling your way to Him who, after He has driven away all your earthly props, can give you His own word and His own promises to rest upon ; and it is not a painful or fatiguing search to which I am now directing you. It is not a search the labour and the difficulty of which are beyond the reach of agitated, and oppressed, and fearful humanity ; for He is not far from you, and He has revealed Himself *a very present help in the time of trouble,* and He is ready, even now, to meet your approaches ; and He asks you not merely to draw near, but to draw near with *boldness ;* and for what ?—that you may have grace to help you *in the time of need.*

The very last chapter I have read is the sixth of John. I have got I think some comfort and establishment from it. It is a marvellously free overture that is there made to the helpless and the sinful. If we receive by faith the body and the blood of Christ, He will dwell in us and we shall be complete in Him.

Let us not, however, remit our prayers for the recovery of the interesting patient in subjection to the will of God. My last excursion with him to Roseneath raised very high my estimation of his religious earnestness. He at that time discovered a mind deeply and seriously at work about the concerns of the soul, at the same time weaned from all delusive confidence in his own attainments, and evidently seeking for a surer foundation. I walked with him some weeks before through his own properties, and there witnessed the fruits of his beneficence, and heard the blessings upon him of those who were ready to perish. I heard him afterwards express the sense he had of his own nothingness, and confess Christ as the alone Author of salvation. Let us hope the good deeds done in his body were done unto that Great Judge who will acknowledge and reward them, and proceeded from that faith which gives an interest and a part in his better righteousness.

Be assured of my sympathies and my prayers, and believe me, my dear Madam, yours most truly,

THOMAS CHALMERS.

LETTERS TO MR. ROBERT BROWN.*

No. CXXXV.

Anstruther, 24th July 1818.

MY DEAR SIR,—I take the liberty of doing now what I should have done during my last excursion from Glasgow, that is, congratulate you on your returning health, and express my earnest wish that all the earnestness inspired by your recent visitation may indeed yield unto you an abundant supply of the peaceable fruits of righteousness. I am quite aware of the consciousness you have of a want of permanent interest and seriousness about these things, and many are those who feel an unsatisfied longing which they know not how to appease; and never do I myself approximate more nearly to a full and settled state of mind in reference to God, than when I feel divested of everything in myself, and am seeking to the offered righteousness of Christ as my hiding-place and my plea before Him.

We are apt, from the very frequency of a term, not to extend our attention to its real meaning. The righteousness of Christ imputed to those who believe is a phrase so familiar that it loses its impression. But hearken diligently to this joyful intimation, and your soul shall live. Your sin put to Christ's account, and His righteousness put to your account, totally alter your relation with God. To this new and delightful relation you are invited. It is unto all and upon all who believe; and not till this be really apprehended by you will the darkness, and the distance, and the enmity of heart, which are between God and the sinner, be done away. Give earnest heed to this word, and the daylight will dawn in your heart. Trust in Christ, and you will be sealed with the Holy Spirit of promise,

* Married to a sister of Mrs. Parker

and through the love of God shed abroad in you be a new creature.

My poor father is upon the bed of his last sickness. He was struck with palsy on Friday, and has since been inarticulate. He has an inward peace, of which we all know the cause ; and it softens the whole distress of this mournful occasion. He accepted long ago of justification by faith ; and the faith that is in him has been the living principle of a life both of prayer and of performance.

May I entreat your zeal and exertion in behalf of my parish. Make no premature exertion in your own person, but you may perhaps help me to some new agents. Let us not at the same time hurry this matter. But I would feel as if my lines had fallen to me in pleasant places, and I had indeed a goodly heritage could I bring St. John's under a thorough system of moral and spiritual cultivation.

Mrs. Chalmers unites in best compliments to you and Mrs. Brown. Our children are well.

Do give me a letter addressed to Anstruther, Fifeshire.— Yours most truly, THOMAS CHALMERS.

No. CXXXVI.

Anstruther, 10th August 1818.

MY DEAR SIR,—I received your most interesting letter, and I can assure you that you mistake the nature of my engagements altogether, if you think I would delay to answer it. Such an interesting topic as it embraces, so far from being extraneous to any business of mine, ought in fact to be incorporated with it, and to constitute its main and favourite article.

It is well that you have all these restless and unsatisfied longings. They will serve, I trust, the salutary object of weaning you from yourself. Be assured that long after the mouth has learned to ascribe all sufficiency to Christ, the heart may still adhere to a remainder of feeling respecting its own sufficiency, and the remainder must be given up, and the whole matter of salvation be given over to Him who is the alone author of it. Even after we profess the righteousness of Christ to be all our justification, there is still a tendency on our part to work for it. Now, the first Christians had peace and joy from the outset. They trusted in Christ, and were then sealed with the Holy Spirit of promise. The Spirit came to them not in the act of their performing the work of the law, but in the act of their hearing with faith.

The question of acceptance is a question between you and the Lawgiver. Roll over this cause upon Him who alone hath magnified the law, and made it honourable by fulfilling it in your stead. Let not any righteousness of your own enter as an element into the solution of it ; for this will darken and perplex the solution, and take off altogether from its clearness and its certainty. There remains another question between you and the Son—" What shall I render unto the Lord for all His benefits ?" Doubt not that He has completed for you the benefit of justification, and the less you doubt of this the more powerful and ardent will be the gratitude which prompts this latter question. And O how complete is that Gospel which not only inspires a sentiment, but affords power for carrying it into effect, which gives strength as well as the will to render back to our Saviour those mercies which are well-pleasing in His sight, and which, perfumed by the incense of his merits, ascend also as spiritual sacrifices acceptable unto God.—My best compliments to Mrs. Brown, believe me ever, yours most truly, THOMAS CHALMERS.

No. CXXXVII.

Dunblane, 9th July 1819.

MY DEAR SIR,—I know that I do not need to urge upon you any attentions that may be right or necessary towards our Sab-

bath-school teachers. You are fully persuaded of the excellence
of the institution and of the importance of extending its interests as far as you can. But I beg leave to suggest to you that
while you may carry personal exertion to a degree hurtful to
your health, you may without fatigue do as much good by the
simple and easy putting forth of your personal influence. In
other words, if you are still unwell, I charge you to spare yourself as to the work of your own particular school; and I offer
the hint, that though you may be apt on that account to regret
the diminution of your usefulness, you may in fact more than
replace all that you lose in this way by usefulness in another
way, even by the stimulus of your occasional intercourse and
conversation with those of them who have health for personal
fatigue and exertion in the direct work of a teacher.

May I suggest that it were desirable that any attentions
which you or Mr. M'Culloch or Mr. Falconer can bestow, should
be somewhat equalized by their being a little extended to those
of the teachers who have not got in so far within the limits of
that organizationship which subsists among the members of our
society. At the same time do not overdo. A small party
once in the month or two months would be a very full contribution to this object.

I have to entreat an interest in your prayers. I feel a woful bereavement of spirituality—an exceeding dimness as to
any sense or perception of God—no distinct impression of the
evil of sin—and I am sure no adequate thoughts of my Saviour
either as to the worth of His sacrifice, or the glories of His
character. Many think me profound in the mysteries of the
kingdom of Heaven : I know myself to be the veriest babe ;
and that there may be talk and argumentation about these
things without the spiritual discernment of them. But let me
comfort myself in this, that even to the simple exercise of
trusting does God award His promises and encouragements ;

and they who walk in darkness and have no light may yet trust. I have just been reading Alleine, I hope with profit. There is a closeness, and a pertinency, and a power in the writings of the good old Puritan, of which we fall greatly short in these days of feebleness and degeneracy.—Offer my most respectful compliments to Mrs. Brown, and believe me, my very dear Sir, yours most truly, THOMAS CHALMERS.

I desire to be particularly remembered to your brother. I hope that both you and he have had great comfort in your respective surveys.—T. C.

No. CXXXVIII.

St. Andrews, 10*th April* 1826.

MY DEAR SIR,—Both Mrs. Chalmers and I received with deep emotion the distressing intelligence conveyed to us by your letter. We had, indeed, observed it before in a newspaper, and were informed of some further particulars by a gentleman from Glasgow. But we had not learned till we received your letter the very mournful circumstances in which poor Mrs. Francis Brown has been left by the death of her husband—a situation so powerfully fitted to call forth the sympathy of all her friends, and to exercise their faith in the mysterious Providence of that God, who, however dark in His ways, does all things wisely and well.

That, indeed, is a great alleviation which you have specified, even the apparent religious state of your brother previous to his dissolution. And I must confess that I felt a peculiar gratification in your description of the letter which you received upon this subject, both on account of her who wrote it, and of her to whom it was addressed. Theirs is the fellowship of one common suffering. May they partake largely of one common consolation, and may the death of a friend so near and dear to both unite their hearts and their hopes in that Gospel, the faith of which can irradiate even the darkest visitation.

I enter fully into the anxieties which you express because of Mrs. Francis Brown, whose situation cannot fail to draw forth the tenderest solicitude of all her friends. I can scarcely imagine anything so painfully and peculiarly interesting as her present situation ; and I pray that, in the desolations of her state, she may experience an upholding confidence in Him who bears respect to the stranger in a strange land.

I was much touched and gratified by the last half of your letter, and by the just and striking reflections at the close of it. I feel with you that the world has a sad power of fascination over the heart, and that to wean us therefrom, there are crosses and extremities in life which appear to be indispensable. May your soul prosper more and more under the discipline of God's providential hand ; and let our experience of the vanities of the creature effectually shut us up unto God in Christ as the strength of our heart and our everlasting portion.

Give my affectionate condolence to Mrs. Brown. Assure her both of my own sympathy and that of Mrs. Chalmers, and of my prayers for her comfort and spiritual improvement in this the hour of her visitation. We long also to be remembered to your Mrs. Brown ; and I entreat you to believe me, my dear Sir, yours very truly,   THOMAS CHALMERS.

No. CXXXIX.

Edinburgh, 17th April 1832.

MY DEAR SIR,—I can assure you it was not without emotion that I heard of the death of your excellent, steady, consistent, and altogether exemplary mother, whose memory I shall ever cherish as one of the finest specimens I ever knew of cardinal worth, and all those virtues which mark a stedfast and withal a sober-minded Christian, well-grounded in the faith, and thoroughly intelligent both in the doctrines and moralities of the Bible.

Mrs. Chalmers fully participates in the feelings which I now express, and we unite in offering our sincere condolence and sympathy on this affecting occasion. May it prove a lesson to us all of the evanescence of the passing world, and the wisdom of being followers of those who through faith and patience are now inheriting the promises.

Nothing brings home more experimentally to my heart the lesson of my native carnality than the constant need which there is of having the doctrine of mortality so repeatedly told to me ; and it does shew how prone we are to cleave to the dust of a perishable world, that though told of death over and over again, yet do we persist in living here as if here we were to live for ever.

May we at length learn wisdom, and, living a life of faith on the Son of God, may we, when our last change arrives, be found in readiness for a blessed translation into His presence, where there is fulness of joy and pleasures for evermore. With our kindest regards to Mrs. Brown, I ever am, my dear Sir, yours most truly, THOMAS CHALMERS.

No. CXL.

Edinburgh, Morningside, 1*st June* 1845.

MY VERY DEAR SIR,—I should have responded sooner to the melancholy intelligence of a month back, respecting your daughter Isabella. The intimation was a moving one to us all ; and the invariable effect upon myself is, that it makes me feel as if domesticated in the household of mourners by being thus made a partaker in the griefs of so affecting a bereavement.

I have often reflected upon it as a singular mark of the Divine forbearance to myself, that, though now about thirty-three years a family man, my household has never yet been visited by death. I feel as if this laid upon me a fearful responsibility; nor am I ever more powerfully impressed by the languor and weakness of faith, than when I contrast the vivid interest that we feel in the temporal good of our children, with the sad practical insensibility of our hearts to the wellbeing of their unperishable souls.

I rejoice to understand that you and your family are at Fairley. I expect to spend a fortnight there soon. It will be to me the scene of many pensive reminiscences; but I shall feel it a comfort, now that the burden and heat of our day are over with us both, to hold fellowship with yourself as one of my old friends and associates through years that have long passed over us.

Offer my kindest regards and sympathies to dear Mrs. Brown, and also to the Misses Brown and your sons. May the bereavement under which you suffer be sanctified both to you and yours. Let our affections be weaned from a world the dearest and nearest objects of which may be so speedily withdrawn from us ; and seeking the city which hath foundations, let us be followers of them who, through faith and patience, are now inheriting the promises.—Ever believe me, my dear Sir, yours very truly,   THOMAS CHALMERS.

LETTERS TO MR. PATRICK CHALMERS.

No. CXLI.

Kilmany Manse, 21*st May* 1812.

DEAR PATRICK,—I have been too long of answering your letter, from the perusal of which I obtained the truest satisfaction. It would give me great pleasure to hear that you had read the books recommended in my last, and how you liked them. I look upon Baxter and Doddridge as two most impressive writers; and from them you are most likely to carry away the impression, that a preparation for eternity should be the main business and anxiety of time. But, after all, the Bible should be the daily exercise of those who have decidedly embarked in this great business; and if read with the earnest sense and feeling of its being God's message—if perused with the same awe, and veneration, and confidence, as if the words were actually coming out of His mouth—if, while you do read, you read with the prayer and the desire that it might be with understanding and profit,—you are in a far more direct road to "becoming wise unto salvation," than any other that can possibly be recommended to you. There is no subject on which people are readier to form rash opinions than religion. The Bible is the best corrective to these. A man should sit down to it with the determination of taking his lesson just as he finds it; of founding his creed upon the sole principle of "Thus saith the Lord;" and deriving his every idea and his every impression of religious truth from the authentic record of his will and of his doctrine.

I was at Anster last week, and found them all in tolerable health. There is now a very fine appearance on our fields. The good weather was long of setting in, but it has set in at last, and the country is in all its glory. I have purchased a horse lately. I ride about ten miles a-day upon it, and find myself much the better of the exercise. The keep is rather expensive, but health and comfort are worth the purchasing; nor will I grudge the whole rent of my glebe upon my riding expenses. I let my grass-field again this year at £8, 6d. per acre, and get about forty guineas for my land. This will nearly all go upon the horse-tax, maintenance, and person that takes care of him. My beddel takes care of my horse and garden for 10s. a month.

People here are all in their usual state of health.   Are you to be over soon ?   I expect Sandy to be with me a few weeks soon.   My Sacrament is to be held on Sunday the 21st of June.   Let me hear from you.—I am, yours truly,

THOMAS CHALMERS.

No. CXLII.

Kilmany Manse, 18th November 1812.

MY DEAR PATRICK,—I have been most negligent in not writing you sooner.   I hope you are to be on this side soon, in which case you will of course spend some time at Kilmany. Mrs. Chalmers has neither seen you nor Charles.   Will you write me soon, and give me an account of your employments and your prospects ?   I am no judge of farming ; nor am I competent to offer any observations upon it.   I trust that you continue to give satisfaction to Mr. Cowan, and should rejoice to hear that the concern was now a prosperous one.

I hope you have never lost sight of the important subject of your last correspondence.   It would give me pleasure to understand that, amid all your other pursuits, you kept firmly and perseveringly by the Bible.   If we would only think of it as God's message, as a letter from our greatest friend, as a record of His will for our salvation, I know not what apology could be thought adequate to justifying our neglect and inattention to it.   I should like to hear from you on this subject.   It is the greatest and the happiest event of life, when the mind takes a decided hold of eternity, and when it becomes its first care to seek the kingdom of God and His righteousness.   I hope you have not merely begun, but are advancing in the inquiry ; and I give it as the result of my own experience and my own feelings, that you will never feel the firmness of your ground till you have laid on the foundation of Christ, and put your confidence in that name, than which there is no other given under Heaven whereby men can be saved. A true faith in Christ works by love, and love aims at obedience. Again, a true faith in Christ is followed by the gift of the Spirit, (John vii. 39 ; Gal. iii. 14 ; Rom. viii. 32 ;) the Spirit gives strength for the execution of the aim, and you actually yield obedience. In this way your faith will not be dead ; it will abound in fruit, and you will rise from one degree of grace unto another, till you arrive at a meetness for the inheritance of the saints in light.—May such be your progress, and such your destination. Be up and doing ; and let the numerous calls given us, both by the Bible and by experience, have the happy effect to stir you up in the ways of wisdom and of piety.

You would hear of Mr. Johnson of Rathillet's death.—Write soon.—Yours most truly,   THOMAS CHALMERS.

No. CXLIII.

Anstruther, 18th January 1813.

MY DEAR PATRICK,—I am glad to observe that your society at Pennicuik is fairly set agoing. I however must decline the honour of being a member of it. The whole amount of the advantage would be 4s. 4d. additional to the cause, which I have it in my power to send by nearer and more convenient channels. The truth is, that I find I have gone too far in the way of connecting myself with other societies, and have frittered away in smalls what would have made a handsome sum at home, where it would have done more good in the way of example and effect among my immediate neighbours. I am besides called upon to preach occasional sermons often, and do not like to pass without a suitable offering to the collection. You must see that having a neighbourhood and a parish of my own to attend to, I must resist these foreign applications. I must stop somewhere ; and knowing that from my acquaintance in different parts, I shall probably be exposed

Q

to similar applications afterwards, I think it right to begin with you, in the confidence that you will perceive that in refusing your application, I do it on proper and reasonable grounds.

I hope that your society will have a happy influence on the minds of its individual supporters. If so much zeal and activity should be employed in the work of sending the Bible to others, it seems quite obvious, that it ought not to be neglected for ourselves, or suffered to lie beside us unread, unopened, and unattended to. It gives me great pleasure to think that this in all probability is the effect in your case ; and one great sentiment with us all should be, that we ought not to think that we have yet attained or are already perfect. The career of Christian sanctification is boundless, and it is our duty to press forward ; and when one looks to himself and feels his woful deficiencies in the mildness, the patience, the charity, the holiness of the Gospel, he must perceive how much he has yet to aspire after. We should at the same time never forget in what way the above virtues are formed and have their increase in the soul : they are the fruits of the Spirit, Gal. v. 22. And as the Saviour is the dispenser of the Spirit—as it is through faith in Him that the Spirit is given—as without Him we can do nothing—hence the necessity of laying all upon this foundation, of a vital union with Jesus Christ by faith, that He may be our sanctification as well as our redemption.

I should have been happy to have heard of your calling on Mr. Anderson. I got a letter from S——, but he says nothing of it. Could any prudent or effectual method be devised of bringing S——'s mind under the influence of the truth, it were most desirable. Give your attention to this particular. There is a danger sometimes in the imprudent use of means ; but prayer for one another is a resource which is always at hand, and can never be carried to excess. Do write me soon. Tell me of your numbers in the Bible Society of Pennicuik. Give me all the information you have about other parishes. It will be a wonderful sum if the parish system can be realized over the whole country. Grace desires her kind love to you.—Yours most truly,

THOMAS CHALMERS.

No. CXLIV.

Glasgow, 2d *September* 1818.

MY DEAR PATRICK,—I received yours some time ago, and yesterday had a visit from Mr. Thomas Thomson, with whose appearance and conversation I was much pleased. I regret that I was so particularly occupied—it being a day of meetings and of parish business with me. He went off this morning for Edinburgh. I would not have known how to address you but for him ; and I am glad to think that you have the opportunity of intercourse with such a family as that which he belongs to.

I trust that the impression of my excellent father's death will ever remain with us. His meekness, under all the crosses and provocations of life, formed a most memorable trait of his character. Above all, let us labour to emulate him in his exalted piety—a piety founded on the faith of the New Testament in all its peculiarity and in all its power. I hope you will read his favourite authors, Newton and Harvey ; but still more, that the Bible, accompanied with earnest prayer to God, will be with you that daily exercise which shall at length make you wise unto salvation.

Anster has now become sadly different to me from what it was. I now feel towards it as if it had sustained a fatal and irrecoverable mutilation. The remembrance of my father's Sabbaths, and of the whole routine of his week-day employments, always stood associated with all my thoughts of the place ; and these associations are now irretrievably broken up. There is a tender melancholy in these recollections. There is a sorrow which nature herself prompts and awakens, but it is grace alone which can impart the godly sorrow that worketh repentance unto salvation never to be repented of.

I trust that you will give all your strength to the one thing needful ; and that your zeal, and earnestness, and integrity in the service of your earthly master will, in fact, with you be so many offerings to your Master in Heaven—spiritual sacrifices unto God through Jesus Christ our Lord. Could the love of God be instated in our hearts in its rightful supremacy, every thing else would find its right place. Enter into reconciliation with Him through the atoning blood and justifying righteous-ness of the Mediator, and render unto Him, as the God of your redemption, the fruits of gratitude in all holy and affectionate obedience.

I shall be very glad, indeed, of an occasional letter from you ; and, be assured, that the details of your situation and employ-ment—accounts of the neighbourhood and country—and, above all, the news of your spiritual progress and welfare, would be highly interesting to me.—I am, my dear Patrick, yours most truly,   Thomas Chalmers.

LETTERS TO MRS. MORTON.

No. CXLV.

St. Andrews, 6th February 1824.

My ever dearest Jane,—I should have written you long ago ; and, indeed, mean to write you at a rate of much greater frequency than I have been in the habit of doing for some time. I am now in far more favourable circumstances for doing so ; for, even though I do have the labour of an extraordinary preparation for my new office, yet I am in very great ease and tranquillity when compared with the bustle and manifold fatigue of my former occupation. All that I shall require will be a regular exchange of letters with you; and I shall regard each arrival from you as the signal for an immediate exercise in the way of writing, that will be at all times agreeable to me.

I can easily leave this for Anster in a chaise after breakfast, spend some hours and dine there, and then return in the evening. This makes a very pleasant family—pop-in to my mother and aunt. I took down Mrs. Chalmers and the two eldest children in this style on New Year's Day. It rained incessantly, but my aunt, notwithstanding, insisted on our trailing to W. Anster with her. I made a second excursion of the sort about a week ago.

We keep very much aloof from the society of St. Andrews, while, at the same time, we are on perfect good terms with them all. They are very convivial, and we want a simple and easy intercourse. Mr. Duncan, whom you may recollect as our occasional visiter at Kilmany, is now Professor of Mathematics, and, in this respect, is quite suited to us.

Perhaps there is no town in Scotland more cold, and meagre, and moderate in its theology than St. Andrews. I do feel the Sabbaths to be very heartless in regard to the public services; and Mrs. Chalmers half threatens to be a Seceder upon our hands. I will not hinder her; but, as to myself, I do feel that bating the deficiency of warm ministerial addresses from the pulpit, I ought to make greater progress here than at Glasgow, where I was cumbered with many things; while here I may at least wait upon that which is good with far less distraction.

I am more persuaded than ever of the nothingness of man, that his wisdom consists in reliance upon God, in closing with

Him as his reconciled Father in Christ Jesus, and casting the whole burden both of his fears and of his corruptions on that Saviour whose blood should wholly dissipate the one, and wholly cleanse from the other. He permits us at times, as He did His disciples of old, to be overtaken with a storm, and even to have the visitations of terror because of unbelief. But His voice is soon heard again—" It is I, be not afraid."

Give my kindest compliments to Mr. Morton, Elizabeth, Miss Thomson, Mr. and Mrs. Edkins, Mr., and Mrs., and Miss Bliss. —I am, my dearest Jane, yours very truly,

THOMAS CHALMERS.

No. CXLVI.

St. Andrews, 9th June 1824.

MY DEAREST JANE,—I would have replied to your welcome epistle very soon after its arrival, but it came on the eve of my setting out for Edinburgh to attend the General Assembly, the bustle of whose operations prevented me from attending to anything else. Be very sure that I shall punctually exchange all your letters, and that too at pretty short intervals.

I now go up to the General Assembly in the capacity of elder for the burgh of Anstruther Easter—an honour to which, I believe, I shall aspire yearly; and in virtue of which it may perhaps please God that I should endeavour to serve the interests of His Church upon earth. We lost one question this year in the Assembly, but we gained two more; and the gain far more than outweighs the loss. I do think that there is a very great improvement in the spirit and temper of that body.

I never was more convinced of the benefit of my transition to St. Andrews than on my return to it just now from Edinburgh, where its tranquillity forms so delightful a contrast with the fatigues of the great metropolis. It was a most severe succession of one pressure after another, when I went from the

General Assembly to the anxieties and the manifold distraction of St. John's in Glasgow.

I took Anster in my way. Poor Isabel is no better; but I am glad that Helen is with her, who reports most favourably of her state of mind. I feel a most unfortunate barrier in the way of oral communication with certain of my relatives on the topic of religion. But I write her an occasional letter, for which she seems grateful and well pleased.

In less than a fortnight I go to Glasgow, and am to spend six weeks there in a course of ministerial duty. I have got a vast deal of labour before me in the composition of my lectures, so that I fear it is utterly out of the question my being in Gloucestershire this summer.

I rejoice to hear of Patrick's good fortune, and also of your own preferment to a better house. May you long enjoy health and comfort within its walls. Tell Mr. Morton that I do not envy his trusteeship, and I fear that he will find it land him in a peck of troubles. It is no doubt honourable to be the object of so much confidence as the charge implies; and I only wish he may not find it at length a very harassing and vexatious one.

But let us look beyond the toils and troubles of life to its latter end. I have recently felt some very vivid gleams of delight when thinking of the sacrifice by Christ for our sins, and how the whole guilt of them is removed thereby. Christ crucified is the great corner-stone of the spiritual edifice; and the more simply that we keep by this truth, the more shall we breathe of that pure element in which joy, and health, and activity are most felt. I need, however, to be saved from constantly relapsing into a carnal and worldly frame of spirit. We need, and we ought, to pray for each other.

Our children are all in good health. The weather of St. Andrews, of which we heard such formidable accounts, agrees remarkably well with the family. Mrs. Chalmers desires her best compliments. We move into a larger and better house soon.—I am, my dearest Jane, yours very truly,

THOMAS CHALMERS.

No. CXLVII.

St. Andrews, 20th August 1824.

MY DEAREST JANE,—I should have replied long ago to your letter; and, indeed, would have done it immediately, had it not come to me in the midst of great and manifold urgencies. I was then in Glasgow, whither I went for six Sundays, and officiated in the chapel of St. John's. I think that I never spent a season of more crowded occupancy between the preparations of Sabbath and the expected attentions, of which I laboured with all my might to acquit myself to my old acquaintances. In returning home I came round by Anstruther, where I saw Isabel somewhat recruited in health, though it were wrong to hold out any intervals of ease that she might enjoy as being more than a temporary respite from a state of disease which, we have every reason to fear, is incurable. It should make us the more thankful that such being her prospect on this side of the grave, her prospect on the other side of it is peculiarly bright and peaceful. You know that she is very close, and with me she has been quite general. But she is communicative with Helen, who represents her as in a very happy frame of spirit, which has been growing upon her from the commencement of an illness, of which she very early conceived that it was to terminate in death.

Since I came to St. Andrews I have been wading through oceans of business that had accumulated during my absence; and have been furthermore pestered a good deal with another odious plurality that we have done our uttermost to resist and testify against, though, we fear, without any success. During the whole of this throng, however, I have never lost sight of the obligation in which I stood to reply to your last communication, nor have I abated in the least of that regard which I entertain for you.

And if the principle of good-will might remain entire in the bosom of a friend, although he does, from circumstances, withhold for a time the expression of it, will you refuse the same justice to your Father who is in Heaven? All the sensible comfort that you enjoy may be regarded as some such token or memorial of His graciousness, as the letter of an acquaintance. But, though at times He forbears to send such a token, it is not because He has forgotten to be gracious. He may have other reasons for it. He may wish to exercise you again, as He has often done in the times that are past. Your business, meanwhile, is to be still and know that He is God; to build the hope of your safety, not upon your own faith, but upon His faithfulness; to look outwardly to His truth, instead of inwardly to your own deficiencies. You will never mend them by keeping your eye in the direction towards yourself, but towards the mercy-seat, whence grace to help will descend upon you as well as mercy to pardon. I like that death-bed experience of Dr. Dwight, who, when asked by his friends how he felt, made no other reply than that there was mercy in God through Christ Jesus. You at least have this reply always to make under all the variety of your fears and your feelings; and you have just as full a warrant as any other sinner has for appropriating to yourself the benefits of the Gospel mercy. Your fluctuations do not affect the truth of God; and if you will stick by that truth under all the clouds and desertions that pass over you, this is a stronger effort of faith than if you only kept it amid the smiles and the brightness of a cheering manifestation.

My visit to Glasgow and my attendance on the General Assembly together, consume at once one half of my summer

R

vacation. Both I deem to be very important duties, and this year they have only left me three months for carrying forward the still very unfinished preparations of my office in St. Andrews. In these circumstances I could not, without most serious inconvenience, attempt Gloucestershire this season; and this inconvenience so far from being lessened, is in my mind aggravated by a most provoking call that I have recently had to preach a sermon in Stockport. I had said some civil thing to them two years ago, when last in Manchester, in reply to a deputation who then applied to me, and I was then under the imagination that it would quite suit me to be in England at any rate at the time of the anniversary. My circumstances now have wholly changed; but this is not enough for these gentlemen who call what I said a promise, and insist on the performance of it. It can at most be but a post-haste expedition within a fortnight of the sitting down of our College, and the few days I shall give it in the month of October I can very ill spare.

This letter has been delayed one post in consequence of a visit from a Prussian clergyman who came in upon me just after I had got this length. He is a very pleasant conversable man, but it is with the utmost fatigue that I can apprehend his broken English. Our family are upon the whole very well. It is their school vacation at present; and Mrs. Tennant with three of her children, who were play or schoolfellows of ours in Glasgow, are now with us. There is a bathing process going on, against which Grace in particular has a most violent antipathy. I think it might be of use both to you and to Isabel were you to write a letter to her. I do this occasionally. It is a curious thing that I should labour under such difficulty in speaking to people whom nevertheless I can address with all fulness in a letter.—With kind love to all your family, believe me, my dearest Jane, yours very truly,   THOMAS CHALMERS.

No. CXLVIII.

St. Andrews, 23d December 1824.

MY DEAREST JANE,—I am quite ashamed of the date of your letter, but I have been much occupied. However, I should have felt the impulse of poor Isabel's death, and sent you off my first and recent impressions upon the subject. There was much to soothe and gratify in her latter end. Hers was a striking exhibition of the Spirit working silently, yet effectually, on whomsoever He listeth, and doing His own office upon the heart of a chosen one who has made a singularly quiet passage through the world, and of whom, I can assure you, my dear Jane, that I have the pleasing belief that she is now in heaven. I know not when I felt so much gratification as last July in Glasgow, on receiving a letter from Mrs. Chalmers, giving an account of a day that she had spent in Anstruther, and stating both what she saw of Isabel herself and what she had learned from Helen respecting her. I hold it most interesting to perceive in one who knew nought of the controversies of our faith, yet who manifestly had great peace and great joy in the simple reliance of the faith itself, to perceive how all the blessings of the Gospel might be realized upon such a one. Never was there a more patient sufferer; and the evident peace, and even joy, that were within, call for our most grateful acknowledgments to that kind Redeemer who suits His grace and His light to the trials of those who are His own children.

Since beginning this letter, (for it is now several days since I began it,) I have seen your letter to Helen. I grieve to hear of your ill health, but sincerely hope that Clifton will do you good. Have you met with my friend Dr. Stock there? Give him my kindest compliments should you see him.

We are going to spend the New Year at Anster. Poor Isabel makes a blank in our sadly reduced family. My mother has much of the comfort and complacency of a well-experienced Christian. Her physiognomy is most expressive of that abundance of peace which Isaiah compares to a deep and mighty river. Never was there a more cardinal person, or one all the elements of whose character were more solidly constituted. She is, I am confident, ripening for heaven ; and it is my desire, though I miserably fail in the execution of it, that I shall contribute my uttermost to the peace and enjoyment of her remaining days.

It was quite necessary, in point of repose, that I should leave Glasgow ; but I must not disguise it from you that St. Andrews has its trials. There is a most inveterate hostility to the evangelical spirit, and a sad public corruption, against which I have hitherto remonstrated ineffectually. Over and above all this, our Sabbaths are truly barren and dreary, from the miserable lack of unction in pulpit services. I have taken up a Sabbath-school which somewhat supplies the want to myself and my family, it being held in my own house, and attended by not more than thirty scholars. I was greatly delighted yesterday by a passage from the excellent Halyburton, who bids us suspect ourselves if our zeal runs all to public, to the neglect of private and personal Christianity. My clear line is to give all my force to the latter when my way is so hedged up against doing much in behalf of the former. My classes give me some precious opportunities however. I this year lecture upon both Moral Philosophy and Political Economy, and in both, particularly in the former, I can lift many testimonies on the side of the Gospel. My students I have great reason to rejoice in, being both well-educated and, many of them, remarkably well-disposed. I forgot to mention that Mrs. Chalmers, under the destitution of evangelical truth in our established pulpits, goes very often to the Dissenters, and incurs some obloquy on that account, which we care not for. Our dear children are all in good health, and we have the advantage of a first-rate school for their education.

And now, my dearest Jane, let us resolve to put our trust in that God who will not refuse His grace and guidance to all who truly seek after Him. Let us linger not in confidence to Him, seeing that He Himself has laid the foundation, and invites us to take our rest thereupon. In the quietness and confidence of His blessed Gospel we shall have strength.—I am, my dearest Jane, yours most truly,   THOMAS CHALMERS.

No. CXLIX.

St. Andrews, 26th February 1825.

MY DEAR JANE,—I trust that we shall get now into a more regular train of correspondence than heretofore ; and nothing, I assure you, would give me greater pleasure than if we could sustain a monthly exchange of letters.

I was sorry to understand that a sort of discordant politics had got in amongst the families of the coast-side. But for all such matters, I refer you to Helen, than whom and my wife, when they do meet together, I never witnessed a more exclusive brace of conversationists, keeping every other body out of the concern, and sitting apart by themselves to their own dear gossip, to the utter neglect of such poor outcasts as myself or any others that happen to be in the house along with them.

Helen will probably come to St. Andrews soon on her way to Glasgow, where she proposes to spend some time with Mrs. Charles.

It delights me to observe what you write of Patrick, who is a very cardinal fellow. I rejoice to hear both of his health and prosperity. I have not heard from James these many months. When there are long intervals of correspondence between us, he always takes it into his head that it is I who am in fault. I believe that it is very generally himself.

I am reading just now "Sheppard's Thoughts on Devotion." I understand him to be a banker in Frome, and a great friend of Foster's. It is a very impressive book, and combines two elements which seldom exist in union together—great science and great spirituality. I would recommend it to you; it is much prized by pious and intelligent Christians in this quarter.—I am, my dearest Jane, yours most truly and affectionately,   THOMAS CHALMERS.

No. CL.

St. Andrews, 17*th June* 1825.

MY DEAREST JANE,—I have of late had several offers to leave the University and return again to the Church. I had sometime ago the offer of one of the vacant churches in Edinburgh; and yesterday I was waited upon by a deputation from Dr. Gordon's Kirk-Session, with the proposal that I should succeed him. But it was not upon light grounds that I relinquished the clerical for the professorial life; and I am more and more confirmed in the belief that a chair in a college is a higher station on the field of Christian usefulness, than a parish anywhere in Scotland. Could one acquit himself rightly of his duties as a professor, it is incalculable the good which might be done to the guides and the clergy of our next generation.

I have met with things in St. Andrews which have somewhat helped to alienate me from its college, but not from a college life or college occupations.

I rejoice to hear from you of the Christian good that is doing in your neighbourhood. It is most true what you say, that Christianity has a most refining influence on the general habit and manners of even the poorest who embrace it. In the case of Sandy Paterson of Kilmany, it transformed a clodpoll into a perfect gentleman; and it shews that a delightful society awaits even this passing world, should the millennium ever be established in it.

Mrs. Chalmers and I spent some days in Kirkaldy lately, the occasion that you must have heard of, the loss of Sandy's youngest child. Both he and his wife were in great tenderness ; and in each of them there is, I trust, a religious feeling mixed with it. What a blessing should they henceforth take this direction ; and what a lamentable delicacy it is, a delicacy of which I feel myself the victim, that restrains one near relative from urgently and affectionately, and in season and out of season, being instant with all who are near and dear to us, that they should be up and doing for the salvation of their souls.

We had a delightful visit two days ago from Mr., Mrs., and Miss Babington. They left us this morning. He was the great friend and coadjutor of Mr. Wilberforce in Parliament, and after himself being a member for thirty years, has lately retired from political life. He is the most decided Christian I know—a man of education, judgment, and of truly engaging manners. It has given a great impulse to us both. I got acquainted with him while in England about two and a half years ago, and I feel myself much obliged and honoured by this attention. The whole conversation was quite delightful.

We expect shortly a visit from my mother and aunt. They will come up in a chaise and return to Anster in the evening. My mother indeed is a most cardinal person. She is quite well at present. James Duncan's wife is her great protégée just now. You are aware of her manifold trockifications with the poor folk. The part relating to her which is to be most rejoiced in, is her solid and well established confidence in God as her reconciled Father—a confidence which ministers the utmost peace to her heart, and diffuses a calm and a complacency over the whole system of her affairs.—I am, my dearest Jane, yours very truly,   THOMAS CHALMERS.

No. CLI.

Glasgow, 4th October 1825.

MY DEAREST JANE,—Perhaps I am never in more unfavourable circumstances for writing at length, than when performing my six weeks campaign in Glasgow. You know that last year I preached for that number of successive Sundays in St. John's Chapel, founded by myself ere I left the place, and this year I am doing the same. I wish to maintain this habit, both to keep up my intercourse with my old people and the exercise of preaching. But what with the exuberant hospitality of the one, and the necessary preparations for the other, this may well be called the *hurricane* season of my year.

You perhaps know that Mrs. Chalmers and all my family are with me on this occasion. It is rather an unwieldy concern; but I am the better enabled thereby to meet the demands of my very kind friends. It was a most severe personal fatigue when singly I had to cope with all the invitations of all my acquaintances ; but now I can divide myself and accept of them by proxy, insomuch that at present I have my wife and a bairn with myself in one place, and a servant and two bairns at a second, and my remaining bairn at a third.

I find it a great advantage to spend my mornings in practical reading rather than in study. My present book is " Owen on Spiritual-Mindedness"—a book which, when you have perfect leisure, I would recommend to your perusal. May the God of all grace and goodness perfect your recovery, and give you many days of comfort on earth to serve Him and be a blessing to your family.—Believe me, my dearest Jane, yours very truly,   THOMAS CHALMERS.

No. CLII.

St. Andrews, 15*th November* 1825.

MY DEAREST JANE,—I rejoice to observe that you enjoyed Sheppard so. My own practice is to read a little before breakfast of some practical treatise every morning. I have already told you of several books that have thus fallen in my way. I think that I have already recommended Romaine, and I have now very great pleasure in recommending "Owen on Spiritual-Mindedness." It is a book which gives palpable directions for the cultivation of this grace ; and I trust that I may derive some important help from it.

We arrived here only a fortnight ago, having protracted our stay in Glasgow as long as college terms would admit of it.

Our three eldest children are in full attendance on Mrs. Cowan—Anne considerably advanced in her music, and giving us a regular afternoon *deave* with her practisings—Eliza fagging as she can at French and Geography—and Grace learning and losing her spell-book time about.—I am, my dearest Jane, yours very truly,   THOMAS CHALMERS.

No. CLIII.

St. Andrews, 5th January 1826.

MY VERY DEAR JANE,—I would have written sooner, but your letter expressed a wish for information about Anster, so that I resolved to put off till I had finished my New Year's visit there. The excursion was to me a very interesting one. Mr. Bell's assistant of Crail, came for me in a gig on Friday the 30th, and took me down there. I have long had a reverence and affection for Mr. Bell, and he is the only coastside minister that was in office when I was a school-boy. I spent Saturday and Sunday with him, having preached to a full church in the afternoon. On the Saturday I had a most delightful walk with Mr. Tod the assistant, from Crail harbour along the beach to Fifeness, and onward to Banderston. We returned by Balcomie, which we visited, and Pittorrie, my grandfather Hall's house, which I recollect to have been in when I was in frocks, and most distinctly recognised the room into which I was admitted to see my grandmother forty-three years ago. There was a dinner given by Mr. Bell on the Friday to all the clergy of the neighbourhood. The most interesting of whom to me was honest cloghering and sniftering Mr. Wilson, who is still cloghering on. I made calls on Miss Coldstream, William Cowan, and Lizzy Hill, a servant of my mother's thirty-six years ago. I left Mr. Bell in his gig early on Monday morning, called at Barnsmuir, where Miss Fortune, now of sixteen, bears a striking resemblance to her mother, Christian Rankine. This whole road was to me full of interest, presenting such well-known objects as Keplie Dooket, with the echo, Innergelly avenue, Third-part avenue, Clishmacclash, &c., &c. I breakfasted in Kilrenny Manse, and was most cordially entertained by Mary Forrester, whose little son of nine weeks old formed an interesting novelty in the group. Got to Anster early in the forenoon. The chaisefull came down from St. Andrews, containing my wife, three eldest bairns, and Miss Hutcheson of Glasgow, now with us. I settled my trust accounts with my mother and aunt; they are both at present remarkably well. We had to leave them before tea from the darkness of the weather at present, and boisterous wind that would have blown out the carriage lights. Helen was still at Lathallan, but she has come to us this day and proposes to spend some little time with us.

I had great pleasure in hearing from Mrs. Duff, the sister of Dr. Barron of Gloucester, of your visit to him, and of his favourable report of you. I sincerely hope that you continue at least in tolerable health, and that you are enabled as heretofore to cast your dependence and to feel your delight in our all-kind and merciful Saviour; so free of access, and so willing as well as able to save, even unto the uttermost, all who come unto God through Him.—I am, my dearest Jane, yours most affectionately,   THOMAS CHALMERS.

No. CLIV.

St. Andrews, 22*d March* 1826.

MY DEAREST JANE,—I have had an excursion to the coast since I wrote last. My mother in good general health, and a state of mind which is truly admirable. Though quite by herself now, (Helen being at Kirkaldy,) she is never without resources, having always some work on hand, and to use her own language, God is very kind to her in supplying her with many a comfortable meditation.

My object in going down was to preach at Kilrenny, which I did to a very full audience. I went down to Anster on the Saturday—walked to Kilrenny after breakfast—preached there in the afternoon—dined with Mr. Brown, and walked in the evening to Barnsmuir with Mr. Fortune I spent the night there, and he drove me up next morning in his gig to St. Andrews. I felt great interest in being with Mrs. Brown (Mary Forrester) at Kilrenny, where her father was minister. The pleasure was damped, however, by the recollection of poor Anne Rankine, who lies with her infant at her side on the east of General Scott's tomb ; and over her, in the churchyard wall, there is a marble tablet with an inscription to her memory. There is no slight resemblance between Miss Fortune and her mother ; and she is now older than Christian Rankine was, when in 1799 I first was introduced to Barnsmuir.

You touch on a matter of great importance and great tenderness, when you advert to the religious training of your children. It is marvellous how obtuse we are on the subject of their eternal interests. How little we persuade them to the things which belong to their eternal peace ; and how little we pray for them. It is a sad evidence of the weakness of our faith when the imperishable souls of those who are dearest to us are not cultivated and not cared for.—I am, my dearest Jane, yours very truly,   THOMAS CHALMERS.

No. CLV.

St. Andrews, 12th April 1826.

MY DEAREST JANE,—I received yours in course, and am truly delighted to observe that you are in such health. May your soul prosper more and more and be in health ; and amid all these intermediate concerns between us and death, that is the interests or cares of a present life, may we forget not that there is a great and enduring interest which overpasses all and absorbs all.

It is out of the question my mother going to England. Mrs. Chalmers has asked her to live with us, and there is the most perfect convenience for it. Still, however, she cleaves to Anster, and will not leave it, she says, as long as Chirsty is her servant. There is a peace and deep serenity about her spirit which is altogether delightful ; and destitute as she is of all teasing curiosity, I am quite sure that whenever she consents to come to us, she will be a most delightful inmate. I really hope that such an arrangement may take place soon.

My practical author at present is Howe. The book of his which I am now at hand with is his " Redeemer's Tears." I never read a sentence of his works before, and I think I shall like him vastly. He is more lucid than Owen, writes with greater taste, and is often, I think, more striking, if not so profound. He is a very judicious and learned as well as pious author. There is more of tenderness, too, about him than Owen.—I am, my dear Jane, yours very truly,

THOMAS CHALMERS.

No. CLVI.

St. Andrews, 30th October 1826.

I cannot be thankful enough for Mrs. Chalmers's excellent recovery. She is now daily a few hours in the dining-room. Her attendant has been one of the Misses M'Clellan, our Helen's sister-in-law, who makes a very agreeable inmate. Besides her, Miss Collier is now upon a visit to us. You may remember her at Dairsie. She is a very decided and cultivated Christian, and has lived for several years with Mrs. Coutts. We are much the better of an influence of that sort under our roof; nor am I aware of an interest of greater magnitude, or that should come nearer to the heart of a parent, than the Christianity of his children. I hope that I should prize it as the most precious indication of God's friendship and fatherly regard, that He visited any of my household with such demonstrations of their sinfulness on the one hand, and of Christ's sufficiency on the other, as might lead them to that faith by which they are saved.

My book at present is Baxter's "Saints' Rest,"—very impressive. I think him particularly so on the awful and affecting subject of our responsibility for each other's souls. I should like more of courage and wisdom in the work of dealing with people on the great topic of their eternity.—I am, my dearest Jane, yours very affectionately, THOMAS CHALMERS.

No. CLVII.

St. Andrews, 10th January 1827.

MY DEAREST JANE,—I have lately, connected with the New Year season, made two distinct visits to Crail and Anstruther. On the one occasion I preached at Crail, and on the other at Kilrenny. When at Crail I visited Mrs. ——. . . .

The next or the Anster visit was still more interesting. Mr. Fortune, now at Barnsmuir, sent his gig for me on the last Saturday of the year. I got down to dinner, and met a company of coast-siders,—Mr. Brown of Kilrenny, Mr. and Mrs. Wilson of Anster, Hall Pringle and his sister from Largo, &c. I stopped at Barnsmuir all night. The two eldest daughters are farther advanced than were Kirsty and Susan Rankine when I first knew them, and, indeed, have a very strong resemblance,

both in mind and appearance, to the Barnsmuir ladies of that
generation. Miss Fortune is now at Leuchars, waiting on Mrs.
Watson, who has had a daughter, and is, I understand, doing
very well.

On the Sunday morning we walked in a family group from
Barnsmuir to Kilrenny—a beautiful day, and most interesting
road, all the turns and objects of which you well know. I
preached in the afternoon at Kilrenny, and stayed all evening
and night in the manse,—interesting from the presence of Mary
Forrester, who, in spite of her " twa bairns," is the same giggler
as ever. She has a deal of genuine humour, and is, I farther
hope, in the way of receiving good impressions from her husband, who is a most powerful and evangelical preacher. The
monument to Anne Rankine and her infant child in Kilrenny
churchyard is a very interesting object : it is upon the north
wall, a little way from General Scott's large mausoleum.

After breakfast I went to Anster, where I found my mother
trocking among wives—the same peaceful and independent
person as ever.

This narrative has occupied more room than I intended. I
shall therefore conclude with a remark of our excellent mother's ;
she reads a good deal, and among other books, " Owen on
Spiritual-Mindedness." She observed, however, that she had
not so much comfort in reading those books which led her to a
view of her own heart, for there she saw nought but corruption ;
but she found great satisfaction from trusting in God.—I am,
my dearest Jane, yours most truly,   THOMAS CHALMERS.

No. CLVIII.

Anstruther, 14th February 1827.

MY DEAREST JANE,—Our excellent mother died this morning
at half-past eight o'clock. She was entire in reason and recollection to the last ; and though she lost all power of articulation

within an hour and a half of her death, yet previous to that she gave forth many tokens of her solid and established trust in the great Redeemer, and, interspersed with these, many wise and judicious directions relative to the disposal of ordinary affairs.

You will forgive the brokenness and imperfection of my present narrative. My dear wife is nursing; and though she has been down in a chaise four times since the commencement of the illness, yet cannot be away from St. Andrews for a night. She had a deal of precious converse with my mother yesterday, who really was in a state of great ease ; but the symptoms of approaching dissolution came on at eight at night, and became more and more aggravated for upwards of twelve hours, when her sufferings were ended.

I am the alone occupant of the house in the meantime, and have all the superintendence. When to this you add that I was up all last night, you will not wonder if in this first letter on the subject of this great bereavement you find me so hurried and so unsatisfactory. But it is an adequate subject for a series of letters ; and I shall be most happy, in my replies to your future communications, to amplify on the interesting topic of our dear mother's last moments.—With kindest regards to Mr. Morton, believe me, my dearest Jane, yours most truly and affectionately,   THOMAS CHALMERS.

No. CLIX.

St. Andrews, 24th February 1827.

MY DEAREST JANE,—Mrs. Chalmers and I were again at Anster to-day. I had gone down by myself yesterday on foot, she came this day in a gig, and we got up together. I am still engaged among the details of business ; but I feel, beside this, an indescribable attraction in the place, softened by the tender and mournful recollection both of years and of people that have gone by. David Barclay took me to the churchyard, where I visited the hallowed spot of my mother's fresh and recent grave. I feel strongly inclined to inclose our family burial-ground. It is bounded on the south by a projecting stone that comes out from the middle of the east gate of Anster Church : that stone is the monument of Captain Anderson, a remote progenitor, who brought home in his ship the wood which roofed the kirk of East Anster when it was first built. . . . The Chalmerses have just been ninety years in Anstruther, and after the death of my aunt Jane, there is no further prospect of our being connected with the place.

A day or two after my mother's death I wrote down a few memorabilia of her last illness : this I shall copy over in my next or succeeding letter. I would have done it at present, but my visit of this day has supplied me with topics which I might have omitted had I postponed them. Perhaps my next visit in a week may supply me with some other topics of immediate interest, as I mean to rummage her scrutoire, where I know that I shall meet with some records of her deep and devoted piety. I have already met with a most interesting record of her charity in a small paper book which she appropriated to an account of her various distributions. I prize it as the best of legacies, and should like to prosecute her Anster benefactions. There is one half of the book blank, and I mean to begin where she ended. I feel a tender and melancholy pleasure in doing so.—Believe me, my dearest Jane, yours most affectionately,

THOMAS CHALMERS.

No. CLX.

St. Andrews, 17*th April* 1827.

MY DEAREST JANE,—I have been again at Anster. The business I expect to be finally settled by the month of June. The house will be sold by the beginning of May. I like to recall the associations of former years by taking an occasional night in it. My aunt is complaining at present.

In my mother's scrutoire, which I have opened, there are many old manuscripts ; and, among others, the birth-day prayers and dedications of the last years of her life. I had great pleasure in going completely round, about a fortnight ago, among all the people whose names occur in her charity-book. These amounted to eighteen ; and I left with each of them a trifle for her sake. Maggy Hutchison was, perhaps, the most interesting of the cases, who, with her aged bedfast mother, Mrs. Duncan, are breathing the atmosphere of contentment and piety. She was teaching a few children, and there was an air of comfort and peace in the dwelling. I have not forgotten a characteristic adage of hers, uttered at Mrs. Wilson's table years ago, that " Nature was easily sufficed."

My book at present in the mornings is Serle's " Christian Remembrancer"—a highly spiritual performance.—Believe me, my dearest Jane, yours most affectionately,

THOMAS CHALMERS.

No. CLXI.

St. Andrews, 20th October 1827.

MY DEAREST JANE,—I enjoyed very much my visit to Ireland, and was certainly treated there with great kindness, and received many honourable attentions. I was in four counties, Donegal, Derry, Antrim, and Down. The marine scenery of Antrim is the finest I ever saw ; and there is nothing which has imprest me so much in visible Nature as the Giant's Causeway, with the precipitous beach on both sides of it.

I was a good deal pushed by the kindness and attentions of the folks at Belfast. Among others, a person wrote me a letter and transmitted along with it his album, requesting an insertion from me there, along with the other eminent persons who had honoured it by their hand-writing. I sent it back without any reply ; and just because of my repugnance to an act which

S

carries with it the consciousness that I too must be a very eminent man like the *lave* of them. It is a most indelicate request ; and I do think, if people are amateurs and collectors of handwriting, the way is, just to get hold of any scrap of a card or letter that he may have written to another upon any familiar occasion, and batter it upon one of the pages of the portfolio. It is really too much to make the man himself accessory to this sort of vanity. You can accommodate, I have no doubt, your friends with abundance of my hieroglyphical scrawls.

Of all the books I have recently read there is none which has delighted, and I hope impressed, me more than Leighton's "Commentary on Peter." What a precious thing it is to get a fresh and powerful impression of religious truth. You are quite right, that in ourselves we neither can do aright, nor feel aright, nor even believe aright. Yet that should not hinder us from looking in the direction whence help cometh. It is a great matter that we are encouraged to persist in the mere attitude of *waiting*. We would be in the right and desirable state all at once. But it would appear that this is not the way, for we are called upon to seek till we find ; to wait the Lord's time, who in due time will raise us up ; to give earnest heed to the Word of His testimony *till* the day dawn and the day-star arise in our hearts.—May He, who is all grace and good-will, give you great peace and joy in believing, and cause you to abound more and more in the comfort of the Scriptures through the power of the Holy Ghost.—Believe me ever, my dearest Jane, yours most affectionately, THOMAS CHALMERS.

No. CLXII.

22d *November* 1827.

MY EVER DEAREST JANE,—I received yours of the 16th, and am quite grieved to find that you are still the invalid. I know that you are in good hands ; and it is my prayer, that He who can cause the peaceable fruit of righteousness to arise from His visitations of distress, may be with you as a comforter and a strengthener on the present occasion. I rejoice, that in the midst of the outward distress, you allege a happiness and a thankfulness to be within. It is certainly a very great matter of gratitude and rejoicing when God is pleased to uphold a tranquil and even happy frame in the midst of outward tribulations. But it is right to remember that your safety does not even depend upon this, but on that kind and all-powerful Saviour who never fluctuates, being the same to-day, yesterday, and for ever.

Fetch, then, all your supplies from Him—lean upon Him : do not even make a fatiguing work of so leaning, but rest quietly on the assurance that you are in the hands of one able, and as willing as He is able, to sustain you. May the blood of sprinkling be upon your conscience ; and as you think of the full and finished work of a Saviour's atonement, may you delight yourself greatly in the abundance of peace secured to you by such a peace-offering.

All here are well. Compliments to all.—Believe me ever, my dearest Jane, yours most affectionately,

THOMAS CHALMERS.

No. CLXIII.

St. Andrews, 4th March 1828.

MY DEAR JANE,—I do think it pertinacious in Mr. —— to keep up this constant annoyance with his album. When it does come I shall simply transmit it with my inscribed compliments ; and he may be thankful that I do not inscribe further my reprobation of the system of albums, and the dread in which I stand of the applications of album-holders. It is still competent for him to batter my line to you about him in the book if he so chooses.—I am, my dearest Jane, yours very truly,

THOMAS CHALMERS.

No. CLXIV.

St. Andrews, 13th March 1828.

My dearest Jane,—The album came to me by Glasgow some days ago. I was comforted to find that some of the contributors had written texts, which I have done too. It was not your joking, but their pertinacity, which annoyed me. I am always pleased with the ingredient of humour in your letters. I shall have an opportunity for sending back their album to Glasgow. The best contributions in it are those of Olinthus Gregory and Hannah More. It is a species of English indelicacy which I could never tolerate ; and the ladies of that land are particular nuisances in that way.

You perhaps remember a venerable brown-skinned folio that my father used to read upon the Sundays. It was a complete body of Boston's works. I have great pleasure in the perusal of it. It has formed a morning reading to me for some time ; and I have now got over his " Crook in the Lot" and his " Fourfold State,"—both of them very precious, and the latter abounds in very impressive passages. I, of late, have betaken myself to early rising, getting up every morning at six. This habit will be of great use to me in Edinburgh. My chief anxiety as connected with that place is, on account of Mrs. Chalmers, whom I particularly wish to protect from a repetition of that throng and pressure to which we were exposed in Glasgow.—Believe me, my dear Jane, yours very truly,

Thomas Chalmers.

No. CLXV.

Edinburgh, 29th November 1828.

My dearest Jane,—I am now in a more amazing bustle than I ever was in my life ; but it being the first month of my residence in Edinburgh, I trust it will subside. I have now a written paper in my lobby, shewn by my servant to all and sundry who are making mere calls of attention, which is just telling them, in a civil way, to " gang" about their business. If any-thing will check intrusion, this at length must. I used to have about twelve letters a week in St. Andrews, I have now upwards of fifty, so that I must write you more shortly, though I hope not less frequently than before.

Erskine's Essay to Baxter is one of the best things he has written. His last work on " The Freeness of the Gospel" has made a great, and, I trust, a salutary impression on Mrs. Chal-mers. It is exceptionable in regard to the wording of some things ; but altogether, in respect of principle and substance, is unspeakably precious.

We have got a governess from St. Andrews for a few months till we know more of Edinburgh ; but our elder girls will take lessons from without by and by.—Believe me, my dear Jane, yours very truly, THOMAS CHALMERS.

No. CLXVI.

Penicuick, 11th *September* 1829.

MY DEAREST JANE,—I received yours of the 1st with great tenderness of feeling, in which Mrs. Chalmers abundantly shared. We are both most thankful for the degree of recovery which the Father of mercies has been pleased to confer upon you. He knows your frame, and it is now your part to possess your soul in peace and in patience. Rest in the Saviour. He likes His people to lean upon Him, and to support them when their strength is gone. A day of complete and glorious emancipation is coming, when they who believe in Him shall be loosed from their infirmities, and sin and sorrow shall be alike unknown.

It was, indeed, a severe family visitation that we have been called upon to endure. There is no death that has more sen-sibly moved and affected me. May the impression be lasting and profitable to us all. The poor widow is bearing up wonderfully, and God will care, I trust, for her and her family.—Believe me, my very dear Jane, yours most affectionately,

THOMAS CHALMERS.

No. CLXVII.

Edinburgh, 6th October 1832.

MY DEAREST JANE,—I have spent a day with the Denbighs. I think much of her ladyship, both in respect of sound intelligence and good principles. She evinces great good sense in this,—that while she travels in Scotland, she selects as the appropriate objects of her inquiries, all that is special, and peculiar, and characteristic in Scotch theology. She has been in quest of our national and popular authors in this line, and, besides, interests herself with the old points and passages of our ecclesiastical history. I was much pleased with her conversation as a whole, but with one drawback—felt, I believe, by all parties during more than the first half-hour of our being together : they neither understood readily my Scotch, nor did I understand readily their English. In this respect of mutual understanding I am far better off with the English of London than the English of the provinces ; and accordingly for several hours we got on very ill—I a barbarian to them, and they barbarians to me. However, it got always the longer the better, especially after we had dined ; and after the whole matter was closed by an act of family worship at their request, I retired from them with the full impression that the barbarous people had treated me with no little kindness.

Miss Moreton gave me a sketch which she had made of Mr. Morton—far the most vivid resemblance of a human head and face that I ever saw done with the pencil. Tell me if you would like to see it, and I shall send it to you on the condition that you return it, as Miss Moreton said she could present you with a similar sketch afterwards. I shewed it to Dr. Welsh, Professor of Church History, and the most enlightened of our phrenologists. He pronounced upon it as a very remarkable head, and instanced more especially activity with great shrewdness and intellect as among the chief characteristics.

If you had any anxiety about it, I could get Dr. Welsh to make a minute study of Mr. Morton's head, with the view of drawing a character. It were a curious experiment as to the soundness of phrenology as a science, besides being interesting in other respects. I observe that Lady Denbigh has some faith in it.—Ever believe me, my dearest Jane, yours most truly, THOMAS CHALMERS.

No. CLXVIII.

15th February 1833.

MY DEAREST JANE,—These are peaceful times, yet not such as should interfere with that most important of all history, the unseen history of minds reposing in the faith of the Saviour, and ripening for heaven under the operation of His sanctifying grace. May such be the prosperous history of you and of yours till we have obtained our secure establishment in the land of everlasting quietness.—Believe me, my dearest Jane, yours most truly, THOMAS CHALMERS.

No. CLXIX.

Edinburgh, 27th *February* 1833.

MY DEAREST JANE,—I received in due time your sprightly communication, to which I might not have replied so soon, but to express the great interest I feel in your proposed movement to us in summer.

Mrs. Chalmers was greatly amused by the new title wherewith you have dubbed her. I confess myself to have been relieved by the Irish Church Reform Bill, the only flaw in it (although that may be one of deadly mischief) being the secularization of the sum which they expect from the sale of Church lands. But you are quite right in possessing your soul in patience and quietness under all the events of Providence, assured always of this, that God reigneth.—Ever believe me, my dearest Jane, yours most truly,   THOMAS CHALMERS.

No. CLXX.

Edinburgh, 6th June 1833.

MY DEAREST JANE,—Since writing you last a letter, which is probably waiting for you at Cupar, I have become wretchedly bilious, and must make another retreat into the country. I shall go probably to Kinghorn, and if at all safe or right for me I will venture east for half a day to the hot and confined and dusty town of Kirkaldy. If I am not able for this, you will have, I hope, the candour to put down my non-appearance there to its right cause—even that candour the want of which I fear has incurably distempered the footing on which I stand with some of my nearest relatives and connexions in this world. Oh, when will the system of human intercourse be left to its own free and spontaneous workings, and cease to be a constrained and hypocritical interchange of jealous exactions and claims of attention upon the one side, of cold, heartless, and formal, but reluctant compliances upon the other ?

Give my kindest regards to Catherine, and ever believe me, my dearest Jane, yours most truly and affectionately, your bilious and beloved, your stomachic and sentimental, your cholical and cholerical brother, who with sincere good will subscribes himself, ever yours,   THOMAS CHALMERS.

No. CLXXI.

Steamboat between Boston and Lincoln, 29th July 1833.

MY DEAREST JANE,—I have been detained a week longer than I expected, and it will be, at least, the middle of August before

I reach Scotland. I beg you will write immediately on receipt of this, and let me know your movements. My address, if you write soon enough, is at the Rev. Mr. Gray's of Sunderland. I want particularly to know about what time you purpose to be at Woodhouselee, for it will depend upon this whether I shall go first there, or go immediately to Kelton. Few things would give me greater pleasure than some quiet day of converse with you at a distance from bustle, and where we could talk over both the prospects of the future and the recollections of other days.

I spent yesterday at Boston, where I heard two very cold sermons in the church, but a better one from a clergyman in the evening, also of the Establishment. During the day I was called upon by Mr. Aitken, formerly of Fife, and who tells me that we had met before at a house in Gloucestershire; he farms in the neighbourhood, and has a visit from Mr. Morton when he comes to Spalding. I had lost my recollection of him—an infirmity that, I fear, is growing upon me. But we had sufficient points of sympathy in his being a Scotchman, and, withal, brother to George Aitken, an old parishioner of mine. He introduced his son to me, a fine-like lad, who is learning a business at Boston.

I hope I am legible in spite of the *dinnel* of the steamboat. We are now approaching Lincoln, whose lofty cathedral has a very noble appearance. Our passengers come chiefly from the fens—and amphibious-looking creatures they are, with a dialect not very intelligible to me, and a certain degree of shyness, which perhaps, however, it is natural for them to observe towards all other land animals.

May the God of all comfort stablish you more and more, both in the promises and precepts of the Gospel; and with kindest regard to Catherine and Mr. and Mrs. M'Clellan, ever believe me, my dearest Jane, yours most truly and affectionately,   THOMAS CHALMERS.

T

No. CLXXII.

Norham, 10th August 1833.

MY DEAREST JANE,—I have been at Berwick to-day, and I am now at a place eight miles up the Tweed from it. I mean to work my way to Woodhouselee from this by the line of separation between the two countries, and always studying to keep as near to it as I can, with one foot, if possible, in England, and another in Scotland. This will bring me down Liddesdale ; and for night-quarters I mean to chap at every manse-door I can fall in with.

I am only sorry that I shall not be able to convoy you homewards, but I will be able I hope to stop with you at Woodhouselee till the 23d. Give my kindest regards to Mr. and Mrs. M'Clellan and Catherine, and ever believe me, my dearest Jane, yours most truly,   THOMAS CHALMERS.

No. CLXXIII.

Penicuick, 24th June 1834.

MY DEAREST JANE,—The doctor prescribes for me one continued holiday all summer, and I mean as much as possible to take his advice. It were well if, in this season of exemption from all strenuous effort, I could find my rest and refuge in God as the strength of my heart and everlasting portion, having whom all the enjoyments of a world that passeth away might be renounced without a pang.—I am, my dearest Jane, yours most truly,   THOMAS CHALMERS.

No. CLXXIV.

Penicuick, near Edinburgh, 25th August 1834.

MY DEAREST JANE,—I am grieved to observe by your letter of the 10th that you have suffered so much lately from ill health. Will you let me know in your next which half of your head it was that felt the greatest pain ? Any peculiar symptoms which I feel are on the right of my head and side ; but of late I have become more confident of a full recovery, and do feel that its holiday summer which I have spent, with its exemption from fatigue and ease, has been of great use to me.

I am much interested by your aspirations after a nearer conformity to the image of the Saviour, and I desire fully to sympathize with them. It is well to look unto Him as our example, as well as look unto Him as our propitiation. I hold it a remarkable expression, and a remarkable coincidence, that in both of these capacities He is said to be *set forth* to us, and set forth by God. What a two-fold power of comfort and of direction there is in this ; and if we give earnest heed unto Him in the aspects under which He is set forth unto us, we may rest assured of the promise given to those who hunger and thirst after righteousness, even that they shall be filled.—I am, my dearest Jane, yours most affectionately, THOMAS CHALMERS.

No. CLXXV.

Burntisland, 27th December 1834.

MY DEAREST JANE,—I have come here for a few days during our Christmas vacation, and I gladly avail myself of my first country holiday to answer your affectionate letter of inquiry.

I have been engaged in class-work for six weeks, and have acquitted myself of it greatly beyond my anticipations. I am much thinner, being now 168 lbs. weight, whereas I at one time was 205 lbs., but muscularly I am as strong as ever ; and as to my head symptoms, noise, hissing, pulsation, accompanied with numbness in my extremities, although they continued with me till within these few days, I am marvellously free of them since I left Edinburgh. On the whole, I think that even my head is knitting with greater strength and soundness again.

As to my being a Tory, I am certainly a Conservative, though not in the party, but in the general and ordinary sense of the term. I believe that under our late Government the country was drifting fast into a state of anarchy, and I fear that our present administration forms in all human likelihood the last barrier—may it be an effectual one—against a tremendous civil war.

But to pass to more satisfactory topics. Have you read Owen on the 130th Psalm ? This is my last great work ; and I would strongly recommend it as eminently conducive to our establishment in that way, which is at once a way of peace and of holiness.—I am, my dearest Jane, yours most truly and affectionately,   THOMAS CHALMERS.

No. CLXXVI.

Burntisland, 20th October 1835.

MY DEAREST JANE,— . . . In the hope that you will accept of this my contrite acknowledgment, I now proceed to the subject which, whatever the diversity of our tastes or our employments may be in other things, should at all times cement by the feeling of a common interest those who possess as we do the doctrines, and I trust the hopes of the Gospel of Jesus Christ. I am thankful to say that no reading so occupies and engages me as the biography of those who have made it most their business to prosecute the sanctification of their souls ; and, in particular, let me name the "Life of Sir Matthew Hale," lately published by Williams, as also Venn's "Memoir and Correspondence." He is the author of the "Complete Duty of Man," which I am now reading, and which, as a practical system of evangelical doctrines and duties, I feel inclined more to recommend, as a family book for the adult sons and daughters of a family, than any I know. It is now becoming a deep concern with me "to watch over the souls of my children ;" and we both have so strong a common interest in this, that I cannot refrain from mentioning a book which you would do well to encourage the perusal of amongst those who are near and dear to you.—I ever am, my dearest Jane, yours most affectionately,

THOMAS CHALMERS.

No. CLXXVII.

Edinburgh, 18*th February* 1838.

MY DEAREST JANE,—There should be no such word as forgiveness betwixt us. You altogether mistake my feelings, if you think that there is anything to forgive. I am well pleased every time I receive a letter from you ; but you must not think of tasking yourself to such an exercise. A letter from any of your family is tantamount to a letter from yourself, when occupied or unwell, which, I am sorry to think, you often are. But bear up under the conviction that God is faithful as well as merciful to forgive all who apply to Him in the name of Jesus ; and be well assured, that as your fears of alienation or displeasure on the part of your earthly friends here turned out to be groundless, be assured that still more groundless are your apprehensions of displeasure in God, whose darling attribute is mercy, whose strange work is judgment, and who rejoices in the confidence which His own creatures rest in His own name, as the Lord God merciful and gracious, long-suffering, and abundant in goodness and truth, forgiving iniquity, transgression, and sin. And though He says of Himself, that He will by no means clear the guilty, yet has He found out a way by which He might at once be a just God and a Saviour—just, yet the justifier of those who believe in Jesus.

I saw your Alexander, whom I love, yesterday. We met at the church-door. John, who Professor Forbes tells me, is one of the ablest and most scientific of his students, has lately added skating to his other accomplishments ; and when I saw him two days ago on the ice, I found him a good proficient in that part of education also.—I am, my dearest Jane, yours most truly,   THOMAS CHALMERS.

No. CLXXVIII.

Edinburgh, 3d January 1839.

MY DEAREST JANE,—Our place is not *Eveningside*. It is true that it is on the other side of Edinburgh from Morningside, and hence the denomination which I in the fertility of my genius chose to annex to it. But remember, afterwards, and address me at Edinburgh, as the brilliancies of invention, however congenial to minds of a high order, like yours and mine, serve rather to bewilder than to guide the prosaic movements of a postman or letter-carrier.

Our family are at present in tolerable health. Thomas Chalmers Hanna, my grandson, of a year and a half old, has been with us for some months—a delicate skift of a creature, but a great favourite notwithstanding ; the object of a very general attention ; the centre of a circle of friends and admirers ; the little despot of an establishment, all the members of which do him homage, and are subordinate to his sway.

I trust your health is mending, and, above all, that your soul prospers, and is in health. Let us keep on the foundation of Christ's grace and righteousness, and there is no fear of us. I feel quite assured that the more we look to the Gospel in its freeness, the more shall we experience of its sanctifying power, of its present salvation, the pledge and earnest of that future salvation which it so richly offers to all who will.—I ever am, my dearest Jane, yours most truly,   THOMAS CHALMERS.

No. CLXXIX.

Kirkaldy, 6th April 1839.

MY VERY DEAR JANE,—I should have replied a great deal sooner to yours of January the 9th. I have only this week finished the labours of our College session, where I am very much engrossed; and even at the best I can only write briefly and generally. I saw both John and Elizabeth very lately. I rejoice to hear of his teaching a Sabbath-school. His is a bright order of talent; and it is a great blessing when men of power become also men of deep and decided piety, which combination I pray God that your son may realize. The strongest of my instinctive likings is towards Alexander—a fine laddie-looking fellow, with an approach to a "lint-tap," and at that age of tooth-shedding when chasms and vacancies occur along the front gums.—Everything is beautiful in its season.

Part of my family is now at Burntisland, which I left this morning, and am now with my father-in-law at Kirkaldy. Grace, Mrs. Hanna, and the grandbairn or oy, are now on this side of the water—the last mending, the two former colded, and not the better of that raw, penetrating east-wind which is felt so severely along the coast of Fife at this season of the year. That easterly *haar*, by the way, is an exception: it may be the beneficial result of wise and beneficent laws, but I cannot say of it as I did of Alexander's toothless apertures—it is not beautiful in its season.

My kindest regards to all—Mr. Morton, Catherine, Anne, Lucy, and John. May they rise around you and call you blessed. I have been reading lately in Fisher's "Marrow of Modern Divinity"—a truly refreshing work, full of the freeness and richness of that blessed Gospel which holds forth, on the footing of a gift, all that is most precious for sanctification here and everlasting salvation hereafter.—I ever am, my dearest Jane, yours most affectionately and truly,

THOMAS CHALMERS.

No. CLXXX.

Kirkaldy, 23d October 1839.

MY VERY DEAR JANE,—I have first to begin with an affecting piece of intelligence, the death of Captain Pratt, my father-in-law, which has brought me and Mrs. Chalmers to this place, where we remain several days. The death even of our most aged friends, however much expected, is always sure to strike and to solemnize when it happens ; and it is, indeed, most marvellous that, familiarized as we are to this most certain of all events, it always comes upon us as with the force of a new lesson which we had yet to learn.

I have not seen the book entitled " Union or the Church made one," but I have read the other production of its author, entitled " Mammon," and think that there is great truth of principle in the work, and that, too, forcibly and impressively propounded.

I have been a great traveller this year, (as far as Sutherland-shire,) and been acting the part of a sturdy beggar in behalf of Church Extension. The sum realized in the course of my itinerancies has been about £14,000. I am scarcely yet recovered from the exhaustion of these efforts, nor do I mean to repeat them.—With my best regards to Mr. Morton, and earnest prayers for the health, and more especially for the spiritual wellbeing, of one and all of the family, I ever am, my dearest Jane, yours very affectionately,   THOMAS CHALMERS.

No. CLXXXI.

Edinburgh, 15th December 1839.

MY DEAREST JANE,—I have not written you since the death of our poor brother James—a touching and most melancholy event—and of which I have already written to Helen, it having been my purpose to hold a special communication on the subject with each of the surviving family ; but the bustle and agitation of our various affairs in this place have sadly retarded the execution of my purpose.

We are greatly too reserved on the matter that principally concerns us. There is an unaccountable delicacy in speaking to each other of the things of the soul. I did feel that sensitive repugnance in the case of poor James, though I occasionally dropped a hint or intimation in writing to him. Still I often had my compunctions on his account, and therefore you can imagine the interest and satisfaction which I felt in your daughter Anne's letter, where she spoke of the confidence he felt on his death-bed in the merits of the Saviour.

Let us all address ourselves to Him as the alone refuge and propitiation of sinners. We cannot surely trust Him too much ; nor is there temerity or presumption in venturing our all upon so sure a foundation. Let us not fear that if our dependence be strong enough, we shall fail in our preparations for eternity ; as the simpler and stronger our faith, the more fervent will be our love, the more abundant as well as affectionate will be our obedience.

I grieve to hear that you are unwell. Cling with full reliance to Him who knows how to save us ; rejoice in the midst of tribulation ; feel the peace and assurance of that blood which cleanseth from all sin.

Give my kindest regards to all—to Mr. Morton, Catherine, and all the family. Tell Anne how much I rejoiced in her letter, and that I shall always be delighted to hear from her. Mrs. Chalmers unites with me in all that is sympathizing and kind.—Yours most affectionately,

THOMAS CHALMERS.

No. CLXXXII.

Edinburgh, 23d February 1840.

MY DEAREST JANE,—I should have written much sooner, but could not, under the suspense and uncertainty of dear Alexander's illness. God has been pleased to take him away from you ; and in the death of that very fine engaging boy has given us another demonstration of the evanescence of a world, the best-loved objects of which are liable to be so suddenly and affectingly wrested from our grasp.

I rejoiced to hear from Mr. Morton that you were prepared for the decisive intelligence before he left home. Often have I thought of Mr. Wilberforce's remark, that the faith of immortality gives a certain firmness of texture to the mind. Could we but realize our future and better world, it would lighten the effect of those calamities to which all flesh is heir in this earthly pilgrimage.

I was glad, though only for a moment, to see poor Elizabeth on the day of the funeral. We shall be anxious to hear how she and Mr. Morton got home.

I am heartily tired of public life, and long, if God be pleased to spare me for such an old age as my mother enjoyed, as if at the gate of Heaven, and with such a fund of inward peace and hope, as made her nine years' widowhood a perfect feast and foretaste of the blessedness that awaits the righteous. If I live I shall be sixty on the 17th of March, entering the seventh decade of my life. It has been a fond speculation of mine, would that it were realized, to make that decade a Sabbatical one ; bidding adieu to all official business, save that of my Professorship, and spending the remainder of my days in the studies and exercises of sacredness. It greatly enhances my desire for such a consummation, when I think of the bright and beautiful serene which sat on the evening of my mother's life. There are few things I should like better, during the currency of such a latter-day period, than the tranquil visit of two or three weeks to Chester Hill. But let us not dwell too confidently on these visions of the earthly future, but rather look forward to the city which hath foundations, whose builder and maker is God.—I remain, my dearest Jane, yours very affectionately, THOMAS CHALMERS.

No. CLXXXIII.

Edinburgh, 20th March 1840.

MY DEAREST JANE,—It gives me real gratification and thankfulness to observe the support which you experience from the hand of God under the heavy affliction that He has been pleased to lay upon you. He knows how to temper His own visitations; and how delightfully alleviating must be your recollection of those traits which mark a work of grace on the dear object of our regret and tenderness.

I have now entered on threescore, and desire to give up the remainder of my days on earth to a busy work of preparation for Heaven—a work of greatest difficulty, nay, impracticable, without the aids of that Spirit who alone can help our infirmities, and perfect strength in weakness.—I ever am, my dearest Jane, yours most truly and affectionately,   THOMAS CHALMERS.

No. CLXXXIV.

Burntisland, 26th June 1840.

MY DEAREST JANE,—I have not written you since poor Mr. M'Clellan's death. I have exchanged letters with Mrs. M'Clellan, and I am glad to perceive that, though greatly distressed, she has been so well supported under the heavy visitation. Our friends and contemporaries are fast breaking up; and each new summons will, I trust, prove a useful as well as an affecting memento to us who are spared.

Our church matters are in sad confusion, owing to the faithlessness and want of real patriotism in public men. The Whigs used us shamefully; but this I very much laid my account with, and have therefore been still more chagrined and disappointed with the treatment of the Conservatives. I have heard that all is fair in politics, even as all is fair in horse-dealing. It is truly wretched, however, to think that the morality of public

and parliamentary men should be on a level with the morality
of a horse market.

I mean to retire from all public business, but I have some
closing accounts to wind up, which may occupy some weeks yet.

With best regards to you and yours, I ever am, my dearest
Jane, yours very truly,   THOMAS CHALMERS.

No. CLXXXV.

Burntisland, 14th July 1840.

MY DEAREST JANE,—I am much interested by what you tell
me of the Ducie family ; and knowing, as I do, Lady Denbigh,
I should like to hear from you of her safety. She seemed to
me a person of great sensibility, as well as of great intelligence
and worth.

I am engaged with Mrs. Chalmers to be at Dunkeld on the
day of their Sacrament, which takes place on the first of August.
After our return thence, it is possible that we may have to go to
Ireland ; but this is not altogether determined. It seems we
held out some hope to the Hannas of Belfast ; but I do trust
that we shall not miss the opportunity and great enjoyment of
your society while in Scotland. I confess that, as a chield gets
aulder, the force of the Scotch proverb that, " Bluid is thicker
than water," is felt with all the greater force by him.

I look back with the greatest interest on the history and
character of both my parents, and particularly on the days of
widowhood of my mother, who evinced a strength of Christian
principle throughout, and a depth of peace and assurance,
settled on the merits of the Saviour, which are not often
equalled.

I mean to write Helen in a few days ; and, meanwhile, with
best regards to Mr. Morton, Catherine, Elizabeth, Anne, and all
the rest of your family, in which Mrs. Chalmers joins, I am, my
dearest Jane, yours very truly,   THOMAS CHALMERS.

No. CLXXXVI.

Edinburgh, 23d November 1840.

MY DEAREST JANE,—I hope you would receive my last letter to you, which seems to have crossed your last letter to me. I did not advert to your being at Cheltenham till Helen here told me. She is in a quiet and complacent frame, and altogether I am much interested by her visit, as well as by the prospect of your being with us in spring. There is something affecting in the thought of a common gathering amongst the members of a once numerous family, recalling, as it were, their scattered forces, and meeting together once more ere time shall complete its work on the remaining few, by laying each one after another successively in the dust.—With earnest prayer for God's best blessings on you and yours, I ever am, my very dear Jane, yours most affectionately,

THOMAS CHALMERS.

No. CLXXXVII.

St. Andrews, 17th April 1841.

MY VERY DEAR JANE,—You will be surprised at the date of this letter ; but I have come to repose here for a few days after the fatigues of the session, and the debilitating effects of my late influenza. I am the guest of Professor Duncan, still an inveterate, and, I fear, hopeless bachelor. By October next, we shall have been acquainted for fifty years, or half a century. I told him lately that when we were first acquainted we were "twa callants," but that now we were "twa carls." You can easily imagine the delight I enjoy in a visit to my own university, and under the roof of an hospitality as free and open and easy as that which obtains between two student lads.

I like Lady Denbigh. I greatly admired both her sense and her piety when I met her in Scotland. I have no wish, however, to be in London; but should I go, I should rejoice in availing myself of her very kind invitation, and also in coming round to you by the railroad.

Let me know particularly of Catherine. May the Giver of all that is good restore her to your wishes and prayers, yet prepare us for His own holy and righteous will, and so spiritualize our hearts, that their affections may be withdrawn from the world, the nearest and dearest objects of which can so speedily be withdrawn from us.—I ever am, my dearest Jane, yours very affectionately,   Thomas Chalmers.

No. CLXXXVIII.

Burntisland, 18th May 1841.

My very dear Jane,—The reason why I did not express the delight I shall feel on your visit to Scotland is, that I waited till I could express the still greater delight of a visit from you in our own house. When I last wrote, we were a family of invalids, with no less than four of us occupying each a separate apartment; but now I have reason to bless God that we are gradually getting better, and that we shall have accommodation both for you and Catherine, with a method of providing for Mr. Morton a most comfortable night-quarters in the town, when he comes to spend days with you. You we expect to have for weeks, or, still better, for months; and as sea-bathing, I understand, is good for Catherine, I can assure you that this is the best bathing-quarter I know anywhere, our house being a very small way from a beach of fine sand. Mrs. Chalmers joins me in the earnest expression of our joint wish that you will accede to this arrangement, and we shall manage to have Helen over too. I am sure you will admire the beauties of our scenery, and be charmed with the kindness of our small and simple society, made up chiefly of the Youngs, who are the magnates of this place, and related to Mrs. Chalmers. Our children begin bathing in June, and will have great pleasure in joining Catherine.

I mean to be constantly at home all summer, spending it in quiet study, after having renounced all the bustle and publicity of other days. It is a favourite speculation of mine that, if spared to sixty, we then enter on the seventh decade of human life, and that this, if possible, should be turned into the Sabbath of our earthly pilgrimage, and spent Sabbatically, as if on the shore of an eternal world, or at the gate of the upper sanctuary, in the outer courts, as it were, of the temple that is above—the tabernacle in heaven. What enamours me all the more with this idea is, the beautiful retrospect of my mother's widowhood, all of which she spent in spiritual enjoyments, and in deep religious peace. With her the season of final retirement from the world was a season of preparation and piety, and I can image nothing more impressive than my recollection of her dying scene. May we die the death of the righteous, may our latter end be like his.—With best regards to Mr. Morton, Catherine, Anne, Lucy, and the young gentlemen, in which Mrs. Chalmers joins, I ever am, my very dear Jane, yours most affectionately,

THOMAS CHALMERS.

No. CLXXXIX.

Burntisland, 30th August 1841.

MY DEAREST JANE,—I am grieved to find from your letter that Anne is so poorly. May she be speedily restored to health and strength ; and above all, may God's will be our will. It is good to be reminded of the precariousness of this world's blessings ; and surely it is high time for us in particular to be looking heavenward and homeward. There is not a better attitude, I believe, both for peace and holiness than a quiet resting in Christ as the Lord our righteousness.

Catherine left on Saturday with Mr. and Mrs. M'Clellan,

and my brother Charles. She is now at Castlebank, and proposes to go to Wishaw and Skirling. She did not just take
with the bathing, and it is thought that going about a little
may be of service to her. I hope to see more of her here also,
for Charles, now at leisure, can conduct her to us at any time.
I have not seen enough of her, nor talked enough to her; and
I cannot sufficiently lament the engrossments which have
hitherto dispossessed better and higher themes, and restrained
my converse on them with my nearest and dearest relatives
more than it ought to have been. I have seen, however, as
much of your Catherine as makes me like her very much, and
think highly of her. She is indeed a great favourite with us
all; and I do hope, that when she comes next, she will find
me more disengaged, for we have been sadly bustled of late.
May God give us grace and wisdom for being Christianly
useful to each other in our journey through this wilderness of
estrangement both from the light and love of heaven. Best
regards to Mr. Morton and the girls, and particularly to dear
Anne. All here unite in kind remembrances.—I am, my
dearest Jane, yours very truly,   THOMAS CHALMERS.

No. CXC.

Burntisland, 29th September 1841.

MY DEAREST JANE,—I rejoice to hear of the betterness of
Anne; and do hope that all these family trials and changes
will issue in the spiritual wellbeing of us all. Would that
we could make them subserve our discipline for eternity, one
of the most essential preparations for which is delight in
praising God—a higher acquirement, I do think, than even
delight and devotedness in prayer. It is a great help, however, that in the exercise of praise we should not trust to the
mere resources of our own meditation, but seek help in the
Bible. And I have never, I think, approximated so much to

the spirit of praise, as when reading, not in a cursory manner, but with intentness and fixedness of thought, on the subjects laid before us in the Psalms of David.

The archetypes of the real words in Scripture will serve us better than the conceptions which come at will or random into our minds, or when left to seek for them, without this aid, by dint of our own meditative energies alone.

I hope we shall begin to build in spring. If God be pleased to spare us, I shall be delighted to have a visit from you when we enter it. We are at present in the bustle of preparation for our departure to Edinburgh, whither we mean to go by the 9th of October.—I am, my dearest Jane, yours very truly,

THOMAS CHALMERS.

No. CXCI.

Edinburgh, 12*th October* 1841.

MY VERY DEAR JANE,—That is a very precious tract which you have sent me, and written, too, by one of superlative talent, though not overborne with the drudgeries and preparations of any great literary office. It is altogether like himself; and I confess that I like to see a vital and practical subject in the hands of such a man as Foster. It reminds me strongly of his Preface to Doddridge's " Rise and Progress."

Dear Catherine left us yesterday. She is a universal favourite among her Scotch relatives; and there is something to me most beautifully touching in the quiet, gentle, and unobtrusive style of her piety. May she be preserved a comfort to you in your declining years; and may one and all of your children rise around you and call you blessed. I rejoice to hear that Anne is mending so fast. May her and our souls prosper and be in health; and may we all make sure of the only thing worth minding, an interest in Christ, and access through Him to our reconciled Father in heaven.

U

I write sparsely you will observe. I am again sunk in arrears, and would really require to write with a rail-road speed by means of a fifty-horse power to get over my daily work, with six letters a-day to the bargain.—I ever am, my very dear Jane,   THOMAS CHALMERS.

No. CXCII

Edinburgh, 31st December 1841.

MY DEAREST JANE,—I expected to write you at length during our holidays; but I staid in Edinburgh, and have found myself quite overborne by its senseless and ceremonious calls, so that I am forced to get through my twenty or thirty unanswered letters with as few sentences as possible; and for this purpose, I am now skulking in another house than my own.

We were out at Castlebank the other day at a great New-year's festival; and I, as being now the patriarch of our immediate relationship, give the New-year's day dinner to-morrow. Yesterday I was at Duncan Cowan's; and he, Alexander his brother, and I, formed the three carls of the party.

My best regards to all. What a rapid flow of years and seasons! May we learn wisdom, and find our way to Him who alone has the words, and who alone has the gift of life everlasting.—I ever am, my dearest Jane, yours most affectionately,

THOMAS CHALMERS.

No. CXCIII.

Edinburgh, 19th February 1842.

MY DEAREST JANE,—Your letter of the 8th of January has been long by me unanswered. I have been somewhat on the sick list, and more especially from want of sleep for several weeks now. Mrs. Chalmers and I went this day week to Castlebank in quest of sleep for me, and we returned yesterday.

I am rather better, though far from being perfectly restored to the use of my sleeping faculties.

I enjoyed my visit greatly; and when after tea and supper, the three matrons set them down by the fire-side to their respective stockings, I thought it quite in keeping with the quietness and domesticity of the scene.

We heard while at Castlebank, that Catherine and Anne had been in London. What a precious emollient amid all the varieties of human distress is the faith by which I trust that both of them are actuated. And what a mighty accession to the comfort and true wealth of a family when the gospel in its spirituality and power makes entry within its threshold, and operates as a leaven for good both within its own limits and in the vicinity around. I bethink me, when I write thus, of these excellent ones of the earth, Mrs. Heskine, Miss Bliss, and Mrs. General Blackwell, to all of whom I beg you will present my cordial and respectful acknowledgments.

My next birth-day is coming apace, when I shall have entered my sixty-third year. There is, upon that occasion, a general convergence towards our house of the immediate relationhood; and I look for the families both of Skirling and Dunkeld shortly.

May the Lord prepare us all for our last and greatest change. I have got hold just now of one of Owen's little practical works, which greatly interests me. It is upon the respective dominions of sin and grace.

Give my best regards to one and all of your household. I hope John is enabled to prosecute his studies, though business, of course, must first be attended to, and full acquittal made of it.—I am, my dearest Jane, yours very truly,

THOMAS CHALMERS.

No. CXCIV.

Edinburgh, 17th March 1842.

MY VERY DEAR JANE,—I received yesternight your very affecting letter, where, however, I can read of mercy mingled with
judgment, and am truly glad to find that both you and dear
Anne experimentally know what it is to rejoice in the midst of
tribulations. There is an expression which I think was quoted
by yourself in a letter of many years back, and which I think
singularly applicable to the present state of suffering which God
has been pleased to lay upon you both : it occurs in Deuteronomy xxxii. 36—" For the Lord shall repent Himself for His
servants, when He seeth that their power is gone." He will
have respect unto your weakness. It is not willingly that He
afflicts you. He will cause that when you are weak, then you
shall be strong—not, it may be, by the removal of the infirmity,
but by making the power of Christ to rest upon you.

How delightful the attitude in which the pitying Saviour is
represented to the eye of faith, as touched with a fellow-feeling—as having been Himself tried even as we are—and as able
(and willing as He is able) to succour them who are so tried.
I know not a more precious expression of His character, did we
but realize it, than that used by the Apostle when he tells us
of the meekness and gentleness of Christ. Let us cast on Him,
then, both the burden of our sufferings and our cares, and He,
not permitting us to be tempted beyond what we are able, will
provide a way of escape, that we may be able to bear it. I feel
much obliged by the effort you have made, under illness, to inform me of your state. Give my best regards to all under your
roof, and may the visitation which has come upon poor Anne
prove a blessing in disguise both to her and to the family.

I send a tract, written by a former student of mine, which I
think among the best I have read, it lays down the Gospel

with such simplicity and freeness. I should like to know Mrs. Heskine's opinion of it, for it is not always that our Scotch manufactures are adapted to the English taste. All here join in the most cordial and sympathizing regards to you.—Believe me ever, my dearest Jane, yours most truly and affectionately,

THOMAS CHALMERS.

No. CXCV.

Dunkeld, 28th April 1842.

MY VERY DEAR JANE,—I have written both Mrs. Chalmers and George on the melancholy event of Mr. Weakner's death, which, though I never saw him, has interested and affected me not a little.

I have come here to recruit a little between the rising up of my class and the meeting of our General Assembly, and am greatly delighted with the beauty both of the weather and of the scenery.

I have assisted at Mr. Mackenzie's sacrament, and been much pleased both with his ministrations and those of some of his auxiliaries—all my own students—and I cannot fail to be gratified by the very superior and more effective style of the pulpit services now than in our younger days. I am quite sensible that talent is but secondary to piety—that gifts are but secondary to graces in a minister of the Gospel, and I therefore am all the more thankful that, besides being men of power and high scholarship, very many of our young preachers are men of faith and prayer, who preside at fellowship meetings, and have been the instruments of great and promising revivals in various parts of Scotland. In short, amid all our troubles, we have great reason to thank God and rejoice when we look to the rising generation of preachers and young clergymen in our Church.

Mrs. Mackenzie was detained by bad health, and is still in

Edinburgh. We expect her, however, to-morrow (Friday.) Our main family anxiety at present is about our little grandson Tommy, at Skirling, who has fallen so unwell that Mrs. Chalmers, though in delicate health herself, has gone to Skirling, whence I wait for accounts, in which I am much interested.

Give my best regards to all your family, and more especially to Catherine and Anne—the nurse and the invalid—who, I trust and pray, will be sustained in their respective lots by Him who is a very present help in the time of trouble. I am sure that there is not a better medicine for the soul than direct intercourse with Himself by prayer. To His care and keeping would I commit you and yours ; and may He verify on you all His own blessed declaration, that He will make all things work together for good to those who love God.

I am delighted with the acceptance of the tract I sent you. It is the composition of another of my students, Mr. Bonar of Kelso.—Ever believe me, my dearest Jane, yours most truly,

THOMAS CHALMERS.

No. CXCVI.

Rosstrevor, 30th July 1842.

MY VERY DEAR JANE,—The danger of my present situation is not of being spoiled, in the common sense of that term, but of being soured and irritated by the turmoil of those manifold calls, and invitations, and urgencies wherewith I am continually beset, and by which all rest and freedom are denied to me. I make my escape from this in a few days, leaving my family for a week or two. Whatever the lionizers may imagine, there is great discomfort brought upon the lion, who has nothing for it but just to run off in the hope that both his lioness and her cubs may be permitted the enjoyment of some comparative repose.

And yet the kindness of the people here is truly of a most

genuine and heartfelt description. What inspires me with this conviction is, that there is so much of real Christianity amongst them. Lady Lifford—a very excellent and devoted person—comes here occasionally for summer-quarters. She is not here at present, but she has been a leaven for good in the neighbourhood, and the savour of her example seems to have told on the vicinity, where I have not met with a greater number of families, within the same compass, in any mere country place, more ready to entertain, and that with obviously congenial feeling, the best and highest of all topics. I have refused all their dinner invitations, but go out in the evenings, which generally conclude with the exposition of Scripture and prayer.—I ever am, my dearest Jane, yours with greatest affection,

THOMAS CHALMERS.

No. CXCVII.

Edinburgh, 30th November 1842.

MY DEAREST JANE,—I have just time to say, that our Convocation has done nobly, and that 400 good ministers are ready to cut connexion with the Establishment, should no relief from the effect of the decisions on the case of Auchterarder be granted to the Church.—I ever am, my dearest Jane, yours very truly,

THOMAS CHALMERS.

No. CXCVIII.

Edinburgh, 31st December 1842.

MY VERY DEAR JANE,—I was myself very much affected by the death of Lady Denbigh, yet do not feel that I have a sufficient opening for a letter to his Lordship. I quite agree with you in thinking of her as about the most amiable and estimable and withal intelligent Christian I had ever met with.

I very much regret to hear of Anne's continued illness, while Catherine's slight relief is matter of thankfulness, though I hear from other notes later than yours, that she has again relapsed.

I very much sympathize with you in all these family visitations, and pray that the sweetening and sustaining influences of the Christian faith may be so with you as that you shall be enabled to rejoice in the midst of tribulations.

I enjoy Morningside, and on no account more than that the society is of a so much more local and domestic character. We had a Christmas dinner from Helen on Monday, with all the relations and parish ministers. Yesternight we had our cakes at Charles's house with the Cowans and others; and to me, as patriarch now of the whole concern, belongs the New-year's dinner on Monday, when the whole of the relationhood are asked, and the parish minister with his new married wife is to come, and Patrick from Wishaw, now at Merchiston, stops to take part in it.—I remain, my dearest Jane, yours most affectionately,   THOMAS CHALMERS.

No. CXCIX.

Edinburgh, 29th January 1843.

MY VERY DEAR JANE,—I received your last some time ago, and after that a very beautiful letter from your Anne, which gives me a view of her mind, for which her friends cannot be sufficiently thankful. There is no such accession of riches to a family as that which is brought to it by the conversion of one of its members to God. May you and yours abound more and more in these spiritual treasures. I can truly say that, if clearly confident of all under my roof being in a state of grace, I should feel and rejoice in it as a nobler inheritance than all which this vain and transitory world can bestow.

We have all been much affected by poor Miss Edie's death— a most gentle and amiable creature, and latterly, a most spiritual and decided Christian. The last message to my daughter Eliza at Dunkeld was, that " to die is gain." The death took place at Dundee.

I beg to offer you my very cordial and sincere congratulations on the prospects of dear Elizabeth, upon which I shall not expatiate at present, as I mean, if God will, to write herself soon upon the subject.—Ever believe me, my very dear Jane, yours most affectionately and truly, THOMAS CHALMERS.

No. CC.

Edinburgh, 9th April 1843.

MY VERY DEAR JANE,—We have at length got into our new house, and within these few days I have given up my class. But another heavy work has been laid on me, that of Convener to the Financial Committee of our Free Church, so that I must still claim the privilege of an engrossed man, and will not be able to write so fully or frequently as otherwise.

It should be very solemnizing when one reflects on the nearing of death and eternity. I am as old now as my father was when I was ordained the minister of Kilmany. Let us be awake to the realities before us and above us. I feel more and more the fundamental and all-pervading importance of faith. Let us take God at his word, and we shall believe that Christ's blood washeth from all sin ; and that He hath made Him sin for us, that we might be made the righteousness of God in Him. With confidence in these sayings, we shall not only have peace and joy, but all the principles within us of new obedience. The benefit of the sacrifice and the gift of the Spirit are inseparable.

My kindest regards to Mr. Morton and your family, especially the invalids. Mrs. Chalmers has been very ill of late, but is mending slowly.—I ever am, my dearest Jane, yours most affectionately, THOMAS CHALMERS.

No. CCI.

Edinburgh, 14th June 1843.

MY VERY DEAR JANE,—You would have been struck with the contrast presented by our out-going clergy between their anxious and wo-begone aspect before they had taken their decision, and their perfect relief and light-heartedness after it. Never was there a happier assembly, with a happier collection of faces, than in our Free Church, with consciences disburdened, and casting themselves without care, and all the confidence of children, on the Providence of that God who never forsakes the families of the faithful.

I am delighted to think that my daughterhood are so heroical on the subject. Rather than surrender the Christian liberties of our Church, they would live all their days on doses of porridge, and *scud berrfit* on the green of Burntisland. There's a specimen of our Scotch lasses! If the evangelicals of the English Church had but a tenth-part of their pluck and hardihood, they would either clear their Establishment of its Puseyism, or scatter so corrupt a hierarchy to the winds—I ever am, my dearest Jane, yours very truly,

THOMAS CHALMERS.

No. CCII.

Edinburgh, 24th December 1843.

MY VERY DEAR JANE,—I grieve to hear of your and Anne's continued illness. But a realizing sense of the Gospel and of its precious comforts will make up for all. I have been reading lately, and with the greatest interest, certain books on the Assurance of Faith, which are full of comfort. They give substantially the same doctrine with Hervey in his "Theron and Aspasio," and "Marshall on Sanctification,"—great favourites, both of them, if you recollect, with my father. John Newton also is very much in the same spirit, and so are Boston, and Colquhoun, and Romaine. Their great lesson is, to come unto Christ as we are, instead of waiting for qualifications to come, which, separate from Him, we never can arrive at. The proper guard against all abuse of this doctrine is, that when we do come, it should be for a whole salvation, for

strength as well as pardon, for holiness as well as reconciliation with God. But surely we cannot too soon take up with
Him that we may take Him along with us in the prosecution
of this holiness.

But the great security for our being right is, that we draw
direct from the Bible. May you and yours have the full enjoyment of its exceeding great and precious promises. What a
precious chapter the 4th of Isaiah is! I feel a growing interest
in the Old Testament, where we have the truths of the Christian
presented to us in the types of the Jewish dispensation.—I ever
am, my dearest Jane, yours very truly, THOMAS CHALMERS.

No. CCIII.

Edinburgh, 3d March 1844.

MY DEAREST JANE,—I have been sadly remiss in writing you,
but such is the number of my students that I am greatly over-
driven. I have about three times a greater number of first
year's students than I had last year in the University, when
preparing our young men for the Established Church. I am
obliged to teach two classes, and the whole number of my enrolment is 209. The truth is, that our Free Church has given
a great impulse to the ecclesiastical profession; and young men
preparing for business have given it up for the ministry—and
these, some of the best I have. Altogether it is the most
talented and intellectual, besides, I believe, the most pious and
devoted set of students I ever had.

Beside the ill health that is annoying you, the transition
which you are on the eve of making, away from the situation that Mr. Morton has occupied for thirty years, forms
another and a distinct trial. But there is a rich provision
both of duties and encouragements in the Bible for all the
varieties of human experience. How precious, for example,
are the closing verses from the 29th to the end of the 6th

chapter of Matthew.   He who says, " I will make all thy bed in thy sickness," says also, in effect, "that as the day comes the provision will come."   I believe that never since the day that His promise was uttered, has it failed of accomplishment to a single human creature praying in faith that it might be verified upon him.   It is remarkable how our Saviour restricts the period for which He allows us to feel thoughtful within certain limits, and forbids us so to feel for a single hour beyond the next midnight, Matt. vi. 34.   But it deserves to be remarked, that the proper translation for " take no thought," is " be not thoughtful ;" the same in the original, as Phil. iv. 6, " be not careful," and it is so translated in Matthew too, in the older English translations of our Scripture.   We are allowed to take thought on the subject of a provision for our families ; nay, our not doing so is denounced as a highly cri- minal neglect, 1 Tim. v. 8.   Only in so providing and casting our thoughts onward, we must not suffer our minds to be corroded or distracted from God and godliness, by an excessive or distempered care, (1 Cor. vii. 32,) but cast all our care upon God who careth for us.

The upshot of this whole argument is, that while we have no warrant to pray for a fortune, or for more than what is need- ful for the body, we have every assurance that if we pray for daily bread—for day by day our daily bread—according to the faith of this our prayer, so most certainly shall it be done unto us.

My kindest regards to Mr. Morton, Anne, Catherine, and all the others.   I rejoice in the success of John's paper.—I ever am, my dearest Jane, yours most affectionately,

THOMAS CHALMERS.

No. CCIV.

Morningside, Edinburgh, 15th *September* 1844.

MY DEAREST JANE,—My illness arose from over occupation, and I have been forced to give much of it up.   Matters were fast hastening to such an attack as I experienced ten years ago, and which laid me aside for a good many months. I am getting greatly better of my retirement and repose, but have quite the feeling, that were I to plunge again among the endless details and tracasseries which have so engrossed me for a long time, I should just be where I was again. In these circumstances, my clear policy and duty are, to take things easily.

Did you ever see one of the Kelso Tracts entitled, " Believe and Live ?" I have mislaid my copy, else I should have sent it to you. It makes so patent the perfect freeness and simplicity of the gospel; it would confirm you much in the habit of which you tell me in your last, when you say you are obliged to " be still." The little work I speak of is eminently fitted to minister great peace and joy in believing. It supplies you with a basis which you may at once lean upon—interposing nothing between the Word of the Creator and the reliance of the creature. As He speaks, so you believe. As His word is, so your faith is ; and when positioned thus, then do we experience that " in quietness and in confidence we shall have strength." Let us keep fast this confidence, and the rejoicing of our hope, even unto the end.—Yours very truly,

THOMAS CHALMERS.

No. CCV.

Edinburgh, Morningside, 17th November 1844.

MY VERY DEAR JANE,—I am glad you have read the tract " Believe and Live." Some complain of its being too free; I can only say that nothing short of such gospel freeness as it represents would come up to the exigencies of my own state: nothing short of the appropriating faith which can say that Jesus loved me and gave himself for me ;—a faith which, the stronger and more assured it is, will be all the more fruitful in grateful and devoted obedience.

My session has commenced. I have somewhat less to do than I had ; but my strength is proportionally less. We have all been labouring too much in the Free Church, but I hope are learning wisdom in this respect.—Yours very truly,

THOMAS CHALMERS.

No. CCVI.

Edinburgh, Morningside, 5th January 1845.

MY DEAREST JANE,—I have deferred too long my reply to yours of the 22d November. Let me now send you the remembrances of the season, and the assurance of my earnest desire and prayer for you and yours. We are all in average health at present ; only Mrs. Hanna alarms us somewhat by the obstinacy of her cold. She and her son, little Tommy, who is a very fine fellow indeed, spend the winter with us. I was truly concerned to hear of Catherine's illness, and shall be interested to know how she is. May the repeated intimations of the precariousness of all earthly comforts lead us to set our affections, and also to labour and pray that the affections of our children may be set on things above.

I am reading with great interest a recent work, " Elliot on the Apocalypse." It is a learned, and critical, and, I think, very complete work. I look on prophetical studies as very confirming, though I hold as of first importance a Bible reading, and practical books that may influence the heart on the side of practical Christianity.—With kindest regards to Mr. Morton, Catherine, Anne, Lucy, John, and Thomas, in which all here join, ever believe me, my dearest Jane, yours very truly, THOMAS CHALMERS.

No. CCVII.

Edinburgh, Morningside, 4th May 1845.

MY DEAREST JANE, — This is a very sad and sorrowful bereavement. Death, though long looked for, is always sure

to strike and to solemnize at the last ; and what an enhance-
ment of affliction when it tears away the object of a long
cherished affection, and desolates the heart under the breach
of one of the nearest and dearest of all earthly relationships.

I was greatly moved by the brief effusions both of your
Anne and Lucy on the mournful occasion—different in character, but the outpourings of such a grief as our blessed Saviour
hath sanctioned and exemplified in His own person, both when
He wept at the tomb of Lazarus and when by the mouth of His
apostle He bade the disciples who were in heaviness from the
loss of their friends, to sorrow not even as others which have no
hope. And what a precious alleviation to think of the faith
and piety of dear Catherine, of whom I am thoroughly persuaded that she slept in Jesus, and so has added one attraction more to the place of glory and blessedness above. May
we who are left behind be followers of them who, through faith
and patience, are now inheriting the promises ; and may the
sorrow of nature be ripened and transformed into that godly
sorrow which worketh repentance unto salvation never to be
repented of.

I have often spoken of it as a signal instance of God's forbearance and mercy, that though now in the thirty-third year
of my family life, He has been pleased to spare me hitherto
the pain of a family death—none such having yet occurred in
a single instance within the limits of my own household, even
indeed since I was the master of a house, which is forty-two
years ago, having entered the manse of Kilmany in May 1803.
What a fearful reckoning and responsibility does this bring me
under. Let me no longer despise the forbearance and long-
suffering of God ; but watching over the souls of those for
whom I have to account, let us henceforth, both for them and
for ourselves, labour to realize an interest in Him who alone
hath the words, and who alone hath the gift of life everlasting.

This sad event has saddened and solemnized all the relationship here.   Grace, I know, will be greatly affected by it.   She
left us a few days ago, along with Fanny ; and they are now at
Fairley in Ayrshire.   Mrs. Hanna is in that neighbourhood at
present, and in the meantime better.   But both she and Eliza
have had symptoms which make me feel the precariousness of
all that is earthly.   Indeed, my own personal feelings ought to
be sufficient remembrances for me.   I am now more than half
way from sixty to seventy ; and certain it is, that though free
of any specific complaint, there has been a general decay of
strength during the last year, which tells me that I should
forthwith set my house in order, and be in readiness for the
coming of the Lord.

But this readiness is a duty which lies upon all of every age
and condition ; and may the death over which we have been
called to mourn bring the lesson forcibly home to us.   May the
event be sanctified and blessed to all your family.   Though in
itself not joyous but grievous, may it yield to you and yours
the peaceable fruits of righteousness.   Let us stand, my dear
Jane, more disengaged than ever from a world that will soon
pass away ; and with the feeling that we are strangers and
pilgrims here, let our doings plainly declare that we seek a
country beyond the grave—that our affections are set on the
things which are above—that we are looking forward to a city
which hath foundations, whose builder and maker is God.—
Ever believe me, my very dear Jane, yours most affectionately
and truly,   THOMAS CHALMERS.

No. CCVIII.

Edinburgh, 19th October 1845.

MY DEAREST JANE,—I observe from your letter of the 1st,
that you still dwell on the thoughts of your dear Catherine,
and I would not forbid this ; mellowed and mixed up as these

thoughts are with the sustaining hope that you will meet her again. The Gospel does not lay an interdict upon your sorrow, though it would dissuade you against being swallowed up of too much grief. But you have fled to the best refuge ; and He who is touched with the fellow-feeling of our infirmities, knows how to adapt His succour to the necessities of all who trust in Him. It is a shifting world ; and I see more and more of its vanity and precariousness. I can understand the sentiment of Job, that I would not live alway ; that is, alway here. The old patriarch knew that his Redeemer liveth ; and let us comfort ourselves with the blessed assurance, that because He liveth we shall live also. Let us verify the experience of the apostle who said, that " Christ liveth in me," and then shall we live a life of faith on the Son of God.

When you write Mrs. Heskine remember me to her and also to Miss Bliss in the kindest manner. I should like to have a place not only in the recollections but in the prayers of these good people. I get an occasional note from Mrs. Blackwell— the effusion of a spirit breathing the utmost affection for all that is good and aspiring, I have no doubt, Godward and Heavenward.

Last month I went to Anster, where, in Mr. Ballardie's house, I married Mr. Couper of Burntisland, one of our Free Church ministers, to Miss Williamson. I took up my night-quarters at Barnsmuir for two nights—was loaded with kindness by the two Mr. Fortunes, the sons of Christian Rankine—met with Mrs. Watson, who came down from Leuchars on purpose to be with me ; and we indulged together in the affecting reminiscences of forty-five years back. I learned much from her and Miss Menzies (still there) of the deathbed both of Mrs. Fortune and Mrs. Brown, Christian and Anne Rankine.—Kindest regards to all, and ever believe me, my dearest Jane, yours very truly, THOMAS CHALMERS.

[Captain Rankine of Barnsmuir had three daughters : the eldest, Christian, married to Mr. Fortune ; the second, Anne, married to the Rev. Mr. Brown of Kilrenny ; the third, Susan, married to the Rev. Mr. Watson, minister of Leuchars, a parish not far from Kilmany. The following series of letters is addressed to different members of this much loved family.—See " Memoirs," vol. iv. p. 441.]

No. CCIX.—To the Rev. Mr. Watson.

Kilmany Manse, 16th December 1814.

My dear Sir,—Agreeably to a promise I made to Mrs. Watson, whose interest in the matter I feel myself much indebted to, I have to inform you that I have at length sent a letter of concurrence in my late appointment to one of the churches of Glasgow. The prospect of my departure gives me a greater tenderness than ever for all my friends, and especially do I feel a very deep interest in all those clergymen who are placed around my much-loved and much-regretted parish. Were I taking leave of the world I would feel myself released from all those delicacies which are so apt to restrain the converse of human beings upon their greatest concern. Now I feel something of the same kind of emancipation upon merely leaving the neighbourhood, and you will therefore bear with me when I express the pleasure I have often felt in witnessing the decided tendency of your mind towards pure and Scriptural Christianity. It is my earnest prayer that you may abound more and more ; that you may obtain grace to be found faithful ; that you may be enabled manfully to hold forth the Word of Life in the midst of all the contempt and resistance it may meet with ; and that rising superior to all the disgust which the peculiarities of the Christian faith excites in the unrenewed heart, you may give a single and well-sustained aim to the great work of fitting a people for eternity. May God pour down such a blessing on your parish that there may not be room to receive it ; but that flowing over into other parishes, it may prove a leaven for good beyond the field of your immediate exertions.

Give the assurance of my friendship and my prayers to Mrs. Watson. She has been beyond measure kind and indulgent to me, and I have every reason to be thankful for the privilege of her countenance and society. Let her persevere in seeking earnestly after the way of peace, and she will find it. God never said to any " Seek my face in vain ;" and if she betake herself to the guidance of His Spirit, and the faithful reading of His Word, she will find all the perplexities which darken the outset of every anxious and inquiring Christian to merge at length in the delightful sunshine of a mind resting upon the promises of God, and running with enlargement and pleasure in the way of all His commandments.—May she long live with you as a fellow-heir of the grace of life ; may the influence of her example be felt and followed by all her relations ; may her children rise and call her blessed ; may she have a part in the resurrection of the just, and be a bright and shining star in that heavenly region where there is no sorrow and no separation.—Yours most affectionately, THOMAS CHALMERS.

No. CCX.—TO THE REV. MR. WATSON.

Glasgow, 26*th January* 1818.

MY DEAR SIR,—Though it be long since I received your last letter, and I have since seen you personally, yet I assure you that I have too much value for a friendly connexion with you and your relations to let down our correspondence. I was much pleased and impressed with the contents of your last communication, in as far as they went to exhibit your own earnest desire for a warmer spirit of Christianity in your neighbourhood, though I fear that your representation of it in this respect is but too just ; that the most satisfactory thing that can be said of it is, that all is comfort and quiet in the enjoyment of the good things of this life.   How strikingly does this express the prevailing character of all neighbourhoods in our land ; how much does an interest in time predominate everywhere over any interest in eternity ; how little, alas ! do the objects of the latter excite a real earnestness and a real seeking after them ; and how faithfully do I describe the heart of every natural man when I say, that it is altogether occupied with the cares, and the interests, and the objects of the world to the exclusion of Him who formed it.   The great problem is, how to set up this in our own souls and in those of our neighbourhood ; and I am sure that no truth comes more forcibly recommended to us by all experienced in the utter powerlessness of man in this business.   Our faith stands not in his wisdom, but in the power of God.   And this truth, instead of quelling our activity, ought just to give the right direction to it—even that of preaching His Gospel, or dealing out as faithful stewards the treasure which He has been pleased to put into earthen vessels ; and praying in faith for a blessing from Him who alone giveth the increase under all the discouragements there of an unpromising soil.   Know that your labour in the Lord shall not be in vain, and forget not the maxim which a devoted missionary, Elliot, transmitted to us as the fruit of his own experience, " that prayers and pains can do anything," &c.

I cannot express to you how much I feel interested in the best concerns, both of yourself and of dear Mrs. Watson.   I spent an evening with much enjoyment lately at Pilmuir.   God grant that all of us may so believe and so abound in those fruits of righteousness which are by Jesus Christ, that we may be found to praise, and honour, and glory in the day of reckoning. —Yours most affectionately,   THOMAS CHALMERS.

No. CCXI.—To Mr. Fortune.

Glasgow,   1823.

My dear Sir,—I have just received your most distressing intimation, the more severe as it was wholly unexpected. In Mrs. Fortune I have lost one of the most intimate and most interesting associates of my early life, and I received the intelligence of her death as a solemn and affecting admonition offered to my own heart of the vanity of all that is below.

I beg that you will compose your feelings under the overwhelming dispensation; and still more do I entreat, that from the tomb of her that is nearest and dearest to you, you will hear that voice of wisdom which bids us cease from time, and give all our hopes and preparations to eternity.

It is my earnest prayer that this awful visitation may work a saving and a sanctifying influence, both to your own heart and to the hearts of those related to her and most interesting to myself. May this deep sorrow shut us all up unto Him who alone can open for us the gates of that city where sin and suffering and separation are unknown. Do remember me in the language of truest sympathy to Mrs. Rankine, Mrs. Watson, and Mrs. Brown.—I am, my dear Sir, yours very sincerely,

Thomas Chalmers.

No. CCXII.—To Mrs. Watson.

Glasgow, 9th June 1823.

My dear Madam,—I have recently heard, and with great tenderness and grief, of the increased illness of poor Mrs. Brown. I think much of the dear sufferer, and it is my cry and prayer to God that she may be upheld in the sore struggle through which God is pleased to bring her to Himself; that grace may prevail over nature, and her affliction—which, after all, is light in the high reckoning of eternity, because but for a moment—

may indeed work out for her an exceeding weight of glory. In her and in Mrs. Fortune I feel that two of my most interesting ties with Fife are broken ; and I do feel more solicitous than ever that you should spare yourself as well as you can the agitations of that trying scene where you are now called to watch and to witness the agonies of one who is in every way so dear to us all.

There is a text that perhaps Mrs. Brown might feel a preciousness in ; it is Deuteronomy xxxii. 36. It upheld the peace and patience of one of my old hearers on his deathbed. He had lost the power almost of thinking, and felt that the sickness and the pain made such inroads upon his mind that he could not be satisfied with any of its exercises ; and so he simply laid it all upon God. He ceased even to try a right process of meditation, but lay still in a sort of resigned abeyance, hoping at the same time, that though his powers of thought, and sentiment, and even prayer, were altogether gone, yet God's power and God's pity were unfailing.

There is a song of triumph that awaiteth all those who die in Christ, and have come out of great tribulation ; and even here the rapture and the glory of it may be partially felt ; it is " unto Him that loved us, and washed us from our sins in His blood." Oh, there is a charm in the thought of its cleansing and peace-speaking power, and that by it the way of access for the guilty is now a consecrated way—consecrated by the blood of a Divine expiation—and in which if we are found, the justice of God will not overtake us, and His mercy will rejoice over us.

I should be sorry to fatigue the mind of your much-loved sister by too great a variety of topics. One text may perhaps be her aliment for hours together. One precious clause is often enough to uphold a dying Christian, and more might distract and annoy her. When Fletcher died, it was after many hours of spiritual exultation, through which he constantly reiterated that " God is love."

Say all that is tender in my name to her on whom the hand of God has been laid. He will at length compass her about with songs of deliverance, and the merciful High-priest, touched with the feeling of her infirmities, saith unto her, " It is I, be not afraid."—Believe me, yours most affectionately,

THOMAS CHALMERS.

No. CCXIII.— To MRS. WATSON.

Glasgow, 9th July 1823.

MY VERY DEAR MADAM,—The intimation from Kilrenny Manse reached us on Saturday, and aroused a deep emotion among us all, though we could not but feel relieved by the thought, that so great sufferings had terminated. After all they are but for a moment, and will now be looked back upon by the glorified spirit as the instruments of her present complete purification—as the steps by which she hath reached her present advancement in heaven. I have now only to entreat that you and Mrs Rankine will be calm. Be still, and know that He who visited you with this sore bereavement is God. It is not the violence of your grief that I fear : it is its despondency ; and therefore would I have you to bear up—to take such part, as health and strength will enable you to do, in the cares and duties of every-day life ; and instead of giving way to overmuch sorrow, be assured that the calls of family and relative obligation are partly the provisions of a kind and wise Ruler for diverting the mind from that which, if singly and exclusively dwelt upon, might overbear it altogether.

And what a season, too, for growth in grace—for the fruits of the spirit—for that righteousness which the chastening hand of God yieldeth unto all those who are exercised thereby. Your hearts are now exceeding soft, and tender, and broken

under an awful visitation of Divine Providence, and they offer
a likely soil for the showers and influences of Divine grace.
The sorrow of nature is not godly sorrow, but it may be turned
to it; and now is the time for deep impressions of the worthlessness of time, of the vast magnitude of eternal things, of
the evil of sin, of the value of the Saviour, of the exceeding
urgency of that gospel call whereby we are entreated to seek
God now, and to enter into reconciliation with Him through
Christ, that we too may be provided against that day when we
shall be summoned into His presence, and that other day when
we shall stand before his judgment-seat.

And what an alleviation to your present sorrows, that you
are not called upon to sorrow as others who have no hope ;
that, on that deathbed which you have so recently witnessed,
there was a brightness and a glory which softened all its
agonies; that, amid the cruel sufferings of the flesh, there was
a Spirit that bore up her on whom God was pleased to lay the
hand of a refiner ; and that, in her case, death was disarmed
of its terrors and its sting, and she was more than conqueror
through Him who loved her.

We must now give up all thoughts of the world as a resting-
place.   It will mitigate the evil when it comes, that we lay our
account with it.   Forewarned, forearmed — we should not
think that any strange thing has happened to us ; and I know
nothing that more lightens the hardships of life, and more
reconciles us to them, than that previous settlement of mind
which a faith in this prediction of our Saviour is fitted to inspire,—" In the world ye shall have tribulation."

There are no deaths which could have carried home this
lesson with greater energy to my own heart than the two
which have occurred in your family.   I desire to find that I
am sanctified, even as I feel that I am solemnized, by them.
May they shut us all up more closely and more tenaciously

unto the faith ; and walking softly and tenderly under the impression throughout the remainder of our pilgrimage, may we retain to the end of our days the attitude of strangers and pilgrims who have not taken up with the world as a residence, but use it merely as a road.

Give my most affectionate condolence to Mrs. Rankine and poor Mr. Brown.—I remain, yours most truly,

THOMAS CHALMERS.

No. CCXIV.—To Mrs. WATSON.

Skirling, 21*st September* 1845.

MY VERY DEAR MRS. WATSON,—I feel deeply sensible of your goodness in having joined me at Barnsmuir, as it added prodigiously to the interest and the enjoyment I felt in my visit to the place of my tenderest recollections.

When in Kilrenny churchyard, I was so engrossed with the tablet appropriated to dear Anne, that I have carried away an imperfect remembrance of that which was raised for Mr. Brown. I saw enough of it, however, to observe that it was placed there by the parochial community as a tribute and acknowledgment for the great worth of his Christian services in the midst of them. I omitted, in the variety of our other topics, to state the very great satisfaction which I felt in such a testimony to his devotedness as a minister of the gospel.

I cannot expect, nor would I dare to ask, for a sight of any of Mrs. Fortune's letters, however intense the feeling might be on my perusal of them. But there is one request which I have the boldness to make, and which I flatter myself that you will not deny. You stated that there were certain texts or passages of Scripture to which Mrs. Brown often referred in the course of her last illness. If you have any memorials of them, I cannot adequately express the value I would feel for a list of

Y

them. You would not need to write them out. The chapter and verses will be sufficient.

I shall, if God will, have returned to Edinburgh by the 1st of October, after which a letter from you would be truly acceptable.

Give my love to your daughters,* and kindest regards to Mr. Watson.

I entreat a place in your prayers.

I hope we shall meet in heaven ; but let us never forget, that without holiness no man can see God.

I purpose writing to Mr. William Fortune in a week. Since I have retired from public business, and have some leisure for looking back on my chequered existence, the scenes and society of Barnsmuir form those parts of the distant retrospect on which I most love to repose.—My dearest Susan, yours most affectionately,   THOMAS CHALMERS.

No. CCXV.—To Mrs. Watson.

Edinburgh, 23d October 1845.

MY VERY DEAR FRIEND,—I must delay no longer to acknowledge your very welcome letter with the packet I received from your daughters, and for the contents of which I have the greatest value, both the testimony to one whom I never can forget or think of without emotion, and the letter from Kilrenny, with your own precious notes respecting the last illness of her who obviously died in the triumphs of the faith.

The picture you sent is superior to that at Barnsmuir, and in some respects more impressive ; but there are in it a force, and vivacity, and decision which, though at the distance of a thousand miles from aught that borders on the masculine, yet are not so true to the original as the other, which presents, I think, a more faithful exhibition of that sensitively and ex-

* I forget if Christian has Rankine also in her name.

quisitely feminine expression which formed the peculiar charm and grace of her character.

It were well if these tender reminiscences of the distant past led us onward in thought to the much nearer futurity which now awaits us both. My God, do Thou sanctify these strong affections of nature, and raise them to the things which are above, so that we may be prepared for that heaven where our dear and blessed Saviour has gone before us, and where we may both love Him and love our fellows without frailty and without a flaw.

I have written William,* and scarcely looked for a reply. He has not written back, and this is very natural : he must not be urged to write, it must be done spontaneously, and this is much better. There is in my heart a derived and descending love from the mother to the children, which I feel a pleasure in cherishing, though you are the only person in the world with whom I could talk about it. I felt a comfort and relief in our recent conversations, and am not without hope that ere another twelvemonth elapse we may have the same opportunity for the same enjoyment.

Meanwhile let us pray for the souls of these dear youth. George I look upon as an altogether new acquaintance, and I think him a very likeable person.

Give my best regards to Mr. Watson, and also to the Misses Marianne and Christian, whom I had pleasure in meeting and conversing with. If Miss Brown be with you, present to her my kindest remembrances.

My winter campaign is on the eve of commencing, and I gladly anticipate its engrossments by these few lines to you. No bustle, however, of other affairs will lessen the interest I shall always feel in your communications, nor I hope prevent my replying to them however briefly.

I pray for a blessing upon your own soul. Heavenly Father,

* Mrs. Fortune's eldest son. See p. 261.

save me from being deceived by the mere counterfeits or sem-
blances of Divine grace. May my love for my fellows be genuine heaven-born spiritual love—such a love to my brethren as
is like unto the love of Thyself. Let us feel towards each other
as fellow-travellers to eternity ; and though, reverting to the
dear and long-departed object of my fondest recollections, I
have not lived with her in one mansion, may I share with her
in one blessed resurrection, and join her among the choirs and
companies of the celestial above.

I like Miss Watson's idea of getting a copy of the picture ;
but before that, I wish to compare it with the one at Barnsmuir. I think a compound of the two would be as perfect as
a black profile can be. You are very good to allow me the
custody of yours, which I purpose, if God will, to return into
your own hand.

With earnest prayer for every blessing on the head of my
very dear sister and friend, I ever am, yours most affectionately,   THOMAS CHALMERS.

No. CCXVI.—To Mrs. Watson.

Burntisland, 1st February 1846.

MY VERY DEAR MRS. WATSON,—I received yours of two or
three weeks back, and read it with much feeling and pleasure.
I should have replied sooner, but am at all times much bustled,
and therefore I am glad to avail myself of a few leisure moments here, for the purpose of acknowledging your kind favour.

It is no ordinary recollection that I have of Barnsmuir, and
should rejoice if through grace and wisdom from above, it
could be made to subserve that highest of all good which has
fruit in eternity.

We are strangely compounded creatures ; and much do I
need a sanctifying influence to spiritualize the strong affections of nature, and give a right and holy direction to them.

I feel the powerlessness of all human argument; and know not
if I have made any good impression on the son of her who
occupies far the most interesting place in my retrospect of
days long gone by. I was favoured with a reply in which I
could discern talent and good feeling and intelligence. May
the all-powerful Spirit grant what He and He alone can give—
the unction which remaineth—the grace which has fruit and
holiness, and in the end life everlasting.

My best regards to Mr. Watson and your dear daughters.
I am quite uncertain of my movements this summer. I had a
letter from Jane lately, who says how much she was interested
by my accounts of Barnsmuir, and how delighted she would
have been to meet you there.

I saw Miss Inglis lately, who tells me that Miss Menzies was
better.—My dearest Mrs. Watson, yours very affectionately,

THOMAS CHALMERS.

No. CCXVII.—To Mr. WILLIAM FORTUNE.

Edinburgh, 5th October 1845.

MY DEAR SIR,—I meant to have written much sooner and
told how greatly I was impressed by my visit to Barnsmuir.
You may not be able to enter into all the feelings which are
associated in my mind with the tender recollections of half a
century. They were powerfully awakened when I stood before
the tomb of your aunt in the churchyard of Kilrenny, and have
just now been revived with tenfold force by the perusal of certain documents which have been kindly put into my hand, and
from which I have gathered particulars new to myself, but
most deeply affecting, relative to the death of Mrs. Brown, and
to that of your dear mother, for whom I have cherished during
the long period of fifty-five years, such regards and remembrances as can never be effaced.

You will forgive me, then, if under a near and urgent and

practical sense of the realities of an eternal though unseen world, I implore both you and your brother whom I love, not to suffer the evanescent objects or interests of time, to shut out from your hearts the solemn considerations of the coming judgment and the coming eternity. I have now come to that period of life when I may be said to be hovering on the confines of both worlds. I can attest from experience the vanities and disappointments of earth, and that truly it is not here where the firm footing of our interest lies. The dear brother who, though younger than yourself, has yet gone before you, has left behind the lesson, not only that time is short, but that we know not how short. The two sisters, loveliest of women, who died within a few months of each other, died more than twenty years ago, and yet were both of them my juniors. The lessons of our common mortality, though not yet within the circle of my own immediate family, yet within the circle of a very wide acquaintanceship, have flown thick about me ; and such is my affection for your now long departed relatives—such my affection both for you and your brother for their sakes, that I entreat you not to make a resting-place of that earth which passeth speedily away, but to aspire Godward and Heavenward, and be the followers of those who through faith and patience are now inheriting the promises.

And do not think, my dear Sir, that that knowledge of God and of Jesus Christ, which is life everlasting, is something so lofty and mysterious as to be beyond the reach of your attainments. The Bible, if read with diligence, and the Spirit given to pour light upon the Bible, if prayed for with sincerity and earnestness, these are the great agencies and means by which even the poorest and humblest of men might be made wise unto salvation. And there are other helps beside the Scriptures not to be neglected, for by them we might be the better enabled to understand the Scriptures. But tastes and understandings are various, and the books suited to some are comparatively useless to others. The human author who did me most good was Wilberforce, by his work on the "Christianity of the Higher and Middle Classes." And yet I know some who felt no interest in this book, though some of the following might perhaps prove more impressive and profitable,—Baxter's "Call to the Unconverted;" Alleine's "Alarm;" Doddridge's "Rise and Progress of Religion in the Soul;" Baxter's "Compassionate Counsel to Young Men;" Guthrie's "Trial of a Saving Interest in Christ;" Bradley's "Sermons," &c. But, after all, let me state in a single sentence what the likeliest expedient is for passing out of darkness into the marvellous light of the Gospel. It is the PRAYERFUL READING OF THE BIBLE. "Search the Scriptures; for in them ye think that ye have eternal life, and these are they which testify of Him who is the way, and the truth, and the life;" and ask for God's enlightening Spirit: "Ask till ye receive, seek till ye find, knock till the door be opened to you," (Matt. vii. 7-11.) Do indulge these overflowings of a heart which feels the strongest interest in one and all of your dearest mother's family. O that God would endow me with the wisdom for arousing your souls; and that His Holy Spirit poured forth upon us from on high would prepare us for an entrance on that exalted region, where the spirits of the just made perfect rejoice for ever in the presence of God.

Give my kindest regards to Mr. George and Miss Menzies. Tell her that our interviews and conversations, though brief, were to me very precious, and that the memory of them is sweet. They have left a sorrow behind them, and given me an intense desire for her comfort under the loss of that dear youth to whom she was a second mother.—I ever am, my dear Sir, yours with most cordial and sincere regard,

THOMAS CHALMERS.

[*The Manse of Inchture,* 16*th November* 1850.—DEAR SIR,—On looking over some of my old papers some time ago, among a number of letters from Dr. Chalmers to different members of my family, I found the following to my father, which I think as interesting as any given in the first volume, and which I am about to copy verbatim, leaving you to make any use of it you like.

That you may understand it, it is only necessary for me to say, that the occasion of it must have been an application on the part of my father for Dr. Chalmers's influence on his behalf, with the view of obtaining the presentation to the parish of Bendochy, then vacant, and which he ultimately succeeded in doing, mainly through the exertions of the late George Kinloch, Esq. of Kinloch, who was a particular friend of my father's. The attachment alluded to was that for my mother, the eldest daughter of Dr. Adamson, first or senior minister of St. Andrews, to whose influence I have heard Dr. Chalmers say he was mainly indebted for his presentation to Kilmany. Indeed, I have a letter before me to my mother, in which the Dr. says,—" seeing it was to your father I stood indebted for the first great preferment of my life." This obligation Dr. Chalmers seems never to have forgotten, as it is again and again alluded to in his letters not only to my father and mother, but also to myself : and I remember his giving frequent expression to it in his intercourse with my mother, as well as to his desire that he could in any way return it, so late as in 1831. Among other efforts to carry this desire into effect, there was none which gave a finer or more striking token of its intensity than that attention he paid my mother on her deathbed, when almost every day for six weeks, in the busiest period of, I think, his first session in Edinburgh as Professor of Divinity, he visited and prayed, and did what he could to comfort spiritually our dying parent, and my brother and myself, in the prospect of our bereavement. I beg to be kindly remembered to Mrs Hanna.—Yours most faithfully,   JOHN ADAMSON HONEY.

The Rev. W. Hanna, LL.D.,
of Free St. John's, Edinburgh.]

No. CCXVIII.—LETTER TO REV. MR. HONEY.*

Kilmany Manse, 2*d May* 1812.

MY DEAR SIR,—I this day arrived from Dundee, and found your letter waiting me. The wax has effaced the date of it ;

* See Memoirs, vol. i. pp. 433-435.

but I am sorry that a single day should have been lost in so urgent a cause. I guess a letter to be the most impressive form of application to Mr. Morison, and have accordingly written him to write Mr. Kinloch. I have no acquaintance with Mr. Chalmers in Dundee, but propose being there on Monday, when I shall speak to my only two acquaintances there, and shall try to reach him through one or other of these channels.

I shall give you an account of the last three years, and leave you to judge whether my conduct is at all palliated by the circumstances. I took ill in May 1809, got so well in July as to spend the summer in Anster a-sea-bathing: took ill again in October, and was thirty-one weeks kept out of my pulpit: spent great part of another summer at Anster, and from November 1810 to September 1811, was confined with a pupil, besides being in such a state of health that every excursion I made from my own bed, and from my own regimen, was sure to land me in the confinement of a week or a fortnight. I am now better—greatly better; and now that I have got something like health, my wish is to keep it, and not to throw it away. I am bilious to a great degree, and nothing but the most scrupulous attention to regimen and exercise can keep it down.

Amid all this, I had projected at different times an excursion to your house, and still persist in my intention of paying you a visit. I was sorry by the way that I missed your call at Kilmany. I often think of you, have as warm and friendly recollections of you as ever, and rejoice in the prospect of being relieved from one painful contemplation, which I assure you is often present to me, viz., my sitting in a place where you, hitherto unprovided, would most assuredly have been, had your boldness in declaring a certain attachment been equal to the sincerity with which you conceived and the constancy with which you maintained it.

Z

I am glad, that while you intimate your having heard of me in the new capacity of a serious man, you offer to keep me in countenance. It is the dread of being laughed at which keeps men from announcing themselves ; and I hope that you will be superior to it. Have you read Foster's "Essays ?"—the best book I have seen for effecting a transition from the school of elegant literature to the school of the New Testament. Read Wilberforce's "View of Religion in the Middling and Higher Classes," and Doddridge's "Rise and Progress of Religion in the Soul." Embark with energy in this new career, and you will find it the most splendid and animating you have ever tried ; nor can I see upon any principle, even of philosophy, how we can stop till we have found our conclusion and our repose in the peculiar doctrines of the gospel.—Give my kindest regards to Mrs. Honey ; and believe me, yours with much regard,   THOMAS CHALMERS.

Let me add to the above Fuller's "Comparative View of Socinianism and Calvinism."

N. B.—I kept this letter open till I received Mr. Morison's answer, which I hereby enclose for the purpose of your making any use of it with Mr. Kinloch that may seem right.

The Rev. John Honey,
Care of Adam Adamson, Esq., Academy, Perth.

[DEAR SIR,—The letter, a copy of which I enclose, is interesting, not only because of its intrinsic merits, but on account of its exhibiting the germs of those schemes of Christian philanthropy which the writer afterwards developed, and prosecuted with such unwearied zeal and such remarkable success. In his diary he speaks of having brought his pamphlet on the Bible Society to a close, on the 22d of September. He seems afterwards to have been much occupied with the business of Church Courts, and has several entries which show the mortification he experienced at the resolution which the Synod adopted, and the earnestness with which he prayed for grace to direct and sustain him: but there is no notice taken of his writing this letter. If we had not had the document before us, we might have been led to infer from no entry having been made on the 20th October—that that day had been spent in leisure and recreation. This letter may, therefore, be considered a proof that the account contained in his diary, ample as it is, exhibits only a part of the intellectual labour in which he engaged.—I remain, yours truly,   JAMES BRODIE.

To the Rev. Wm. Hanna.]

No. CCXIX.—LETTER TO THE SECRETARIES OF THE FIFE AND KINROSS BIBLE SOCIETY.

Kilmany Manse, 20th October 1813.

DEAR SIRS,—I have been very much to blame in delaying an answer to your last. I was otherwise a good deal occupied. I beg you will not slavishly adhere to every word of the subjoined. It is perhaps too long, and retrenchments from it to make room for paragraphs of your own or others may be advisable. You should all mention at the foot of it, that if any shall wish to form Penny Societies in their neighbourhood, they may obtain the requisite information by corresponding with any person or persons whom you shall fix upon for that purpose.

In pleading the cause of any institution, the great question which it lies upon us to answer is, What good will it do? The object of the Bible Society is to provide Bibles for those who have them not; and the most effectual answer to the above question is, the assembling together a few facts to shew the good which this has done.

1. Our first fact goes to prove that the Christianity of the Bible gains a readier access into the hearts of the ignorant than the Christianity of sermons, and systems, and human compositions. When missionaries went to Greenland, you may be sure they had the ignorance of a most raw and unfurnished population to contend with. They thought they would go

systematically to work, and, before laying before them the religion of the Bible, they attempted to give them some ideas of what has been called *Natural Religion.* They expatiated on the existence, and the unity, and the attributes, and the love of God. The poor Greenlanders did not comprehend them ; and, at the end of many years, the missionaries were mortified to find that they had not gained a single proselyte to the faith. On this they resolved to change their measures, and, as a last desperate experiment, they gave up all their preparatory instructions, and made one great and immediate step to the peculiar doctrines of Christianity, bringing them forward in the language of the Bible. The effect was instantaneous. When told of sin and of the Saviour, the ears of savages were constrained to listen to the message, and their understandings opened to receive it. There was something in the hearts of these unlettered men which responded to the views and tidings of the Gospel. The demonstrations of natural religion fell fruitless and unintelligible upon their ears ; but they felt the burdens of sin and of death, and pleasant to their souls was the preacher's voice, when it told that unto them " a Saviour was born." They live in the very outskirts of population, and beyond them there is nothing seen but a wilderness of snow, and nothing heard but the angry howling of the elements. Who will say that the enterprise is chimerical now, when, by the single influence of Bible doctrine, a Christian people have been formed in a country so unpromising—the limits of the visible church have been pushed forwards to the limits of human existence, and the tidings of good-will to men have been carried with acceptance to the very last and outermost of the species.

2. Our next example shall be taken from the Esquimaux of Labrador—a rude and wandering race, who hunt for furs all summer, and live all winter in caverns under ground. In this case, as in the former, missionaries laboured among them in the

first instance. They communicated to their hearts an interest in the subject. They translated portions of Scripture into their language. The Bible Society has presented them with the Gospels of Matthew and John. The arts of reading and writing are fairly introduced among them ; and so great is the excitement which lies in Christianity, that a few of its teachers have achieved a mightier step in the progress of civilisation than with any other subject, or upon any other occasion, the work and the perseverance of many centuries could have accomplished.

3. Philosophers reason upon the influence of climate ; but there is a power in Christian truth which carries it over all these accidental varieties. Christianity is gaining her proselytes in every quarter of the globe ; and we now turn your attention from the bleak and dreary regions of the north, to a country lying under the fierceness of a vertical sun. We allude to the Tamul Christians on the coast of Coromandel. They were formed, about a century ago, out of native idolaters by the society in London for propagating Christian knowledge ; and Christianity has been kept up and extended among them by a translation of the Bible and the labours of successive missionaries. New impressions of the Tamul Bible are preparing for them ; and, instead of that obstinate superstition which we are so ready to ascribe to the natives of India, we have beheld Pagans, and the descendants of Pagans, capable of reading the Bible, and in the attitude of eagerness to receive it.

4. But to bring our list of examples to a close. Our last shall be given you from the Records of the Baptist Mission in India— one of the most flourishing missionary concerns now in operation, and which, since the year 1746, has doubled its number of proselytes every three years. The Scriptures have of late been translated into the Bengalee language. The New Testament has reached a third edition, and the Old is now in circulation. By a letter, dated the 26th October 1810, it appears that

nineteen had applied to Dr. Carey for baptism; and mark the decisive importance of the fact, eighteen of these were indebted under Divine grace to the translation of the Scriptures for their conversion. This is what may be called the turning-point of the whole business, and it is here laid in full and authentic exhibition before you. The Bible is translated into the language, and put into the hands of an idolater. That Bible is read; it is brought into contact with his mind, and the faith which cometh from the Word of God is the consequence. He turns from dumb idols to serve the living and the true God; and the Scriptures are glorified by their having made him wise unto salvation, through the faith that is in Christ Jesus.

Our limits restrain us from expatiating. These are only a few facts out of the many, a few gleanings out of the information already before the public; nor can we offer a survey, however general, of the decided aspect toward Christianity among the various peoples on the face of the globe. From the poor African, and his eagerness for the *white man's book*, to the learned Arab who is beginning to suspect his Alcoran, and is on the eve of being presented with the Bible of Christians, in his vernacular tongue, we see symptoms full of promise, and call upon all our countrymen to share in the glorious work of carrying the promise forward to accomplishment.

We have only spoken of the foreign operations of our Society, and can merely advert to its reviving and purifying influence in the interior of Christendom; how it recalls the veneration of Christians from modes and vanities to the one charter of our faith; how it recognises the Bible as the great and only directory of religion; how it spreads the most effectual antidote against the corruptions of human systems; how it brings the good men of all parties into contact with one another; and how, in the very act of circulating the Bible, it circulates the infection of its own spirit and its own piety along with it.

The rich have done much for the cause ; but we invite the men of all ranks to share in it. We address the lower orders of society, and wish to convince them that, though the individual offering may be small, the number of individuals is great, and that the accumulation of their littles will form into a mightier sum than all the united gifts which the rich have yet thrown into the treasury. A penny a week from each householder in Fife amounts to £4000 a year. The same from each householder in Britain amounts to half a million in the year ; and this is a sum larger by eight times than any yearly income which the Bible Society has yet received from its wealthy and numerous subscribers. It is true that the Missionary Society has also its claims ; and it is for you to give your own directions to your own benevolence. We trust that societies for such objects will grow and multiply among you. We do not despair of seeing the day when every parish shall have a Christian society—when not a district of the land shall be left uncultivated, but shall yield a produce to the cause of the Saviour ; when these lesser streams shall form into a mighty torrent to carry richness and fertility into the dry and desolate regions of the world ; and when Britain, high in arms, and in political influence, shall earn a more permanent glory by being the dispenser of light, and peace, and the message of heaven to the remotest nations.

We exercise no other control over you but that of persuasion ; and sorry should we be if a single farthing came in upon us of constraint, and not of a willing mind. What you give, give cheerfully, and let it be no more than you can spare. There are some who depend on charity for their subsistence, and these can never give what they receive from others. There are some who have not yet arrived at this state of dependence, but are on the very verge of it. To them we address a passage from the Bible,—" If any provide not for his own and specially for those of his own house, he hath denied the faith and is worse than an infidel." There are others again, and these, we apprehend, form by far the most numerous class of society, who can maintain themselves in humble but honest independence, who can spare a little and not feel it, who can do what Paul advises them, lay aside their penny a week, as God hath prospered them, who can share that blessedness which the Saviour speaks of when He says, that " it is more blessed to give than to receive," who, though they cannot equal their richer neighbours in the amount of their donations, can bestow their something, and, at all events, carry in their bosoms a heart as warm to the cause, and call down as precious a blessing from the God who witnesses it.

" What !" say some, " will you take from the poor ?" No: we do not take. It is they who give ; and shew us the man who complains of it ? To him would we say,—" It is you, and not we, who do an injustice to the poor. It is you who impute to them a grossness and a want of generosity which do not belong to them. It is you who have the indelicacy to sit in judgment over their circumstances and feelings. It is you who think of them so unworthily, that you cannot conceive how truth and benevolence should be objects to them, and that after they have got the meat to feed, the house to shelter, and the raiment to cover them, there is nothing else that they will bestow a penny upon." They may not be able to express their feeling at a suspicion so ungenerous, but we shall do it for them. " We have souls as well as you, and precious to our hearts is the Saviour who died for them. It is true we have our distresses ; but these have bound us more firmly to our Bibles ; and it is the desire of our hearts that a gift so precious should be sent to the poor of other countries. The Word of God is our hope and our rejoicing. We desire that it may be theirs also ; that the wandering savage may know it and be glad ; and the poor negro, under the lash of his master, may learn of a Master in heaven, who is full of pity and full of kindness. Do you think that sympathy for such as these is your peculiar attribute ?—know that our hearts are made of the same materials with your own, that we can feel as well as you, and out of the earnings of a hard and honest industry we shall give an offering to the cause ; nor shall we cease our exertions till the message of salvation be carried round the globe, and made known to the countless millions who live in guilt, and who die in darkness."—Yours truly,

THOMAS CHALMERS.

LETTERS TO THE REV. DR. CHARTERS OF WILTON.

No. CCXX.

Kilmany Manse, 18th November 1812.

MY DEAR SIR,—I have been most wanting to the duty and reverence I owe you in not writing sooner. It gives me great concern to hear of Mrs. Charters. I hope that she may recover, and, at all events, it is my prayer that she may be supported in this the day of her visitation, that she may have great peace and joy in believing, and be able to join in the triumphant exclamation of the Apostle—" Thanks be to God who giveth us the victory through Jesus Christ our Lord."

I have been a good deal hurried since marriage. My wife has read your marriage present, (for which accept our best thanks,) but I am ashamed to say that I have not. I have been inquiring for " Henry on Meekness," but have not found it. Mrs. Chalmers is constitutionally meek, beyond most women of my acquaintance. Constitutional meekness is amiable, and companionable, and pleasing, but I would not say of it, that it was virtuous, till it rested on a religious principle. My article on Christianity is now printing, I believe. I was not able to take it in person to Edinburgh from being confined with rheumatism. I am now well again.

I have received your pamphlets, and have given some of them away. I shall be most happy to see those on Justice and Old Age. It would delight me to pay you another visit soon, but I cannot risk the exposure of winter, and my travelling next summer will depend on a number of circumstances.

I am sure you would be charmed with the eighth Report. Our County Society is doing nothing, and, what is worst of all, it has suspended the far more efficient operation of districts and parishes. My parish has been operating at the rate of £30 a year and upwards. There is another forming at Balmerino, a contiguous parish. This system carried over the face of the county of Fife would produce £3000 a year, instead of the paltry £150, which, I understand, is all that they have been able to realize on the more extended scale of a County Society. Would it not be a fine spectacle to see the parish system extended over Scotland, and a whole people combining their energies in a cause, the very supporting of which is an exercise of piety.

My prayer to God is, that He may bear up your old age with His best consolations, that He may bless you in the evening of life, and, when He calls you hence, that He may take you to Himself, and make you for ever happy in His presence.

Mrs. Chalmers joins me in compliments, and believe me yours, with great esteem,   THOMAS CHALMERS.

No. CCXXI.

Glasgow, 26th December 1816.

MY DEAR SIR,—I at one time thought I should have been able to visit you in the month of November, but I find the engagements of my new situation often to thicken upon me in such a way as to disappoint all my wishes and to disarrange all my plans. It would be a great pleasure to myself to spend some days in your neighbourhood, but at present I really cannot specify any future week in which I am sure that it would be altogether convenient.

My health has improved greatly within these few months, partly, I believe, from having betaken myself to horsemanship, and partly from my having shaken away from me that load of secular duties which, in shape of attendance on the various institutions of the place, and of ministering in things temporal to the need of a crowded population, frittered away all the time, and vulgarized all the habits, and put to flight all the literature and all the spirituality of our clergymen. This is what I wrote to you about formerly ; and be assured, my dear Sir, that all my fears, before I entered Glasgow, upon this subject, were fully realized by the facts which met my observation. And I have no doubt that the evident depression which has taken place in the theology and general science of our city ministers is, in a great measure, referable to the vicious system of associating them with so much of the public management of city and Government affairs.

Be kind enough to remember me to Miss Hardy and to Mr. and Mrs. Usher.

I have no intention at present of publishing my last charity sermon in Edinburgh. I am just now in the press with a thin octavo volume, comprising a series of discourses on the infidel argument of astronomers against the truth of Christianity. Fuller, in "The Gospel its own Witness," gives a chapter to this discussion. I enter more at large into it, and shall send you a copy when it comes out, which I expect to be in the end of January.

Mr. Smith, a principal bookseller here, told me some time ago that he had sold more of your sermons and of Blair's, than of any other author's.

I pray God to bless and sustain the evening of your days,

and that whether we meet on this side of the grave, we may be found without spot and blameless on the day of the coming of our Lord.—I am, my dear Sir, yours most truly,

THOMAS CHALMERS.

No. CCXXII.

Kirkaldy, 14th September 1820.

MY DEAR SIR,—I can assure you that it is often matter of regret, if not of self-reproach to me, that I have not returned your kind visit, and gratified my own feelings by renewing my old intimacies with a neighbourhood to which I feel very strongly attached. It is all due, I can assure you, to the force of circumstances; and were it not for the claims of relationship in Fife, I am quite sure that Roxburghshire would be the quarter of a very early excursion. I am fearful of promising, but I cannot think of despairing of seeing you once more on this side of time.

My feeble essays to do good can scarcely yet bear to be mentioned. I have certainly been amply supported in them by the aid of a number of well-principled men in Glasgow, and I am more persuaded than ever that it is only through a vigorous and well-conducted ecclesiastical agency that any decisive influence can be brought to bear on our vicious and rapidly deteriorating population.

It is my earnest prayer that you may inherit the blessing promised to those who maintain a patient continuance in well-doing. I have looked lately into Cotton Mather's "Essays to do Good," and thought of you all the while. I only learned so much as the existence of this great American philanthropist a few weeks ago. That, by the way, is one of the miseries of our great town,—I have no time for reading, and have suffered the whole literature of the country to get before me. Give my kindest compliments to Miss Hardy when you see her. I ascended the Terrace very lately, in the hopes of meeting with my old friend there, and learning of you ; but I found a new name upon the door. I beg to be remembered to Mr. and Mrs. Usher of Courthill. May God bless and sustain you.—I beg you to believe me, my dear Sir, yours very affectionately,

THOMAS CHALMERS.

No. CCXXIII.—To W. ROGER, ESQ. OF GLASGOW.

Charlotte Street, 18th February 1817.

MY DEAR SIR,—I was very much touched and gratified by the address which was read to me in your presence, and which you had the kindness to leave in my hands. I consider it as peculiarly valuable on two accounts. First, as an expression of approbation and regard on the part of my hearers; and, secondly, as a memorial of their deliberate sentiments on a subject which has long engaged and interested my own thoughts.

The experience of every month confirms me in the opinion that a minister of religion should be allowed to give all his time and all his strength to such objects as are strictly and substantially religious, and that the violation of this principle not only entails upon him a world of personal vexation and discomfort, but that it also goes to impair the effect both of his pulpit and parochial ministrations.

Were I called upon to specify the one measure by which the people of a parish could contrive to throw the most inviting charm over the situation of their clergyman, I should say, by rendering such an homage to the importance of his employment as to shield it from everything that can at all tend to harass or to disturb it, and permitting him to relieve the fatigue of study by varieties of his own choosing—by such varieties as he himself finds to be most congenial to his own taste, and temper, and sense of duty, and not by such varieties as custom, or accident, or arbitrary regulations may have accumulated upon his office for years, and perhaps for generations before he had entered it.

This charm has been lately held out to me, and that, too, for the purpose of drawing me away from a scene of duty which I count to be one of the most important within the limits of our National Establishment ; and I will frankly confess to you that I am not able to compute what might have been the extent of its influence had I not been assured, both by my experience of your past services and by the warmth and sincerity of your present professions, that you were willing to guard the office I now hold from all those intrusions by which its peace or its sanctity might be violated.

I feel myself placed on high vantage-ground in declining all those personal services which have for their object the further-ance of civil and secular accommodation among my parishioners. You have empowered me to state—what I am sure, from the reason and liberality which characterize the functionaries of this city, they will find to be most abundantly satisfying—that the public agency which I withhold in my own person I am willing to provide in a tenfold degree in the persons of others who have kindly undertaken to relieve me of every labour that is not strictly professional.

I thank you most cordially for your kind recommendation and offer in respect of ministerial assistance, and only lament the necessity I am under to accept of it. I trust that it will not tempt me to remit my diligence in the business of my pro-fession, and that its whole effect will be to secure, both for my parishioners and my hearers, the benefit of a more entire ministration.

With sincere prayers for the comfort and usefulness of our future connexion, and an earnest request that you, and the other gentlemen with whom you are associated, may give me a place in their intercessions at the Throne of Grace, I beg leave to subscribe myself, my dear Sir, your most affectionate friend,

THOMAS CHALMERS.

LETTERS TO THE REV. J. W. CUNNINGHAM OF HARROW, LONDON.

No. CCXXIV.

Glasgow, 8th January 1818.

MY DEAR SIR,—I received your very kind letter some time ago, and do count it a very great refreshment to obtain from you an occasional communication. Since writing you last, I have had the good fortune to receive your small work on " Benefit Societies," which I can assure you I read with much interest and satisfaction. These institutions have certainly the advantage over saving banks which you ascribe to them; and if delivered from the accompaniment of dissipation and excess, which I am sorry to observe go along with them in your part of the country, might have an important effect on the habits and comforts of the lower orders. They generally, however, set out on too liberal a system of allowances, which brings them to their termination in a few years. And such is my conviction of the complete means being with the poor themselves, to be altogether independent of relief from others, that I rejoice to observe any demonstration of this in any way that may induce foresight and economy amongst them; so that if, in point of fact, savings banks shall present a greater allurement to economy than any other institution, I should rejoice in their being encouraged and multiplied throughout our land.

You ask me how I liked the review of my " Discourses" in the " Christian Observer." I have lived too long in the rough element of severity and invective not to feel that it treats me with great moderation. There is an evident tone of friendship about it which would have reconciled me to much greater freedoms than it has actually used. And I still retain the same feeling of kindness towards its conductors, and the same opinion of its being by far the first of our religious periodicals in respect both of talent and Christian spirit, that I have long entertained.

Perhaps I ought not to say to you what I honestly think and feel of the evangelical clergy in the Church of England, that they are the great Christian luminaries of our country at this moment ; nor in all the other denominations of religion put together have I met with a goodlier number of devoted and spiritual men spending their zeal and earnestness and talent on the best of causes.   There is one peculiarity with which I feel myself most frequently, and I admit most justly charged, and that is a pleonastic exhibition of the same idea.   And yet when one thinks of the passage where the power of demonstration is likened to a hammer breaking the rock in pieces, who does not feel that in such a process the hammer is often directed to the same point of application ? And be assured that there never yet was any cause carried, or any object practically driven, but by a succession of similar and repeated strokes.   This is the case in Parliament.   It is so also in the pulpit.   And though I have no reason to believe that I shall ever contribute much to the establishment of any right position, and the overthrow of any wrong one, yet I have no doubt that an extensive impression will never be made on the public mind by a bare and didactic exhibition of truth, however rigid and faultless the whole conduct of the argument may be ; and that with our nature, constituted as it is, there must be reiteration, and variation, and impassioned urgency.

I have not had yet the pleasure of seeing your sermon on the funeral of the Princess Charlotte.   Hall is eminently beautiful and impressive, and I really think it among the foremost of his productions.   My own I am ashamed to speak of, and indeed it can scarcely be intelligible out of Glasgow, where the question of churches was perhaps about the next in interest to the main and overwhelming interest of that period.   I feel some little value, however, for the appendix, for which I am altogether responsible on the footing of *voluntary* authorship.

I long for a more realizing sense of spiritual things. There is a darkness which no light of argument can disperse. There is a light which never can be reached but by knocking at the door of that sanctuary that we cannot open. May God make to each of us the revelation which He maketh unto babes ; and may such be our fellowship with the Father and the Son, as to stamp the recognisable character of Heaven on our fellowship one with another.

Have you ever attended to the doctrine of the disinterested love of God ? I fear that Edwards, Witherspoon, and the American divines have a little darkened the freeness of the Gospel offer by their speculations on the subject. They seem to put all the discredit of selfishness on the love of gratitude, and would suspend the act of acceptance by faith, till somehow or other it could be made contemporaneous with the dawn of love to God on account of His own excellencies. This I do think is a forbidding of those whom God has not forbidden, and I cannot but preach the Gospel without reserve to all men in every state of moral disease.

Do let me hear from you soon. May I request you to give my kindest remembrances to Mr. Wilson when you see him. There is no man in the world whom I have a greater love for than Mr. Wilberforce ; but I have such an impression of the way in which he is harassed and overdone by extensive calls upon his attendance, that I am fearful to intrude upon him even with compliments.—I am, my dear Sir, yours most affectionately, THOMAS CHALMERS.

No. CCXXV.

Anstruther, 11*th August* 1819.

MY DEAR SIR,—I should have acknowledged your kind communication long ago. I am here on a visit to my mother and for sea-bathing, having reduced myself to a state of con-

2 A

siderable languor, as inimical to mental as to bodily exertion. I observed with the utmost gratitude your readiness to assist me in the matter of my publications. I feel my thorough need of such assistance; and have to confess a very uncouth and primeval ignorance of many of the proprieties of our language, aggravated as it is in my case by carelessness and a kind of impatience to arrive at the conclusion of every undertaking.

Since I received yours, I have seen the " Christian Observer " upon my last Work ;—very kind, and breathing the partialities of friendship. He speaks of sensibility to the lash of criticism. On this subject I have often admired a couplet in Beattie's " Minstrel,"

> " Him, who ne'er listened to the voice of praise,
> The silence of neglect can ne'er appal."

It were untrue to general nature, as well as to my own individual experience, did I profess to have fulfilled the first of the above lines, and therefore have no title to the privilege expressed in the second. But it is good to know the way of arriving at that privilege, even to love the praise of God and not the praise of men. Nor do I know a more memorable remark of Foster's, than that—of all the propensities of unrenewed nature, the appetite for praise needs to be kept under the severest castigation.

By the way, have you seen his " Missionary Sermon ? " What a marvellous composition !—how rich in sentiment, and how replete with matter so weighty and dense, that in my hands it would have been expanded into a large octavo volume ere I could have felt it to be in a right condition for being addressed to the general mind of the country. I underrate, I believe, the capacity of my readers ; and in my anxiety to convey a lucid impression, I nourish a diseased tendency to useless and excessive illustration.

I saw one of your excellent ones of the Church of England lately, Mr. Stuart of Percy Chapel. I have now seen many of the most distinguished of both our Establishments, and without flattery, there is one mighty point of superiority that you have over us. You know that a man may look with an observant eye upon a particular affection, and yet not possess the affection itself. To have a just perception of the laws and the phenomena of anger, it is not necessary to have an irritable constitution ; and it is not the most passionate who are worst fitted to acquire the metaphysics of human passion. Now, this is just as true of our good as of our bad feelings. It is just as true of the spiritual as of the sensual part of our nature ; and I do think that while the orthodox of our Church come forth with their didactic expositions of Christianity, and intellectually assign the right place to faith, and love, and holiness, the evangelical of yours shew forth all these graces in real and living exemplification. We theorize about the virtues of the new creature : you actually breathe these virtues. I have seen many good epistles written with pen and ink, and all about Christ too, by our clergy ; but I have not seen so many living epistles among them. We talk about religion ; you talk religion. And as far as I have remarked, while the matter has come as abundantly to us in word and even in argument, (λόγῳ, either *verbo* or *ratione*), it has come far more abundantly to you in power.

When in the same room with Mr. Stuart, I felt as in a pure and holy atmosphere, and learned how greatly more efficacious, in the way of especial influence upon others, is the devotion which emanates from an actually renewed heart, than the demonstration which emanates from an able and enlightened understanding.

I have seen the tracts of some of your seceders. I would call them able and impressive expositions of *one half of the truth.* Why are they more fearful of touching on the personal graces of the believer than the apostles were before them ? Why will they only look to the sun through the open window of a chamber, when the first teachers looked also to the light, and heat, and visibility which were introduced through the open window into the chamber itself ? Still it is most true and worthy of all acceptation, that without the sun and without the open window, all would be void, and dark, and cheerless in the apartment. Still it is true that the gospel attitude is that of looking unto Jesus, and beholding with open face the glory of the Lord. But why do Antinomians obliterate the succeeding clause, about being changed into the same image from glory to glory, even as by the Spirit of the Lord ?—With best wishes and many prayers both for your personal and ministerial comfort, believe me, my dear sir, yours most truly,

Thomas Chalmers.

No. CCXXVI.

Glasgow, 25th March 1823.

My dear Sir,—I should have replied to your kind letter of the 26th of December long ago, but I was then in sad agitation about my purposed movement to St. Andrews, and am still in a state of great engrossment with duties and preparations of various sorts. I have, however, now the comfortable prospect of at length being unwarped out of a situation, the fatigues and details of which I at length found to be utterly incompatible with the attention which I conceive due to such distinct and general objects as have been offered to me.

In regard to a topic for a missionary sermon, I at one time thought highly of the civilizing influence of Christianity, as an argument fitted to propitiate those who were indifferent to the cause on its higher and more appropriate merits. My experience, however, has led me to distrust the efficacy of all those attempts which are made for the purpose of conciliating to a Christian enterprise those who are not Christians ; and, after all, I am more disposed to confide the whole hopes of success to the strict and sacred operation of evangelical motives on men of evangelical minds, though I cannot deny, at the same time, that the earth may be, and often has been, made to help the woman.

What would you think of the universality of the law written in the heart as an invitation to missionary undertakings ? There is no controverting the existence of a moral sense among the rudest barbarians—the accusings and the excusings of it within them—insomuch that the idea of sin is at once under-stood among them without a formal or circumlocutory defini-tion. Thus in all countries you have a ground upon which you can at once enter—a John the Baptist in every heart, who has already in some measure prepared the way of the Lord, pre-cursors even in the strangest territories who are there before you, and whose office it is to make your message welcome, or at least intelligible ; as much, in fact, of moral intimation, al-ready given unto all, as will secure, and in a judicial way, their acquittal or their condemnation when we go forth preaching unto all—enough to guide them to the understanding and recep-tion of the Gospel if they follow the light that is already in them, and enough to attach to them the most fearful of penalties if they reject or turn from it. I am aware that within the short compass of a letter I cannot qualify enough so as to free the argument of all exceptions ; but you will perceive in the general how an impressive reasoning on the side of the mis-sionary cause might be built on the universal moral light which, however obscurely, is spread over the world—a light at all events that enters into the character and conduct, and so leaves an accusing or restless conscience in every heart ; thus preparing the way for the tidings of a Saviour, and making

Him precious to some, while to others He is the savour of death unto death. I should be much comforted by a letter from you. I am still hopeful of being ready, on English Pauperism, by the month of May or June.—Believe me to be, my dear Sir, yours most affectionately,

THOMAS CHALMERS.

No. CCXXVII.

Edinburgh, 17th March 1832.

MY DEAR SIR,—I have asked Mr. Whittaker to send you a "Letter to the Royal Commissioners for the Visitation of Colleges in Scotland," lately printed by me ; and my precise reason for so doing is, that you might be enabled to estimate the justice of your friend Lord A.'s complaint against me, because of an offensive communication which I had presumed to make to him and his fellow Commissioners.

I am in all my principles and feelings a thorough Conservative—none more so. But they are our Tory corruptionists who have brought us into our present helpless situation. There was no rudeness in the manner of my communication that could be alleged as at all offensive. But the substance of it was disagreeable to his Lordship, who dislikes honesty and truth when associated with independence.

If the Commissioners shall respond to my statements, am I at liberty to notice in any future argument how unpalatable my memorial was to Lord A. ?

I have written Mr. Collins to send Whittaker copies of my "Eight Years' Experience in Glasgow," if the pamphlet be yet in print. I should really like you to see it.—I am, my dear Sir, yours most truly,   THOMAS CHALMERS.

I shall be most thankful for any abstract which you may publish of my views on Pauperism.—T. C.

No. CCXXVIII.—To Rev. Dr. Wright of Stirling.

Glasgow, 14*th February* 1823.

My dear Sir,—I write under the impulse of lively gratitude to yourself for what you wrote of me to Mr. Muir, who was kind enough to read it to me. I hold it to be a most excellent recommendation that I should write the number of sermons which you suggest, and I sincerely trust that it will not be lost upon me. It is my desire to join in the sentiment of the Psalmist on this subject, "If I forget thee, O Jerusalem, let my right hand forget her cunning, and let my tongue cleave to the roof of my mouth, if I do not prefer thee above my chiefest joy." It is satisfactory to myself that I have ever held a professorship as a higher station, even speaking Christianly, than a church. I never quitted this sentiment even when I had not the most distant hope of a chair; and now that I have had the offer of one, and accepted of it, I have just acted on the principle which I at all times felt and have at all times avowed. But it is still a matter of great thankfulness to me when I can get any of my brethren among the senior clergy to view the thing even with tolerance, though not with positive approbation. I am much comforted by the testimonies of Dr. Davidson and Mr. Gordon of Edinburgh. I request a place in your prayers. Should I be spared, I look forward now with great confidence to the occasional enjoyment of your society. Here I was overborne and had no time for general intercourse or general objects. The unbounded leisure and command of summer give me a scope for all sorts of excursion, whether of mind or body.—With kindest compliments to Mrs. Wright, and earnest request that you would send me a letter, I entreat you to believe me, my dear Sir, yours very affectionately,

Thomas Chalmers.

No. CCXXIX.

Dumfries, 3d September 1822.

MY DEAR SIR,—I reached this in safety about eight o'clock, and have comfortable prospects of my journey. And I can assure you that it forms no small addition to my comfort when I reflect on the arrangements that I have left behind me, and by which you have kindly consented to keep stedfastly and constantly by my congregation of St. John's till I shall return to Glasgow; and you will indeed confer upon me a great benefit by resisting all the urgency that might be employed for the purpose of drawing you to preach elsewhere. I esteem it a very fortunate circumstance, that by your services, which are so satisfactory to my people, I feel disburdened of the uneasiness that I might otherwise have when away from them; and that I am thus set at large for the prosecution of a journey which I deem to be most important, in a way that is satisfactory to myself.

Yet be assured that a single and undivided attention to the peculiar work of a Christian minister is the way of peace and of pleasantness. I envy those who have escaped the distraction of all other pursuits and all other speculations. And yet I cannot blame myself for my labours on the argument of Pauperism; and I sincerely hope, that instead of going forth upon it, it has intercepted and laid hold of me, so that I have only followed the call of Providence and duty when I suffered myself to be involved in it.

Tell Mrs. Chalmers that it may yet be three days ere I finish the long folio epistle which I am preparing for her. I have this night nearly completed one page of it.—Do believe me, my dear sir, yours very truly,   THOMAS CHALMERS.

No. CCXXX.

St. Andrews, 20th November 1823.

My dear Sir,—I enjoy very much the repose and quietness of my new situation, and promise to get on very comfortably; but be very sure that all the felicity of the circumstances immediately around me is not unmingled with much regret and tenderness because of those in Glasgow whom I have left behind me. I am not insensible to the force and the value of your friendship in particular; and have sometimes thought of my own apparently cold and passive exhibition under the many ardent demonstrations that you have given of it. The truth is, that my extreme occupations in Glasgow put me into a state that was quite unnatural, and now only have I begun rightly to estimate and to feel the manifold kindnesses that surrounded me there.—Yours most truly and affectionately,

THOMAS CHALMERS.

No. CCXXXI.

Burntisland, 21st September 1832.

My very dear Sir,—We have this day received the sad intimation of Mrs. Smyth's death, and you may well believe that both I and Mrs. Chalmers feel very deeply for you under this afflictive dispensation.

It is our earnest prayer that the Heavenly Comforter may be with you in your present trying circumstances, when all earthly comfort and sympathy are so unavailing, and may He who grieves not willingly any of His children pour a healing and a sanctifying medicine into your cup of discipline.

That uncertainty of life and awfulness of death which we often preach, we do not often practically or adequately feel. But never, I should imagine, does death make a more realizing demonstration of itself than in circumstances like yours,

2 B

where it has made inroads upon your dwelling, and torn asunder the nearest and dearest of all earthly relationships.

This is a sore bereavement. May your widowed heart find its solace and relief in the promises of the Gospel. May its faith bear you up amid the agonies of wounded nature, and then shall this visitation, though not joyous but grievous, yield unto you the peaceable fruit of righteousness.

My heart bleeds both when I think of yourself and when I think of your motherless children. Cast the whole burden upon the Lord and He will sustain it. What power and preciousness of adaptation do we often meet in short and single clauses of the Bible ; and I doubt not, my dear Sir, that your now exercised and experienced spirit has by this time made fresh discoveries both of the divine wisdom and the divine tenderness which are stamped upon its pages.

Mrs. Chalmers unites with me in deep condolence both for you and your afflicted family, and with the sincerest regards of us both, ever believe me, my dear Sir, yours with utmost sympathy and regard,   THOMAS CHALMERS.

LETTERS TO THE REV. DR. MACFARLAN OF GREENOCK.

No. CCXXXII.

St. Andrews, 15th April 1824.

MY VERY DEAR SIR,—I cannot resist the impulse of my present joy and gratitude on the receipt of a letter from Glasgow this morning, by which I am led to cherish the pleasing and delightful hope that you may be minister of St. John's.

Just now I am in a perfect hurricane of business, preparing for our public examinations, and I shall just therefore say, for your encouragement, that I stake my whole credit on your finding it the easiest and most manageable city parish in Scotland, and that what many deem the bugbears are indeed the facilities of the parish. I shall be most happy, my dear Sir, to enter with you upon any details that you may require of me, and at present I can do no more than bless the Providence that has evolved itself in a way so gracious.—Do believe me, my dear Sir, yours most affectionately and truly, Thomas Chalmers.

No. CCXXXIII.

St. Andrews, 9th September 1824.

My dear Sir,—I most honestly rejoice at the pleasure you feel in your situation. I think that you will find this much enhanced by your parochial visitations, in which exercise I had always more satisfaction than in any other which belonged to the office.

As to my Sacrament examinations, I requested from the pulpit that all who intended to communicate for the first time should meet me in the vestry at one particular hour—say ten P.M. upon a Tuesday. I had previously marked on little slips of paper "half-past ten," "eleven," "half-past eleven," &c., which I dealt out to those assembled individually; and upon which each came back to me at his own specified time that forenoon —and this afforded me half-an-hour's conversation with each. The length of this exercise to myself depended on the number who came forward; and if that number was too great, I gave slips of paper for the next day (Wednesday) at "ten," "half-past ten," "eleven," &c., marking Wednesday, however, to separate them from the catechumens of Tuesday. I thus, sometimes in one, and at most in two forenoons, got over the main burden of my Sacramental examinations. If any did not satisfy me, I prescribed chapters of the Bible for their reading, and assigned the time when they should call upon me in my own house for further conversation. I must say, however, and

I was surprised at the discovery, (for which, however, a satisfactory cause may be assigned,) that I found the candidates for
the Lord's Table in Glasgow, generally speaking, to be much
better prepared than those in Kilmany.

Besides all this, I, on the recommendation, and according to
the practice of Dr. M'Gill, convened all whom I resolved to
admit as communicants in the vestry at three, P.M., on the Wednesday previous to the Fast-day, when I gave them an address
in cumulo, and then distributed to them their tokens and a
certificate that I had that day admitted them to be communicants.   It was generally in the interval between the separate
conversations and this meeting that each got a testimonial from
the proper elder, and shewed it before I gave the token.   At
the end of each separate conversation I gave to the individual
on a slip of paper the day and hour of this general address as a
memorandum.

Let me entreat that you will neither be over-fatigued by your
visitations nor overwhelmed by your sacramental work.   I shall
be most happy at all times to furnish any details that may be
required of me.—I am, my dear Sir, yours very truly,

THOMAS CHALMERS.

No. CCXXXIV.

Edinburgh, 21*st December* 1842.

MY DEAR SIR,—I have seen Dr. Abercrombie, and attempted
to rectify and undeceive him as to my desire of hastening or
precipitating the crisis.   The truth is, that the success of my
attempts is directly fitted to avert a crisis if anything will.
Will you look at Regulation Seventh of the enclosed ? and I trust
you will allow the right middle way is to be *provisionally* in
readiness for the worst.   I also send the copy of a subscription
paper, which is also *provisional.*   Such an attitude of preparation as I long and labour for would place the Church on right

vantage-ground for negotiating with Government on the footing of an independent party. Whether with or without a general meeting of your congregation an association, whether congregational or parochial, could be easily got up anywhere. Our association at Morningside yields already at the rate of £250 a year. Oh, when will men know how to discriminate between what is an imaginative picture, and what a sober and practical reality !—I ever am, my dear Sir, yours most truly,

THOMAS CHALMERS.

No. CCXXXV.

Edinburgh, 4th August 1845.

MY DEAR SIR,—I now sit down to give you my reasons why I cannot attend the Assembly at Inverness. They may be summed up in two :—

First, There is something more than personal inclination on my part ; there is a positive feeling of duty that has resolved me henceforth to live the life of a student. For this purpose I have already signified by a formal act, my retirement from the public business of the Church. It were a rescinding of that Act and the exposure of myself again to other and future applications should I go to Inverness. It is not the time taken up with that solitary movement, but it is the struggle that I should have with subsequent applications which I am most anxious to save. And meanwhile I issue these refusals with a clear conscience ; for truly it is a higher department to have to do with the understandings and consciences of my students, than to wear out any more of my life in the outward business of the house of God. But,

Secondly, That business is infinitely better done by the timely retirement of the veterans from the stage, and the consequent calling up of younger and stronger men. I am fortified in this idea by two very recent examples. I was urged to

be a member of the last Assembly, and such was the over-
weening importance attached to this by some, that they absurdly anticipated a decay of interest in the Assembly should
I not be there.   Now, I put it to yourself—Do you ever recollect an Assembly the proceedings of which were conducted in
a finer spirit, and with higher ability, and with greater effect
upon the public mind ?   Again, Mr. Guthrie applied to me to
launch the Manse Scheme at the first meeting about it which
he held in Glasgow.   This also I resisted; and is not that
scheme progressing at a rate most encouraging to all the friends
of the Church ?   I perfectly agree with you in thinking, that
the Assembly of Inverness, now that it is determined on,
should be made as impressive as possible, so that the larger the
confluence to it from all parts the better.   This I am urging
upon all my acquaintances who should and can go, whether
they are members or not.   But for myself, it is out of the
question.   Will you forgive me if I state an illustration which
has occurred to me in connexion with this subject ?   To parade
me onward to Inverness appears to me as ludicrous as to
parade thitherward a congeries of old bones; for it strongly
reminds me of the delusion under which Cobbett laboured
when he brought Tom Paine's bones from America, and carried them through England, in the hope that they would operate as a charm in every neighbourhood wherever he presented
them.—Ever believe me, my dear Sir, yours most truly,

THOMAS CHALMERS.

No. CCXXXVI.

Edinburgh, 7th August 1845.

MY DEAR SIR,—Our two last letters crossed each other.   In
regard to my going to Inverness for the purpose of an address
on the Sustentation Fund, I beg to submit the two following
considerations :—

In the first place, it has been my uniform experience that the Associations have remained as sluggish and lethargic after such an address as previous to its delivery. Witness my Assembly's address at Glasgow, and my more recent addresses there, since which time the Associations just yield as little as ever. The only way of advancing the Sustentation Fund is by an agency who might severally deal with each of the localities piecemeal and at close quarters. I did no sensible good by a series of at least twenty public addresses in the north of Scotland. All the good I have done is by correspondence or personal converse, either in my own person or the persons of the agents whom I employed.

But 2*dly*, My feelings and principles on the subject are well known, and more especially my strong dissatisfaction with a number of the Highland ministers and congregations. On the other hand, they do not at all sympathize with me in my sense of the religious importance of this subject. They call it secular, and seem to speak as if my confidence was placed in carnal weapons. This was the feeling, I afterwards heard, of the *men* whom I dealt with at Arran, and I believe it to be a pretty general feeling in the north. Now, put these two considerations together ; first, my general experience of the uselessness of these addresses ; and secondly, my special experience of the positive dislike to the subject in the north ; and then I ask you to conceive with what utter heartlessness, or rather with what inward recoil of spirit I behoved to go to Inverness, there to obtrude an unpalatable subject upon an unwilling auditory.— I who am not a member and would be felt by many as a most unwelcome interloper, were I to go upon such an errand. Nothing, my dear Sir, could force a way through such a barrier but a special invitation from the Assembly where they have met, and this too at the instance of twenty, thirty, or forty Highland ministers themselves; after which, and when they

had put the censorial staff into my hand, I should feel at freedom to wield it with all faithfulness, though at the same time
I hope with all delicacy. But be assured that there are paragraphs in your closing address to the last Assembly which will
do infinitely more good to the Sustentation Fund than all I
could hope to do by going to Inverness.—Ever believe me, my
dear Sir, yours most truly,   THOMAS CHALMERS.

No. CCXXXVII.—IN REPLY TO A LETTER REQUESTING SOME DIRECTIONS ON THE SUBJECT OF PRACTICAL CHARITY.

Glasgow, 6th November 1821.

MY DEAR SIR,—I received a letter some days ago from the
person who signs himself " Christianus," and with which I
would have been still more gratified had he subscribed his
real name.

I think that the best school for benevolence is a limited
district, which it is competent for any individual to assume as
the field in which he chooses to exercise his philanthropy. I
would take one of the poorest vicinities in the whole town, and
measure off for myself a population of, say fifty or a hundred
families, and the topic of introduction I should choose would
not be an inquiry into their temporal necessities, (for this
might call forth a reaction most appalling to the adventurer,
and most corrupting to the people whom he means to benefit,)
but rather an inquiry into the state of health and the education
of the young ; or the accommodation that there is with respect
to schools and churches ; or something, in short, that would
begin your acquaintance with the people, without exciting any
sordid or mercenary expectation. You will not find it so formidable an affair to secure a welcome from the families, among

whom you may reiterate as often as you will on the same topics, but never in the ostensible capacity of an almoner, assuming always the higher capacity of a friend to their children, and a zealous advocate or promoter of all that can conduce to the improvement of principle and moral habits among the population. In this way they will not obtrude their necessities so readily upon you; while you, on the other hand, when their necessities in any particular way force themselves upon your observation, may secretly and without the knowledge of others relieve them. You will thus find the work of charity a very quiet and manageable process; for, in truth, there won't be half a dozen families among the hundred who will stand in real need of your money; while, perhaps, one-half of the whole would have been the sordid expectants of your generosity had you injudiciously announced yourself as the general almoner of the district that you had assumed.

Meanwhile, ply all the families with kind and moral attentions, stimulate education, recommend cleanliness, encourage church-going habits. Be not too obtrusive with your money; let the people pay for all themselves as much as possible, and, at the same time, shew that you grudge no expense that would serve their best interests by being generous in every case of unquestionable distress; by setting up, if you will, a little library in the district, to which, however, there ought to be small quarterly payments on the part of the people themselves. Set up a local Savings' Bank if you think it would promote frugality, and study by all possible means to make the people thrive—not so much by any imparted liberality on your part, as *thrive* by teaching them the power of their own resources and their own capabilities.

I have not nearly exhausted this favourite subject; but I send you to the best school when I send you to the school of your own experience. Blunders, and failures, and discourage-

ments are unavoidable ; but you are in the best place for pro-
fiting by these, when you confine yourself to a local territory,
where you are ever growing in acquaintanceship and mutual
regard with the people, than when you throw yourself at large
over a boundless field.   Mr. John Campbell, Tertius, W.S., has
done the very same thing that I now recommend to you, and
if you are disposed to consult him, he is qualified to supplement
the deficiencies of my present communication.—Yours truly,

THOMAS CHALMERS.

No. CCXXXVIII.—To a Friend.

St. Andrews, 13*th November* 1825.

MY VERY DEAR SIR,—I have no *peculiar* mode of addressing
the Gospel to any one class of human creatures. It is a wide and
general proclamation of mercy to all, and whatever the age or
condition of the sinner, still he is welcome to Christ ; and
coming unto Him he shall in *no wise* be cast out. All are
warranted to approach, even with boldness, to that throne of
grace where they shall receive both mercy to pardon and grace
to help in every time of need.

It is a wonderful plea that the Psalmist urges for pardon,
" Pardon mine iniquity, *for it is great.*" That greatness of transgression, which would preclude the hope of forgiveness from
an earthly superior whom we had offended, is the very argument
which we are encouraged to make use of in praying for pardon
from Him, whose thoughts are not as our thoughts, and whose
ways are not as our ways. May you, my dear Sir, and all with
whom you are connected, have great peace and joy in thus
believing ; and sure I am, that when Gospel peace enters,
Gospel holiness will follow in its train. Have you read Romaine's "Treatises on Faith?"—they are very precious.—Believe
me, my dear Sir, yours truly,   THOMAS CHALMERS.

No. CCXXXIX.—ON MAN'S RESPONSIBILITY FOR HIS BELIEF.

St. Andrews, 15th March 1826.

MY DEAR MADAM,—Lord Byron's assertion, " that man is not responsible for his belief,"—an assertion repeated by Mr. Brougham and others—seems to have proceeded from the imagination that belief is in no cases voluntary. Now, it is very true that we are only responsible for what is voluntary, and it is also true that we cannot believe without evidence. But then it is a very possible thing that a doctrine may possess the most abundant evidence, and yet not be believed, just because we choose to shut our eyes against it ; and our unbelief in this case is owing not to the want of evidence, but to the evidence *not being attended to.*   Grant that belief is not a voluntary act, it is quite enough for the refutation of Mr. Brougham's principle, if attention be a voluntary act.   One attends to a subject because he so chooses, or he does not attend because he so chooses.   It is the fact of the attention being given or withheld which forms the thing that is to be morally reckoned with.   And if the attention has been withheld when it ought to have been given, for this we are the subjects of a rightful condemnation.

It is enough to make unbelief a thing of choice and a thing of affection, that we have power over the direction of our noticing and investigating faculties.   You are not to blame if you have not found some valuable article that you had lost in an apartment of thickest darkness ; but you are to blame if you might have opened the shutters or lighted a candle, so as to have admitted enough of light for the discovery.   Neither are you to blame if you find not the hidden treasure of the Gospel, provided that it is placed beyond the reach of all your strenuousness, and of every expedient that can be used for its discovery ; but you are to blame if you have not gone in quest of it, or if you have wilfully and determinedly shut your eyes against it, or if you have not stirred up those powers of your mind over which the mind has a voluntary control to the inquiry after it. The Discerner of the heart will see where the lurking perversity lies, and make it manifest of all who remain in darkness, that they loved the darkness—of all who have not come to Christ, that they were not willing to come.

Christianity lays no unreasonable service on men, and far less that service which were most unreasonable of all—the homage of your belief without offering such evidence as, *if attended to,* will constrain the belief. Our religion has its proofs, and it also has its probabilities. Its proofs can only be gotten at by patient and laborious inquiry, and when they are so gotten at they carry the belief along with them. Its probabilities again may, some of them, be seen at first sight, and though not enough to compel our belief, yet they form a sufficient claim upon our attention. They form that sort of precognition which entitles Christianity, at least, to a fair and full trial, and, if not worthy all at once of a place in our creed, it is worthy of a further hearing. Now, all I want is, that that hearing shall be given, that the evidences of Christianity shall be studied, that the Bible shall be read with patience, and prayer, and moral earnestness, and on the principle that he who seeketh findeth, I have no apprehension of such a course not terminating in a full and stedfast conviction that the Bible is an authentic message from heaven to earth, and contains in it the record of God's will for man's salvation.—I am, my dear Madam, yours most truly,   THOMAS CHALMERS.

No. CCXL.—DIRECTIONS TO AN ANXIOUS INQUIRER.

St. Andrews, February 1826.

DEAR MADAM,—I have been asked by Miss —— to write you on the subject of certain difficulties to which I believe almost every inquirer into the way of salvation is subjected. It is very possible that aught I can say may not produce an immediate impression on your mind, for I have often experienced the very great tenacity wherewith the obstacles to a free and full reception of the Gospel stand their ground in the mind of many a labouring seeker after truth ; but it is a great thing that you are in earnest if you are not at rest ; and in the meanwhile it is the part of every true friend you have to state to his uttermost ability such considerations as might, with the blessing of God, be helpful to your progress.

I would first, then, say to you, that you are not to wait till you have mourned enough for sin ere you accept the Saviour. You complain that you have not such deep views of sin as experienced Christians speak of ; but how did they acquire them ? they are the fruits of their experience in Christ, and not of their experience out of Christ. They had them not before their union with the Saviour. It was on more slender conceptions of the evil of sin than they now have that they went to Christ, that they closed with Him, and that they received from His sanctifying hand a more contrite spirit than before—a more tender conscience than before. Do as they did ; wait not till you have gotten their deep sensibilities till you go to the Saviour. Go to Him now ; go to Him with your present *insensibility ;* bring it before Him as part of your disease, and He, the Physician of souls, will minister to this and all other diseases. But, generally, you complain that you are ignorant of how to go—how to believe. Now, this has long been a stumbling-block to many ; their thoughts are *how* they are to believe, when their thoughts should be *what* they should believe. They look inwardly for the work of faith, when they should look outwardly for the object of faith. " For every one thought," says Richard Baxter, "that he casts downwardly upon himself, he should cast ten upwardly and outwardly upon Jesus, and upon the glorious truths of the Gospel." You say that you have no

doubts of the freeness of Christ's salvation, and of His willingness to save you.   Dwell upon this ; persist in this ; stand in
the Gospel attitude of looking upon Jesus, and light will at
length arise within you.   In the act of looking, you may have
to wait a longer or a shorter time for your coming enlargement ;
but surely it is worth the waiting for.   Meanwhile your business
is prayer ; a diligent attention in the ordinances of religion ;
reading of God's Word ; and, above all, a keeping of the sayings
of Christ : " He that keepeth my sayings, to him will I manifest myself."   Be assured you are in good hands, even in the
hands of Him who will not break the bruised reed nor quench
the smoking flax.—Believe me to be, dear Madam, yours truly,

THOMAS CHALMERS.

No. CCXLI.—TO THE COUNTESS OF D——.   A LETTER OF
CHRISTIAN ENCOURAGEMENT.*

MY DEAR COUNTESS,—It is my earnest prayer to God that
your superintendence of the Sabbath School, established in the
very interesting district in which you reside, may be abundantly
blessed, and that it may be productive of lasting benefit to its
sequestered inhabitants ; that a religious population may arise
around you ; and that God, by His Spirit, may carry home the
lessons of His Word to all to whom they are administered.

When one thinks of the certainty of approaching death, and
the greatness of the coming eternity, one cannot but think that
the only important history which is going on in the world is the
unseen history of human souls ; nor do I know a more interesting event than that of a heart alienated from God, and labouring
under a distaste for the method of salvation by the Cross, when
it becomes at length reconciled to all the peculiarities of the
Gospel, and is called out of darkness into God's marvellous
light.   In these institutions of Sabbath Schools there is always,

* Communicated by the Rev. T. Grinfield, Clifton.

indeed, a secondary advantage to be derived from the acquirement of those habits of regularity, and subordination, and all
those minor accomplishments which conduce to the formation
of good subjects and good members of society ; and when
education is received in subserviency to those temporal blessings,
it is no doubt of considerable temporal advantage, and must be
so considered even by those who have no taste for religion, and
take no concern for the high matters and interests of eternity.
But really when we look to the insignificance of the present
scene, and read believingly the Bible, and there learn the lesson
of what a wretched being man is by nature ; and when we are
made to understand that there is only one way of recovery, and
to consider how great and how radical a change must take
place in our hearts ere we can be admitted into the kingdom
of Heaven, and that we must submit with the docility of a little
child to these sayings, that "through faith in the blood of
Christ we are justified, and through the washing of regeneration we are sanctified;"—when these views open in their
significancy and magnitude upon the understanding, then a
mightier object will be seen connected with a Sabbath School.
It will be valued chiefly on spiritual and sacred grounds, and
the main anxiety will be, that they who repair for Scriptural
education shall become wise unto salvation through the faith
that is in Christ Jesus.   Now, to fulfil this higher object, it is
necessary that every higher expedient should be resorted to ;
that the children should be spoken to with affectionate concern
by their teacher, that he should add to his admonition the force
of his example ; that parents should warmly co-operate in the
great object, and add all the force of their example and admo-
nitions ; that unanimity should prevail amongst all connected
with it ; and that the prayers of intercession should frequently
be lifted up for the prosperity of a cause so righteous.   It is
my earnest and real desire that all the inhabitants of your

place may experience in rich and satisfying abundance the
comforts of the Christian faith, and may grow every day in the
graces of Christian obedience. It is, indeed, a wondrous silence
which immortal beings observe in their intercourse with each
other on the most urgent and greatest of all topics, that of their
souls ; and I sometimes think how they will look to each other,
and upbraid each other, should they meet on the same common
ground of condemnation on the great day of reckoning. Believe me, I feel nothing but the prompting of anxiety and
tenderness when I entreat my fellow-Christians to persevere
in a course of earnest and laborious striving for the kingdom of
Heaven. The Gospel invitation is free, but the Gospel require-
ment is strict : there is a change of heart demanded, as well as
a change of external conduct. But, oh how delightful that the
prayer of faith maketh all things possible, and that, though we
begin in darkness, and helplessness, and error, if we follow the
Saviour, He will shew unto us the light of life.—Yours very
truly,   THOMAS CHALMERS.

[3d *April* 1852.—DEAR SIR,—My daughter tells me that you wish to
know the date of the letter I had the pleasure of receiving from the venerated Dr. Chalmers. I cannot say exactly, but I think it was about the
year 1834, or 1835, or 1836. It was on the occasion of a discussion I had
with some clergymen of the Church of Geneva, about the Divinity of our
blessed Saviour. I cited Dr. Chalmers, as the head of the Presbyterian
Church, consequently Mr. M.'s *chief,* as being peculiarly opposed to a heresy
which, I think, tends to subvert the foundations of Christianity, and I took
the liberty of writing to the great and good man himself, to confirm the
truth of the opinion which I had ventured to assert as being his.—I am, my
dear Sir, your obedient servant,   CATHERINE OSBORNE.
    The Rev. W. Hanna.]

No. CCXLII.

MY DEAR LADY OSBORNE,—You must forgive my writing in
another hand, as I am very much over-worked. And I hope

to be further excused if I do not go into the subject of your letter at any great length.

It appears to me that there are two grounds upon which an error in Theology might be fatal :—first, the error might be so opposed to the clearest light of scriptural evidence as to imply the utmost moral unfairness in the examination of holy writ, or a hard rejection of the Divine testimony. With my views of what I hold to be the obvious sense of the Word of God, I could not be an Arian without incurring this delinquency. The second ground on which an error in theology might be fatal is, the great moral and practical importance of the doctrine which is either vitiated or disowned. I could not renounce my opinion of the divinity of Christ, without at the same time renouncing what I at present regard as the most essential and characteristic principle of the gospel. Dilute this article of Christianity, and you in the same proportion dilute other articles of the faith,—no less vital and fundamental than itself,—as the value of the Atonement, the depth of the enormity of the guilt that calls for Divine expiation, the need of a regenerating influence from on high, the unchangeableness and authority of Heaven's law, and the dignity of its moral government. Those are the great elements of the Christian system ; but by detaching the sentiment of Christ's divinity, we should take all the force and the spirit from them.

This doctrine strengthens and impregnates the whole of practical Christianity ; and whether it be the trust, or the gratitude, or the obedience of the gospel we are urging, they can only be urged with effect along with the belief that Jesus Christ, the author and the finisher of the faith, is absolutely and from eternity God. The first chapter of Revelation, the beginning of the Gospel of John, Romans ix. 5, 1 John v. 20, Philippians ii. 5, 8, and the first chapter to the Hebrews, appear to me the most decisive passages of the New Testament

2 c

in favour of the godhead of Christ: and the Old Testament appears to be the more impressive and convincing the longer I attend to it; for this let me refer you to the sixth of Isaiah, quoted in John's gospel, and applied by him to the Saviour; Isaiah viii. 13, 14, quoted in the same manner by Paul in the Epistle to the Romans; Isaiah ix. 5, 6; Jeremiah xxiii. 5, 6, where the Lord our righteousness is Jehovah; Micah v. 2; Zechariah xiii. 7; Malachi iii. 1. I entreat you to excuse the brevity and the imperfection of these hurried statements. The subject on which you have called me to express myself is fitted for an elaborate dissertation; and nothing like adequate justice can be done to it within the compass of a letter, written in great feebleness and amid manifold engagements.—I have the honour to be, &c.,   THOMAS CHALMERS.

No. CCXLIII.—TO HIS ELDEST DAUGHTER, ON PARTAKING FOR THE FIRST TIME OF THE SACRAMENT OF THE LORD'S SUPPER.

Early Vale, 23d October 1832.

MY DEAR ANNE,—Though I have as yet said little to you about the Sacrament, it is not that I do not feel, and feel deeply, the importance of the step which you are about to take. I have long and earnestly regretted that the solemn urgency of my occupations should have left me so little time and so little strength for attending to my family, and more especially to that highest interest of all, the state of their religion, impressed as I am both by the weight and importance of the obligation, and also by the solemn responsibility which the Apostle lays upon ministers for the souls of their people, though surely not more solemn than the responsibility of parents for their children, who ought therefore to watch for their souls as they *who must give account.*

I hope that I may have much free conversation with you both respecting the Sacrament, on the Fast-day preceding it on Thursday. But meanwhile I should like you to ponder the following considerations bearing upon the subject :—

1. You should not look on your past sinfulness as any barrier in the way of approaching the Lord's table ; and you cannot too soon or too confidently overpass this barrier by believing thoughts of that blood which was shed for the sins of the world —of that propitiation to which one and all are invited to look for their acceptance with God.

2. Neither should you look on your own impotency for acceptable obedience as any barrier ; and you cannot too soon or too confidently overpass this barrier by believing thoughts of the all-sufficiency and strength of that Spirit who is freely given to those who ask, and more especially to those who, fleeing for refuge to Jesus Christ the Master of the great solemnity in which you are to join, lift up their supplications for aid and ability to do the will of God in His all-prevailing name.

3. If you have faith in the two great truths which I have now specified, this will encourage you to go forward to the table of the Sacrament ; and yet instead of putting the question to yourself, Have I faith in these truths ?—I would rather that you dwelt on the contemplation of the truths themselves. It is by thinking directly of the truths, and not by thinking reflexly on what the state of your own mind is in regard to them, that you come to a right decision and establishment of purpose on this subject.

4. But there is one most important subject of self-examina tion on which I would make the whole question of this sacramental observance to turn. I would never stir a doubt as to the efficacy of Christ's blood, or your own welcome to the participation of its benefits ; and neither would I stir a doubt as to the readiness of the Spirit to perfect strength in your weakness. But there may be a doubt, and this I would have you to clear up, on the state of your own will and your own

purposes. Are you willing to be all and to do all that God would have you? Is it your purpose, in singleness of heart, to be His only and His altogether? Are you honestly desirous of making yourself over wholly unto Him, or, in other words, of submitting yourself entirely to God? These I hold to be the proper questions for putting to your conscience on the present occasion. When thus employed, you are counting the cost of the Christian profession ere you enter upon it; and great, I promise, will be your peace and joy, sure will be your progressive holiness, if in good faith and with firm integrity you resolve henceforward, and with reliance on the Divine grace, to be not almost, but altogether a Christian.

I bid you both recollect not merely the momentous personal interest which each of you has in this great concern, but the immense benefit of your Christian example to the younger children. May this prove, then, a decisive step in the history of your lives—a sure step to that heaven for which it is our highest interest as well as highest duty to prepare.—I ever am, my dear Anne, yours most truly,   THOMAS CHALMERS.

No. CCXLIV.—To MASTER J. MORTON.*

Edinburgh, 21st March 1832.

MY DEAR JOHN,—I would have given this letter partly to you and partly to your mamma, making it in that way a proper counterpart reply to the communication from Chesterhill of March 8th; but I feel that I cannot do justice to your very interesting epistle without devoting the whole of this sheet to it. I allude more particularly to your desire that I should tell you something of religion—that highest and most important of all subjects.

The only advice I shall give you at present will be a general,

* Eldest son of his sister Mrs. Morton.

but I have no doubt that if followed it will prove a very effective one. The Bible is able to make you wise unto salvation. I do not want to overtask you with the reading of it, but it is right you should read it by little and little, and that frequently. And I would, therefore, first recommend that you should peruse so much of it every day, and bring to the exercise all the attention and all the understanding you are able to do.

But, again, the Bible itself tells us that no man can understand or feel it aright by the mere natural and unassisted exercise of his own faculties; and that it is the office of the Holy Spirit to make the Word of God clear to our judgments, and powerful in its effect upon our hearts and lives; and it furthermore tells us, that God gives His Holy Spirit to them who ask it. My earnest recommendation therefore is, that as you read, you would also pray that God may open your understanding to understand.

My third and last recommendation is grounded on the saying, that the prayer of the wicked is an abomination to God; and that if we regard iniquity in our hearts, God will not hear us. Therefore, while observing my first and second directions to read the Bible and to pray, forget not my third, to be diligent in keeping God's commandments, doing all which His Word tells you to be right, refraining from all which His Word tells you to be wrong. Thus will you grow in the knowledge of the way of salvation. He who seeketh findeth; and you seeking to know God and Jesus Christ whom He has sent, will find the way of righteousness and peace, and have your feet firmly established on that good path which leads to Heaven.

Give my kind regard to your father, mother, brothers, and sisters.—I am, my dear John, your affectionate uncle,

THOMAS CHALMERS.

No. CCXLV.—Advice to a Young Clergyman.

Edinburgh, 12th *November* 1838.

My dear Sir,—I shall say nothing of practical or devotional reading and study, indispensable though they be to the upholding of the best and highest functions of our being, but speak chiefly of intellectual pursuits and professional business.

And first, it were of immense value to lay it down as a rule to which you should doggedly and determinedly adhere, that of giving two or three hours daily for at least three days in the week, and, if the calls of immediate business allowed, for more days than this, to some high subject of professional literature. I pressed this on Mr. Douglas, constitutionally one of the most indolent men I know, and the result was his work on the " Advancement of Society," &c. Your " Exegesis on Miracles," and your " Sermon on the Sacrament," convince me that if you would but select your topics and do likewise, you could, by dint of perseverance, furnish products of sounder and still higher quality than those to which I refer.

And the same habit of so much time for this elaborate mental exertion might not only issue in superior authorship, but superior sermons, of which it were well that you had a certain and increasing number when called to preach on great public occasions, or to first-rate auditories.

My reason for being satisfied with three days in the week for the more transcendental effort which I now recommend is, that I suppose your ordinary pulpit preparations are managed in a different way, and might require perhaps two or three days each week, not to be encroached upon by any call on your mind, during these days, for a more fatiguing exercise.

So much for the creative efforts of thought and composition. Additional to these, I would have one or two hours a day for the perusal of the more arduous kind of books, such as might subserve the preparations which I have now recommended, and store the mind with all that is most profound and philosophical in the themes which you propose to elucidate.

If these directions were fully and regularly acted up to, I would willingly allow the remainder of the time for light reading, society, and parochial duties. And, in reference to the latter, I would, as I could find the instruments, devolve as much as I profitably could upon others, whether in the capacity of elders or Sabbath-teachers, without, at the same time, precipitating these arrangements beyond the real worth of the agents who shall or may cast up one by one, and to those you might rightly commit the management in question.

But what is all in all, is a systematic distribution of time. It is not by irregular efforts, however gigantic, that any great practical achievement is overtaken. It is by the constant recurrence and repetition of small efforts directed to a given object, and resolutely sustained and persevered in. In this way you will work yourself into a deep and cleaving interest in topics which at first may have been repulsive. Edwards's Works supply a rich assortment of such topics ; marks of conversion, marks of a work of the Spirit, original sin, necessity, sacrament, &c. ; see also Butler's " Sermons," Davison's " Prophecy," and many other authors whom I could mention ; but I would rather the concentration of your strength on a few themes, than that you should be a universalist.

I think that there might be a most beneficial expenditure of all your time, and that the interest of every hour of it might be completely filled up between the two objects of, first, a great mental product, and, secondly, a great practical effort in your parish. I do not want to shut out hours of ease and relaxation ; but the fatigue of the other hours will make these last all the more enjoyable. It is a most valuable experience of Brainerd—that the regular distribution of time is essential

312 CORRESPONDENCE OF DR. CHALMERS.

to one's religious prosperity ; and of Elliot—that through faith in Christ Jesus, it is in the power of prayer and of pains to do everything.—Yours most truly, THOMAS CHALMERS.

[In August 1831, the late Mrs. Grant of Laggan received a letter from a lady then in Italy, describing the character of a young Italian Artist, in whom she was much interested, of remarkable genius, but unfortunately imbued with sceptical opinions on religion, which she had in vain endeavoured to remove. She begged that Mrs. Grant would submit a statement of the case to Dr. Chalmers, and solicit the favour of his benevolent aid in suggesting how the erroneous views of the young man might be best combated ; a request which Mrs. Grant with considerable hesitation complied with, by sending her correspondent's letter to Dr. Chalmers. The following answer was returned by Dr. Chalmers to Mrs. Grant.]

No. CCXLVI.—LETTER TO MRS. GRANT OF LAGGAN.

Edinburgh, 2d September 1831.

MY DEAR MADAM,—I am sure you will excuse me from entering in my own person on an argument with one who, from the account you have sent me of him, has yet to acquire the very first elements of a subject on which he speculates so adventurously, and yet with so little information.

I must therefore confine myself to the recommendation of certain books, which, if not read and studied by him, really makes the task which your friend has put into my hand in every way as hopeless as that of teaching optics to the blind, or teaching philosophy to children.

Taylor's " Process of Historical Proof ;" Taylor's " Transmission of Ancient Books to Modern Times ;" Paley's " Evidences of Christianity ;" Lardner's " Credibility ;" " Lardner on Jewish and Heathen Testimonies to the Truth of the Gospel ;" Paley's "Horæ Paulinæ ;" Butler's " Analogy ;" Leslie's " Short and Easy Method with the Deists ;" Littleton's " Conversion of St. Paul."

I hope that the perusal of these may have a favourable effect, though I must confess that the union of so much confidence with so much ignorance tempts me to despair.

That there should be no time to read, and withal such trust in the conclusions of his own confessedly uninformed mind, forms a composition which it is truly most difficult to deal with, and makes it an impracticable task to put down the determined but withal superficial infidelity of our age.—Ever believe me, my dear Madam, yours most truly and with great esteem,   THOMAS CHALMERS.

P.S.—Your friend should continue, however, to treat the person with great tenderness, and to make him the subject of her prayers.—T. C.

No. CCXLVII.—To T. ERSKINE, ESQ. OF LINLATHEN.

Anstruther, 10th August 1818.

MY DEAR SIR,—I was obliged to leave Glasgow on the day of that night in which you were to have visited me, and left a line explanatory of the cause, which was a sudden call to wait on my father during an illness that has since turned out to be his last. He died here on the 26th of last month ; and I propose moving homewards to-morrow.

Be assured that there is nothing that could be more agreeable to me than to enter with you into a regular, though it should not be a frequent correspondence. I derived too much advantage from the personal interview I had with you, not to desire a continuance of intercourse in the only other way it can be maintained when at a distance from each other.

I shall forbear at present giving a full and deliberate opinion on your " Translations of St. James." The doctrine you educe from them I hold to be undeniable and highly important ; and I feel benefit from the view you give of holiness, in that you

2 D

rescue it from the humble office of evidencing our judicial state, and would raise it to an importance that were absolute and terminating. I see that many of our divines lay something like an exclusive stress on the object of making our title clear by our works; whereas the character of being zealous of good works is a character the formation of which is stated as an object in itself of Christ's coming to this world, and is essential to our preparation for the next.

It just occurs to me that in James ii. 18, the contrast between the two terms is of a wider description than between faith in dormancy and faith in action—it is between faith viewed as one distinct object, and works viewed as another. But I trust I shall look over the whole Epistle with greater care, and be able to express myself more fully and decisively respecting it.

My father, I have reason to rejoice, was a thorough Christian. His favourite treatise was the "Theron and Aspasio" of Hervey, where the forensic benefit we have derived from Christ is the main topic of his argument. But does not the principle of self-preservation direct our primary attention to this matter, and should we actually conceive a trust in the Saviour for righteousness, who can say that a transition so much fitted to change and to brighten the prospects of man shall not also bring along with it new affections, new desires, new principle, and all the elements, in short, of regeneration.

The Spirit cometh by the hearing of faith. They who trust in Christ are sealed with the Holy Spirit of promise.—Believe me, my dear sir, yours with great esteem and regard,

THOMAS CHALMERS.

No. CCXLVIII.—To T. ERSKINE, ESQ.

Kirkaldy, 15th October 1818.

MY DEAR SIR,—I am here on an excursion from Glasgow, for the purpose of taking back Mrs. Chalmers who has been spending the whole summer in Fife. You may not yet have heard of the matter which chiefly engrosses the interest and the feelings of the people of Glasgow at this moment :—poor Dr. Balfour was seized with apoplexy on Monday upon George Street, and taken into the nearest house, where he still lies, and is not expected to live another day.

I received your manuscript a few weeks ago, and have read it, I assure you, with great satisfaction. To pronounce upon it critically would require a more elaborate examination than I can possibly afford ; but I can at least say, that I never read James with a more entire impression of the unity of what at one time appeared disjointed, of the significancy of what at one time appeared dark, of the pertinency of what at one time appeared irrelevant, than I have done through the medium of your translation. There is a light, and a power, and a moral impression about your performance, that there is not about the version of the Apostle in our authorized Scriptures ; and if you can substantiate on good philosophical grounds all the reformations that you propose, you will indeed offer a very valuable, as well, I am persuaded, as a very acceptable contribution to Biblical literature. If you have confidence in the soundness of your various renderings, I regard the work as altogether worthy of publication.

You have certainly succeeded in sustaining a more continuous process of argument and reflection by your version than one can discover to be in the common one.

You will confer a great favour upon me by an occasional letter. What I feel the need of is, that power of faith which must ever accompany the reality of faith, and which, if wanting, may well lead us to suspect the reality. What I have long experienced of my own mind is, that it is quite possible to describe the whole range of Christian doctrine in the terms of a consistent and satisfying argumentation—to make use of all the terms in theology, and bring them into good logical arrange-

ment, just as you make use of the symbols of an algebraical
process, and conduct that process in a way that is unexception-
able, while the quantities represented by the symbols are not
at all present to the mind throughout the whole process of the
investigation. I long for more of the life and freshness of an
actual contact with these things—for the kingdom of God as
abundantly in power as it is in word—in short, for such manifestations of the first and elementary ideas, as I am persuaded,
no play or performance of natural talent can ever conduct me
to. It is here that I feel my helplessness—it is here I believe
where the accomplished philosopher is on a footing with the
most untaught and illiterate of the peasantry—it is here, I am
persuaded, where light must be created and sent into our hearts
by the immediate hand of God, instead of being excogitated
by the labouring of the human faculties. I am awake to a
sense of necessity and dependence; and I await the performance of the promise, " Awake, O sinner, and Christ shall give
thee light." It is given to prayer while it is withheld from presumption—it is given often to the intercessions of others, while
it is withheld from all that a man can ask or do for himself;
and believing as I do that when a man goes in quest of Christian truth in proud dependence upon himself, he gives an ungodliness to the very outset of his inquiries; that God must be
acknowledged in this way, as well as in every other, ere He
direct our path. I have too high an opinion of prayer as an
engine of mighty operation, not to feel a desire that I may
have a part and an interest in your prayers, that God may
visit me with such communications of light and of love, as to
give me a distaste for the world, and a spiritual relish of Him
as the strength of my heart and my satisfying portion.

I am in the press just now with a volume of congregational
sermons. I feel the poorness and the barrenness of them all;
and yet somehow or other I have prevailed upon myself thus to

come forward with them. I see a mighty and untrodden interval between the state of my own mind and the spirituality of other Christians; but I have the hope of being the more confirmed by all this in the attitude of the Apostle who had no confidence in himself, but rejoicing in the Lord Jesus was enabled to serve God in the Spirit.

I shall return your manuscript to Mr. Stirling. I hope I have not done wrong in showing it to a neighbour who takes an interest in these things, but who, I am persuaded, will read it with a simple view to his own edification. It is my prayer that you may be useful, and eminently so, in the Church of Christ. What we want is labourers, with or without ordination: either may wield the instrument of God's Word, and in the hands of neither will it return void. Have you seen Edwards's " Treatise on Prayer ?" A season of revival in the Church is generally preceded by a season of prayer. I stand sadly in need of your devotional frame all the day long—of the religion of feeling—of a real sensibility towards Him who is both a just God and a Saviour—who has so wondrously blended in one demonstration the infinity of His love with the infinity of His holiness.—Believe me, my dear Sir, yours most truly,

THOMAS CHALMERS.

No. CCXLIX.—To T. ERSKINE, ESQ.

Edinburgh, 29th December 1843.

MY DEAR SIR,—I read both your letter and that of Madame de Stael with much interest and affection. These are trying and sifting times, but I have the confident hope that good will come out of them. In particular I am most happy to observe that our Free Church ministers are manifesting a vigour and a spirituality which I never before witnessed, even in them, and which, under God, I can only ascribe to their being actuated by the feeling and the conscious freedom of now emancipated men. Meanwhile things are evidently converging to a crisis which I trust will usher in a brighter day both of Christian love and Christian liberty.

I most cordially agree with you in thinking that our journey through Normandy should never be forgotten. In good earnest I assure you that I often look back upon it as the most brilliant and interesting passage of my bygone life, though the death of the poor Duchess casts a deep shade over it.

I should rejoice if we met eye to eye. I feel convinced of a radical and essential unity betwixt us, however diverse and distorting the media might be between our respective visions and certain of those questions on which we may chance to differ. My fatigues compel me now to write by my daughter Grace, who with Mrs. Chalmers desires kindest regards.—I ever am, my dear Sir, yours most truly,   THOMAS CHALMERS.

No. CCL.—To REV. JOHN FOSTER.

Glasgow, 8th November 1821.

MY DEAR SIR,—I lately saw Mr. Jeffrey, the editor of the " Edinburgh Review," and spoke to him at some length about the conduct and character of that widely-spread journal. I told him how much it would add to its usefulness, did he not prohibit all his general contributors from ever touching on the subject of Christianity, and, making room for a theological department, admit an occasional article on that subject from one who was soundly acquainted with it, and able to render it impressively to his readers. My time is so much occupied that I have abandoned that sort of literature entirely. But I took the liberty of suggesting you as one whose occasional contributions would be of eminent service to the work ; and to yourself I add, that through the influence and diffusion of that work, such a direction may be given to your labours as to be of the first consequence to the best of causes. Mr. Jeffrey requested me to

write you, and express the pleasure it would give him could
you be prevailed upon to send him an article ; and I may here
suggest to you, that from the very general character of that
work hitherto, it were greatly better, instead of advocating one
species of Christian partisanship against another, to advocate
revelation in general against infidelity, or to expatiate in those
more Catholic tracts of thought and sentiment, where one might
keep from that sort of controversy which is so often confounded
by a superficial public with the narrowness of sectarianism.

Do let me know what you think of this. I shall only say,
that I would prefer to see your lucubrations in the " Edinburgh"
rather than in the " Eclectic Review," because of the greater
publicity and influence that they would thus attain ; while I
still persist in another opinion that I have long expressed on
the subject of your literary labours, and that is, that I regret
you do not give more of your strength to the rearing of such
works as may come out ostensibly and independently from your
pen—being thoroughly persuaded that you can publish nothing
in this way which will not prove a permanent accession to the
Christian literature of our country.

I can truly say for myself that I read no compositions
with greater excitement than your own. I perused both your
" Missionary Sermon" and your book on " Popular Ignorance"
with unmeasured delight ; and one passage more especially, of
the latter, has kept a very tenacious hold of me, that in which
you adventured, and with marvellous success, to pourtray the
popular imagination of God—a description that came home so
much to my own consciousness as to assure me how idolatrous
and mean were all my conceptions of the Deity.

There is one thing more that I beg to propose to you ere I am
done. I am aware of your taste for landscape, and of the full
gratification it would find in the scenery of our Highlands. I
have myself gone a very little way into that sublime and

interesting region, and I would most willingly give up three weeks to the enterprise of penetrating right through to the most northerly point of Scotland, were it in the capacity of a guide and companion to you. I beg that you would think of coming to Glasgow next summer, and taking up your abode with me till we set out on this expedition.

Meanwhile you will oblige me greatly by as speedy an answer as you can afford to this communication. Mrs. Chalmers joins in kindest regards to you.—I am, my dear Sir, yours very affectionately,   THOMAS CHALMERS.

No. CCLI.—To Rev. Dr. Ryland.

Glasgow, 18*th February* 1818.

My dear Sir,—I return you many thanks for the kind present of "Fuller's Life," and also for your very excellent pamphlet on "Antinomianism,"—both of which I received from the hands of your son.

I can assure you that I read the latter with much interest and pleasure. It revived all my recollections of the excellent Jonathan Edwards, to whose principles on the subject of Freewill I have long been a decided convert. You have given a very clear and judicious exposition indeed, of the perfect consistency which obtains between the absolute sovereignty of God on the one hand, and the fitness of bringing forward the urgency of Gospel calls and Gospel invitations on the other. I trust that your performance will do much good. It reminds me of your conversation when I had the pleasure of meeting you at Bristol, and which I shall not soon forget. I feel greatly indebted to you for the question you proposed to put to him who said, "I have come unto Christ,"—"*What have you gotten from Him?*"

I rejoiced in recognising it as a very prevalent feature in your connexion, your horror at Antinomianism;—and it is my prayer that, both by doctrine and example, you may succeed more and more in vindicating the truth as it is in Jesus, as being, indeed, altogether according to godliness.

I have read nothing with greater excitement for a very long time than Hall's "Sermon" on the late lamented death. It is, indeed, a very rich and wonderful composition, and I think more impregnated with theology than any of his former works. It whets the appetite more than ever for a volume of congregational sermons from him. Do wrestle this point with him till you have prevailed. I read lately his and your excellent prefaces to his father's work.

Mr. Foster is now in your neighbourhood. I know nothing that would more interest me than a communication from him. I carried away with me a very great affection for him, and I retain it. There appeared a vile unchristian attack on him lately in one of our Magazines; and I heard nothing around me but indignation against it. He has many admirers in this part of the country. Your son I see occasionally. I entreat a part in your prayers. Oh, that we felt more and more a child-like dependence on the teachings of the Holy Spirit! May God prosper your abundant labours, and cause you to rejoice in the fruit of them.—I am, my dear Sir, yours most truly,

THOMAS CHALMERS.

No. CCLII.—MR. J. E. RYLAND.*

Edinburgh, 2d March 1831.

MY DEAR SIR,—I received your melancholy intimation of Mr. Hall's death with the greatest emotion, and consider it as a severe blow to the Church universal—as an event to be deplored not by his own flock and family alone, but by all the friends of our common Christianity.

I felt a particular interest in your narrative of his death; and was struck with the coincidence between his dying testi-

* Author of the "Life of Foster," &c.

monies and those of Fuller, Dwight, and others of our best established Christians. The "humble hope" of his last moments deserves to be enshrined among the most precious of those *memorabilia* which he has given to the world.

Will you tell Mrs. Hall (to whom I expect to write shortly) that I do feel a melancholy satisfaction in her having selected me, as one of those friends of her venerable and illustrious husband, who should be especially apprized of the sad event that afflicts and solemnizes us all.—Believe me, my dear sir, yours most truly,   THOMAS CHALMERS.

No. CCLIII.—MR. J. E. RYLAND.

Edinburgh, 17th November 1843.

MY DEAR SIR,—I should have acknowledged long ago your letter of the 17th of October, announcing the death of John Foster—a man of gigantic intellect, and whose writings have earned for him an imperishable name ; but who I trust is now enjoying a better and a higher immortality. I ever had the greatest veneration both for him and Mr. Hall, who, along with Dr. Ryland, Andrew Fuller, Drs. Carey, Marshman, and Ward, made up altogether a very bright constellation, and which serves to signalize the Baptists of England more than any other denomination which I at present recollect.

I forget whether Mr. Sheppard of Frome is a Baptist. I am much interested by this renewal of our correspondence. It is now twenty-one years since we met at Bristol, and I am now made to understand by your letter that you are settled at Northampton.

Mrs. Chalmers unites with me in kindest remembrances, and I entreat you to believe me, my dear Sir, yours very truly,   THOMAS CHALMERS.

No. CCLIV.—To Mrs. Paul.

St. Andrews, 20th October 1827.

My dear Mrs. Paul,—I have read the MS. on Prophecy which you kindly put into my hand, and I can assure you with a strong conviction of its soundness. I perfectly agree with the writer in thinking that there has been a very culpable negligence of this important department of that Scripture whereof it has been said, that all is profitable. I myself am in for a full share of the blame, and I do hope that I shall not merely feel the obligation of giving more earnest heed unto prophecy, but that I shall henceforth act upon it. The perusal of your paper has freshened the impulse which I received some months ago from reading the work by Irving, and I certainly have of late attained a growing sense of the duty which attaches to this branch of sacred study. I am now reading in ordinary the Book of Isaiah, and derive occasional aid from M'Culloch's "Lectures ;" he is not a millenarian, which I am now very much inclined to be ; and the other day read with great pleasure the 26th chapter, the latter verses of which appear to describe the impotency of human and ordinary efforts to Christianize the world, (verse 18,) and then (verse 19) the commencement of the great era which is ushered in by the first resurrection.— Believe me, my dear madam, yours very affectionately,

THOMAS CHALMERS.

No. CCLV.—To Rev. C. Bridges.

Edinburgh, 2d January 1834.

My dear Sir,—I gladly avail myself of the opportunity which the Christmas holidays afford me of acknowledging your most esteemed letter of October last, as when engaged in teaching my classes I find both my strength and time very much engrossed, having two distinct courses of lectures and upwards of 200 students to deal with.

I feel the greatest value for your kind and instructive communication, and more particularly for those parts of it which I
can turn to a useful purpose, whether in the way of suggestion
or of warning, as to the special business of my own profession.
I deeply feel my need of effort and prayer, that my whole course
may be more and more spiritualized, assured as I am of the
possibility of delivering all the lessons of theology in the
strictest form of sound words, and with the fullest adherence
to the letter of the truth as it is in Jesus, while the real unction
and vitality of the Gospel spirit may be altogether wanting. I
shall feel the utmost value in connexion with this all-important
object both for your advices and your prayers. It is only by a
manifestation from Him who is the Sun of Righteousness that
the demonstrations of a professor can be brightened from the
moonlight to the sunshine, of which you have so impressively
told me, and have not only the greater light, but also the heat
of the higher luminary imparted to them.

I have a distinct lectureship this winter on the methods and
the machinery of Christian education, which subject leads me
not only to the vindication of religious establishments, but also
to what may be termed the spiritual tactics of a parish ; and I
can assure you that there is not one sentiment which you have
either written or spoken in my hearing which I more thoroughly
sympathize with than the mighty importance of maintaining unbroken the conjunction between the ministerial and
the pastoral. I think myself prepared to shew that it is the
dissolution of this sacred union that, instrumentally speaking,
has so weakened the influence of the Christian ministry all over
the land, and more especially in our large towns. When on this
subject I shall have occasion to make extracts from your admirable work on the various official and professional duties of
clergymen.

I often think of your parish, which, as a hallowed abode of

peace and piety, supplies me with far more interesting recollections than anything I have seen in England. May the Giver
of all grace continue to bless, and that abundantly, your ministrations among the dear cottage families around you, and pour
down such a blessing that there may be no room to receive it.

I beg that you will offer my best regards to Mrs. Bridges,
and to Miss Wakefield, if still with you. In their work and
labour of love amongst the young, and particularly among your
own dear children, may the pleasure of the Lord prosper in their
hands.—I ever am, my dear Sir, yours with greatest esteem and
attachment, THOMAS CHALMERS.

No. CCLVI.—To REV. C. BRIDGES.

Burntisland, 12th April 1836.

MY DEAR SIR,—I take great blame to myself in having
deferred so long to write to you. It is true that I am much engrossed, and not so able for fatigue as I have been ; but nothing
can justify the remissness of my correspondence with one whose
communications, and, above all, whose prayers, I so highly value.

I have seen Mr. Drummond since I last received your letter.
I highly approve of your proposal to publish Fox's " Martyr-
ology," though, I fear, I can do little to promote its success in
Edinburgh. I am completely over-done, and am obliged to
take flight into the retirement of the country.

I hope you see Mr. Bickersteth occasionally—for I should
like that, the first time you met him, you would deliver this
message from me. When I wrote him last I had only entered
on the perusal of his work on " Prophecy," and not proceeded
far in it ; and certainly, from the beginning of his volume, I
understood that he was doubtful on the subject of Christ's personal reign—in which sentiment I stated that I agreed with
him. I now find, however, that he is decidedly for that opinion ;
and I am very far from being decidedly against it. But I have

not yet got beyond Mede upon this question, who certainly left it indeterminate, though I am now far more confident than I wont to be, that there is to be a coming of Christ which precedes the millennium—a millennium to be ushered into the world by a series of dreadful visitations, for which, I fear, we are fast ripening—in the train of which all our present structures, whether civil or ecclesiastical, will give way, that room might be made for a universal empire of truth and righteousness.

I beg my most grateful regards to Mrs. Bridges ; and if Miss Wakefield be still with you, I would offer her, too, my best acknowledgments.—Ever believe me, my dear Sir, yours most cordially,   THOMAS CHALMERS.

No. CCLVII.—LETTER TO THE REV. HORACE BONAR.

Edinburgh, 9th January 1847.

MY DEAR SIR,—Would you allow me to suggest "Alexander on Isaiah" as an admirable book for your review.   As far as I have looked into it, it seems a work of extraordinary merit.   The author is an American professor at Princeton. I feel quite assured that your brother, were he to address himself to the work, would go through it *con amore*.   I cannot close this communication without expressing my entire satisfaction with the doctrines and the progress of what I call your South Country School, of whom I hold yourself, Mr. Purves of Jedburgh, and Mr. Campbell of Melrose, to be the trio of its representatives.   It is not of your prophetical, but of your theological views that I now speak, though to the former also I approximate much nearer than I did in my younger days.*

---

* Ps. L. 1–6.—" This is a remarkable psalm, and the subject of it seems to lie within the domain of unfulfilled prophecy.   There has been no appearance yet from Mount Zion at all corresponding with that made from Mount Sinai.   And I am far more inclined to the literal interpretation of this psalm, than to that which would restrict it to the mere preaching of the Gospel in the days of the apostles. It looks far more like *the descent of the Son of Man on the Mount of Olives*, with

But speaking of the latter, nothing can be more precious than the manner in which you expound the things that are *freely* given to us of God. I feel assured that no other doctrine will regenerate the world.—Give my kindest regards to Mrs. Bonar, and ever believe me, my dear sir, yours very truly,

THOMAS CHALMERS.

LETTERS TO DR. JAMES BROWN.

No. CCLVIII.

Edinburgh, 30th August 1833.

MY DEAR SIR,—It is owing entirely to my having been so long from home, that I have not till now requested your ac-

all the *accompaniments* of a *Jewish conversion,* and a *first resurrection,* and a *destruction of the assembled hosts of Antichrist.*"—(*Posth. Works,* vol. iii. p. 51.)

Ps. LXVIII. 18–35.—" Mixed up with all the literalities of the typical, the great antitype shines forth in this high, sacred composition. We have positive evidence for Christ in this psalm, in Eph. iv. 8,—after which we need be at no loss for objects in the future triumph and victory of His cause adequate to the loftiest expressions which we here meet with. . . . There is every likelihood of allusions here to the great contest of the Book of Revelation. . . . But God has in reserve for His people still another restoration. He will bring them again as of old, from Bashan and the Red Sea to their own land. His people will '*see Him whom they have pierced,*' *perhaps when his feet stand on the Mount of Olives,* and Jerusalem will again become the great central sanctuary by becoming the metropolis of the Christian world."—(*Ibid.* p. 69.)

ISA. LXV. 17–25.—" It is delightful to mark how an expression so general as that of the new heavens and the new earth, and therefore of the great and general renovation, should be blended with the expression of God's special kindness to his ancient people—proving that the Jews are to bear a prominent part in the establishment of the next economy. We are greatly wanting in the details of the millennium ; and perhaps from the want of Scriptural data for the determination of them. We cannot think of those who bear part in the first resurrection that they will again die ; but will none of the righteous die ? And if not, what is meant by the child dying a hundred years old ? And in contrast with him, the sinner, who, though he should live a hundred years, will be accursed. We doubt not that there will be *two contemporaneous societies at that period*—the righteous and the wicked, who are without, and will not be permitted to hurt or to destroy in all God's holy mountain. Again, will there be a change in the laws of animal nature—that the carnivorous shall cease being so ; or are these things only figurative ? The earth, with its curse fully removed, will be greatly more productive, and so as that men shall not labour in vain, as now."—(*Ibid.* p. 339.)

ceptance of my last work ; and I feel very much flattered by your favourable opinion of it. This is but the second day of my return from England.

I agree in all you say on the subject of Mr. Duncan's work, with the exception of your single remark upon its dedication, than which he could have done nothing more rightly and appropriately. It is the common feeling of us both, that whatever of the academic spirit, or of the purely academic enthusiasm, either of us may possess, we are far more indebted for it to you, than to all other teachers put together. Of all my living instructors, I have ever reckoned first yourself, then Professor Robison of Edinburgh, and, lastly, Dr. Hunter of St. Andrews, as far the most influential in the formation both of my taste and intellectual habits. I have read the Preface, and I think the book promises vastly well. My two eldest daughters, who have mastered the first four books of Euclid, are to attempt the perusal of it ; and I mean to accompany them. Such is my confidence in Mr. Duncan's powers of lucid conveyance, while he at the same time sustains the purity and dignity of the science, that I have no doubt of their fully understanding him.

I shall do all I can for the volume, but that is little. A review from your pen in the pages of the " Edinburgh " would make its fortune.—With best regards to Mrs. and Miss Brown, I am, my dear sir, yours most truly,   THOMAS CHALMERS.

No. CCLIX.

Edinburgh, 16th February 1834.

MY DEAR SIR,—I agree with you in thinking that the appointment of Ivory would shed very great *éclat* on our University. Whether he would make a good working professor, I know not ; but I shall take every fair opportunity of stating what I do know of him as an illustrious savant.

On the subject of your second note, which I presume to be yours though subscribed only with your initials, I agree with you in deprecating the universality of popular preaching throughout the Church, if by this is meant flimsy, or vulgar, or untasteful, or irrational preaching. But there is one ingredient of popularity which I should like to see in all sermons, grounded as it is on the adaptation of the peculiar doctrines of Christianity to the felt wants and exigencies of our moral nature, and to the workings and aspirations of which nature the peasant is as feelingly alive as the philosopher. For example, his conscience tells him, often more powerfully and just as intelligently, that he is under the condemnation of a violated law; and so it falls with all the greater acceptance upon his ear, that unto him a Saviour is born. The doctrine of the atonement, in fact, urged affectionately on the acceptance of the people, and held forth as the great stepping-stone, by which one and all are welcome to enter into reconciliation and a *new life*, (for a fully declared gospel is the very reverse of Antinomianism,) I hold to form the main staple of all good and efficient pulpit-work. I need not say how much my recent illness has endeared to me the propitiated forgiveness of the New Testament—a forgiveness to which we cannot resort too early, and on which we cannot, if honestly desirous of conforming ourselves to the whole word and will of God, cast too confidently the whole burden of our reliance.

The interest you have taken in me inclines me to mention, that on Saturday week I received the notification from Paris of my appointment as a Corresponding Member of the Royal Institute of France. The place which they have assigned to me is in the Academy or Department of the Moral and Political Sciences.—I am, my dear sir, yours most gratefully,

THOMAS CHALMERS.

No. CCLX.

Burntisland, 30th August 1836.

MY DEAR SIR,—It is with no common interest and satisfaction that I received your kind note ; and am much gratified with your remembrance of me, who have fallen so much short of my own desires, and what, had it been possible, I should have regarded as one of my most incumbent duties, that of testifying, both by my frequent calls and frequent inquiries, how deep the respect, and how cordial is the attachment, I have ever felt for you. I need not say how much I am gratified by the approval you have given to my last published sermon. I have long thought that great injustice has been done to the theology of the New Testament, by the inadequate representations of Orthodoxy in regard to its practical character ; and that if these were more insisted on, it might serve to recommend its precious overtures of welcome and good-will ; its proclamation of forgiveness ; its full and free amnesty, even to the chief of sinners ; its grand disclosure of pardon to all who will, through the medium of an atonement, by which the law is magnified, while the transgressors of the law are taken into full reconciliation ; and so a fairer exhibition of the righteousness of the Christian system might gain the acquiescence of many in these doctrines of salvation and grace, by which so many are nauseated, because they do not perceive the goodness and the virtue with which the acceptance of these doctrines is inseparably associated.

I cannot express the earnestness I feel that you, my dear Sir, may enjoy the comforts here, and be admitted to all the triumphs hereafter of a firmer faith in the Gospel of our Lord and Saviour Jesus Christ.

With kindest regards to Mrs. and Miss Brown, ever believe me, my dear Sir, yours most cordially and with great esteem,

THOMAS CHALMERS.

No. CCLXI.—To Mrs. Brown.

Burntisland, 13*th November* 1836.

My dear Mrs. Brown,—I cannot adequately express the deep emotion which I felt on receiving the melancholy intelligence of Dr. Brown's death—one of my most respected and earliest friends, and of whom I have often said, that of all the professors and instructors with whom I ever had to do, he is the one who most powerfully impressed me ; and to the ascendency of whose mind over me, along with that of Professor Robison's of Edinburgh, I owe more in the formation of my tastes and habits, and in the guidance and government of my literary life, than to that of all the other academic men whose classes I ever attended. But, in addition to his public lessons, I had the privilege of being admitted to a long intimacy with your departed husband, and of enjoying the benefits, as well as the charms, of his most rich and eloquent conversation ; besides receiving from him many written communications, which I have kept by themselves, and prize as a great literary treasure. Of these, the most interesting is the last, received from him not many weeks ago, and on the most momentous of all subjects. You may be well assured that, when such a master-mind as his thought fit to disclose itself on the high themes of religion, I could not but feel alive to the manifestation of a sensibility on this greatest of all concerns, the knowledge of which I now feel to be inexpressibly precious.

It is my earnest prayer that you and your daughter may be supported on this trying occasion by Him who is the Giver of all comfort, and who alone can sanctify and bless His own visitation. May we all be led to the wise and right consideration of our latter end ; and laying hold of the offered atonement of the Gospel, may we henceforth sit at the feet of Him, who alone hath the gift, and who alone hath the words of life everlasting.

I exceedingly regret that I was altogether disabled by circumstances from attending the funeral. Either to-morrow or Tuesday I hope to call upon you at Beaumont Place.

With my best regards to Miss Brown, I entreat you to believe me, my dear Madam, yours with deepest sympathy and respect,   THOMAS CHALMERS.

[*Rectory, Hornsey,* 16*th August* 1852.—MY DEAR SIR,—A discussion took place at the close of 1837 at the monthly meetings of the Society for the Promoting Christian Knowledge, in the course of which the proper designation of the Episcopal Church in Scotland came to be considered. Some members, who sympathized with the very High Church party, desired to describe the Scottish bishops as bishops of the Church *in* Scotland, or *of* Scotland, thereby ignoring the Established Church. Eventually it was determined, by the recommendation of the bishop of London, to make use of the designation which the bishops claimed to themselves—"Bishops of the Scottish Episcopal Church," by which no offence could be given to any one. Thinking that some incorrect rumour might reach Dr. Chalmers of the discussion, I wrote to acquaint him with the true state of the case. The accompanying letter is his answer.—With kind compliments, I am, yours truly obliged,   RICHARD HARVEY.

The Rev. Dr. Hanna.]

No. CCLXII.—LETTER TO REV. MR. HARVEY.

Edinburgh, 6*th February* 1838.

MY DEAR SIR,—I owe you many apologies for my delay in replying to your letter; but I am really borne down by arrears of correspondence, and business of various sorts.

I regret that anything should have occurred which might mar the cordiality that ought to subsist between the two Establishments. There are several here who will feel the disownal of us far more deeply than I can at all sympathize with. I feel confident that the exclusive principle which was manifested at your meeting must wear out of credit with the ministers of the Church of England; and that a notion so utterly senseless and fantastic will at length be entertained by so very few, as that we shall at length afford to look on them with the most benignant complacency.

The epithet "Episcopalian" would have saved the credit of the meeting, and, I should imagine, have satisfied all parties. " The Episcopal Church either of or in Scotland."

When you write Mr. Le Bas, offer him my kindest regards. I rejoice to hear of his preferment ; and I hope that I shall meet him in my visit to London, which, if God will, I propose shall be towards the end of April. I have not forgotten my last delightful visit to Hornsey ; and I look forward with the greatest pleasure to the renewal of it.—With most respectful acknowledgments to Mrs. Harvey, I ever am, my dear Sir, yours most gratefully,   THOMAS CHALMERS.

No. CCLXIII.—To MR. JOHN SHEPPARD.

Edinburgh, 25*th April* 1833.

MY DEAR SIR,—I should have acknowledged long ago the kind gift of your acceptable volume,* which I have been perusing with very great interest and pleasure ; and which, highly as I esteemed your " Thoughts on Devotion," I regard as a far richer production, abounding as it does in the views of a deeper experience, and having in it much greater fulness, as a repository of pearls and precious things. I have taken the liberty of referring to it in my " Bridgewater Essay," now in the press ; and I know that a review of it has appeared in our " Scottish Presbyterian," favourable, though not equal to my own impression of its merits.

My habit in reading a book is to mark with approbation, or the contrary, as I move along. I find that I have given my most intense approval to the following passages :—page 18 ; bottom of page 20 ; top of page 157. These I single out as

---

* " Essays on Christian Encouragement," &c.

being double marks. The single marks are innumerable, and yet represent, but feebly, the delight I have felt in the perusal of your volume.

I have not, though quite honest in the marks I affix to all my readings, jotted down a single passage as questionable or that I differ from.—Ever believe me, my dear Sir, yours most respectfully and with greatest regard, THOMAS CHALMERS.

No. CCLXIV.—To Mr. JOHN SHEPPARD.

Edinburgh, 16*th November* 1833.

MY VERY DEAR SIR,—Your very kind letter of the 30th of July I should have acknowledged long ago ; but I have been a great wanderer this season, and for a good many months have been marvellously little at home.

I need not say how much I have been gratified by your remarks of approbation and kindness on my last work—an abundant compensation, I assure you, for the hostility which I have been doomed to experience so abundantly at the hands of the English reviewers, who, with the exception, as far as I have yet seen them, of the " British Critic," seem bent on running me down. One ought not to be sensitive about a matter of this sort, and it would argue a particularly morbid constitution not to be abundantly comforted under all their severities by the approval of the wise and the good.

I have received your Sermon on the death of Mr. Hughes, whom I had the pleasure of knowing. I am much delighted with it ; and as I have only room for one remark, I was greatly struck with your felicitous illustration in page 25, on the hostility by which the British and Foreign Bible Society was assailed, and where you have so justly and forcibly characterized, in particular, the attacks that were brought to bear against it from this pugnacious quarter of the island.

I cannot express the tenderness I feel in being made to

understand from your letter that you have been labouring under depression ; I wish I could prevail upon you, my dear Sir, to look more objectively, and less subjectively, than you appear to do—more to the outer truths, if I may so express it, of Christianity, and less to the inner lineaments which these may have impressed on the tablet of your own character. I should not feel myself justified in offering this advice, did I not feel assured that, after all, it is by the direct exercise of faith, that all these virtues of the new obedience are engendered within us which furnish the materials of a reflex self-examination. I have derived great comfort from a little tract, entitled " Brief Thoughts on the Gospel, and the Hindrances to Believe it."

With the greatest esteem and regard, I ever am, my dear Sir, yours most truly, THOMAS CHALMERS.

No. CCLXV.—LETTER TO DR. SYMINGTON.

Edinburgh, 9th October 1838.

MY DEAR SIR,—I should have replied sooner to your kind letter of some weeks past, but I was unwilling to sit down till I had begun the perusal of your work on the Atonement.

I am now reading it with great interest, and, I trust, with a practical and good impression. It is indeed that doctrine of great price, the very name of which is as ointment poured forth.

I hope I shall be able to write you at greater length on the subject after I have completed the perusal of your substantial and masterly volume. Indeed, I believe I shall have to write you at any rate early in November. Meanwhile, I am marking all the passages as I go along, and will furnish you with a list of them either in writing or when we meet.

My preference in the treatment of a subject is for an exhibition of the direct proofs first ; after which, I do not object that other arguments, after being brought forward as preliminary considerations, should be exhibited in the form of collateral or subsidiary arguments. For example, I agree with Paley in the first sentence of his "Evidences," where he pleads for an immediate entry on the strongest credentials of revelation, and that anterior to any consideration of its necessity. But this question of arrangement is too unwieldy for discussion in a single letter; and I think the chief objection to the usual arrangement is done away when the prefatory views which you exhibit are held forth more in the light of presumptions than as the initial steps of a logical process, which last method has the effect of placing the less obvious probabilities at the basis of the argument, and so of making the whole weak throughout, because weak radically.

On the whole, I feel quite assured, and the assurance will gather in strength as I advance in my reading of your work, that it forms a most sound and valuable contribution to our professional literature.—With best regards to Mrs. Symington and your family, I am, my dear Sir, yours most respectfully and truly,   THOMAS CHALMERS.

No. CCLXVI.—LETTER TO REV. THOMAS BARTLETT.

Edinburgh, 25th January 1839.

MY DEAR SIR,—Your "Life of Butler" came to me about a week ago; and I suspended all other reading till I should achieve the perusal of it. My engagements leave me very little time for this indulgence; but I have now finished the Narrative, and cannot forbear writing you now, though I have not yet entered on the Abridgment which you make of the "Analogy." I mean, however, to look over this also; and should anything occur to me, in respect of its execution, I will send you a second letter.

But recurring to the Memoir, I have perused it with great eagerness, and a very intense feeling of satisfaction and in-

terest. My veneration for Butler gives a magnitude even to
the minutest traits which are recorded of him, insomuch that
I feel as if I had made a real acquisition by knowing of his
fast riding on a black horse, and his habit of stopping and
turning to his companion with whom he was engaged in talk.

Allow me to say that I look on what is peculiarly your own
part as done with great taste and great talent ; and it is not
with the spirit of flattery, but of justice, that I tell you, labouring as you did under the disadvantage of scanty materials, that
the work is greatly indebted to your own reflections, that
you have imparted to it a strong literary interest, and have
managed to infuse into it as great a biographical charm as the
fewness of the known incidents would allow.

Page 222.—I shall here transcribe an extract from my class-
book on Butler's " Analogy." Dr. Ryland, in his edition of
" Andrew Fuller's Works," says in a note,—" I heard Mr. Venn
of Yelling give an account, however, to Mr. Beveridge, who related his conversation with one of his chaplains, to whom the
bishop remarked, ' that it was an awful thing to appear before
the Moral Governor of the world ;' when the chaplain, whose
views were more clearly evangelical, referred him to the
obedience of Christ by which many are made righteous ; and
the dying bishop exclaimed, ' O, this is comfortable,' and so
expired." What I now give brings Butler's expression still
nearer to that at page 226.

Even if you had done no more than collect the scattered
remains of such references as were made to Butler by various
Authors during his life and after his death, that of itself would
have justified the volume ; for though these references are
taken from printed books or pamphlets, they, even at this time
of day, are as little known as if they had been extracted by
you from manuscripts and letters.

I shall only add, that nothing can be more agreeable than

2 F

your kind notice of myself. Pages 335, 336, brought back to me
a very vivid and most interesting recollection.*—With my best
regards to Mrs Bartlett, believe me ever, my dear sir, yours
most respectfully and cordially,   THOMAS CHALMERS.

[*Princeton*, 10*th March* 1848.—REVEREND AND DEAR SIR,—Having
learned from the public journals that you were engaged in preparing a
Memoir of the late great and good Dr. Chalmers, and that you desired to
have letters which he had written transmitted to you, it occurred to me to
doubt whether I had not a duty to discharge in reference to this request.

Though I enjoyed the precious privilege of corresponding with him, yet
but few letters passed between us. We were both too busy, and especially he
in the great concerns in which he was called to act, to devote much time
to letter-writing. I think the letters which I received from him were not
more than *three*. Of one of them, and the longest, I enclose herewith a copy.
The others have, I scarcely know how, passed out of my possession ; for, as
the handwriting of *such a man* could not fail of being the object of intense
curiosity and of deep interest with the multitudes on this side of the Atlantic, who admired his talents, and venerated his name, I found it difficult to
retain in my possession any scrap that bore the impress of his hand.

In one of my letters to this beloved and illustrious man, I begged him,
with an importunity never addressed by me to any other person, to favour
the American Churches with a visit. I know not that I ever had so ardent a desire to behold the face and to hear the voice of any other human
being : and now, painfully aware, of course, that I can never enjoy this
privilege, I feel a kind of solicitude that I never felt before, for the accomplishment of the great biographical trust committed to your hands.

I rejoice to have seen all the works of this venerable servant of Christ,
that have been placed within my reach ; but I must say, that those from
which I have received the deepest impression of the real glory of his character, have been his *posthumous writings*. Of the vigour and elevation of his
mind, I had enjoyed proof enough from the many volumes which had long
since fallen under my notice. But from some of his most unstudied writings which have lately met my eye, I have received impressions of his
moral and heavenly grandeur of soul, greatly beyond those which I had
received from the multiplied and rich productions of his genius. I thank
his God and my God that I have been permitted to see these last effusions

* See Memoirs, vol. iii. pp. 388, 389.

of his heart and his pen. They have much enlarged my views of his Christian greatness, and, I hope, have not been without benefit to my own soul.

But among all those who will take such a deep and tender interest in your work, there are, perhaps, few less likely than myself to enjoy the pleasure of seeing it completed. Being far advanced in my 79th year, and daily admonished by many infirmities that I must soon " put off this tabernacle," it is not very probable that I shall survive the publication of your precious Memoir. But be it so : this will be of small importance to any one. Many in both hemispheres will read it, enjoy it, and be, I trust, the better for it ; and in the meanwhile I shall be, I hope, so happy as to join the great and beloved man himself, whom all have for a time lost, and to see him face to face in a more enlightened and happy world, and to unite with him in the endless praise and enjoyment of that precious Saviour, whose atoning sacrifice and perfect righteousness are " all my salvation and all my desire."—I am, Reverend and dear Sir, most respectfully, your friend and brother in Christian bonds,   SAMUEL MILLER.

To the Rev. Wm. Hanna.]

No. CCLXVII.—To REV. DR. SAMUEL MILLER.

Edinburgh, 28th *December* 1840.

MY DEAR SIR,—I owe you many apologies for not having replied sooner to your letter of the 28th of January of last year. The truth is, that my whole attention has been absorbed by the questions and the difficulties of our own Church ; and I, positively, have had no remaining strength or time for the American controversy, of which you have sent me so full and interesting an account in your kind communication. It is well, however, that there was no immediate practical necessity for giving one's mind to the subject, seeing that, so far as I know, there was no application made by your seceding party for a recognition of their views by the General Assembly of the Church of Scotland.

I hope you received a former letter of mine on the subject of your book respecting the " Eldership," which I have ever recommended to my classes as the best I know on its own especial topic, beside being an admirable general vindication of the Presbyterian polity. I am much interested by your argument for the separation of the two orders of elders and deacons, the conjunction of which I have ever deprecated as the most incongruous of all pluralities.

With earnest prayer for your continued public usefulness and personal comfort, and in humble hope that we shall meet in heaven, I entreat you to believe me, my dear Sir, yours most respectfully and cordially,   THOMAS CHALMERS.

No. CCLXVIII.—To REV. THOMAS GRINFIELD, CLIFTON.

Burntisland, 28th April 1841.

MY DEAR SIR,—It is impossible not to be highly gratified by your letter of the 20th, in which you speak so favourably of my " Treatise on Natural Theology." I labour under the discountenance of one principal Review, and the positive hostility of another. First, the " Edinburgh," chiefly (I believe) from a difference in our politics : secondly, the " Quarterly," whose editor, a Scotchman, has been my unrelenting adversary for more than twenty years. It is therefore all the more pleasing when a literary and professional man like yourself gives his attention to my various theses, and records a favourable impression of them.—Believe me ever, my dear Sir, yours very truly,   THOMAS CHALMERS.

No. CCLXIX.—To REV. THOMAS GRINFIELD, CLIFTON.

Burntisland, 16th June 1841.

MY DEAR SIR,—I should have much sooner acknowledged your last of May 1st ; but I have been in feeble health, and much and painfully engrossed with the troubles of our Church.

I got an interdict served on me this day which I mean to disregard ; and on the identical principle which would decide an English Bishop to disregard the mandate of a civil court, either to admit or exclude a man from holy orders.

I read your pamphlet* with great interest a few days after its arrival, and cannot but augur great good from the establishment in your important city, of such an Association as that before which it was read. I was much pleased with the " Lecture;" and while I thank you most cordially for your most kind mention of myself, I must also express my satisfaction at the testimony you give, and which you have so well established, to the harmony of the two faculties of reason and imagination; an important principle, truly, and sadly overlooked by those heartless Statists and Utilitarians, who think that nothing can be true which is beautiful, and nothing beautiful which is true.

You have succeeded, though against the authority of Samuel Johnson, in demonstrating that sacred subjects admit of being represented in the style and with all the effect of the highest poetry.—Ever believe me, my dear Sir, yours most gratefully and cordially, THOMAS CHALMERS.

No. CCLXX.—To REV. THOMAS GRINFIELD, CLIFTON.

Burntisland, 1st *September* 1841.

MY DEAR SIR,—Your letter has been too long unanswered; but we are still in the thick of our Church contests, with a majority (I hope and believe) of our Establishment in readiness to give up their connexion with it, rather than submit our ecclesiastical affairs to the Erastian control of the civil power.

I gave orders to my bookseller to send for your acceptance each volume of the series as it comes out. I expect vol. xxi. to be published on the 1st of October. It consists of altogether new matter, and on a subject which I should like to be well understood in England, that of Pauperism—a question far from being either practically or doctrinally settled in either of the two countries.

* " Lecture on Imagination and Poetry, with a Special Reference to the Poetry of the Bible," delivered before the Bristol Book Association.

The manifold distractions of our Church controversy have interrupted the forthcoming of my works, which will now be resumed.   I feel that any vigour I ever had, whether in litera-ture or in public life, is rapidly abating.   There is a higher and more satisfying pursuit than either, and in which I pray that God by His grace might advance and perfect us both.   May our souls prosper and be in health ; and for this greatest and best of all communications, I would seek more and more unto Him who alone hath the words and alone hath the gift of life everlasting.—I ever am, my dear Sir, yours very truly,

THOMAS CHALMERS.

No. CCLXXI.—To REV. THOMAS GRINFIELD, CLIFTON.

16th December 1841.

MY DEAR SIR,—I received your " Syllabus of Lectures on Milton," and feel quite sure that your converse in this mode with the citizens of Bristol must have a refining and elevating influence on the public mind of your city.   I take your friendly advice as very kind, prompted, as I am sure it is, by the breathings of a real wish for my safety and wellbeing.

I am always delighted by a letter from you, being ever, my dear Sir, yours most affectionately and with great esteem,

THOMAS CHALMERS.

No. CCLXXII.—To REV. HENRY BELL.

Edinburgh, 16th January 1836.

MY DEAR SIR,—I have just time to request your acceptance of a copy of the fourth edition of my " Bridgewater Treatise."

I look back with great pleasure and much thankfulness to our Matlock visit, and to all the kindness we received from you —a pleasure only marred by the recollection of my own im-patience of feeling at the delay in our getting off, from some mistake of the coachman.   What a bright and beautiful world we live in, and how abundant in all the means of enjoyment, but for the sad perversity of our own distempered spirits !

Mrs. Chalmers, who has been long an invalid, joins me with Eliza in kindest remembrances both to yourself and Mrs. Bell. —Ever believe me, my dear Sir, yours very affectionately and truly,   THOMAS CHALMERS.

No. CCLXXIII.—To REV. HENRY BELL.

Edinburgh, 28th October 1846.

MY DEAR SIR,—I have read so much of your volume, and like it exceedingly. I think there is great beauty in its composition, and that its literary merits stand very high. But I was still more struck with the amount of thought in it, and more especially with the instruction deduced from the passages, or rather from the clauses that you comment upon. I have marked particularly what suggests a new argument for the plenary and universal inspiration of the Bible. I rather regret the anti-Calvinism that you have discovered ; but let that pass. I have finished lecture second, and am only sorry that at the commencement of my winter duties, my perusal of your work must go on very slowly. I have no doubt of its favourable reception.

I am much interested by what you state of Professor Lee's " New Theory of Hebrew Tenses." I should like that you made known that your views for the application of the pluperfect to the 1st and 2d verses of the 1st chapter of Genesis would bring philology and geology at one. My own sense of the meaning was made known to the world in 1814, and shewn to Professor Buckland in 1835, who adopted it in his " Bridgewater Treatise," but without acknowledgment.

Have you seen Elliott's " Horæ Apocalypticæ ?" He makes a very unwarranted attack on our Free Church, and has been ably replied to by Dr. Candlish, in a pamphlet of which I will send you a copy.

Mrs. Chalmers joins me in the kindest regards to you and Mrs. Bell. I cherish a most pleasant recollection of our last visit to you. If the venerable Mrs. Fox be still alive, offer her my most affectionate remembrances, and the same to Dr. Douglas Fox and all the family.—I am yours, &c.

THOMAS CHALMERS.

No. CCLXXIV.—TO THE REV. TIMOTHY EAST, BIRMINGHAM.

Edinburgh, 23*d January* 1847.

MY DEAR SIR,—I shall have great pleasure in recommending your volume to my students. I would have applied myself more closely to the whole subject some time ago ; but the truth is, my theological course is one of three years' duration, and I do not get at the subject of the divinity of our Saviour till next month, when I shall have occasion to state my favourable impression of the merits of your work ; after which you will hear what the result is to be. I am much pleased with the new lights into which the argument has been cast by you, and I think it of great advantage to the students that they should, after studying the critical and scientific arguments, be thrown abroad as it were on a general work like yours, which takes its own independent and very intelligent view of the doctrine. I shall probably read out to my students those passages which I have marked, as having in them the characters of originality along with great weight.

Forgive me for saying that I think you have expanded too much in the latter part of the volume, which admits, in my opinion, of a good deal of compression, without any sacrifice of the sterling quality of the argument.

I did not congenialize with the instance which you gave of the Bishop of Exeter, which, whether correct in itself or not, had better have been avoided. I have not yet finished the perusal of it, having about 150 pages more to read. I am not aware of any work on the subject so well adapted for general and family reading ; and I have often regretted, that beside having works on each of the great doctrines of Christianity, altogether of a critical and controversial character, we should not have works made up of those kind and impressive appeals, which form the main staple of your volume, and which may be read and recognised of all men.—With many apologies for my long delay, I am, my dear Sir, yours very respectfully and truly,   THOMAS CHALMERS.

No. CCLXXV.—TO THE REV. EBENEZER BROWN
OF INVERKEITHING, FIFE.

Glasgow, 15th December 1821.

MY DEAR SIR,—I received your much esteemed note yesterday. I am quite aware that its suggestions are not only very kind, but very necessary ; for I am sure that both in language and in spirit we lie under many temptations to depart from the simplicity that is in Christ. I can truly say that I have the utmost relish for those evangelical authors whose style is that of great homeliness, while clearly and forcibly expressive of the great truths of the Gospel ; and, lastly, I have read with great satisfaction your work of " Romaine on Faith," whose ever pervading idea is just that of Jesus Christ and Him crucified. The constant presentation of this truth, so far from being offensive to a spiritual man because he heard it before so often, is like the constant presentation of the same food, agreeable and welcome to him because he is hungry ; and it is indeed a tremendous thought that by the wisdom of words the cross of Christ may be made of no effect.

There is one thing, however, that ought to be adverted to ; the difference of styles is somewhat like the difference of

dialects.   You would not have a plain Yorkshire minister when
he comes to your neighbourhood attempt to preach in the
dialect of Fife.   His own dialect is the best for his own people.
And in like manner there is a style proper to every one,
whether it be natural or acquired, which perhaps is the best for
one class of ministers, though unsuitable to another.   God inter-
posed with a miracle of tongues that the Gospel might be
preached to every man in his own language ; and it is perhaps
in unison with this principle of His administration that He
rears a diversity of authors who may speak to the people each in
his own style or dialect the wonderful works of God.   I have
much more to say upon this subject, but I must postpone the
subject till we meet and talk about it.

May I entreat your prayers, for which, I assure you, I shall
have the same value that I would for the prayers of a venerable and much loved father.   May the God of all comfort
rejoice your heart with the tokens and demonstrations of your
usefulness ; and let it be our united supplication to Him, that
He would pour down of that Spirit upon our land, without
which all human exertion is powerless as infancy.

Give my best compliments to your brother when you write
him or see him, with whom, as with yourself, I have had some
very congenial and much valued fellowship.—I am, my dear
Sir, yours most affectionately,   THOMAS CHALMERS.

No. CCLXXVI.—To the Countess of Elgin.

Edinburgh, 1st June 1826.

MY LADY,—Your Ladyship's very kind letter was long of
reaching me, partly from Mr. Whyte's ignorance of the place
where I first resided when I came to Edinburgh, and partly
from the change of place which I have undergone during my
stay in the metropolis.

I feel myself greatly flattered and obliged by your Ladyship's

goodness in having again tendered me so pressing an invitation
to come to Broomhall; and there is nothing which could afford
me greater enjoyment than to renew the Christian and intellectual gratifications which I have had the happiness so often
to experience there. This is an object which I shall study to
achieve in the course of my present college vacation. Just now
there is a very particular avocation which makes it impossible
for me to go anywhere but the east of Fife, and that is, the
marriage of a sister, which takes place early next week. I shall
be much occupied both before and after that event with home
matters; but I am not without hopes of being able through the
summer to realize that converse which, I crave your Ladyship's
forgiveness for saying, has left a fragrance behind it, and the
remembrance of which is sweet.

We have lost ground *numerically* this year on the plurality
question, but we have not lost heart; and it is my feeling that
bating this and another distressing division, this Assembly has,
on the whole, had a very promising aspect, and the spirit of our
Church is unequivocally improving.

I beg my most respectful compliments to the Ladies Bruce,
and to Lords Elgin and Bruce, who I know are at present from
home.—I have the honour to be, my Lady, your Ladyship's
most obliged and obedient servant, THOMAS CHALMERS.

No. CCLXXVII.—To the Countess of Elgin.

Edinburgh, 6th March 1830.

MY LADY,—I received your deeply interesting letter—the
perusal of which, I can assure your Ladyship, has given me
unfeigned satisfaction. I hold the faith and the feelings
therein expressed to be altogether legitimate—warranted as
they are by the terms in which the Gospel overtures are
framed, and which direct us to look for the primary object of

our confidence, not inwardly upon ourselves, but outwardly to the Saviour.

I have repeatedly expressed my regret that the admirable general lesson of Mr. Erskine's book should have had the burden of one questionable and obnoxious expression laid upon it; and which I foresaw would frustrate and overbear the good of his publication by the interminable controversy that would arise from it. All men are not pardoned—but all men have the pardon laid down for their acceptance; and the latter is just as effective an exhibition of the Divine character as the former, without the heavy exception of being unscriptural, and liable to be abused to Antinomianism.

I feel that I could talk on this subject far better than write; and therefore I look forward with great interest to my purposed visit to Broomhall, so soon as we are fairly settled in our new house, which I expect will take place in the middle of April.

With most respectful compliments to Lord Elgin, I have the honour to be, my Lady, your Ladyship's most obliged and obedient servant,   THOMAS CHALMERS.

No. CCLXXVIII.—To the Countess of Elgin.

Edinburgh, 2d June 1831.

My Lady,—I beg to send your Ladyship the pamphlet on the Poor Laws, along with Sir John Sinclair's and two tracts of my own. The one on the National Debt may not be very interesting, yet if sound, and I cannot find out a flaw in the reasoning, leads to a conclusion of great practical importance.

I regret that I cannot lay my hands on Mr. Drummond's or Mr. Irving's letter on the subject of Miss Mowbray, and I suspect they are still in her father's hands. I have, however, the satisfaction of sending Mr. Campbell's.

I returned in time to be present at the discussion of Mr. S.'s and Mr. Irving's cases. Mr. S.'s very appearance at the bar of the Assembly involved in it a practical bull, and the decision was inevitable. Of all the motions that were fabricated on Mr. Irving's question, I think the one adopted was the best.

I grieve for poor Campbell. He was probably right in *idea*, but if he obstinately persist in couching that right idea in a wrong phraseology, he may not be the less dangerous as an expounder of truth. The man whose sound views may save himself, might still, by abandoning the form of sound words, mislead others. Yet I cannot help being in great heaviness on his account.

It is ominous that Spencer Drummond, who is now in Edinburgh, should at this moment have seceded from the Church of England because of its tenet of universal redemption, when our own tenet of particular redemption has driven Mr. Campbell beyond the pale of the Scottish Establishment.

I never leave Broomhall without the feeling of its being the most congenial moral atmosphere I breathe anywhere. My regret at parting from it at this time was aggravated greatly by what I perceived were the sufferings of Lord Elgin. It is our duty earnestly to pray for their alleviation.—I have the honour to be, my Lady, your Ladyship's most obliged and obedient servant, THOMAS CHALMERS.

No. CCLXXIX.—To LADY MATILDA MAXWELL.

22d October 1843.

DEAR LADY MATILDA,—I very sincerely regret that I cannot avail myself of your kind invitation—obliged to leave on Wednesday, and engrossed every moment before it. I must confess myself to have been greatly touched by your allusions, both to your dear father and to poor Lady Elgin, whose tragical death moved and affected me greatly.

I should have rejoiced if I had had it in my power to have taken refuge for a few days in the asylum of peace and friendship which your goodness has proposed for me; there to have renewed the associations of former days, and to have had a brief but happy breathing time from the fatigues and anxieties of this stormy period.

I beg that you will offer my most respectful acknowledgments to Mr. Maxwell; and with earnest prayer that we may all meet in that Heaven where separation is unknown, and charity ever reigneth, I always am, my dear Lady Matilda, yours with greatest esteem and regard,   THOMAS CHALMERS.

No. CCLXXX.—To Lady Carnegie.

Glasgow, 3d February 1823.

MY DEAR LADY CARNEGIE,—I have looked over the papers which relate to Ireland, and shall give them over to Mr. M'Gregor as your Ladyship directed me.

I feel the weight and magnitude of the object to be such that I would not venture on any deliverance without the actual survey of an Irish district in person, and the leisurely attention of many weeks to the topic in all its bearings. I shall therefore satisfy myself at present with a few remarks that have occurred to me during the perusal of those interesting documents which have been put into my hand.

1. I rejoice to observe a progress towards that subdivision of effort which is so requisite. In proportion as this is carried forward will there be a relief felt from that unwieldiness which has hitherto stamped such an impotency on all the plans of a very ambitious and extended benevolence.

2. So much am I impressed with the truth of the above remark, that I should have greater comfort in the meantime did I contribute my subscription to one complete and concentrated operation on a single parish than to a thin and evanescent sprinkling of good over a whole country. I feel quite assured that the exhibition of a model in philanthropy will do more for

the cause than a magnificent aim with an execution that lags at a most hopeless distance behind it. The success of a process upon an experimental farm would give a far more beneficial impulse to agriculture than a large grant from the Exchequer, to be divided equally among all the parishes of the empire.

3. I feel the more comfort in advancing this suggestion that I do not thereby supercede or discourage any extended operation which may be going on at present in the county of Clare. I simply recommend as an addition to the whole that there shall be the singling out of one manageable parish in which there may be immediately established a full system of the means of moral and economical amelioration devised on the soundest principles, and which shall not be suffered to labour under the want or the shortcoming of any one instrument that is fitted to give efficacy to the experiment.

4. I liked the small pamphlet very much, and chiefly because of the intercourse which its plans would necessarily produce between females of the higher and lower orders. All my experience has convinced me that from no human influence does a more rapid civilisation ensue than from the personal attention of ladies to the children of the poor.

5. I liked the simplicity of its objects, viz., the cleanliness and personal habits of the peasantry, and to which I would superadd, as far as practicable, their education, comprehensive of reading to all, and sewing to the girls.

6. It is a mistake to think that there is no limit to profitable work ; we can no more provide work for the employment of all in a well-peopled country than food for the subsistence of all. I should like to see every plan delivered from errors in political economy ; and be assured that there is no permanent amelioration to be looked for but in such an elevation of mind and manners throughout the general mass of the natives as that, under the impulse of their own improved taste, they shall at length

become the willing agents in raising and improving their own condition. You will always find that, in the absence of poorrates, the average style of comfort among the people determines their habits, whether of prudence or of precipitation as to marriage. Should a higher demand for comfort be at length introduced among the peasantry of Ireland, this would restrain these improvident connexions which I hold to be a palpable and immediate cause of wretchedness in every population. Now, this is not to be done in a day ; let us be thankful if it should be done in a century, and meanwhile let each of us suit his movements to the mediocrity of his powers, more satisfied with doing a small thing thoroughly well, than with the short-lived glory of a splendid enterprise that vanishes in smoke.—I am, &c.,

THOMAS CHALMERS.

No. CCLXXXI.—To LADY O'BRIEN.

MY DEAR LADY O'BRIEN,—1. I should even think Ennis to be too wide a field, and I should prefer a district of the town with a population of three thousand, and this district the poorest in the place.

2. A chapel to be built in it, with a minister who had the zeal and spirit of a most devoted missionary, but who at the same time, totally free of all partisanship, could so manage his addresses, both from the pulpit and in private houses, as never once to advert to such a distinction as that which obtains between Catholics and Protestants. This I think he may do under the single impulse of a desire for the spiritual and everlasting good of all, and without any dereliction of that faithfulness which is incumbent upon him as an expounder of God's will for man's salvation.

3. The way to mark that more special reference which the chapel has to the district than to the general town is, first, by holding out the preference for seats to those who reside within

the limits of the district; and secondly, by the minister's assiduous cultivation of it as the peculiar vineyard of his household and week-day attentions.

4. Let not the sittings be gratuitous. If the people are poor, let the seat-rent be the smaller on that account; but let there be a rent however trifling, that the people may have a feeling of property in their assigned pews, and more especially that there may be a distinct and tangible right by which to fence the local congregation from the intrusions of the town at large.

5. The demand for seats may at first be small, but the unwearied ministrations of the clergyman from house to house will make it great. Whatever vacant room is over after the local demand has been met and satisfied, should then be exposed to the whole population.

6. The minister will soon obtain such an ascendency over the families of his district as would render him the efficient instrument for stimulating all those economic and educational processes that might be judged expedient.

7. He should be a man who, standing between the rich and the poor, could as fearlessly tell the latter of their duty in respect of industry, independence, cleanliness, &c., as he could tell the former of their duty as the stewards and almoners of Heaven's bounty.

8. And he should know that it is utterly impossible to achieve one valuable object of philanthropy by letting forth all the streams of affluence on the relief of indigence, that this last duty should be performed unseen, and without the publicity which combination is sure to give it; and that the only visible movement in behalf of the poor, (in ordinary times,) should be for the purpose of moralizing and enlightening them; it being always understood that every scheme, even for their temporal comfort, will fail, which is not founded on the basis of their own improved hearts and habits.

2 G

9. The minister will be greatly the better of a band of associates, with each having the management of his own sub-district, and being thoroughly impressed with kindred principles to his own, both in regard to the economics of the people and their higher interests.

I am aware of many difficulties which might be felt in the perusal of the above sketch ; but I shall not anticipate them, and rather leave them to be started ere I attempt to do them away.

N.B.—The effect of repeated domiciliary visits, when conducted with kindness and *judgment,* is altogether unknown, and even the obstinacy of Catholic prejudices is not able to withstand it.—Yours, &c.,   THOMAS CHALMERS.

No. CCLXXXII.

Glasgow, 12th May 1823.

MY DEAR MADAM,—I have perused with great interest the letters of Lady O'Brien, and have transmitted them to Mr. M'Gregor. I still think, that instead of taking any other part in the more extended movements which are going on for Ireland than subscribing for them as others do, her Ladyship would serve the cause more effectually by concentrating her strength upon a third part of the town of Ennis.

The regeneration of a country is never to be accomplished in any other way than by a piecemeal operation—by each individual philanthropist doing his part within a sphere that is commensurate to his influence and to his powers. When the Spirit of God writes in many hearts the sacred law, then the owner of each individual heart will go forth upon that portion of the field which is within his reach, and do with all his might that which his hand findeth to do. It is not the local system that will regenerate our land, but a host of spiritual men must go forth in the day of God's power, and calculating aright on the most effective way of distributing their forces. I think that the result of this concentration would be the adoption of the local system with a busy operation of separate and parochial activities over the face of our kingdom. Still it is the Spirit of God that is the prime mover ; still the helplessness of man and the need of prayer must ever obtrude themselves on the notice of Him that looks to the whole question, and attentively regards all the parts and all the bearings of it. Without the descent of living water from above, the local system does not more for a country than the best apparatus of aqueducts for irrigation could fertilize it without rain—as little for it as the agricultural processes of Egypt could avail without the annual overflow of their great river.—I am yours, &c.,

THOMAS CHALMERS.

No. CCLXXXIII.—To SIR ANDREW AGNEW, BART.

Lochryan, 31*st August* 1838.

MY DEAR SIR ANDREW,—The inclosed paper is very well drawn up, nor am I aware of any amendment that can be made upon it. Allow me, however, earnestly to suggest, that before the managers of the new church at Leswalt attempt distant places they would make a thorough operation on their own neighbourhood. It is not, as you well know, large individual subscriptions that I am contending for, but a general and diffused application by which all who are willing might have the opportunity of making their contributions, however small. I would fain hope that if this were done, the adequate funds might be obtained without the necessity of going beyond the confines of Wigtonshire.

The reason why I do not add my own name to those of the gentlemen who have subscribed this paper is, that from the position I hold I should be exposed to similar applications from all quarters, and so be placed under the necessity either of giving my name in every instance, or of giving offence by refusing it in those cases where I judge it were better that the most strenuous attempts were made to realize the whole sum necessary in home produce rather than foreign aid.

Before I close, I cannot adequately express the deep sense I have of your great kindness and liberality to myself. It is a great contribution you have made to our cause, that from the moment of my touching Stranraer to the moment of my leaving it, you have franked and taken charge of the whole intermediate locomotion, comprising two Presbyteries.* After you had

---

* *"Saturday, August* 18*th.*—Left Fairley at ten. Looked with great interest to the coast all the way from Girvan to Lochryan; it being quite new to me, and maintaining throughout the character of a simple, remote, and solitary glen. Got to Stranraer about nine. The town looked impressive as we approached it—it forming a crescent, and its twinkling lights spread before us in this form. Sir Andrew Agnew waiting our arrival. He introduced us to Colonel M'Dowal; and took us (me and Mr. Collins) in his carriage to Lochnaw Castle, six miles off.

" *Tuesday,* 21*st.*—Went to the Presbytery at twelve. Spoke at great length on Church Extension in a meeting-house, to an audience more limited than it would have been, had not the public misunderstood the intimations. Made the acquaintance of Mr. Symington, Cameronian minister here, for whom I have great value.

" *Wednesday,* 22*d.*—The work of this day has been two-fold; first, the forming a Parish Association for Leswalt, which was done in Sir Andrew's house—the parish minister, and several elders, farmers, and others, having met and adopted our regulations. Went at two, in Sir Andrew's carriage, to Portpatrick, where I held another meeting with the minister in his manse, and elders, and farmers, and others; and where also Colonel Hunter Blair, Colonel Vans Agnew, Mr. Blair, M.P. and Captain Little, attended. Had a good deal of talk here; and after having settled this business, went forth to the harbour, and enjoyed exceedingly the bold rocky beach. Then scrambled along the beach in another direction from Dunskey Castle. Got at length into a den beautifully wooded, and watered with a noble fall, which conducted us to Dunskey House, belonging to Colonel Hunter Blair, who had many visitors.

" *Thursday,* 23*d.*—I rose about seven. Walked out to a beautiful den, which terminates in the beach. Then laved my hands in the Irish Sea, and returned again through the den, beautifully wooded, and furnished with chairs and wooden bridges; and I thought that had Helen and Fanny been with me, how objectively they would have gazed at the rushing cascade, and the airy seats placed at different points for the best views. Spoke to a crowded audience in Mr. Symington's church on Church Extension, to my own and the people's satisfaction. Went off to Lochnaw Castle.

"*Friday* 24*th.*—Sir Andrew's carriage took us to a most beautiful bathing-cottage on the sea-side, where the family reside often for many weeks together. It is situated most romantically in a secluded recess on the beach, with braes, and

done so much, I did not object to your settling with the driver at Glenluce, so as that there might be no exception to the munificence of such a help to me through so large a tract of country; but after you had done so much you should have done no more; and, allow me to say, it was ultra or beyond all that ought to have been done that you should propose to bear any part of my

rocks, and famous scrambling heights, on each side of it, and before it the sea, with an expanse of fine yellow sand at low water. Mrs. Chalmers and I are invited to take up our residence there, *en famille*, for as many weeks in summer as we like; and well do I know how the explorations, and the climbings, and the shell-gatherings, and the bathings, would be enjoyed by Helen and Fanny in this deep and peaceful solitude.

" *Sunday, 26th.*—Another day of complete rest. Enjoyed the quietness of the sacred Sabbath morn. Had family worship and exposition in the evening; and as Sir Andrew and I were next day to take leave early, I bade a grateful and affectionate adieu to the rest of the family.

" *Monday, 27th.*—Instead of taking the direct road to Wigton, Sir Andrew was kind enough to take me round by the coast, for the sake of its interesting scenery. A plain, pristine, russet-looking country, poor in produce, but not of unpleasing aspect, with rocks peering forth of the verdure everywhere, and a beach which presents a number of fantastic and impressive forms. Had the kindest possible reception from Colonel Vans Agnew.

" *Tuesday, 28th.*—A general movement to Wigton, four miles off, at one. Several carriages put into requisition. We landed at Mr. Young's, the clergyman of Wigton—a most beautiful village, both in respect of its site and its interior, placed on a gentle eminence, where it commands a noble view of Wigton Bay. The church quite full, as indeed I had been led to expect from seeing at least twenty carriages on the street when we entered the town. I delivered my address from the precentor's desk; and it went off apparently with the entire and cordial approbation of the audience. Sir Andrew took me out in his carriage to Cumloden, not the seat but the cottage of Lord Galloway. It was a ride in the dark of about nine miles, through, I was told, a very beautiful country, chiefly along the Cree. Passed through Newton Stewart, and about a mile on reached Cumloden, where Lord and Lady Galloway (their visitors having all retired to bed) gave us a very flattering reception.

" *Wednesday, 29th.*—Cumloden is a most enchanting place; a large cottage spread over a great extent of floor, with but one good story of numerous apartments and attics above it. A highly-decorated lawn of shrubbery and clumps of trees, and at one place a bushy flower garden; a brawling river, tributary to the Cree, of rapid descent, and which a shower swells into a torrent; a noble Alpine background of northern hills, on the confines of Galloway and Ayrshire, with beautiful glimpses of nearer objects, as the tower of Minigaff Church, &c. Walked with Sir Andrew to Minigaff, about a mile off. Every step disclosed new charms of landscape. Minigaff itself has a manse like a rectory, with a most gentleman-like approach; and the view from its front door, comprehending the banks of the expenses after leaving Stranraer. When Mr. Symington told me that you insisted on settling for the chaise-hire to Cairnryan, I felt doubly ashamed of all your goodness to me, though doubly grateful for your kind feelings both to myself and to the great object of Church Extension in Scotland.

Will you forgive me if I entreat that you will not exceed in

wooded Cree, rolling past and before it its dark moss-coloured waters, is one of the most exquisite I ever saw. Walked to the church, at whose door there was a number of carriages. A large meeting of people whom I addressed on Church Extension. Mr. Blair took me in his carriage to Penningham House, his mansion.

"*Thursday, August 31st.*—Went in cavalcade with a riding horse and two open carriages six miles up the Cree, to a small church now building for a simple and upland population. Delighted with the scenery on the banks of this river, more especially when the Minwick enters it, which one might trace upward through a most romantic and remote glen, but at the entry of which into the Cree, also, we are presented with a truly interesting panorama of level cultivation, skirted by rocky eminences, and expanding upward into ascents of a bolder character, which terminate at length in a noble Alpine boundary projected upon the sky. After our upland survey of this new parochial locality, with its rising church and now completed school, was driven forward by Mr. Gordon to Newton Stewart, and then took leave of my numerous conductors. The views over the Cree from this to the parish of Minigaff are truly glorious. Went alone into Sir Andrew's carriage. Rode sixteen miles in it by myself over a plain, pristine, peat country, not without its charms, however, and which kept my interest perpetually alive, from my having with me a map of Wigtonshire, by which I could verify the hills, rivers, and places. Passed the Church of Kirkcowan half a mile on my left. Got to Glenluce about three. Sir Andrew joined me there, and we got on six miles farther to Dunragget, the seat of Sir James Hay. The Misses Hay, and particularly Susan, greatly interested in my movement here. It seems two Glasgow voluntaries—the Rev. Messrs. King and Anderson—are now hanging upon my rear, and held a meeting after me at Stranraer, which has turned out a failure. They tried to evade the hissing by stating that they would understand every hiss to be directed against the doctrine which they were opposing; and then Mr. Anderson fell foul of me, and they, unmindful of his interpretation, began lustily to hiss; he, as unmindful of his own position, felt greatly annoyed, saying, What, will you hiss the great Dr. Chalmers? Left Dunragget about seven. Landed in Mr. Symington's, where I took leave of Sir Andrew, and who undertook to order a post-chaise for me to Cairnryan, the place of General Sir Alexander Wallace, whither Mr. Symington and I went, and where we landed about ten, and got a warm welcome, a warm room, and warm and comfortable bed.

"*Friday, August 31st.*—Lady Wallace and Sir Alexander both very cordial. Took leave at ten, greatly rested and refreshed by this quiet family visit. Got into the mail for Ayr. Entered inside; but was so delighted with the scenery, that I soon got outside. Reached Ayr at ten."—*Extracted from Dr. Chalmers's Journal.*—See Memoirs, vol. iv. p. 166.

your public liberalities, for my impression is, and I state it frankly, that your disposition is to encroach on the duty which a man owes to those of his own household. Do indulge me in the freedom I use. You have done more for our cause by your testimony and personal countenance than you could have done by any pecuniary contribution. It is to the multitude of subscribers, and not to the enlargement of subscriptions that I look for the increase of our means.

With best regards to Lady and Miss Harriet Agnew, and to one and all of your dear family, I have the honour to be, dear Sir Andrew, yours most gratefully and respectfully,

THOMAS CHALMERS.

No. CCLXXXIV.—To MR. THOMAS WALKER, FLESHER, GALASHIELS.

Burntisland, 1st July 1840.

MY DEAR SIR,—I received your letter of the 22d, and read it with the greatest interest—admiring as I do greatly both the sentiments which it expresses and the spirit which it breathes. The excellence of that composition, as well as the account I have received of you from your worthy and esteemed clergyman Mr. Veitch, has encouraged me to address you as an acquaintance and a friend.

Next to the approbation of my own conscience do I value such a testimony as yours, and more especially as coming from one in your class of society ; and I feel it to be an ample compensation for all the discouragements which I have experienced in my attempts to extend the means of a pure Christian education for the people of our land.

I can truly say, that after the salvation of the working classes there is no object which I have more at heart than their elevation in the scale of comfort—only to be attained I think, however, through the medium of their own worth and their own intelligence. And I am therefore all the more cheered and gratified in every new instance I meet with of their high capabilities for mental and moral improvement. I do hope that the influence of your example and your exertions will tell powerfully in the diffusion of a spirit and principles like your own throughout the mass of our population.

I spend the winter months in Edinburgh. Should you ever visit the capital at that season, I beg you will call on me and let me make your personal acquaintance.—With many thanks for your kind and encouraging communication, I am, my dear Sir, yours very truly,   THOMAS CHALMERS.

No. CCLXXXV.—To REV. DR. STRACHAN, BISHOP OF TORONTO.

Burntisland, 1st May 1841.

MY DEAR SIR,—I received your letter a few days ago, and have read it with the greatest interest. I spent ten days lately with Professor Duncan, and both he and I put it down to the account of your honest, we have the vanity to think, your intense, and cordial friendship for us that you have given us so kind and affectionate an invitation. Though older, he is stronger and healthier than I ; and I must acknowledge that, apart from engagements altogether, I should, on the consciousness of my infirm and irregular health alone, shrink from a voyage and then a journey of such magnitude. I fear that with me it must ever remain a speculation ; but I am not the less grateful on that account for the effusion of so much regard to one of your earliest companions.

Besides the great kindness of your letter, I was much interested by its subject-matter. I had before read your letter in the *Times,* and think that you have made out a complete case. I can also well believe that no injustice against you either in the public papers or by public men will ever countervail the substantial good-will which your official and personal attentions are sure to gain from all the classes of your extensive diocese amongst whom you expatiate. It is here that the real strength of clergymen lies, and I have no doubt that the knowledge and experience of this go far to explain the passionate hostility felt towards every conscientious and well-principled ecclesiastic on the part of chartists, radicals, and all those who have leagued themselves against social order and the stability of our existing institutions.

I rejoice in your willingness to entrust with so much power every man above twenty-one, "provided his religious principles are sound, and that he felt it matter of conscience to exercise it aright. Give a man a strong feeling of moral responsibility, &c."—Your strictures on De Tocqueville are admirably just, in that he would confide power to a people merely on the score of their secular education. But, on the other hand, our High Church conservatives are as wide of the truth as he who apprehends danger in confiding any ecclesiastical franchise to a people whatever their religious knowledge and character might be, and though they should pass through the ordeal of the most strict and conscientious examination previous to their entry on the roll of our communicants: in other words, nothing can be more blind or ignorant than the prejudice of those hard and impracticable Tories amongst us who spy democracy in the present doings of our Kirk—the most distinguished for loyalty and love of order of any corporation in the known world.

We are steering on the middle path between Puseyism on the one hand and Voluntaryism on the other. I do not say that we will succeed, but it is my firm belief that if we do not, National Establishments of Christianity will and ought to be put down, not for a perpetuity, but till that period when the kingdoms of the earth shall become the kingdoms of our Lord and Saviour Jesus Christ.

Give my best regards to your son whom I met at Pennicuik,

2 H

and of whom I entertain a very pleasant recollection.—I am, my very dear Sir, yours most cordially, THOMAS CHALMERS.

What weighs with Mr. Duncan against the proposed voyage is the apprehended loss of the " President."—T. C.

No. CCLXXXVI.—To PROFESSOR DUNCAN.

Edinburgh, 29th December 1842.

MY VERY DEAR SIR,—I am just now at holiday time trying to work my way through unanswered letters, among which I find two bearing the subscription of your much-loved name— the one dated the 12th of November, the other, ingrate that I am, the 12th of October.

On the subject of the first I share in the horror you express at the cruelty of slaughtering animals for amusement. I think that their being even slaughtered for food is one of the greatest enigmas of our present mysterious world. The day is coming, however, when " the mystery of God will be finished," (Rev. x.,) and this, with all other difficulties, will be solved.—Ever believe me, my dear Sir, yours very affectionately and truly,

THOMAS CHALMERS.

No. CCLXXXVII.—To PROFESSOR DUNCAN.

Morningside, 7th September 1844.

MY DEAR SIR,—Can you tell me of any author who treats of the properties and progression of prime numbers? The following is a curious order, observed for some time, in the proportion which the composite numbers bear to all others, and from which I had hoped that the absolute proportions of the composites to the primes throughout the whole infinity of numbers might have been ascertained within an indefinitely near approximation :—

The numbers in which 2 does not enter as an aliquot part are to number at large as 1 to 2, or $\frac{1}{2}$.

The numbers in which 2 and 3 do not enter as aliquot parts are as 1 to 3, or $\frac{2}{6}$.

The numbers in which 2, 3, and 5 do not enter, as 4 to 15, or $\frac{4}{15}$.

The numbers in which 2, 3, 5, 7, do not enter, as 8 to 35, or $\frac{8}{35}$.

The numbers in which 2, 3, 5, 7, 11, do not enter, as 16 to 77, or $\frac{16}{77}$.

See the promise then I had on entering this investigation, that, if you take the primes in order, 1, 2, 3, 5, 7, 11, &c., you would arrive at the general proportion that the composites formed of them successively would so run as to leave remainders, which bore to all numbers proportions expressed by fractions, whose numerators each double its predecessor, as 2, 4, 8, 16, &c., and whose denominators were the products of the two last prime numbers that had been taken up in the progress of the investigation, as, $2 = 1 \times 2$, $6 = 2 \times 3$, $15 = 3 \times 5$, $35 = 5 \times 7$, and $77 = 11 \times 7$. Judge of my disappointment then, when proceeding to the next prime number 13, and expecting the result $\frac{32}{143}$. I found it very difficult, and thus has my goodly progression been most cruelly put an end to.—Yours very truly, THOMAS CHALMERS.

No. CCLXXXVIII.—To PROFESSOR DUNCAN.

Edinburgh, 14th December 1845.

MY DEAR SIR,—I should not have written you on Sabbath, but for the subject on which I mean to address you, and to which I shall confine myself. I have long had the utmost regard for you. There is not a human being whom, without the circle of my relationship, I like nearly so well. But, though affectionate towards you, I have not been faithful. Consider how soon both you and I will be mouldering in our coffins. Heaven grant that we may both share in a blessed resurrection, through our common interest in Him who hath said, "I am the resurrection and the life," &c.—Ever believe me, my dear Sir, yours very affectionately and truly,

THOMAS CHALMERS.

No. CCLXXXIX.—To PROFESSOR DUNCAN.

Morningside, 13*th September* 1846.

MY DEAR SIR,—It has come at last. This death falls upon your heart as if it were a new lesson which you had still to learn. Oh, that this sorrow of nature were ripened and transformed by divine grace into that godly sorrow which worketh repentance unto salvation never to be repented of. Eternal life is not a thing to be got anyhow. There is a precise, definite, and let me add, only and exclusive way laid down for the attainment of it—a way authoritatively pointed out and prescribed by Heaven. He who hath the Son hath life ; he who hath not the Son hath not life. Christ says of Himself, " I am the way, the truth, and the life—by me, if any man enter in, he shall be saved ;" and, " No man cometh unto the Father but by the Son." Let us not quarrel with this way, more especially as it is open to all of us : " Whosoever cometh unto me shall not be cast out ;" " Believe in the Lord Jesus Christ and you shall be saved." It is for God, the offended party, and not for us, the offenders, to dictate the terms and the treaty of reconciliation. Heaven grant that you may be led henceforth to bestow an earnest heed on the Word of His testimony till the day dawn and the day-star arise in your heart. Read the Epistle to the Romans ; and if you furthermore read my printed Lectures upon them, you will have at least my views on the method and way of salvation grounded on my understanding of this portion of the Divine record. May our Father in Heaven bless this exercise to your soul, and so open your understanding to understand His Scriptures that you shall become thereby wise unto salvation.

It is to me a striking coincidence that, on the day before I received the intimation of your brother's death, I attended the funeral of Daniel Ramsay,* an inmate of Gillespie's Hospital, in my vicinity here. I go to perform family worship there this evening, when it will be my duty to improve this event to the survivors—all old persons above sixty. The reminiscences of more than half a century have been powerfully and feelingly awakened by both these events. May they tell efficiently and abidingly upon us both; for the time is fast approaching when we too shall be laid on the bed of our last agonies.

I shall not close this letter till I have returned from the evening service at the Hospital.

I have returned from my household sermon to the old people. The text was, "The time is short;" but, in addition to this argument, I endeavoured to press home the growing callousness of the heart to the invitations of the Gospel; yet, nevertheless, the perfect freeness of that Gospel, the benefits and immunities of which are theirs if they will; and on their acceptance of these, they will receive a new heart here, and the joys of an unfading inheritance hereafter.

It is my earnest prayer that God may thus dispose and enable you to receive that truth which is to be found in His Word, and which, if gifted by the Spirit to understand it, you will find to be the power and wisdom of God unto salvation.— Ever believe me, my dear Sir, yours most affectionately and truly, THOMAS CHALMERS.

* See Memoirs, vol. i. p. 6.

[Copy of Correspondence between the Rev. Dr. Thomas Chalmers, Professor of Moral Philosophy, St. Andrews, and Dr. Thomas Easton, Minister
of Kirriemuir, in reference to the Pauperism of that parish.]

No. CCXC.—Dr. Easton to Dr. Chalmers.

Kirriemuir, 26th January 1827.

Rev. Sir,—My parishioner, Mr. James Aitken Wylie,* having incidentally mentioned that you had been pleased to speak
kindly in your class of my statements relative to the pauperism
of Kirriemuir, I happened to say to him that I was extremely
desirous to obtain your opinion on a question of importance
connected with the subject of pauperism. I then stated to
him the question to which I referred ; and having the utmost
confidence to place in the prudence and discretion of the young
man, whom I have known from his childhood, I took the
liberty of stating to him, that if a suitable opportunity presented itself, he would oblige me by laying it before you. His
answer, written on his return to St. Andrews, has been received, in which he states your willingness to hear from me on
the subject.

The case is this:—It has been my object to meet the pauperism of this large and populous parish chiefly by collections
made by my congregation in the church ; and hitherto they have
been such as nearly to answer the demands made on us. Now,
my difficulty is this. The population of the parish is rapidly
increasing, and it may be expected that pauperism will increase
in a like ratio ; but as the church accommodates a part only of
the population, being seated for 1240, there is no hope that the
collections of my church will be sufficient long to meet the pauperism, that I cannot but foresee is coming upon us. In point

* Then a talented young man of great promise, and now the Reverend Mr.
Wylie, the respected author of many learned works, and more especially of the
" Papacy, its History, Dogmas, Genius, and Prospects."

of fact, the collections are at present, as I ever expect them to be, averaging from £135 to £140 per annum, in halfpence and penny pieces. How then am I to meet the pauperism which must necessarily arise from an increased population? We may expect more cases of insanity, more widows and orphans.

Perhaps one or other of three schemes may be adopted. The first is, let the parish be divided into sections, and let every district provide for its own poor. I fear we are not all Christian enough to trust to this scheme. There are also more poor in one district than in another. Several of our paupers reside in Dundee, and in other towns and parishes.

The second is, let the people add to the amount of their collections. If every individual would contribute a penny weekly in place of a halfpenny, the amount would be doubled. But the far greater part of my numerous congregation is comparatively in moderate circumstances, the heritors and most of the wealthiest of the people being Episcopalians.

The third is, let the church be enlarged, or a chapel of ease be erected. I have had the church examined by an architect of eminence, but his opinion is, that the roof is of a construction so peculiar that it cannot be interfered with. A chapel of ease would be an effectual remedy; but though I have urged the erection of one, I have as yet failed in persuading the people to undertake it. I am afraid, therefore, that unless you can suggest a way of escape, we must at last yield to necessity, and submit to assessments; the many evils of which have often been shewn, but by none so well as yourself.—I ever am, Rev. Sir, your most obedient servant, THOMAS EASTON.

No. CCXCI.—DR. CHALMERS TO DR. EASTON.

St. Andrews, 6th February 1827.

MY DEAR SIR,—I should have replied to your interesting letter sooner. I fear you will think my advice somewhat too general, though I deem it founded on an experience that is quite universal, and which I feel confident that you also will verify should you attempt to enlarge your fund by assessment. The experience is this, that you really do not, by an assessment, make your escape from the difficulties which bring it on. You do not even lighten these difficulties. You may for a time; but you will most assuredly aggravate them in the long run, and will be sure to find that, after all, you have less of comfort, and more of clamour and complaint among your population than at the outset of your compulsory system. Admitting, therefore, fully the existence of the difficulties which you allege, I hold it, on the above consideration alone, to be your true wisdom, rather to acquiesce in them, and manage with your humbler means as you can, than by a forced augmentation of these means, strengthen those evils, which in their present less degree you will find to be far more tolerable.

You state the small accommodation that you have in church for your populous parish, and how from this cause, what would have gone to swell your collection, now goes to the collections of your meeting-houses. On ecclesiastical or Christian grounds, I hold it very desirable that your accommodation should be widened; but I confess that I should not be very anxious about it for the economic object of a more liberal public provision for the poor. My own confidence all along in Glasgow was not upon means, but upon management; and not so much on the positive activity and strenuousness of that management, as on the co-operation of men who thought with myself, that the best way of disposing of every application, was by strict investigation into all the resources of the applicant, to devolve him as much as possible on his own industry, or on the duty of his relatives, or on the sympathy of his neighbours, or lastly, (though we very rarely indeed had recourse to such an expedient,) on the private liberalities of the more affluent. But we were quite sure, that just in proportion to the regularity, and certainty, and largeness of our sessional ministrations, would all these better securities for the relief of distress be slackened in the parish,—and so, proclaiming the insignificance of all that we could do, we devolved the burden on those upon whom Nature and Christianity had devolved it before us, and felt that the indefinitely nearer we came to a cheap and moderate, and withal gratuitous economy on the part of the public body, the more plentifully did relief flow from all those private sources of industry and sympathy which I have now enumerated. It was not my presence which achieved this. The thing goes on more prosperously since I left it; and our chapel district, with a population of 5000, is upheld by a collection of less than £100 in the year.

Try *gradually*, and get hold of men who think right upon this object; and though you cannot fill the parish all at once with them, give each a district as he casts up, and let him fully understand, that that man does his duty best to the Session who gives the Session least to do. You will find that each new elder might nearly relieve you of his own district altogether.

I have just room to assure you, that, with some few modifications, I thought exceedingly well of your book, and hailed it as an accession to a good cause. I should express my obligations for your very handsome treatment of myself in that volume.—I am, my dear Sir, yours most truly,

THOMAS CHALMERS.

No. CCXCII.—DR. EASTON TO DR. CHALMERS.

Kirriemuir, 16th February 1827.

REV. SIR,—Your letter of the 6th current I received in course, and I beg leave to return you my warmest thanks for the trouble you have been at in answering my letter of 26th January last. You have indeed bestowed a great deal of attention on the subject to which it refers. What you say is exceedingly satisfactory, and you may be assured that I am grateful for the recommendations you suggest. The only addition, practically speaking, which I would venture to make—improvement I cannot take it upon me to call it—is to classify the cases of poor, and, if we are driven to the expedient, to allow the heritors to provide for the insane, the fatuous, the blind, and to relieve the others from the church collection.

There is an analogical objection that may be urged against the voluntary relief of the poor, which has often occurred to me, and to which I am desirous to draw your attention,—one which I have never seen alluded to by any one. It is an argument founded on what you yourself have said respecting religious education. You object to the leaving of religious education to the principle of supply and demand, because, you say, that, owing to the corruption of human nature, men are naturally averse to spiritual truth, and it is necessary, therefore, that, by means of endowment, it should be brought to every man's door. But may it not be said that, owing to the same cause, men do not naturally love their neighbours as they ought, and therefore it is necessary that human laws should compel them to relieve the wants of the needy.

As I am aware how very valuable your time is, I do not expect an answer to this letter.—I am, dear Sir, most respectfully yours,   THOMAS EASTON.

No. CCXCIII.—DR. CHALMERS TO DR. EASTON.

St. Andrews, 22*d February* 1827.

MY DEAR SIR,—Your letter is too interesting not to be replied to.

You are quite right in your views of the distinction which obtains between the cases of general indigence and the cases of special and involuntary distress, such as lunacy, dumbness, blindness, &c. There would not be the mischief in assessing for these that there is in assessing for poverty at large, because such an assessment would not multiply its objects, and not go beyond a certain definite amount. Still, however, it is greatly better not to have even this more innocent assessment, for the one is extremely apt to run into the other, and I would far rather struggle to overtake the more special visitations by the collections and purely voluntary subscriptions, than attempt aught so dangerous as the admission of the compulsory into the business of charity in any of its parts.

Your analogical argument in favour of assessments is ingenious, and to myself new. Yet, on a narrower view of the actual similarities and dissimilarities between the course of instruction on the one hand, and the course of the ordinary relief of poverty on the other, I am persuaded it will not be found tenable. When the course of poverty is left to itself, then in proportion to the aggravation of its distress is the strength and efficiency of these counteractives by which it is mitigated, if not done away. Men are more goaded to industry and thrift, their relatives more excited to duty, their neighbours more awakened to compassion, and the rich more alive to voluntary exertion. When the course of ignorance is left to itself, then in proportion to the aggravation of that ignorance is the growing apathy to the evils of it, and an apathy which extends from the uneducated man to his neighbours, just because they too live in-a land unblest by education. The institutions for knowledge, besides, can accomplish their object purely and without adulteration. The institutions for general relief, in as far as they may be said to accomplish their object at all, do so at the fearful expense of every virtue concerned in the administration of charity, putting to flight the gratitude of the recipients, and the spontaneous generosity of the dispensers. —I am, my dear Sir, yours very truly, THOMAS CHALMERS.

No. CCXCIV.—To John Hamilton, Esq.

Edinburgh, 18th February 1840.

My dear Sir,—I beg that you will tolerate my dissertations. With me the uppermost object is to secure our independence. Should we be able to secure it with a less measure of Non-Intrusion, and should we lose it because of our insisting on a higher measure, we shall never be able to hold up our faces either to the Church or to the country. We shall for the sake of the gnat have been giving up the camel. I am not insensible to the importance, in one way, of identifying the cause of the Church with the cause of the people. I feel quite assured, that without them the Conservatives, as a body, would have been on the side of the authority of the Court of Session. This is an important element. But the other is a most important element too. There is throughout a general longing, all over Scotland, for a settlement. Even our lowest measure would satisfy a large majority, both of the Church and of the middle classes in the country, and would be followed up, I trust, by such a pure and vigorous administration on the part of our ecclesiastical courts, as to enthrone our beloved Church in the hearts of the general population.

You know the aspect under which I view an Act of Parliament when it respects the powers of the Church. Its object is not to convey the powers, but to convey and make sure to us certain temporal benefits in the exercise of those of our powers which it defines. If it do not comprehend all the powers, if at a certain point beneath, its temporalities are made to cease, this is not an interdict on the powers which are beyond—no limit on our powers, but on their own bounty. It is this which makes my conscience appear to be so elastic

on the subject of Non-Intrusion ; while on the subject of independence, I am not sure but I go further than any of you.
Paul said, on justification by faith, of those who tried to
mitigate the doctrine and encroach upon it, " to whom I gave
place, no, not for an hour." I say, of the slightest inroad on
the spiritual independence of the Church, " to which I give
place, no, not by one hair-breadth." The time appears fully
come, when, by next General Assembly, every refractory licen-
tiate should be deprived, and every refractory minister deposed.

I should like you to learn Sir Frederick Pollock's notion of
the change which I propose in the style of ecclesiastical legislation. It would clear away an ambiguity which hangs over
the connexion between Church and State, securing for us
certain benefits, if not to the whole extent of the exercise of
these powers, at least up to a certain limit, and leaving us at
entire liberty beyond that limit to do all which is competent
for a Church of Christ. The full and practical observation of
this principle would, by the removal of a flaw, mightily
strengthen the cause of religious establishments.

Speaking of Sir Frederick, I value his co-operation chiefly
upon one account. You are as well acquainted with styles of
Acts of Parliament as he is; but his London and Parliamentary experience gives him the advantage of knowing what the
things are, and what the forms of expression which would be
either most offensive or most conciliatory to the English members. If a man of tact, he will even know how, in the wording of
a matter that would revolt them, if seen in its nakedness,
to put it so that it shall escape the dislike and animadversion
of that very sensitive and high-minded assembly of men, who,
however enlightened within their own province, are downright
ignoramuses in regard to Scottish Presbytery—the object of
contempt because of its littleness in their eyes, and with some
of keen, even of loathing antipathy, because of its imagined

affinity to puritanism—at once hated religiously from the natural enmity of the heart to the truth, and hated politically from the historical recollections of the seventeenth century, which saw a monarch of England brought to the scaffold.

It is right to say, that notwithstanding the tone of this letter, and though I have written Lord Aberdeen, I have avoided the mention of a single word which can in the least fetter, but will rather facilitate the objects of the deputation.— I am, my dear Sir, yours truly,   THOMAS CHALMERS.

No. CCXCV.—To JOHN HAMILTON, ESQ.

Edinburgh, 24th March 1841.

MY DEAR SIR,—You have prescribed for me a truly arduous, and I fear unprofitable task, and the reiteration of the veriest truism, and that for the conviction of minds in a state of hopeless prejudice, and obstinately shut against the reception of it. There is nothing in common between our Scottish Evangelicals and our modern destructives, they are under the operation not only of diverse but of antagonistic influences. The Chartists know this well, and they everywhere oppose us. They are acting most intelligently for the prosecution of their ulterior objects, and in this respect forming a perfect contrast to the Conservatives, who are at present their coadjutors, in pulling at the same rope along with them. My belief is, that acting together they will pull down our Establishment; when the *further* account will have to be settled between themselves, the infatuated aristocracy will find when too late that they have lent a hand to the demolition of the only breakwater which stood betwixt the anarchists and their own order.

These are plain truths, nevertheless I utter them, and that for the purpose of your making them as widely known among your Conservative friends as possible, believing as I do that nothing but plain truths at this time of day will save us.

They are now lending themselves to a policy which must alienate from their cause the flower of our Scottish clergy, and in which if they succeed they will deprive of all its moral weight that Church whose ministrations were never more efficient and prosperous than at this moment, and which ministrations have ever been on the side of order, and contentment, and loyalty, and the other peaceable fruits of righteousness.

But, perhaps, it will avail you more, if, instead of spending your strength on such a demonstration, you make it palpable to their understandings that zealous though we are for the principle of a religious Establishment, there are many hundreds of our clergy, and these the best and most influential among them, who are in perfect readiness for a dissolution of the connexion between Church and State, rather than have an Establishment on the terms which the Court of Session would now prescribe to us.

If this letter be short it is because I hold the warfare of argument to be now over, and that it is no longer a contest of opposite reasonings, but of opposite wills, and opposite determinations. My confidence is no longer in man, but in the righteousness of our cause, and in that, when forsaken by all our earthly friends there is a God above, who, after the purposes of His wise and holy discipline have been fulfilled, will again visit in mercy the Church of our fathers. " We are perplexed, but not in despair."—I am, yours very truly,

THOMAS CHALMERS.

No. CCXCVI.—To SIR GEORGE SINCLAIR.

Burntisland, 18th August 1841.

DEAR SIR GEORGE,—I am very unwilling to believe that we might not obtain the wished-for consummation, by the passing of the Duke of Argyle's Bill, without incurring the delay necessarily implied in the appointment of a Commission of Inquiry.

At all events, I think the only footing on which the Church can come to an agreement with the State in regard to your proposed suspension of all legal actions by both parties, is, to express her willingness that, whatever the civil consequences might be which follow in the train of her decisions on the conduct of any of her office-bearers, and might in the ordinary course of law prejudicially affect their interests—that these civil consequences may, by an extraordinary Act of the Legislature, be remitted in favour of those who should otherwise have suffered from them. The Church, for example, could bear to have their temporalities made over for life to the Strathbogie ministers, and the temporalities of the respective parishes to which they had been presented to the nominees for Auchterarder and Lethendy ; but could not, I imagine, without a surrender of the very principle for which she is contending, consent either to recall the sentences already passed on the former delinquents, or to suspend the actions now pending before her own courts against the latter. The difference between the Church and the State is, that the Church cannot deviate from the path of her conceived duty in matters ecclesiastical ; whereas the State may, on grounds of political expediency, suspend or alter her methods of procedure in the disposal, as seemeth to her good, of things secular. The Church goes all the length she can go when she acquiesces in this unlooked-for stretch and exercise of power.

But for the above consideration I should hail the appointment of a Commission, confident as I am that the fullest inquiry would serve the best for the vindication of the majority of our Church, and that the result would be to soften away many a prejudice, and remove many a misconception, which now obtains on the subject both of their measures and of the spirit and character of the leading members in that body—nay, would demonstrate, not only the perfect innocence, but the Christian, or, which is tantamount to this, the truly Conservative patriotism of all their doings.

Neither do I object to any of the names you mention, and hail with particular satisfaction those of the Duke of Argyle, the Marquesses of Bute and Breadalbane, Sir William Rae—to which your own ought to be added. But my strong preference is, for such an immediate and right settlement as would supersede the necessity of such a Commission; and let me entreat you to consider this as the first and not yet matured view which I have taken of your suggestion.—I ever am, my dear Sir George, yours most truly, THOMAS CHALMERS.

No. CCXCVII.—To Sir George Sinclair.

Burntisland, 30th September 1841.

MY DEAR SIR GEORGE,—You seem not to be aware that I am not a member of the Committee on the Church Question—driven from it, in fact, by the mortifying experience which I had had of the little reliance that was to be placed on the professions of public and Parliamentary men.

I could not therefore give a direct response to your proposition without the usurpation of a power which in no shape or degree belongs to me. May I beg, therefore, that you will present it to some other member of the Committee; and to none could you do it with greater propriety than to Dr. Gordon, our present Moderator; and I shall most cordially acquiesce in the arrangement which you propose, should it seem good to him and to his colleagues.

I am not able to comprehend what is meant by a last opportunity which we must seize upon now, or the cause of the Church might be irrecoverably gone, unless it be that unless the wishes of Lord Aberdeen in London, and his adviser in

Edinburgh, shall be consulted by making his Bill the ground-work of an arrangement, the best and greatest of our national institutes must be sacrified to the vanity or doggedness of the two men. The very thought of this makes my blood boil with indignation. Sir Robert calls out for time and leisure (and most rightly) to mature his civil and economical measures. But there must be an instant soldering, it would appear, of the affairs of the Church ; and so as to lay the irritated humours of a mortified peer and an impracticable lawyer. The thing is beyond endurance.

But let me explain myself in reference to a former letter. Should we get no more than the *liberum arbitrium*, it will be the clear duty of the Church to work it in the best way possible ; and most happy should I be, if it so turned out, that because of its efficacy in securing a succession of evangelical and efficient clergymen, it superseded all further demand for any ulterior changes or reformations.—Ever believe me, my dear Sir George, yours most truly,   Thomas Chalmers.

P.S.—On reading over this letter I find I have been making myself hot by the imagination of a possibility. You, however, must know better, and can perhaps say whether the possibility be a truth ?—T. C.

No. CCXCVIII.—To Sir George Sinclair.

Burntisland, 30th September 1841.

My dear Sir George,—Since writing you this morning, I have seen the report of Sir William Rae's speech at Rothesay ; and I must say that I look far more hopefully to a measure wherewith he has to do than to aught which may be grafted on Lord Aberdeen's Bill, or concocted between his Lordship and the Dean of Faculty. I do think that, after this announcement, the most graceful and becoming thing for both the Dean and the Earl, would be to retire from the concern. The Dean did us great mischief by conjuring up the Strathbogie case, which I have no doubt was gotten up mainly under his auspices and by his encouragement, and which I fear will prove far the most serious obstacle in the way of an adjustment.—I ever am, my dear Sir George, yours most respectfully,

THOMAS CHALMERS.

No. CCXCIX.—To SIR GEORGE SINCLAIR.

Edinburgh, 6th October 1841.

MY DEAR SIR GEORGE,—I return you many thanks for your very kind letter, all the more grateful to my feelings that I had the apprehension of having been somewhat too stout and controversial in my former communications.

I have heard through another channel of the good you are doing. Be assured that if we had but the reasonable prospect of a fair and well principled adjustment, all my efforts should be on the side of peace and charity. I never was a friend to agitation for its own sake ; and would infinitely rather that the circumstances of the Church allowed its ministers to remain quietly at their respective homes, and prosecute the labours of their high vocation in their own parishes.

Since writing the last page, I have seen some friends of the Church, both lay and clerical. Their feeling seems to be, that it will be impossible, after the attempt of the opposite party to disestablish us, to stop the progress of Defensive Associations but by a definite measure, with the character and certainty of which the bulk of the Church and country might be satisfied.— I have the honour to be, yours, &c., THOMAS CHALMERS.*

* For the remaining letters of this series, see " Selections from the Correspondence," &c., edited by Sir George Sinclair, Bart.

No. CCC.—To the Bishop of Llandaff.

Edinburgh, 27th October 1841.

My Lord,—There should, I think, be such a freedom of the Church from civil coercion, that she should be at liberty to apply her own tests on every appointment by the Patron for the determination of the question—Is it for the Christian good of the people that this presentee should be inducted in a given parish as their minister? This we have had since the Revolution till the recent usurpations by our Court of Session. It is true that the congeniality of a man's preaching with the popular conscience has been regarded by the suffering party in Scotland as the element of fitness; and this because of the adaptation between the subject-matter of Christianity and the human conscience. I could say much in defence of this peculiarity of ours, which, till now, has never been invaded from without, though overborne for a century by Moderatism within. But I will not detain your Lordship further than by saying, that I should hold it an immense improvement on the ecclesiastical system in England, as well as on ours, not that you should adopt all our views on the element of the popular will, but that you should have the benefit of the principle which, if conceded to us, would set our question at rest,—" that the power of the Patron and of the Civil Courts should cease from the moment that the presentee is handed over to the Church Courts." This would leave the ecclesiastical power clear for the determination of its own proper questions, that is, for sitting in judgment on all the likelihoods of usefulness on the part of such a presentee to such a parish. The majority of our Church are at this moment willing to endure the deprivation of all their temporalities rather than have the authority of the Court of Session, as exercised within these four last years, forced upon us by the legislature. It will in fact prove the suspension, if not the breaking up, of a religious Establishment in this country.—I am, my Lord, yours, &c.   THOMAS CHALMERS.

No. CCCI.—TO THE BISHOP OF LLANDAFF.

18th January 1842.

MY LORD,—I am glad to observe from your Lordship's letter, that we are like to be protected from the Civil Courts ; but we must be protected from them when giving effect to our own views on the subject of Non-intrusion. We do not ask the Church of England to adopt that principle ; but we ask her to act upon it as our principle, just as a self-regulating body should not be disturbed in the execution of its own by-laws, these not being inconsistent with the order of civil society. Our contest is not for the specific object of Non-intrusion, but for the greater and comprehensive object of independence in spiritual things, so well advocated by the Archbishop of Dublin.— I am, yours, &c.,   THOMAS CHALMERS.

No. CCCII.—TO THE HONOURABLE AND REV. DR. WELLESLEY.

Edinburgh, December 1841.

MY DEAR SIR,—I beg to send you the enclosed statement, with such marks and observations of my own as occurred in reading it. The only thing better than the Duke of Argyle's Bill, which I shall mention at present, were the following up of a suggestion made by the Duke of Wellington, that we should frame a measure of our own and send it up for the sanction of Parliament. We may be said to have as good as done this when we approved, by a great majority, of the Duke of Argyle's Bill, though I have no doubt that we could frame another motion for giving effect to our principle, if this were preferred.

Would the British Government think it justifiable to propose that the priesthood of Hindostan shall either renounce their idolatrous religion or be stripped of their endowments, both the religion and the endowments having been long in subsistence at the time that their country was acquired by us? And the parallel question to this is, Would it be justifiable to force from the Church of Scotland the surrender either of presbytery or any one of what the Church holds to be its essential principles, on the pain of losing her endowments if she refuse, seeing that both presbytery and its principle of non-intrusion were in full operation along with the endowments at a time when this country was annexed to England? In other words, are Scotchmen to be treated worse than Hindoos? I may send another memorial on the subject; but this, as being the latest, is the worthiest of your attention.

THOMAS CHALMERS.

P.S.—It is of prime importance to remark, that the passing of the Duke of Argyle's Bill would not alienate a single clergyman from our Church; the forcing of another Bill might occasion such a disruption as would lead to our overthrow.—T. C.

[The distinguished talent and Christian patriotism displayed by the youthful Marquess of Lorne, in a publication entitled a "Letter to the Peers," not only awakened Dr. Chalmers's liveliest admiration, but filled him with the highest anticipations of the powerful influence which, in his after life, might be exerted by one so gifted and so good, not only upon his own order, but upon society at large. On receiving this publication Dr. Chalmers addressed the following letter to the Marquess.]

No. CCCIII.—To LORD LORNE.

Edinburgh, 28th January 1842.

MY DEAR LORD LORNE,—I have read your work with the most profound interest and satisfaction, insomuch that I fear to incur the semblance of insincerity by telling you all I think of its merits. Let me therefore copy a sentence which I have just written to Lord Galloway, after having entreated him to read your Letter:—" It is a truly admirable and far the best pleading in favour of the Church, on the grounds of constitutional law, that has yet appeared. Heaven grant that it may open the eyes of our rulers, and take them out of that false position which they now occupy—having the names of Conservatives, yet undermining the best and most truly Conservative of all our national institutes." As an address to statesmen, we have had nothing half so good, or that promises to be half so influential during the whole controversy ; and I am sure it will cheer and encourage the hearts of very many of our friends.

In writing to yourself, instead of expatiating on the general merits of your composition, let me enter more into particulars. I like what may be termed the construction of the argument, and think you have happily both relieved and strengthened no little a part of it by your reference to history—more especially when you infer the character of our principles from the nature of the opposition to them, as embodied in the " Black Acts." Again, the deference paid to our Constitutional liberties by the Law of Patronage, in that it enacted but the forfeiture of the emoluments as the penalty of its own violation, is exceedingly well-reasoned and brought out ; and I think it most fortunate that you brought this to bear on that mischievous article in "Blackwood"—the evil influences of which your Lordship's counter observations are so well fitted to neutralize. I furthermore rejoice in the pointed notices which you have taken of the Moderates, and think you particularly felicitous in instancing the check of refusing the supplies in the hand of Parliament as demonstrative of the real nature of the British Constitution, however seldom, nay, even though it should never be put into operation.

I do hope that your clear and masterly distinction between the legal and the constitutional, or between the *leges* and the *leges legum*, will tell on the public understanding, and that your exposure of the Strathbogie ministers will enable men to see in its just light the whole extent of their delinquency ; and I look confidently forward to a reaction of sentiment against the Court of Session from the perusal of your pamphlet.

But far the most brilliant and effective part of your pamphlet is that in which you deal so successfully with Sir Robert Peel's Letter. This will probably interest your readers the most of all you have written ; and there is a truly additional test given to your work by your notices of Lords Aberdeen, Brougham, and Melbourne.

I feel that I have given you a most inadequate representation of all I think and feel on the subject of your work. To supplement this in some degree I shall send you your own pamphlet as marked by me in the course of my perusal of it— a habit of mine in reading. I remember being much interested by falling in with a pamphlet of my own, marked in the same way, and from which I learned what the passages were which had been met by a responding intelligence and good liking on the part of him who read it. I have only resolved now on thus sending the pamphlet to you, so that the marks were just the spontaneous indications of the moment, and I will not add another ; although on looking over it, I find that the part I liked most is marked the least—that is, your argument on Sir Robert Peel, which I must have refrained from marking till I got to its closing passages.

Let me add, that there is a certain command of statement and reasoning which must add greatly to the impressiveness of

your work.   I was afraid, from its being so closely argumentative, that it might not be read with so much interest and
attention by the general run of readers.   I am happy to find,
however, that Mrs. Chalmers pronounces on it as most lucid
and intelligible ; and she is particularly struck with your
exposure of the infirmities of Sir Robert Peel's Letter.
Another lady in our neighbourhood, to whom I sent my own
copy from the shop yesterday, has returned it with a line,
saying, that she never till now saw clearly into the merits of
our case.

You have done us a great service.   Many, very many, of the
Church's best friends will bless God and rejoice because of it.
I shall be delighted to hear of your Lordship's improved health,
and will ever have the greatest pleasure in attending to your
Lordship.—I have the honour to be, my dearest Marquess,
yours most gratefully and most affectionately,

THOMAS CHALMERS.

["I cannot," said his Lordship, in writing to Dr. Chalmers at this period,
"refrain from expressing my deep regret at the nature of the proceedings
of the Presbytery of Edinburgh.   I regret that the Presbytery has urged
upon the General Assembly to engage in an Anti-patronage war, because it
gives ground for the charge that the Church mounts in her demands to
meet and to secure popular applause.   I regret it, because this moving a
'peg higher,' as Dr. Candlish has expressed it, can be justified on no principle that I am aware of, and lowers, in my opinion, the character of her
position.   I do not, indeed, view Patronage as some have done, as if it were
a great leading institution, and as if it were revolutionary to speak against
it ; but I again repeat, that I see no cause or just ground for the Church
demanding what she did not demand before.   I see no 'course of events'
which calls for such a change ; but I do see, and am thoroughly convinced
of the impolicy and inutility of such a change, and I feel sure that those who
have felt themselves 'shut up' to enter an Anti-patronage contest, have
contributed much to 'shut up' the Church from any remaining chance of
settlement.   I do not know how the Duke can preface his Bill in the House
as a 'settlement of the question,' with any confidence or truth, if the

2 K

Church adopts such a course ; nor do I know any means by which he could persuade the Peers that it is their duty to advance in their concessions in proportion as the Church rises in her demands." The able and earnest remonstrance from which these sentences have been quoted elicited the following lengthened reply.]

No. CCCIV.—To Lord Lorne.

Edinburgh, 19*th February* 1842.

MY DEAR LORD LORNE,—Your Lordship cannot be more annoyed than I have often been by the evils that we have suffered from the complication of our question ; and by what I have felt to be the tactlessness of many of our friends, who have obtruded their Non-Intrusion on the attention of Englishmen, when they should have kept by the cause of spiritual independence, or who, in the ordering of this cause before them, have argued independently of the special exercise or application that had been made of the Church's inherent power, when their great strength would have lain in defending the power itself. It is not to be told how much the real merits of our question have been obscured and mystified by this unfortunate complication ; and one great ingredient of force and clearness in your Lordship's work is the close adherence of it to that one principle, on which alone we can expect to engage the sympathies of the English Church, and, I may add, the sympathies of all the churches in Christendom. There is all the difference between the two parts of our controversy that there is between a genus and a species. Your Lordship has done well in confining your view to the genus—the generic or comprehensive principle, which, if once secured, would leave the possession of the species to ourselves.

But two things can be alleged in explanation of this ; and the latter of the two goes far to justify, insomuch as it has pre-cipitated a far more ostensible reference to the principles of Non-intrusion than might otherwise have been expedient.

In the first place, the only exception which Lord Aberdeen and others would lay upon our free discretion is, on the power of giving effect to the dissent of the people, however honest and religious we may judge that dissent to be, unless they are able to substantiate it by such reasons as we can approve of. Now, without entering at present on the rightness of our giving effect to a dissent in these circumstances, (which I think admits of most ample vindication,) let me but advert to the high estimation in which it was held by the Church—insomuch that they elevated it from the rank of a mere judicial principle on which they might act or not according to circumstances, to the rank of a law on which they must act invariably—thus marking a distinguished preference for the object or principle of that law. But it has been disallowed by the Court of Session; and what we want, therefore, is, that the Legislature shall append civil effect to it, through some such Bill as the Duke of Argyle's. Now, what is the return made to this application by Lord Aberdeen's Bill? It is something a great deal worse than a refusal, simply to confirm our law; for this were merely to consign the principle thereof back to its own level, and would leave us to act on it as heretofore as we saw cause. But more than this, he would degrade it immeasurably beneath the place it had before the Veto Law was passed—when we were at least free to act upon it judicially, though not bound to act upon it statutorily. He would take away this freedom, and on the tenderest of all points—that is, the very thing which we so much valued as to make it the object of a universal enactment, he would make the object of a universal prohibition; so that what formerly we may have done at any time, we must never, according to his Bill, do now. By his Bill, then, there are two principles struck at and done violence to : *first*, by an abridgment of our freedom at all—the principle of our spiritual independence ; *second*, by an abridgment of it on this particular question—the ancient constitutional principle of Non-intrusion. It is like the infliction of a double violence; and we are not to wonder at the double resentment or resistance to which it has given rise—or that what they have singled out as the object on which to violate our liberty, should have called forth our special regards or special vindication, as well as the general cause of liberty itself.

But, secondly, and still more urgently. When we did urge our spiritual independence apart from Non-intrusion, what use was made of this by our opponents? They gave forth that we had lost sight of the people, and were intent only on our own power. I can imagine nothing more exquisitely unjust and injurious, than the treatment of the Church in this respect, by the adversaries who were opposed to her. The only part of our spiritual independence that was in jeopardy was the power of giving effect to the dissent of the people; and it is in fact for their cause that the Church has incurred all the plagues and the perils of this controversy. And, on the other hand, the only exception which our antagonists were for laying on our spiritual independence, was the liberty of giving effect to the people's dissent; so that really, after all, their opposition, though ostensibly against us, was virtually and in effect against the people through us. Yet would these opponents of ours brand us with seeking our own aggrandizement, and not caring for the people; and, Conservatives though most of them were, gladly accepted the aid both of Radicals and Voluntaries, in urging home a popular invective and outcry against the pretensions of a domineering priesthood. This was beyond all endurance, and the temptation, or rather the necessity, was quite irresistible, that we should place the principle of Non-intrusion more on the foreground than we had done, that the real object of the Church might be understood, and so her character vindicated against the unworthy artifices of her multiform and motley opponents. I speak on my own historical recollections of what actually happened. At the outset of the Non-intrusion Committee's negotiations with Lord Aberdeen, and when I myself was Convener of it, I held converse as well as correspondence with his Lordship, and was quite willing at that time to exchange the Veto Law for the *liberum arbitrium.* It was reported that he in consequence wrote to the Dean of Faculty, now Lord Justice-Clerk, that he had prevailed on us to give up the Veto Law; and the representation which our enemies grafted on this report, and industriously circulated to our prejudice, was, that we had surrendered the people, and were now standing out on the question of our own power only. This was very hard to bear, when, in point of fact, what we have been standing out for all along, is for the power of protecting the people ; and, to save ourselves from the vile mystification practised against us by these our determined adversaries, we were obliged, whether we would or not, to speak, not in the general of spiritual independence only, but of the special and indeed the only contest for which that independence is at present staked—a contest for the security of Christian congregations against the intrusion of unacceptable ministers.

And now, my Lord, let me refer to an expression in your letter, when you say that the Church, by quitting the argument of her spiritual independence as the alone ground of her vindication, has given up the only position in which she was unassailable. She, in the first instance, has not given up this position, though compelled also to make use of other arguments besides. But what I particularly wish is to direct your Lordship's attention to the distinction between a cause being unassailable in respect of argument, and the same cause being unassailable in respect of practical safety. It is truly a possible thing to make out a resistless demonstration in favour

of our Church ; and yet, if we do nothing more but keep by
the terms of that demonstration, and make triumphant repetition of it, we may in fact be neglecting the only means by
which to save her from destruction. I have already shewn
what practically the effect is, when we make exclusive allega-
tion of our own spiritual power. Our adversaries, with a
singular disregard of all principle and truth, have availed
themselves of this for the purpose of detaching and alienating
the people from our cause. It was a most natural feeling on
the part of our friends, that if, with the mere view of simplifying, we were to concentrate our argument on a single point,
and this to make us controversially stronger, or stronger on
the abstract than we otherwise might be, we should thereby
become weaker in the concrete, and fall before a weight of
adversaries regardless of all argument, and resolved at every
hazard, and though with the sacrifice of every principle, to
overbear and trample on the Church of Scotland. Should it
come to this—should we be crushed by the hand of power,
and our virulent and determined enemies get the better of
us on the field of living contest, it will be a poor consolation
that we had the better of them on the field of argument. We
are not, therefore, to keep by the topic of our spiritual independence alone, when our enemies take such dishonest advantage of this. We are, in truth, fighting not only our own
battles, but the battles of the people ; and why should not
the people be made aware of it ? Are we to forfeit the benefit
of an alliance with those for whose best and highest interests
we are putting to hazard all our possessions and interests in
this world ; and this in order that we might become an easy
prey to those heartless oppressors, who first would asperse and
blacken, and then would destroy us ?

You have estimated well the evil of complicating an argument unnecessarily. But in some cases it may be a necessary

evil. Certain it is that it has cast an obscuration over the real strength and merits of our cause, in the eyes even of what may be called the higher reason of the country; and this is precisely the obscuration which your Lordship's work is so well fitted to dissipate. But even if educated minds are puzzled by the complexities of a question, how much more must we expect this in the minds of the general population? Now, what has the Church been doing for the sake of making out a necessary reformation, with the greatest ease and least possible disturbance? for, essentially conservative as she is, she would like to work out all her improvements in the safest and most pacific way. She for ten years has been labouring to effect a composition between the rights of patronage and the rights of popular conscience, so as to amalgamate these two distinct elements; and she succeeded by means of her Veto Law, which, if let alone, might have secured both the peace and efficiency of our Church for an indefinite period. But she has been precipitated into a warfare upon this question; and with singular moderation has her majority kept by a midway position, between an absolute and unlimited patronage on the one hand, and popular election on the other. She has thus subjected herself to the heavy disadvantage of maintaining a complex, when she might have adopted a simple proposition, and so commanded the cordial, unmixed, enthusiastic support of the great bulk and body of the religious public in Scotland. When I say that in their minds there is not room or comprehension for more than one idea, I say nothing especially disparaging to them; for this is precisely what your Lordship, as well as myself, must have experienced of those of the Conservative and cultivated orders who are now arrayed in hostility against the Church. For the sake of propitiating their understandings, you would cast off Non-intrusion from the controversy, and keep by spiritual independence. Now, for this very reason, we, to propitiate the full understandings of the country at large, should cast off Non-intrusion too, and keep by the one simple and intelligible principle of the abolition of patronage. There is no reason why, if Government and the Conservatives will not grant us the half measure which would have satisfied us, we should not lay hold of all the additional strength that we shall gain by seeking the whole measure— and more especially as the whole measure would satisfy us better. I have no affection whatever for Patronage in itself, nor do I see a single positive argument or principle that would incline me to the *adoption* of it. But as it exists, I for one, on the principle of making the most of things as they are, should have rejoiced in any practical expedient, by which to harmonize the right government of the Church with a state of matters already in being. But these foolish Conservatives won't let us; and with all my native preferences for the position of the *extréme gauche* upon this question, as no other alternative is left me, I most congenially and approvingly will go along with them. This is precisely the movement of our Church at this moment; and if she is charged because of it, with the waywardness of moving from one extreme to another, it is truly owing to no waywardness of hers, but to the impracticable obstinacy of the *extréme droit*, who, whether we look to ecclesiastical or to secular politics, will be found the real, though not the proximate causes, of all the violent and precipitate changes which take place in society.

In the present instance, I can clearly see a most justifiable reason (apart from the policy of it) for passing at once to the lower extreme, rather than attempting to take up with some of the intermediate positions. My general inclination is for a gradual and pacific march of improvement. Leibnitz's law of continuity in physics, I should like to see exemplified in politics also. In spite of all the ridicule that has been cast on bit and bit reforms, it is a style of reform which I greatly prefer to such sudden and large transitions by movements *per saltum*, as was effected for instance through the late Reform Bill. On this principle, I should have been satisfied at first with a mere *liberum arbitrium*—the very least and gentlest modification that could have been attempted on Patronage. But in very proportion to the moderation of my demand, now that it has been resisted, is my conviction of the intractable nature of the element I have had to deal with. Had I treated with Patronage from some of the more distant positions and been withstood, the hope might still have remained within me, that, by taking a nearer position, I might gain from it some mitigation of its rigours. But I have been treating with it all along from the nearest position which is at all possible. Of all men I have made the least and the gentlest demands upon it, and have therefore had the most emphatic evidence of its unyielding and impregnable quality. I of all men, then, am the most logically and legitimately entitled to pass at once to the conclusion, that nothing will serve but the utter extinction of this unruly element. Patronage and the popular will may not necessarily and in their own nature be immiscible, but enough for a practical conclusion that the men in power and in possession will not allow of their combination, and that, therefore, they are immiscible in deed and in actual performance. If the thing will not be regulated, it ought to be destroyed.

It grieves me to say that a process is now in operation which, if continued, will at length open the eyes of all virtuous and sound-hearted men, and convince them that Patronage is a thing which it is impossible to keep terms with. I allude to the profligate system now adopted of treating and trafficking with our licentiates ere they shall obtain a presentation. This tampering with the principles of the future ministers of religion bodes fearfully both for the Church and the country by another generation. It is dropping poison into the fountains of the national morality ; and if not arrested, will so speed the progress of corruption, that it must soon be visited by its own natural penalties, as well as call forth the judgments of offended Heaven on a degenerate land.

But it may well be asked, do we put ourselves into a likelier position for success by taking up the ground of Anti-patronage ? Not certainly if we look singly to the existing dispositions of our legislators ; nor am I at all sanguine that these will be much influenced or operated on through the medium of the Scottish population. On that population—I mean the best and most religious part of them—we are gaining every day ; and if Conservatives, on the one hand, have not scrupled to avail themselves of Radicals and political dissenters in opposition to the Church, we, on the other, might most legitimately rejoice in the accessions made to our strength from the truly Christian and conscientious dissenters who will swell our ranks on the event of that disruption to which many of us are now looking forward, and for which I am happy to say that a most hopeful preparation is now going on. It is our duty to do all we can for the averting of such a catastrophe, but it is also our duty to be in readiness for the worst ; and though I have a great dislike to all agitation when there is no practical call for it, yet, in present circumstances, I must confess that I do look with the most benignant complacency on the Defence Associations which are multiplying so fast in various parts of our country. They will form a ready-made apparatus for the support of a Church in full possession of that spiritual independence which had not been permitted to us within the pale of the national endowments. I trust it may be so well supported and extended as that we shall be enabled, in perfect freedom from the interdicts and tracasseries both of courts and of heritors, to impart without let or hindrance the blessings of Christian instruction to those many thousands who hitherto have been utter strangers to the habits and decencies of a Christian land. Heaven grant that, in this spirit of true charity and Christian patriotism, our ministers might be enabled, in return for their sufferings and their cares, to render this best of services to the commonwealth ; and, by saving the country from that sorest of all distempers, a profligate and irreligious common people, to save our now blind and infatuated aristocracy from themselves.

I have written with all the heaviness of an invalid, and am now rusticating in the country for the benefit of my health. But I could not leave your able and interesting letters any longer unreplied to. I shall rejoice at all times to hear from you, and promise never to inflict so long an epistle upon you in future. It would suit my strength and my engagements better to write not at length on the general subject, but shortly, and on single points of it at a time. Let me earnestly recommend as the object of your attention what may be called the human nature of our question, now that you have acquitted yourself in a style so masterly on the law of the question. I should rejoice if you were to make a study of the workings of this one system and that other throughout the country at large, and amongst the people who live in it. I feel assured it would convince you not of the innocence only, but the positive good of having our Church more popularized. It would dissipate the association so extensively prevalent between a popular system in the Church and democracy in the State, and land you in a conclusion the very reverse of that which is the all but universal faith of those of your own order.

THOMAS CHALMERS.

No. CCCV.—To Lord Lorne.

Edinburgh, 15*th March* 1842.

My dear Lord Lorne,—I received your last letter some days ago. It, in conjunction with your Lordship's truly admirable preface to the second edition of your work, convinces me that substantially we are far more at one than appears to be upon the surface. The most material difference respects the time in which the Church should have simplified the object of her endeavours, and openly announced what many of us have all along felt. Her optimum is the abolition of Patronage. It was the hopelessness of this attainment which restrained her from framing an expression sooner; and it is now her hopelessness of any effectual security against the evils of Patronage which convinces her that the time has now come for attempting the entire removal of it. Had your Lordship been aware of the whole of our correspondence with men in power, and of the treatment we have received at their hands, I feel confident that you would not think we had become hopeless too soon. I shall only instance the last of a long series of disappointments, in that Sir James Graham held out the prospect of an amicable settlement, *provided that we did not agitate the country;* and professes now, that had he understood our object of gaining the *liberum arbitrium,* he never would have entered into negotiation with us at all. Our confidence in public men is now completely shaken; and it is too much in them to expect that we shall lend ourselves any further to the objects of their policy by neglecting to avail ourselves any longer of the only human help which remains to us—the *friendship* of the people—until hostile statesmen shall have finished their last work upon us, and we thrown off by the one party shall have made new provision in the support of the other party, for a refuge to fall back upon.

Meanwhile, can anything be fairer than the warning now

given to the men in power? They know that the Duke's Bill
would bring us all into a state of quiescence; and they also
know that the passing of their own favourite measure would be
gall and wormwood to the great majority of the Church. They
are able to avert the consequence of this if they choose; and
if they do not, whether that consequence shall be the abolition
of the Patronage or the ruin of the Establishment, this is a result which must be laid in either case, not at our door, but at
that of our opponents.

There is one thing, however, which I believe they do not
know, and which, perhaps, it were well they did, for it is a
matter on which they seem to be absolutely incredulous,—and
that is the perfect determination on the part, I believe, of
hundreds of our clergy rather to be driven from their places
than to surrender the spiritual independence of the Church. I,
this morning, received a printed sketch of what will soon be
circulated among the Non-intrusionist clergy, and which will
shew what the prospects are which they now cherish, and
what the provision is which they are now planning to meet the
possibilities that are before them. I cannot think it wrong to
send my copy to your Lordship; and indeed I think it but fair
and desirous that even our worst enemies should be apprized
of what is really going forward, &c.   THOMAS CHALMERS.

P.S.—I have this day seen a Highland minister who assures
me that the whole of his synod (Glenelg) are in readiness to
quit the Establishment rather than submit to a civil supremacy
over the Church.—T. C.

No. CCCVI.—To WILLIAM LAMONT, JUN., ESQ., GLASGOW.

Edinburgh, 9th April 1842.

DEAR SIR,—I regret that I cannot attend a meeting, the
spirit and the objects of which I so thoroughly approve.

It is cheering to observe the progress of our great cause;

and that while, on the one hand, the ministers of our Church, in spite of every effort to shake or to seduce them, remain an unshrinking and undiminished majority in defence of her violated liberties, on the other hand, the public are becoming more alive every day to a sense of her wrongs. So that, between a resolved clergy and an attached and confiding people, let us hope, with the blessing of God, that the best and greatest of our National Institutes will yet stand its ground against all the attempts which have been made, and are still making, whether to vitiate or to destroy it.

I feel that I cannot estimate too highly the labours of your important Association ; and do hope, that under your influence, and within the sphere of your operations, many others will arise in your own likeness, and be instruments in the hand of Providence for the diffusion of sound information and right views of our question, both in the West and throughout the whole of Scotland.

On the subject of patronage, I had long been in the habit of regarding it as practicable to harmonize her initiative voice in the appointment of a minister with the sacred prerogatives of conscience, and the deference I have ever held due to the collective voice of every honest and religious, however humble a congregation. The experience of so many fruitless and fatiguing negotiations have now wearied me out, and forced both myself and many others to desist from this as a vain and hopeless enterprise. The reported attempts of patrons to tamper with the principles of our young licentiates on their entrance into the ministry, and so instil a deadly poison into the very fountain-heads of the nation's morality, have now completed my antipathy to the whole system, and led me to the conviction, that it were best both for the Church and the country of Scotland if it were conclusively put an end to.—I have the honour to be, dear Sir, yours most truly,   THOMAS CHALMERS.

No. CCCVII.—To Alex. Campbell, Esq., M.P.

Dunkeld, 23*d April* 1842.

My dear Sir,—I should have replied sooner to your kind note of more than a week ago. Be assured that the delay does not proceed from any indifference to your proposed movement, in which I earnestly pray that God may speed and prosper you ; and I further hope that you will put the right interpretation on my non-appearance in London at this time ; I stand much in need of repose, and I have come here to recruit between the labours of my class and the meeting of the General Assembly.

You are aware that Lord Lorne dislikes the Anti-patronage movement that is now afloat, and seemed to regret it as a disturbing force in the way of his father's Bill. Now, were I a legislator instead of an ecclesiastic, and disliked the method of popular election, I should be disposed to reason thus :—The passing of such a Bill, it is needless to disguise, would slacken, if not arrest, the Anti-patronage movement, even as the Veto Law did ; and this is a consideration which should not only stimulate the movement of such a measure, but, more encouraging still, will, in all likelihood, enlist others to support him, on purpose to avert what they think a great evil. In my eyes, so far from being an evil, I look forward to it as our final and most secure landing-place ; but, whether you will agree with me in this or not, you will at once perceive that this Anti-patronage movement, *fairly* viewed, should be hailed as an auxiliary, and looked upon not as a conflicting but as a conspiring force upon your side, and all this without prejudice to the opinion of ——, an opinion which I myself expressed in my correspondence with Lord Aberdeen, that the *optimum* of this matter were a Church whose ministers were paid by the State and chosen by the people.

I am most thankful, and I am sure that in this I am sympathized with by thousands, for the true Christian patriotism of your efforts on the side of the Church's independence, and enlargement out of her present difficulties.—Ever believe me, &c.,   THOMAS CHALMERS.

No. CCCVIII.—To JOHN C. COLQUHOUN, ESQ.

1842.

MY DEAR SIR,—I yesterday saw your letter to Mr. Hamilton. You wish the Church to declare publicly, that it would be satisfied with the *liberum arbitrium*. Should it not be enough for legislators to know that this is the lowest measure under which the great proportion of our clergy, I hope the majority, could conscientiously minister in the Church as an Establishment? We cannot say more, and for two reasons; first, the use made of such a declaration by our unprincipled enemies, would be to hold forth the Church to the country as having abandoned the people, satisfied with power to itself; but secondly, and chiefly, it is a declaration which the Church could not honestly make. For my own part, I should greatly prefer such a bill as that set forth by Mr. Hamilton, and still more would I prefer the total abolition of Patronage; yet, for the sake of the immense benefit to the people, which is conferred by an Establishment that is at all tolerable, I would keep by it with the *liberum arbitrium* alone, determined, at the same time, that as far as possible this said *liberum arbitrium* should be so exercised in every one instance, as that no minister should in any case be intruded on a parish contrary to the will of the congregation.

For what purpose should more be required of us than this? Is it that the odium of having sacrificed the people should be shuffled off by Members of Parliament and laid upon the Church? Let each party bear their own burden; and I for one am very glad that an alternative between the *liberum arbitrium* and the popular dissent, should be left with the legislature. Our unequivocal preference is for the latter. If their preference is for the former, let this be brought above boards, that the public may estimate at its real value the profession, not of Liberals only, but of all denominations. I rejoice to think that our majorities promise to be unbroken, and that the modern fines and rebukes of the Court of Session will tell about as little on our noble-hearted Church, as did the boots and halters and thumbscrews of their worthy predecessors before them.—I am, yours, &c.,   THOMAS CHALMERS.

No. CCCIX.—TO ALEXANDER GORDON, ESQ., LONDON.

Edinburgh, 3d January 1843.

MY DEAR SIR,—It is my earnest and anxious desire that you may not be annoyed after so much trouble, if I frankly state to you the difficulties which I feel in complying with the requisition by which I have been so much honoured, and that, too, at the hands of so many high and estimable men.

My greatest objection lies in this, that it is more of a Scotch than of an English or London requisition. I would not like to lecture in London because I was set to it by people here, but because I was drawn to it by people there ; what would be influential with me were a requisition sufficiently numerous, and the more so the better, by men of course possessing weight in society, but still by men desirous of such lectures for themselves, and that because they really want to become informed on the subject of them. It is with this view that I should defer more to a requisition signed by literary and ecclesiastical than by merely official men. To make plain my meaning, I would lay greater stress on any one of such names as those of James Hamilton or Isaac Taylor, or Joseph Bunting or Christopher Benson, or Hallam or Thomas Carlyle, &c. &c., than for

2 L

any half-dozen Members of Parliament, merely as such. I do not say this to the disparagement of those few who have subscribed your requisition ; for, apart from their situation, I can recognise some of great mental power and great Christian worth amongst them. But I want to make it plain to you, that the chief recommendation of names in my eyes would be, that they were such names as afforded a sufficient guarantee for a desirous and intelligent audience. In this view, such names as those of William Hamilton and Alexander Gillespie —and first and foremost of all, allow me to specify your own— are to me of far greater influence than the names of hundreds at a distance from London ; neither do I see that there is any virtue in the names of whole corporations, such as kirk-sessions and others. The most powerful of all requisitions were one subscribed by respectable citizens, amongst whom one could discern men of literature, and ecclesiastics of all denominations.

And then, as to our Church question, I should like you to know how very little desirous I am of enlightening mere statesmen and politicians on the subject. After the repeated disappointments of the years that are past, it is very natural for statesmen to magnify their office, and to imagine that all which is said or done bears a reference to them. The truth is, that in all my future treatment of these topics, my converse will be with secular and Christian philanthropists rather than with statesmen ; indeed, I would shrink from a position or character which I should feel so utterly grotesque as that of an expedition to London for the purpose of schooling the Parliament ; and for doing away every aspect of aught so ridiculous, I feel relieved, as if by the removal of an obstacle in the way, by the recent deed of our Convocation, which will probably bring our whole matter to an issue before I can possibly go to London, which certainly cannot be sooner than the month of April ; and if I do go, it will be for the purpose of addressing those who take an intellectual or Christian interest in the grave ecclesiastical question. The doings and state of the Church of Scotland may supply preface and illustrations for my argument, but it will be an argument not intended, not perhaps fitted for, the apprehension of statesmen, but which, with the blessing of God, might serve, in these extraordinary times, to unite and direct the energies of those who have the Christian good of our people at heart, and who, either with or without Establishments, are ready to co-operate in whatever might best conduce to the spread of truth and righteousness in our land.

Let me entreat that you will take no more trouble in this matter. Forgive all that may appear harsh or ungrateful to you in this letter. If I do go to London, it can only be on a very clear and imperative call of duty, for all my personal tastes and inclinations would forbid the movement—a movement, therefore, which would require a much louder call, and a much clearer and opener path than I yet see before me. I cannot let this letter go without expressing the high esteem and value in which I hold such names as those of Sir John Pirrie and Mr. Plumptre.—With kindest regards to Mrs. Gordon and your family, I ever am, &c.,

THOMAS CHALMERS.

No. CCCX.—To ALEXANDER GORDON, ESQ.

Edinburgh, 2d *February* 1843.

MY DEAR SIR,—Your requisition has now assumed such a shape, both in its substance and in the signatures which are appended to it, that I am now greatly more disposed to entertain it than I was at the earlier stages of our correspondence on the subject.

You are aware that I have all along deprecated the idea of a lectureship in London on the Scottish Church question, and that, from the very first, I have shrunk from the possibility of any such construction being put on any such lectureships being delivered there, as a presumptuous and futile attempt to influence the decision of that question ; and the question had not commenced, at least so as to attract public notice, when I delivered my lectures in 1838 on National Establishments of religion, and the proposed supplement to these will naturally partake of the same general character, being intended for an audience not of statesmen but of *scholars*, who take a literary or professional interest in the subject—a subject of paramount importance, and which will outlast all the fluctuations of this world's restless politics.

I feel the utmost possible respect both for the noble and parliamentary requisitionists whose names were in the first presentation, transmitted some weeks ago, but not without the apprehension that the very appearance of these should foster an erroneous notion of the real design and character of the proposed undertaking. They are the literary and ecclesiastical names both in the first and subsequent presentations which have decided me in its favour, and I now look forward in good earnest to the probability of my sooner or later visiting your metropolis for the fulfilling of the task which you have put into my hands.

But, lest in any quarter there should be a lurking expectation of my appearance there either before or during the discussion of our Church question in Parliament, let me state, once for all, that I cannot possibly attempt the delivery of these lectures till the month of June, or after the rising of our General Assembly, by which time it is to be hoped that the decision of the Legislature, whatever that may be, on the wrongs complained of by the Scottish Church, will be no longer a matter of anticipation, but a matter of history.

I regret that I can only yet hold out a conditional promise

of complying with the request by which you and the other requisitionists have honoured me, and I fear that a whole month must elapse ere I can venture on a definite reply.— Ever believe me, my dear Sir, yours with greatest esteem and regard, THOMAS CHALMERS.

No. CCCXI.—TO ALEXANDER GORDON, ESQ.

Edinburgh, March 1843.

MY DEAR SIR,—Referring to my letter at the beginning of last month, I beg now to state, that the idea of my lectureship in London on the subject specified in our recent correspondence, must, for a time at least, be abandoned.

The prospect of a disruption in our Establishment has led to the formation of a financial committee for the support and extension of the Free Presbyterian Church in Scotland. Of this committee I have been appointed convener, and the importance, as well as weight and labours of the consequent duties, must detain me in Scotland for several months to come. I feel assured that after the turbulence of party passions has subsided, the Church of Scotland will be found, from first to last, to have acted a consistent part throughout all the stages of this controversy.

The call or concurrence by the people in the appointment of ministers has ever been the integral part of our constitution. When the method she laid down some years ago for regulating this part of our procedure was litigated before the Civil Courts, she made appearance for no other purpose than to prevent, if possible, a separation of the temporalities from the cure. In this she failed, as she had often done in former questions of disputed settlements brought before the civil tribunal, and was prepared to undergo all the consequences which had ever followed on any adverse decision—that is, a forfeiture of the benefice. It is the first time since the Revolution that other consequences have been made to follow, that orders are issued forth on our Church by the Civil Courts for the doing of ecclesiastical acts, so that we at their bidding, and by the enforcement too of pains and penalties, must proceed in the ordination of ministers, to establish the pastoral relation between them and their people, however much we might deem the step we should be thus compelled to take contrary to the principles of the word of God, and to the Christian good of parishes. At no stage have we resisted the law.

When the first adverse decision of the Court of Session was appealed to the House of Lords, and confirmed there, we conformed to that decision to the extent of all which had ever followed on similar adverse decisions. We resigned the temporalities ; but more than this was required of us, and, for the first time since the Revolution Settlement, an interdict was by the Court of Session laid across the path of one of our Presbyteries when engaged in prosecuting the trials of one of our licentiates with a view to his ordination. It is true that besides this, such trials, when there is no legal question, are in general preparatory to the immediate entrance on the living and the cure. But the effect of such a question in all past instances, when given against us, was only to dissever the living, and never to intermeddle in any way either with the ordination or the cure. It was for the first time in the history of our Church that this distinction had been violated, insomuch that it was felt to be an outrage by the unanimous Commission of the General Assembly, where there were men of all ecclesiastical parties, although since then a party has been found to acquiesce, not only in this, but in all the subsequent and still larger excesses of the Court of Session, which now claims the power of taking our whole discipline and government in its own hands. The challenge has been made by one of their own number to tell what the inch of ground is on which the Church of Scotland has now a free jurisdiction, or to specify a single question wherewith the Court of Session might not intermeddle so as to bring the Church, even in things of the most exclusively sacred and spiritual character, under its own absolute control.

To be protected from this altogether novel invasion by the Court of Session, we made another appeal to the House of Lords in the case of Auchterarder, and they have again confirmed this second and distinct adverse sentence of the inferior Court. It is only now that we can be charged with resistance to the law should we abide in the Establishment, and refuse obedience to this new usurpation. Rather than incur the charge, we choose to quit a territory where such disobedience can be alleged against us. For our carrying this determination into effect two steps, we conceive, have to be taken—the first is the appeal to the Legislature, not to reverse the decision of the House of Lords, that we know to be incompetent, but to modify or remove the solitary statute passed many years subsequent to the settlement of Presbytery, and now discovered, for the first time, to conflict with the constitutional acts by which, both at the Revolution of 1688, and at the union between the two States, the liberties of the Scottish Church were by solemn treaty granted and secured to the Scottish nation. The Acts on which we have all along rested our security were not once looked at and referred to in the House of Lords, and in the House of Commons the only treatment bestowed upon them is that the principles which they embody—though recognised and ratified by their own predecessors in the legislation of other days—are now denounced as monstrous and intolerable ; meanwhile there has been no change in the claims or pretensions of the Scottish Church, the only change which has taken place is in the principles and will of the English Parliament.

Our appeal to the Church's constitution having thus been

defeated, there remains but one other appeal more, that is to
the Church's conscience—even that resolute and unswerving
conscience, which, after the struggles of more than a century,
won for us our ecclesiastical constitution, which still is vigorous and entire as ever, now that the constitution of our Establishment has been destroyed. We can no more acquiesce at
this day in the power of the State over things spiritual, than
we did in the seventeenth century. It is true that the same
Government which is pleased at the change which has been
effected in the conditions on which, as a National Church, we
obtained our support, might also change the conditions on
which all Churches whatever now enjoy their toleration ; but
even this will not move us. We can no more yield to the Peers
of England their maxim that the Church is the creature of the
State, than we can consent to the dogma of one of their own
philosophers, that morality is the creature of law—the one is
Hobbism in Ethics, the other is the Hobbism of Christianity :
both are alike abhorrent to us. In a few short weeks the re-
nunciation of our connexion with the State will take place by
the deed of the General Assembly.

I once intended, but now give it up as a hopeless and unavailing task, to touch both on the mis-statement of our principles, and the glaring misrepresentations of fact, which, in
the matter of our Church question, have so blinded and bewildered the English understanding. All this has now gone by,
while the general question of the footing on which a National
Establishment of religion might be upheld, or of the harmony
which I hold to be the possible, nay, the most easy and practicable harmony of the legal provision, on the one hand, with
the liberties of the Christian Church upon the other,—this
question, so far from losing its interest, has only now risen to
the importance which it never had before. Let us hope that,
with the blessing of God, events will at length open men's

eyes, and work out what all remonstrance and all argument have failed to effect.—I have the honour to be, &c.,

THOMAS CHALMERS.

No. CCCXII.—To ALEXANDER GORDON, ESQ.

Edinburgh, 17th May 1843.

MY DEAR SIR,—I have now left Dunkeld. Your letter of the 11th has given me inexpressible relief; for personally I have no wish but the contrary to be in London, and without a very clear and imperious call of duty I would rather not incur the fatigues and the hazards of a lectureship there, however brief. At the same time, I think it likely that the gentlemen whom you have consulted have misunderstood both your object, and also my own views and inclinations. I never would have thought of lecturing in London till after the determination of our question by the Legislature. I could not have prevailed on myself to do so before it, and would have recoiled from the semblance of aught so presumptuous and grotesque as that of *schooling* the Parliament. My idea of the proper time, if ever it shall come, for my appearance would have been subsequent either to their resolution of doing nothing, and so leaving us to our present struggles with the Court of Session, or to their resolution of passing such a positive and obnoxious measure as would have forced us out of the Establishment altogether. On either of which events I should have felt it desirable to harmonize our resistance in the one case, or our secession in the other, with the principles which I advocated in my former lectureship on the lawfulness and expediency of National Churches; and such would have been the substance of my reply to any requisition had it been now made to me, so that the only present effect of such a requisition would have been to manifest the interest now felt in London for the Scottish Church;—a manifestation, I do think, fitted to have a wholesome influence upon Government,

2 M

and to make them, perhaps, more wary in their attempts to crush and overthrow us. I am even hopeful that, through your interview with Mr. Campbell, a certain amount of this mediate and precautionary influence may already have been brought to bear upon them ; let us hope and pray, however, that any movement on my part will be superseded by an act of justice done to the Church of Scotland ; and be assured that with no part of your much loved letter do I more thoroughly sympathize than when, devolving the cause upon God, you speak of waiting the *evolutions* of His wise and holy providence.— I am, my dear Sir, yours affectionately,

Thomas Chalmers.

No. CCCXIII.—To Rev. —— ——.

Edinburgh, 19*th March* 1843.

Dear Sir,—Your letter has given me great pain—not that I see a difficulty in the question when viewed in the light of my own conscience, and according to the strength of my own confidence ; but I do feel deeply for the distress of which you have presented me with so affecting a picture, and in particular my heart bleeds for poor Mrs. ——, whose fears are so very natural, and must be so very distracting to her spirits.

Suffer me first to address myself to the question as one of conscience, which I do the more readily because you speak of your own misgivings on this score, when you think of the rightful claims which your creditors have to whatever might belong to you. Do not suspect me of sitting in judgment upon another man's conscience, (1 Cor. x. 29,) but suffer me to state my own views :—If I were compelled to abandon my stipend by that highest of all necessities, (the necessity of principle,) then I should not look upon it as a thing which belonged to me, and that morally I was not more responsible to my creditors for it than if it had been wrested from me by the hand of violence.

And, second, as to the strength of my confidence, I will not rest it on any other foundation than the promise of God. If we go fearlessly on in the way of duty He will make good His own declaration, that " as the day comes, the provision will come." He will not forsake the families of those who put their trust in Him. He hath said to such, " I will never leave you nor forsake you." So that we may boldly say, the Lord is my helper, and I will not fear what men can do to me. I will not at present speak of our prospects. I would not run the hazard of misleading you by presenting you with any calculations whatever upon these. I can only say that the impressive representation which you have set before me will make me all the more strenuous in behalf of our general fund for the support of the Free Church, believing as I do, that many, very many, are our faithful clergy, with whom it will form their main earthly dependence in this matter. I have had much to encourage me, and feel assured that, under God, if the friends of our Church will give it what they might, and what they ought, we shall not only make out a moderate competency for all the disestablished ministers, but be enabled to extend over the whole of Scotland the blessings of a Christian education. I enter fully into the expression of your being paralyzed and unable to do aught for us in your own parish. However much we value the active co-operation of the minister, yet it is not indispensable to the establishment of a local association. We are setting up these even in parishes where ministers are hostile ; and it will be far more practicable in cases such as yours where they are friendly.—I am, my dear Sir, yours most truly,

THOMAS CHALMERS.

No. CCCXIV.—To the Same.

Edinburgh, 20th March 1843.

My dear Sir,—I submitted your letters to one of the leading men in Edinburgh, and will not shew them to any more, as I do not think that any other conclusion can be come to than what he and I agreed upon. You are quite right in supposing that others in this season of toil will be placed in circumstances of great and peculiar difficulty ; and accordingly a representation, similar to your own, was sent to me yesterday. I doubt not there will be more ; and the just effect of them all is, (in the utter hopelessness of doing much, if any thing, in the way of special adaptation of our means to special cases,) to stimulate our utmost endeavours for making good the general fund, that supplemented by the separate efforts of each congregation might lighten, and if so be, do away the privations consequent on the surrender of our present temporalities.

The number of our Associations, I am happy to say, has now reached 405 ; and it is our earnest desire that no parish, however the minister might stand affected, shall be without one. But human helps will prove a vain and impious reliance without a single-minded dependence on Him who can make all things work together for our good. I will not let go my confidence that He will make all to emerge in the good of His Church, and in a surpassing compensation to the faithful adherents of His cause for all their relinquishments and all their losses.—I beg my best regards and sympathies to Mrs. —— ; and in the earnest hope that God will clear up a way of comfort both for yourself and your family, I ever am, my dear Sir, yours most truly,   Thomas Chalmers.

No. CCCXV.—To Andrew Johnston, Esq.

Edinburgh, 20*th April* 1843.

My dear Sir,—I return you many thanks for your munificent and truly encouraging donation of £100 for our Free Church. You say in aid of the New Endowment Scheme. Unless you forbid me, I will assign it to the Building Fund; as in the first instance we shall chiefly look to the yearly produce of our subscriptions and Associations for the sustentation of the ministry. These Associations now amount to 405, and with the fair prospect of being doubled in the course of the summer.

In regard to your important suggestions, it is very certain that both the government sanction of our Veto and the Queen's oath of protection to our constitutional rights have been much insisted on in the course both of our debates at home, and of our correspondence with London. I do not see that any farther delay should be incurred for the sake of a formal restatement of these, more especially as we are now declared, both by the legal courts and by Parliament, to be on the ground of rebellion against the law, if we do not implement their decisions in every such spiritual matter as they might choose to take under their cognizance and control. The sooner we make ourselves off from that ground the better.

Let it be our stay and our confidence that the Lord reigneth; and that He will make all to issue in the extension of His Son's kingdom, and the establishment of His own glory.

Perhaps you could suggest how it is that the sympathy and fellow-feeling of the evangelical public in England could be rendered most available for the promotion of our common cause in this country.

Remember me in the most cordial and affectionate manner

to dear Mrs Johnston, and to the respected families of Sir Thomas F. Buxton, Mr. Gurney, and Mr. Hoare.—Ever believe me, my dear Sir, yours most gratefully and truly,

THOMAS CHALMERS.

No. CCCXVI.—To ANDREW JOHNSTON, ESQ.

Edinburgh, 3d May 1843.

MY DEAR SIR,—I cannot lay my hand on any copy of the speech to which you refer ; but the matter respecting which you inquire may be shortly stated thus :—

I never doubted the perfect competency and power of the Church to pass the Veto Law, and the obligation under which all its courts lay to regulate their procedure by its provisions. When this ecclesiastical law was found not to quadrate with the civil law, I never counted on any other effect from this want of harmony than the forfeiture of the temporalities of the benefice—in itself a very serious evil. To avert this evil, I recommended the repeal of the Veto, but in conjunction at the same time with the condition, which I held to be indispensable, that the Strathbogie ministers should retrace their steps, for that it was of prime necessity to vindicate the authority of the Church over her refractory members. These ministers, instead of making reparation for their disobedience, proceeded onwards in their course to the ordination of Mr. Edwards, for which glaring outrage they were most righteously deposed. On this I instantly withdrew my recommendation, not of one measure, but of several measures, which behoved to stand or fall together —to be adopted or rejected, not singly, but simultaneously.

It was in deference to the good of a National Establishment, or of a legal provision for the clergy, that I wished to bring our law into accordance with the law of the State. But when I found that the interpretation put on my proposal was that I deferred to the legal authority of the State in things spiritual, and also that the Strathbogie ministers proceeded on this interpretation, instead of submitting to the discipline of their ecclesiastical superiors, I gave up the attempt to secure the Establishment principle till it should be freed from the principle of Erastianism. For on any other footing than that of entire spiritual independence, I should hold a National Church to be a moral nuisance.

I know not if I have made myself intelligible. Certain it is that I have now given up all faith in the efficacy of arguments. It is by deeds, not arguments, that the truth will become manifest at last.

You will be delighted to hear that our Associations for the support of the Free Church now amount to 514 ; and we expect by the time of the General Assembly to have more than the half of Scotland organized.

I had a letter this morning from the munificent William Campbell of Glasgow, who now despairs of the Government being brought to reason upon our question, and tenders £2000 for our Building Fund.

With earnest prayer for God's best blessings on you and yours, ever believe me, my dear Sir, yours most gratefully and truly, THOMAS CHALMERS.

[*Durness by Golspie*, 20*th July* 1843,—MY DEAR SIR,—From several causes, which I need not state particularly, I could not possibly leave the manse till a fortnight ago—waiting an opportunity of conveying my furniture and part of my family by sea, from near the shores of Cape Wrath to Thurso, and my wife and the younger branches of the family by land, being a distance of at least 70 miles ; not a house or hut could be got nearer for their accommodation. I have taken a room in the only inn in the district where I at present sojourn, in the midst of a poor and afflicted but sympathizing people—some of whom, I trust, have been taught to put their trust in the Lord. Hitherto we have met together to worship in the field, and we have no prospect, at present, of a site for church or manse from our noble proprietor. My feelings, and that of my family, on leaving the manse, after a happy residence of thirty-one years, I cannot easily describe. Though painful, in some respects, yet I trust it was a willing sacrifice. The cause is good ; Jehovah-jireh is a strong tower. While we have had cause to sow in tears, may we reap in joy. My wife was born in the same manse she lately left empty, left two of our children's dust behind, and accompanied by six, all hitherto unprovided for, to sojourn among strangers, has displayed a moral heroism which is soothing to my feelings.— My dear and honoured Sir, yours very truly,   Wm. Findlater.

The Rev. Dr. Chalmers, Edinburgh.]

CCCXVII.—To the Rev. William Findlater.

Edinburgh, 30th July 1843.

My very dear Sir,—I received your deeply interesting, and let me add, affecting letter on Friday, and the same day made its contents known to Mr. Dunlop, who is Convener of the Distributing Committee, and who feels on the subject of your application precisely as I do ; even that it is a case which must be instantly attended to and met. I hope you will suffer no inconvenience from the delay of a few days, as the Committee does not meet till Friday next, when I am sure that your proposal will on the instant be acceded to and acted on.

Though such matters do not fall within my official range, (mine being the in-gathering rather than the out-giving department,) yet I beg that you will not let that restrain any future communications which you might wish to make to me ; for I shall feel it quite a privilege and a pleasure to attend to them.

Tell dear Mrs. Findlater how my heart bled at the representation of the departure from Durness, and from the house in which she had lived from her birth. May she and you and all your family richly experience the Saviour's promise, that though in the world we shall have tribulation, in Him we shall have peace. May we learn to sit loose to a world that is so fast loosening from our hold ; and may the Giver of all grace fit and prepare us for living together in that city which hath foundations, and where sin and sorrow and separation are unknown.

You will be pleased to hear that our cause is progressing rapidly. Indeed, our chief pressure now arises from the rapidly increasing number of our adhering congregations. Nevertheless, I retain the unshaken confidence, that with God's blessing we shall be enabled to build up all and provide for all.

Give my kindest regards to Mrs. Findlater, and with earnest prayers for Heaven's best blessings upon you and yours, ever believe me, my dear Sir, yours most cordially and truly,

THOMAS CHALMERS.

No. CCCXVIII.—To PROFESSOR SEDGWICK OF CAMBRIDGE.

Edinburgh, 16*th March* 1844.

MY DEAR SIR,—I take it exceedingly kind that you should have bestowed the attentions and the courtesies which you have done on Dr. Candlish.

It appears very clearly to me, from your letter, that very strange exaggerations have been practised on the credulity of those at a distance from us respecting the violence and asperity of our Free Churchmen. I live in the very thick of the controversy, and can give you my solemn assurance that I do not know of more than one or two instances which require to be at all defended—and even those are of a character in no way outrageous. I observe, from the report of the London meeting, that I myself have been made the subject of one of those misrepresentations, and may therefore be regarded as an evidence at first hand on the question of its justness and truth ; and I am confident you will give me credit when I tell that both the meaning and the spirit of the expression which has been imputed to me have been altogether misunderstood and perverted. The truth is, that we are far too busy, too much engrossed with our own weighty affairs, to say much, or even to think much, of our residuary friends. I am well-nigh overborne with matters which engross all my attention and time, having had no less than 210 students at our theological seminary, and of these a number of first-year attendants three times greater than I had last year in the University of Edinburgh. Such is the impulse which our movement has given to the ecclesiastical profession, that the number of theological students preparing for the Free Church in Edinburgh alone, is very nearly double the number preparing for the Establishment in all the four universities of Scotland. We are aware all the while that there is a world of calumny abroad against us, and our best way is to let it spend its force, and not trouble ourselves either with the authors who originate or with the newspapers which give it circulation. "We are doing a great work, and why should we come down to them?"

I must not attempt in this letter to enter into detail on that very voluminous controversy to which you have adverted, but which, at the same time, if your engagements would allow of it, is altogether worthy of your studious and sustained attention, involving as it does great principles, and leading as it will do to the most momentous results. I shall undertake no more at present than fill up this sheet by as succinct and synoptical a statement as I can possibly give within such narrow limits of our Scottish Church question. For the sake of brevity let me endeavour to present you with the leading points in numerical order:—

1. The line of demarcation between the civil and the ecclesiastical was a great topic of contention between the Church and the State in Scotland during nearly the whole of the seventeenth century, which at length, after the persecutions and the martyrdoms of twenty-eight years of the reigns of Charles II. and James II., was terminated by the Revolution Settlement.

2. By this Settlement, the relation in which the Church and the State stood to each other was distinctly and definitely laid down. It forms, in fact, the great charter of our constitutional law and liberties, and was solemnly renewed and ratified by the articles of union between the two kingdoms.

3. By this charter it is provided that the government of the Church is distinct from that of the civil magistrate, and the final jurisdiction in things spiritual was vested in our ecclesiastical Courts. But ours being an Established Church, questions occasionally arose which involve temporalities along with matters of purely ecclesiastical government ; and so it was further provided that, where on those questions the decisions of the civil and the ecclesiastical Courts conflicted with each other, the civil decisions should infer only civil effects, and the ecclesiastical only ecclesiastical effects ; and till within these few years nothing was of more familiar occurrence than the decisions of the Church courts taking effect as to all matters of discipline, and ordination, and Church government, and the contrary decisions of the law courts taking effect by the forfeiture of the temporalities, and of consequence the separation of the emoluments from the duties of the pastoral office. This precluded the respective powers from ever coming into collision, while they operated powerfully and often wholesomely as a check upon each other.

4. In 1712, or twenty-two years after the Revolution Settlement, and five years after the union, the Act of Queen Anne, for the restoration of patronage, was passed. But for more than a century after this, the great constitutional principle of the separate jurisdictions of the two sets of courts—the civil and the ecclesiastical—and the confinement of each within their own proper sphere, was observed inviolable. Contrary decisions were sometimes given on the same question as before, but still the minister, whom the ecclesiastical court admitted to any

given cure, was charged with all its duties, though if, unfortunately, as it occasionally happened, the civil court gave a
decision adverse to his civil rights as minister, he behoved to
relinquish the temporalities of the office.

5. And not till within these three or four years has the discovery been made that the Act of Queen Anne did envelop a
contradiction to the principles of the Revolution Settlement
and the articles of union; a discovery which ran as counter
to all the previous conceptions of the civilians as the ecclesiastics in this country—and upon which the civil courts now do
what, for a hundred and fifty years, they had never offered to
do—overrule the discipline, and ordinations, and all the other
judgments of our ecclesiastical court; thus taking upon themselves the entire government of the Church of Scotland.

6. On this discovery being made, an application came from
the Church to the Legislature—the object of which was to
remodel that one law so as to bring it into union with that
prior and original constitution, upon which our Church entered
into union with the State in 1690, and Scotland entered into
union with England in 1707. It was in fact asking of them
nothing more than to rectify their own blunder, so as that no
subsequent act of theirs should be suffered to violate the prior
constitution which they themselves had ratified.

7. The application to Parliament was disregarded; and
when the Church was thus defeated in her attempts to obtain
redress on the ground of the British constitution, she had no
other choice than to fall back on the ground of her original
principles, appeal to her own conscience, and submit these
anew to the decision of her own conscience—that conscience
which bore her honourably through the struggles of the seventeenth century, and at length won for her a constitution in
which she could acquiesce, but in the violation of which she
cannot acquiesce; and so she relinquishes her connexion with

the State, rather than submit to the government of the civil power in those matters which she deemed to be sacredly and peculiarly her own.

Such is a very brief outline of our question, and I have it not in my power at present any farther to extend it. Let me only say, that so far from upholding such an establishment as that which I have renounced, I, in every pleading for the cause of National Churches, made an express reservation in behalf of the Church's spiritual liberties, which have now been scattered to the winds. I would have been a renegade to my own principles had I remained in an established church; and the only way of fulfilling them was to come out from amongst them.

Let me farther add, that the Free Church of Scotland is probably doing more at this moment for the establishment principle than any other church or community of Christians in the world. We have gone out on the establishment principle, and are so giving that principle all the weight of a disinterested testimony; and are at this moment, I believe, giving, in consequence, the utmost disappointment and offence to many of the Voluntaries. Had we remained in and swallowed all the humiliations which the civil power have laid and are still laying on the skeleton Establishment of Scotland, the principle of Establishments would have been thoroughly brought into utter scorn and contempt, and the triumph of Voluntaryism would have been complete.—I am, my dear Sir, yours truly,

THOMAS CHALMERS.

No. CCCXIX.—To D. M. M. CRICHTON, ESQ.

Burntisland, 16th August 1841.

MY VERY DEAR SIR,—I mean to be at home all this week, with the exception of Friday, and also to be at home on Mon-

day next week.   If God will, I shall be in Edinburgh on
Tuesday and Wednesday.

It delights me to observe that things are fast approaching
to that state in which there will be no room for the slightest
shade of a difference betwixt us.   I long to see you, and talk
with you on a subject upon which our friends are not particularly ripe,—I mean the future economics of our Church, should
the Legislature be so infatuated as to force on a disruption
from the Establishment.

The man who was thought a Utopian when he, seven years
ago, predicted £10,000 a year for Church Extension, and
afterwards realized £50,000 a year, has some claim to have his
views considered, when he now, with far greater confidence,
predicts, with the blessing of God, £100,000 a year for Church
independence, and as much more as will superadd the building
of churches to a secure maintenance for one and all of our
Non-Erastian clergymen.

It were well if you could let me know when I might have
the pleasure of seeing you.—I ever am, my dear Sir, yours with
the most cordial regard and esteem,   THOMAS CHALMERS.

No. CCCXX.—To D. M. M. CRICHTON, ESQ.

Edinburgh, 18th February 1842.

MY VERY DEAR SIR,—I owe you many apologies for having
delayed so long my reply to your letter of the 2d.

Go on and prosper, my dear Sir, and may God abundantly
reward your labours of love.   Let me again reiterate what I
have often said, had we twenty labourers like you there would
be enough of instrumentality at least for arousing Scotland.

With best wishes for you and yours, I ever am, my dear Sir,
yours most gratefully and truly,   THOMAS CHALMERS.

No. CCCXXI.—To George Yule, Esq.

Morningside, 9th June 1843.

Dear Sir,—I am at present so much engrossed that I have not had time to reply sooner than now to your letter of the 2d of this month.

For more than twenty-five years now I have studiously avoided the habit of attending public meetings as encroachments on my strength and time which I could not well bear; and nothing but the exigencies of our Church could have led me to take that part in them which I have recently done.

And now, with my decaying vigour and my increasing engagements, I am in far less favourable circumstances than ever for sharing in a work which I must forthwith leave in the hands of younger and abler men.

There is one strong temptation, however, to attend one or other of the meetings which you propose. I should like for once to dissipate the groundless misunderstandings which still linger, I fear, in the minds of the Evangelical Dissenters, as if there were ever the slightest reluctance either on my part, or on the part of those who think along with me, to co-operate with them in all good works. But there are two reasons which oblige me to resist even this inducement, however powerfully it operates on my own taste and inclinations :—

1. The present state of my engagements, along with a sense of utter exhaustion, from which I do not hope to recover for some weeks, would disable me from doing full justice to my views.

2. An opportunity will occur, in the month of July, at the bicentenary celebration then to be held of the Westminster Assembly, and which, I trust, will be attended by the ministers and members of all evangelical denominations. I hope, in particular, that Dr. Wardlaw will return good for evil, and though

I do not meet with him now, will give us the benefit of his presence on that occasion.

I am going to use a great liberty both with him and with Dr. Winter Hamilton. Will you have the goodness to say to them how kind I should take it if they, and any other members of the deputation, would honour me so far as breakfast with me any morning during their stay in Edinburgh.—I am, dear Sir, yours truly, THOMAS CHALMERS.

No. CCCXXII.—To CAPTAIN BURNETT OF MONBODDO.

Banchory House, 10th *September* 1843.

MY DEAR SIR,—The umbrella came safe to hand. There is another small matter which I have forgotten, Mr. B.'s account for shoe-mending. I am quite ashamed that you should have such trouble about these bagatelles ; and yet things small in material amount may be great in principle. "He who is unfaithful in the least, is unfaithful also in much."

But what most impels me to write at present is to assure you of the delight which your letter has given me. You do me no more than justice when you suppose that I was greatly moved and affected at the time of our separation. I can truly say that no place and no people have taken so strong a hold both of my memory and my heart as your own Monboddo, to which I shall ever look back as I would to a much-loved home, where for the whole of a happy but short-lived week I felt myself domesticated in the midst of beauty and quietness, and, above all, of kind affection—these most soothing appliances to the mind of one who longs for retirement from the bustle and the agitations of public life. But I must not forget what some one of our poets says of the transition from loving much to loving wrong ; nor so fasten my regards on your dear earthly paradise, as to withdraw me from the calls of duty, or the needful preparations for that home in the heavens, where sorrow and suffering, and best of all, where sin is unknown, and, where loving each other with pure hearts fervently, we shall be enabled to serve God without frailty, and without a flaw.

I have just come from a most extraordinary scene. I had given Mr. Thomson the hope that I might preach at his tent in Banchory. He chose to placard this over all Aberdeen; and there assembled about six or seven thousand people. He got the pulpit carried from the tent to his own front entry, and I have preached the identical sermon to them that I did at Auchinblae, to six or seven thousand people assembled upon his lawn. I have been forcibly reminded of the last delicious Sabbath in your place, and which I so exceedingly enjoyed after the service was over, from the time that Mrs. Burnett received me into her carriage, and throughout the whole of that evening, when I was so much regaled, both by my own solitary walks around your house, and at the return of all its much valued inmates, to each of whom individually, I beg again to offer my most affectionate regards.—Ever believe me, my very dear Sir, yours with the greatest respect and regard,

THOMAS CHALMERS.

P. S.—There is nothing which has afflicted me so much for a long time as the description you give, both of your own feelings and those of Mrs. Burnett at the time of our separation. Before you receive this I shall have passed the Mill Inn in the mail for Montrose, and will look to its door with an enhanced interest. Let me entreat a place in yours and Mrs. Burnett's prayers, that Jesus Christ may be the Lord my strength to guide and guard amid the fascinations and trials of an evil world. May Heaven's best blessings rest upon you both.—T. C.

No. CCCXXIII.—To Captain Burnett of Monboddo.

Edinburgh, 23d March 1847.

My dear Sir,—There is a most entire accordance of principle betwixt us in all that you say throughout your last most interesting letter. Drunkenness is the great master-evil in our land. There is a variety started lately in regard to Temperance Associations, which, I think, will take well with many who recoil somewhat from the present constitution of them. An association has been recently formed by the Rev. Mr. Reid here, an eloquent and zealous teetotaller, named a Total Abstinence Association, on religious principles, and without the pledge. It hits my view better than did the former system, and I am now endeavouring to make a conscience of conforming to the object of such a society, and hope to do it better than, I fear, I could have done under the yoke of a written engagement.—Give my kindest regards, &c. &c.,

THOMAS CHALMERS.

No. CCCXXIV.—To the Rev. P. Henderson, Pollockshaws.

Edinburgh, 13th December 1845.

My dear Sir,—There is no express law of the Free Church that such congregations only as are either aid-giving or self-supporting should supplement the stipend of their minister. Such a maxim might be either a sentiment or a principle, but it has not been formed into a law. But to estimate in how far as a principle it is applicable to your case, I should like to know whether you share in the equal dividend or come under the rule of one and a half more. Even though the former, I feel great satisfation in learning from you that your contributions for last year came to £74, 7s. 6½d. If all Associations made up of the poor and labouring classes were to do as well, we should be greatly better off than we are ; and I do hope that your association will not only keep up its present rate of contribution, but gradually and indefinitely extend it. If you are under the rule of one and a-half more, I look upon you as being in very fair and promising circumstances for a much larger income than, I fear, we shall ever attain on the system of an equal dividend. I presume that there is a disposition on the part of your people to supplement your income. Their present contribution would secure for you under this rule upwards of £111. But should they be disposed to make an addition to your income, I beg you to observe, and for the credit of the rule too, that for every £2 additional which they would give to their present contributions, they would get £3 in return ; or, in other words, if they were to make out a supplement of £26, and send it to us through the Association, then, in virtue of their whole contribution being £100, you would receive £150. Be assured that I am the last man that would say this is enough. My view of the matter is, that all our public functionaries are greatly underpaid ; and I should rejoice if matters were so far advanced as that every minister of the Free Church should have £200 a year. I have the vanity to think that, if they would place themselves under my guidance, or rather, as I am no longer fit for action, under the guidance of my views for several years, they should not be long of reaching this point. But letting that pass, if you are among the one and a half rule ministers, your people have an obvious interest in giving at least £26 of their intended supplement to you through the Association to our General Fund, when the whole accruing £100 would come back, and £50 to the bargain. It is true that the people would then have an interest in sending us no more, but in reserving all their additional contributions for a supplement to you. And yet I should hope better things both of them and of yourself, than that you would make a dead stand in your contributions to us so soon as you came to the £100. I do feel confident in the general, that, when there is enough of principle in a congregation to work up their contributions so far as £100, for the sake of £150 to their minister, this of itself is a guarantee for as much more of principle as would lead them to go beyond the £100 for the good and the interest of the Church at large. I beg that you may shew this letter to any you please, as my argument against the equal dividend, and for the principle of each congregation getting as they give. On the other hand, will you suffer me to retain your letter, and to make use of it as a case in point for the support of this principle? I shall be happy to hear from you farther, and am, my dear Sir, yours truly,   THOMAS CHALMERS.

No. CCCXXV.—To SIR GEORGE SINCLAIR.

Edinburgh, 19th September 1846.

MY DEAR SIR,—In regard to the Pauperism, I think it is all over with Scotland. After the matter has been legalized so far, I feel quite unable to suggest any modifications by which the evil to the landlord, and what is of still more importance, to the people themselves, can be either alleviated or done away.

In regard to the other question of our restoration to the Establishment, I look upon this as almost equally hopeless, as the Free Church could not, consistently with her principles, accede to such a movement but upon such conditions as would appear quite extravagant to all secular, and therefore to the majority of our public men. In the first place we should require to be acknowledged as the Establishment; nor could we hold fellowship with the ministers of the present National Church but upon their submitting to our discipline, or being reckoned with for their disobedience to Acts of Assembly anterior to the Disruption. In the second place, we will never again, I hope, come under the yoke of patronage, for the modification that would have kept us in, will not and ought not to recall us.

Thirdly, there behoved to be an entire recognition of our spiritual independence, to the effect, that the civil courts might never intromit with us save in those questions which related to the temporalities of the Church. There is one respect in which we would deal more gently with the clergy of the Establishment than we ourselves were dealt with. Though they never could be recognised by us as ministers of the new-modelled Establishment till they had given the satisfaction specified in the first article, yet they should be life-rented in their temporalities, and the places left vacant would be given to our licentiates.

I feel it quite grotesque writing to you in this manner; but I am desirous of convincing you how little reason there is to expect that there can be such a re-union as that to which you refer.

Allow me to express the satisfaction I feel in renewing my correspondence with you. There is nothing intermediate that should efface the friendly recollections and feelings which our friendly intercourse in other days will ever awaken in my mind.—I am, &c., THOMAS CHALMERS.

LETTERS TO MR. LENOX OF NEW YORK.

No. CCCXXVI.

Edinburgh, 17th January 1842.

MY DEAR SIR,—Your great kindness to our Church entitles you to know that we are still in deep waters, and to all appearance in circumstances of greater danger under our New Conservative than under our old Whig Government. Meanwhile, I trust that a calm and resolute principle of adherence to the great cause of spiritual independence is in steady progress throughout our land; so that when the crisis comes, I hope and pray that our Church will be enabled to acquit herself with

faithfulness and honour; and that, whether she continue or
cease to be a National Establishment, she will preserve unim-
paired her moral weight in the country, and have the support,
as well as the sympathy, of all good men.

In the expectation of hearing from you soon, I ever am, my
dear Sir, yours most gratefully and respectfully,

THOMAS CHALMERS.

No. CCCXXVII.

Edinburgh, 4th May 1842.

MY DEAR SIR,—The Conservatives have used us very ill; but
I have reason to believe are now somewhat staggered at the
resolute and unbending front of the majority in the Church.
They flattered themselves that we would give in rather than
lose our endowments; and they find it a more difficult problem
than they had first counted on, now that they are opening to
the conviction of such a disruption, on the event of their persevering in their present policy, as will lead to the separation from
the National Church of so many hundreds of her best clergy as
could, on the strength of their respectability and influence,
carry the great bulk of the population along with them, and
resolving themselves into a Home Mission, would take possession of the land.

We are now beginning to organize the country into Defence
Associations, that, if necessary to relinquish our present in-
comes, which of course would be left in possession of a Church
then Erastianized, we may from their contributions obtain such
support as might be raised for the Non-Erastian Church of
Scotland.

All, however, is yet in a state of uncertainty. Our Assembly
begins to sit to-morrow fortnight. The appointment of the
Marquess of Bute to be our Commissioner, is variously interpreted. That the object of this arrangement is a special one,
there can be no doubt, as in usual times the office is conferred

on a poor nobleman, whereas Lord Bute is possessed of great
influence and great wealth, and withal had earned the gratitude of our Church by his munificence in the cause of Church
Extension. Some are apprehensive that the object is to con-
ciliate so many as might convert the minority into a majority
on the side of Lord Aberdeen's Bill with some plausible modification. Let me hope, on the other hand, that our majority
will remain firm and unbroken ; and should such be the result
of their experiment, let me further hope that the Government
will be wise enough to conclude that ours is a position from
which we are not to be driven, and that they will desist from
their attempts to force or to carry it.

This is the day in which the Scottish Church question comes
before the House of Commons.—I am, my dear Sir, yours most
gratefully and truly, THOMAS CHALMERS.

No. CCCXXVIII.

Edinburgh, 28th July 1843.

MY DEAR SIR,—I have this morning received your noble
benefaction of £1100. I last evening received a letter from
Mr. M'Millan, overflowing with gratitude to Mr. Johnstone and
yourself, for the similar sum which he had just received at
your hands, and which at once places him in a state of sufficiency and perfect ease. May the Giver of all grace plentifully
reward such sacrifices for the good of His cause and His kingdom in the world.

We are to send out Dr. Cunningham and another on an
American mission. He may go soon enough to take this
letter ; but if not, I shall send by him notes of introduction to
yourself and Mr. Johnstone, not that either of you shall add to
the princely donations which you have already bestowed on us,
but that you may confer the benefit of your information and
advice in regard to the likeliest methods for the prosecution of
their objects.

I rejoice in the liberty you have given as to the disclosure of your name. I have no doubt whatever as to the great expediency of making it known in the way of example and excitement to others; and I shall feel it a great additional favour, if you release me from the tie of secrecy in regard to your former benefactions, and more especially for that object wherewith Dr. Mackay is connected.

I shall instruct Dr. Cunningham to take out all the documents which might furnish you with the information of our doings. Our Financial Committee has now begun to issue a Monthly Statement, and there is an article furnished by myself to its second number, entitled, " The Increasing Prosperity yet Increasing Difficulties of the Free Church," which will at once let you perceive the great importance both of what you have done for Mr. M'Millan and of your second donation, that to the General Fund being allotted to the building of churches rather than to the sustentation of ministers.

I shall be delighted to meet with the artist when he arrives, and will be most happy to give him the sittings which he requires of me.

I am sure it will gratify you to hear that the ministrations of our Free Church clergymen are palpably becoming more powerful and spiritual than they were. May God prosper His own cause by the instrumentality of these devoted and self-denying men.

The Moderates are carrying it with a high hand. In my own parish (Morningside) they have ejected the minister from his *quoad sacra* church, and the service has been carried on in my own house for three Sabbaths to a congregation one day of towards 400 people; while in the residuary there were by all sorts of forced appliances, about 150, rapidly dwindling, and now, I believe, short of a hundred. We are to have a tent during autumn, and expect to have our church built by the beginning of winter.

I beg that you will convey the expression of my grateful regards, and the assurance of my earnest prayers for the two unknown friends who have supplemented so handsomely both the Kirkcudbright and the general donation.—I ever am, my dear Sir, yours most gratefully and cordially,

THOMAS CHALMERS.

No. CCCXXIX.

Edinburgh, 24th *February* 1844.

MY DEAR SIR,—I return you my most cordial thanks for the munificent offering of £1250 from the first Presbyterian congregation in New York. You say nothing as to the destination of it, and I shall therefore leave that undecided till the next General Assembly—making it depend on the then state of our funds whether it will go to sustentation or building.

I am affected by your observation that we shall never meet in this world. Few things would afford me greater pleasure than the quiet of a few weeks, were I permitted to enjoy it, under your hospitable roof. I beg that you will present my best and most grateful regards to the Misses Lenox ; and in the hope of meeting both you and them in Heaven, believe me ever, my dear Sir, yours most truly, THOMAS CHALMERS.

No. CCCXXX.

Edinburgh, 7th *October* 1844.

MY DEAR SIR,—I lose not a moment in acknowledging your munificent donation of £200, in aid of our proceedings in the West Port. I shall not annoy you by the expression of that gratitude which I most intensely feel. May the prayer of Saint Paul, in 2 Corinthians ix. 6-15, be fully accomplished upon you and yours. In a few days I trust that we shall be able to prepare a narrative, with a few extracts from our more recent minutes, respecting our operations in the West Port, and

2 o

by which you will be enabled to know what has been done and is doing in that locality. It seems to be exciting very considerable attention in this part of the country; and for myself I look upon it to be of such paramount importance, that I mean to confine my efforts to the prosecution of the experiment.

Let me crave a part and an interest in your prayers. I have long wished that my last decade, that is, from the age of sixty to seventy, should be a Sabbatical one—a season of peace and piety. Four years of that decade have now passed away; and, instead of retirement and repose, it has been with me a period of bustle and of manifold engrossments. But there is a Providence in these things in which it is our becoming part to acquiesce; and I think it will gratify you to know that your various communications, charged as they have ever been with all that is kind, and genial, and refreshing, have ever operated as cordials to soothe and to sustain me amid the discouragements and the conflicts of an arduous warfare.—Ever believe me, my dear Sir, yours most gratefully and truly,

THOMAS CHALMERS.

No. CCCXXXI.

Edinburgh, 30th December 1844.

MY DEAR SIR,—I have requested my secretary for the West Port to draw up a narrative of our proceedings there. I should like, in fact, to send you quarterly reports from that very interesting locality—at the bottom of the scale it is said both in respect of depravity and destitution, and therefore all the fitter as the field of an experiment for trying the efficacy of educational and moral influences. I do hope that you will look upon the narrative as bearing evidence to a satisfactory progress, for which, however, I desire humbly to acknowledge my entire dependence on the Giver of all grace. There are some with whom I cannot sympathize, who undervalue all mechanism in the enterprises of Christian usefulness, and tell us of the Spirit as the alone agent of all that is really good. There are others again, whose faith stops short at the secondary, and who despise as fanatical the doctrine of a spiritual influence. The way to adjust this difference is not to conflict these two elements, but to compound them. The Spirit does all, but through an instrumentality to which the Bible guides us ; and it were well if we could so combine matters as to work the instrumentality with all diligence, yet pray for grace from on high with all earnestness. If we neglect the former, nothing will be done ; if we neglect the latter, an impressive mockery awaits all the confidence of human activity, and all the proud decrees and anticipations of human wisdom.

I should feel it a great favour if you or any of your friends would present me with your views on American Slavery—a subject on which I am most anxious to be directed aright, detesting as I do slavery in all its forms ; yet not prepared for those impetuous measures for which the ultras on both sides of the Atlantic are vociferating so loudly. I feel the greatest value for your kindness in having obtained Dr. Alexander's deliverance on Dr. Anderson's works. Perhaps you could do me a similar service on this subject of slavery, on which I should like if I could make up my mind by the beginning of April.— I ever am, my dear Sir, yours very affectionately,

THOMAS CHALMERS.

No. CCCXXXII.

Edinburgh, 21st April 1845.

MY DEAR SIR,—I feel exceedingly obliged by your valuable and most interesting statements on the subject of American Slavery. My growing infirmities and the weight of other engagements have determined me to give up the duties henceforth of a Member to our General Assembly, else I should have taken part in the discussions which will certainly take place in May. But as I am in some degree pledged to make some manifestation of my views upon the question, I propose to prepare next week a letter for publication on the subject in one of the newspapers. Meanwhile, I shall derive the greatest aid from your representations, without, of course, committing you in the least by any formal notice of them. Our views are substantially the same, else I would never have written such a letter to Dr. Smyth of Charleston as I did, and upon which Lewis Tappan, on your side of the water, has commented so outrageously.

I received the other day from America the last Report of the Foreign Board of Missions. I observe that the Abolitionists have been trying to extort from them a declaration against slavery. Really this is quite intolerable, that they must thus insist on binding up and implicating their undoubted good thing with all the other good things that are going on in the world, and fasten the burden of their cause upon every other, when in fact, on every principle of good tactics and the right division of employment, each cause speeds infinitely better when prosecuted separately and upon its own distinct merits. I do hope that this obtrusive and ever-meddling impertinence of theirs will have an effectual check laid upon it. It is most provoking, and on no account more so than that it impedes the very object which their own hearts are set upon, but which the hearts of others, as zealous and only wiser than they, are as much and as honestly set upon as theirs are.—I ever am, my dear Sir, yours most gratefully and cordially,   THOMAS CHALMERS.

No. CCCXXXIII.

Edinburgh, 15th July 1845.

MY DEAR SIR,—I will not annoy you by the expressions of my gratitude for the munificence by which you have conferred such facilities and enlargements on our operations in the West Port. If I evinced any feeling of restraint in making our necessities known to you, it proceeded from no distrust in your willingness to give, but, on the contrary, from the feeling that it is ungenerous to take advantage of the well-known liberality of those whose previous benefactions have exposed them to demands and expectations from all points of the compass. There is a species of rapacity, I could almost call it harpyism, even among professing Christians, which has often scandalized me, and which discovers itself by a universal set in from all sides on the man who is at all signalized by his past liberalities. I think that the proper re-action were all the greater delicacy and reserve towards him who had already done and expended so much upon the cause.

I admire exceedingly the Report of your Assembly on the subject of Slavery—done, I think, with admirable tact and wisdom. I very much like, too, the deliverance of our own Assembly (May 1845) on the same question, and confidently hope that you will approve of it. In regard to my letter, it appeared in the "Witness" about the end of April; and had I not thought that you would have seen it there, I should have instantly forwarded a copy to you.* Lest, however, this may not be the case, I have sent orders to Mr. Macpherson to copy it over for you, and send it in his own hand-writing. I do hope that all the ultraism to which we have been hitherto exposed is set at rest, and that the great cause of an ultimate abolition of slavery will speed all the faster and all the surer in consequence.

And now, my dear sir, may I beg that you will now begin to cherish the purpose of a visit to Scotland next summer, that your determination may be formed in time, and that we may be apprized of the month when we may look for your arrival.

* See Memoirs, vol. iv., Appendix, pp. 581-591.

It will give both myself and Mrs. Chalmers the greatest pleasure to receive you and the Misses Lenox under our roof; and, if God be pleased to spare us, I shall have much to say and perhaps something to shew on the methods of Christian philanthropy. Few things would so delight me as the formation of a personal acquaintance with you. We think it possible that Jacob Abbot, now of your city, may be a sojourner in Edinburgh for some time next summer; and with you as our guest, and him as our frequent visitor, I should expect much light to be thrown on the comparative ecclesiastical systems of Britain and America. But his coming is an uncertainty; and do not therefore, I implore you, suspend your movement upon his.— Yours with the utmost esteem and cordiality,

THOMAS CHALMERS.

No. CCCXXXIV.

Edinburgh, 20th October 1845.

MY DEAR SIR,—I avail myself of the Quarterly Report for October to add a few sentences. Your welcome letter of the 25th ult. came to me some days ago; and I have detained this for a few days in the hope that I might be able to announce the arrival of your pamphlet on the instruction of slaves in the South. It has not yet, however, made its appearance. I received, however, by the same post which brought your letter to me, the deliverance of the American Foreign Board of Missions, and I think it a remarkably wise and well-weighed decision which they have come to, and quite of a piece with the high character of that most intelligent and enlightened body.—I ever am, my dear Sir, yours with the greatest esteem and regard, THOMAS CHALMERS.

No. CCCXXXV.

Edinburgh, 17th December 1845.

MY VERY DEAR SIR,—The pamphlet respecting the religious instruction of the negroes in the south reached me some time ago. It delights me to find that so much is doing; and I do hope that, instead of having to report only a fractional good, we shall hear shortly of a movement towards a universal Christian education of the coloured tribes in these States. I along with your letter yesterday received two papers, sent me, I believe, on account of Dr. Leonard Wood's views on the question of slavery. He seems to have taken a sound view, and to have arrived at a right and well-weighed deliverance upon the subject. I feel confident that the abolition of slavery is far likelier to come soon by acting on these calmer and more comprehensive surveys of the matter in all its bearings, than on the extreme views of the ultra abolitionists. I can assure you, that the direction which this business has taken, elevates greatly, in my estimation, the wisdom and force of principle which appear to pervade in general the ecclesiastical mind and philanthropic public of America.

May the Giver of all grace pour His richest blessings upon you and yours.

With affectionate regards for the Misses Lenox, I ever am, my dear Sir, yours very gratefully and with the utmost esteem and regard, THOMAS CHALMERS.

No. CCCXXXVI.

Edinburgh, September 1846.

My very dear Sir,—I observe, and with the greatest satisfaction, your growing sense of the spiritual destitution which obtains among the working-classes of your own land, or the great bulk and body of your common people—the very impression which I received thirty years ago from my first observations of the state of Glasgow, and on which I have been incessantly acting and arguing ever since. There is indeed a very great delusion among those who, satisfied with a superficial and rapid survey of the ecclesiastical state of a country in the number of churches, and the bustle of a full and crowded attendance on the most popular and prosperous of these, infer a sufficiency in the means and methods of Christian education for the community at large. I am very confident, that the more minutely and statistically the matter is inquired into, the more certainly will it be found, that your own America, like our own Britain, labours under the burden of a population miserably deficient in respect to all the observances of a Christian land. I see no remedy for the practical heathenism into which they have fallen, but a vigorous appliance of the territorial system, along with the indispensable grace from on high. I should rejoice in observing your liberality taking its direction towards the supply of your spiritual necessities at home; knowing, as I do, that they are such as might well absorb the means, not only of one, but of many Christian philanthropists, however richly gifted with the blessings of abundance they might be. I repeat, that I should feel it a most selfish and unjustifiable thing on my part, should I continue to divert your attention from what I hold to be far the most profitable and fruitful direction to which you can betake yourself.

I expect to send you a pamphlet which I recently published on the Evangelical Alliance. I had great pleasure in meeting with so many of the American brethren on their way to London. I should like to know your views upon this subject. Do you happen to know Mr. and Mrs. Marcus Spring, and Miss Fuller, all of New York?—they were recently with me. Douglas the slave, and Lloyd Garrison, have recently come to Edinburgh and opened their batteries on the Free Church, which I trust, on the other hand, will stand its ground against them.

I will not relinquish the hope, and never can give up the desire of seeing you in this country. I rejoice that we are still at peace with America. Your remarks on a deviation from orthodox theology being slight enough at first not to endanger salvation, but diverging at length into deadly error, are of first-rate importance.—With best regards to the Misses Lenox, I ever am, my dear Sir, yours most cordially and gratefully,

THOMAS CHALMERS.

No. CCCXXXVII.

Edinburgh, 28th October 1846.

MY VERY DEAR SIR,—I will not attempt any adequate utterance or expression of my gratitude for your letter of the 8th, because I know well that this is not the return which you have much, if any value for. But I feel sure that a better return, and one by which you will be far better pleased, is the simple information, that you have enabled me to meet every existing engagement, and so got me out of all my difficulties. I have no need at present for more money from you; and I have the confident hope beside, that I shall be enabled to proceed in all time coming on home resources alone. At the same time, it is altogether due to the unexampled generosity of your whole treatment of me, to let you frankly know, that should I require it, I shall unreservedly make the statement to you of my wants, though I must again couple this with the announcement of my expectation, that the Christian philanthropy on this side of the water (now more alive to the efficacy of our territorial proceedings) will, as it ought, meet every fair demand which I shall make upon it.

It may perhaps interest you to know, that of the money received, which includes all your own most munificent donations, I got £300 from a lady, and four or five single hundreds from as many individuals. Lord Jeffrey, the celebrated Edinburgh reviewer, is one of these, who takes a most friendly interest in our doings. I had many donors of £50, £20, £10, &c. &c. And what to me was extremely gratifying, upwards of 200 subscriptions from the West Port itself, ranging from the smallest copper coin (half a farthing) to £2.

Do tell the Misses Lenox, with my affectionate regards, that I will not let go the hope of yet seeing them and you in Scotland. But let us never cease to pray, and to prepare for taking up our residence in that eternal city whose builder and maker is God. May He who is now employed in preparing a place for us, prepare us for the place. I was very much interested by a recent letter of yours on the new theology. The old is better. May it come to us not in word only, but in power. Mrs. Chalmers joins with me in kindest regards.—I ever am, my dear Sir, yours with highest esteem,

THOMAS CHALMERS.

No. CCCXXXVIII.

Edinburgh, 2d January 1847.

MY DEAR SIR,—You will observe from my last letter, that I very gladly and gratefully accept of your kind proposal as to the additional payments which place me on a high vantage-ground for the full establishment of our system.

Lord Jeffrey's offering was not in homage to the Free Church, but because of the general merits of our cause, as associated with the enlightenment and moralization of the people. I called on him the other day. He is indeed a very amiable and engaging person, and one of the best specimens I know of the natural man, with great respect, too, for Christianity, even in its most serious and evangelical form. Heaven grant that it may ripen ere he dies into a personal and saving faith.*—With

* 24, *Moray Place, Saturday Evening,* 17*th November* 1847.—REVEREND AND DEAR SIR,—I entrusted my subscription entirely to the discretion of Dr. Chalmers, and cannot have the least objection to its now being disposed of as may seem best to the trustees who have been honoured by his confidence, and are following out his instructions.

I have been very much touched and gratified by what you are kind enough to most cordial and Christian regards to the Misses Lenox, ever believe me, my dear Sir, yours most affectionately and with greatest esteem, THOMAS CHALMERS.

No. CCCXXXIX.

To Dr. D. STEBBINS, NORTHAMPTON, MASSACHUSETTS.

Edinburgh, 30*th May* 1844.

MY DEAR AND VENERABLE FRIEND,—I cannot adequately express the interest which I feel in the relic of Edwards, which you have had the goodness to bestow upon me. Him I have long esteemed as the greatest of theologians, combining in a degree that is quite unexampled, the profoundly intellectual with the devotedly spiritual and sacred, and realizing in his own person a most rare, yet most beautiful harmony between the simplicity of the Christian pastor, on the one hand, and on the other, all the strength and prowess of a giant in philosophy, so as at once to minister from Sabbath to Sabbath, and with most blessed effect, to the hearers of his plain congregation ; and yet, on the high field of authorship to have travelled in a way that none had ever done before him, the most inaccessible places, and achieved such a mastery as had never till his time been realized over the most arduous difficulties of our science.

There is no European divine to whom I make such frequent appeals in my class-room, as I do to Edwards—no book of human composition which I more strenuously recommend, than his " Treatise on the Will," read by me forty-seven years ago,

inform me, as to the degree of indulgence and favour with which that great and good man was pleased, in the large benignity of his nature, to regard my humble efforts in the great cause to which his life was devoted, and can truly say that I still cherish his memory with the sincerest love and veneration.

I am much struck with the appeal in behalf of the Holyrood Church, which you enclose for my consideration, and beg leave to annex a cheque for a small sum, as a contribution for its completion.—I have the honour to be, dear Sir, your obliged and faithful, &c. &c.   F. JEFFREY.

To the Rev. W. Hanna.

with a conviction that has never since faltered, and which has helped me, more than any other uninspired book, to find my way through all that might otherwise have proved baffling and transcendental and mysterious in the peculiarities of Calvinism.

You will not wonder, then, at my value for the memorial which, through my friend Dr. Cunningham, you have put into my hands. I will place it beside the autograph sermon of Edwards, which I received from his grandson, Mr. Dwight, a good many years ago, and which, along with the autograph in my possession of Brainerd and the Missionary Elliot, I cherish as the most precious of my literary treasures.

It is my earnest prayer, venerable father and friend, that yours may be an evening of piety and peace, and that the manifestations of light and love from the upper sanctuary may descend upon your soul ; so that while drawing near to death, you may be ripening for eternity.

But whatever your experiences may be, and they are exceedingly various even with the most experienced Christians, may you at all times be enabled from looking inwardly upon yourself, to look upwardly and outwardly on the great object of revelation—the Sun of Righteousness—so that, like an eminent countryman of yours, when asked on his death-bed about his frames and feelings, you might be enabled to make the constant and confident reply,—" that *there is mercy with God in Christ Jesus.*"—I ever am, my dear Sir, yours most cordially and gratefully,   THOMAS CHALMERS.

No. CCCXL.—To the Rev. Dr. Merle d'Aubigné.

Edinburgh, 24th March 1845.

My very dear Sir,—Excuse my employing an amanuensis, which is better for you, as I have a very illegible handwriting, which, in conjunction with my English, might make it all the more difficult for your perusal.

I very much rejoice in having heard from you. I have been meditating a letter to you for months, to intimate the eager expectancy of the Christian public here for your fourth volume, and also to communicate with you on the all-important subject of Christian union. But I do hope we shall have the pleasure of meeting with you in Edinburgh, when we can talk at large over both these subjects.

Before addressing myself to your special inquiries, let me first state the high sense I have of the Christian and theological importance of your work on the Reformation. It is not of its interest as an historical record that I alone speak ; but, over and above this, I have read no didactic or even devotional human work more fitted to impress upon the reader the precious doctrine of justification by faith, or endear to him what was so dear to the mind of Luther—the sentiment of " The Lord our righteousness."

I rejoice in the commencement of our correspondence. May the Giver of all grace pour on you and yours His best blessings ; and let me entreat you to believe me, my very dear Sir, yours with the utmost esteem and regard, THOMAS CHALMERS.

No. CCCXLI.—To the Rev. Dr. Merle d'Aubigné.

Morningside, 3d June 1845.

MY VERY DEAR SIR,—You asked me to point out the most interesting objects for a small western excursion from Glasgow. It delights me to hear that our Moderator, who is far better acquainted with the localities of that region than myself, is willing personally to undertake your guidance through Argyleshire, and to one or two of our most interesting islands. I should have liked that, as an ecclesiastical historian, you could have seen St. Andrews, the ancient ecclesiastical metropolis of Scotland, and seat of our Scottish Reformation, and I do hope that you will make out Iona, the place of the great St. Columbus, and noted as a religious asylum from very ancient times.

It would have gladdened my heart could I have accompanied you : but I confess myself to be fairly worn out ; and, after my exertion in Glasgow on Sunday, will stand urgently in need of repose.

I need not say how much both yourself and Madame d'Aubigné have grown upon the affections of us all. My own family, in particular, have the utmost desire for intercourse with you both, and should indeed rejoice in it as a great privilege could we obtain a quiet day or two of your and her society in the charming retreat of Fairley, in Ayrshire. The lady whose house we occupy there (Miss M'Call) desires us to invite you ; and my four daughters, whom you have not seen, and who are there before us, have been put into a state of greatest expectancy ; and I feel assured that matters could be so arranged as to fall in with your other movements, and secure you needful rest, as well as expedite your journey.

There is nothing I would more prize than leisurely and uninterrupted converse with you for as long a time as you can possibly spare.—I ever am, my dearest Sir, yours with the utmost esteem and regard,   THOMAS CHALMERS.

No. CCCXLII.—To the Rev. Dr. Merle d'Aubigné.

Edinburgh, 7th February 1846.

My very dear Sir,—I should have replied to yours of the 19th of January sooner ; but I cannot regret the delay, for only a few minutes ago has your new volume been put into my hands, and I have just read its noble preface, so well fitted to silence and to shame all adversaries. My family are now devouring it, and I expect myself to achieve its perusal in a few days. I have already seen some of the proof-sheets, and was much pleased with the spirited and impressive style of the translation.

Many thanks to you, my dear Sir, for your deeply affecting details on the subject of your mother's death. They forcibly reminded me of my own mother's death, which took place in February 1827. She died in the triumphs of the faith.

I observe that the Vaudois Free Church is not without its perplexities, especially on the subject of a Confession. We may get involved in difficulties, too, on the question of the Evangelical Alliance, about which some of our Presbytery are beginning to make a stir. It will not be the knowledge that puffeth up, but the charity which edifieth, that will practically resolve this question.

I beg my best regards to Madame d'Aubigné, in which all our family most cordially join. May I beg that you will also offer my friendly and respectful acknowledgments to Monsieur Gaussen. I read with great interest the opening of your winter session.—I ever am, my dear Sir, yours with great esteem and affection,   THOMAS CHALMERS.

No. CCCXLIII.—To the Rev. Dr. Merle d'Aubigné.

Edinburgh, 14*th February* 1846.

MY DEAR SIR,—I have now finished the reading of your fourth volume, and cannot sufficiently express my interest and admiration. In point of narrative, I believe that the latter half of it will prove the more attractive to the general public. The Swiss Reformation was very much unknown in its details to the people of this country, and I never was more rivetted in my life to any book than when engaged in the perusal of it.

But, while the latter half of your volume is full of interest on the subject of the Church's spiritual independence, and the danger of mixing up the secular with the spiritual, I should hold that the former half of your volume will be still more prized by theologians. The Confession of Augsburg, and the conference between Luther and Zwingle at Marburg, are truly splendid and memorable passages. Go on and prosper, my dear Sir, and be assured that your present volume, with the anticipations which it holds out as to the subject of the one that comes next, will raise very high the interest and the expectancy of the British public.

My very best regards to Madame d'Aubigné, in which, as well as in regards to yourself, one and all of my family most heartily join.—I ever am, my dear Sir, yours with the utmost regard,   Thomas Chalmers.

No. CCCXLIV.—To Miss Brewster.

Anstruther, 19th May 1845.

My dear Miss Brewster,—I cannot take leave of this place, which I quit in an hour or two, without conveying to you the expression of my very sincere regret in not having had the good fortune to meet with you on Saturday. The disappointment was all the more cruel that you left only a few minutes after our arrival, when we found that you had got quite beyond our reach.

I cannot express in an adequate manner the interest I felt in my conversation with Sir David on Thursday. I know well how alive you are to the moral glories that irradiate a church or a nation ; and I do hope that you are not insensible to the glories even of the material heavens which now beam upon us in larger and brighter revelation than ever ; and in proportion to which I think our conceptions should rise of that spiritual economy under which we sit, both being under the control and comprehensive government of Him who sits aloft from view, and gives birth, and movement, and countenance to all things.

It is my fondest hope and prayer that both of us shall have an interest and a part in the yet undeveloped blessedness of that high and holy administration.

With kindest regards to Sir David and Lady Brewster, ever believe me, my dear Madam, yours affectionately and truly,

Thomas Chalmers.

No. CCCXLV.—To Miss Brewster.

19, *York Place, 28th May* 1845.

My dear Miss Brewster,—I can imagine nothing more monstrous than the stupidity into which I fear I must have fallen, if it was really you who sat near the moderator's chair this evening, and on whom I speculated in my own mind for hours as one whom I ought to have known. It is far the most mortifying instance, though very many such have occurred, of my utter want of the organ of individuality; but I never could have fancied it possible that it ever could have happened in the case of one, in whom (forgive me for saying it) I feel so much interest.

It would comfort me effectually if you would have the goodness to let me know where and when it is that I may have the pleasure of waiting upon you.—Ever believe me, my very dear Madam, yours most affectionately and truly,

Thomas Chalmers.

No. CCCXLVI.—To Mrs. Williamson.

Edinburgh, 21st May 1845.

My dear Mrs. Williamson,—I must not suffer myself to plunge into other scenes and occupations without making the grateful acknowledgment of all your kindness to me during the happy days I spent under your hospitable roof. Mr. Mackenzie most cordially joins me in this feeling; and we both agree in this, that we never spent a week where, both within doors and without, there was so much to regale and to gratify, and that without so much as one taint or particle of alloy from the beginning to the end of it. I cannot adequately express the enjoyment I felt both in the revival of the images and recollections of other days, and in the unexcepted cordiality and good-will of my fellow-citizens.

2 P

I have had particular satisfaction in Mr. Ferrie. I think that all his appearances, both in public and private, were in the highest degree creditable ; and I no longer wonder at the general good liking felt for him by the families of Anster. We have been reading his account of our Fife excursion, and there is a great deal of good feeling in it, as well as lively description. Will you tell him how much we were all amused at the reference which he made to the palmy days of my boyhood ? He has misnamed, however, my old friend Lizzy Geens. I had forgot that she was adverted to by Mr. Tennant.

I trust that we may see Dr. Williamson on our side of the water before he leaves Burntisland ; and it is my earnest hope and prayer that he may be long spared to you. May the Giver of all grace pour the richest spiritual blessings on you and yours. I was much delighted with the manifest improvement that has taken place in the spirits of the people, and in the relish felt by so many of them for sacred things. May there be a descent of living water from above on all the households of the town and neighbourhood.—Ever believe me, my dear Madam, yours most affectionately, THOMAS CHALMERS.

No. CCCXLVII.—To MISS MARSHALL, GLASGOW.

Fairley, 17*th June* 1845.

MY DEAR MISS MARSHALL,—It is a precious effect of a few days' domestication in a house that it draws so much closer one's intimacy with all its inmates ; and I have a very great value for the revival that has thus taken place of our old acquaintanceship with your household, as well as the formation of a new acquaintanceship with the younger members of the family. Every additional opportunity I have of observing Mr. Buchanan and his doings, enhances all the more the esteem I have ever felt for his Christian worth and patriotism.

Should you see Miss Watson, will you have the goodness to

let her know that I am quite ashamed of having had so imperfect a recollection of her so long as we were together in your house ? But Mrs. Chalmers has refreshed my decaying memory ; and I can now recognise her as the daughter of that kind, cordial, and most respectable old lady, who, though a Dissenter, looked most benignantly on the good Churchmen who differed from her. But what is still more interesting to me, she is the sister of George Watson, whom I visited on his death-bed, and whose case I have often quoted as one of the most delightful I had ever witnessed, of one who, on the stepping-stone of a simple faith, attained to a clear and confident sense of a reconciled God, and the assured prospect, through Christ, of a blessed immortality.

With best regards to Mr. and Miss Buchanan and your two nephews, ever believe me, my dear Madam, yours very affectionately and truly,   THOMAS CHALMERS.

No. CCCXLVIII.—To CHARLES SPENCE, ESQ.

Morningside, 26th January 1846.

MY DEAR SIR,—Though I am not able to attend your public meeting on the 30th, you know that I feel no want of interest in its object. The truth is, that I look on the Christianization, I will not say of the poor only, but of the general population, as the highest cause of our day—the enterprise which, with the aid and countenance of Divine grace from above, will be prolific of the greatest blessings to the greatest number of our fellow-men.

I do hope that your labours will have the effect of laying more open to the public observation, the fearful destitution which prevails of all adequate means and adequate methods for the religious instruction, and so for the social, the moral, and the spiritual wellbeing of countless thousands, I should even say of the great mass of our city families. May the minds

of men be made more alive to the urgent necessity of something being done far more effectual than has ever yet been
attempted, at least on a large scale, or than has yet been
scarcely thought of.   And be assured that I shall rejoice in it
as of one of the best results attendant on your present effort,
should it have the effect of uniting in one common work of
Christian charity the wise and the good of all denominations.

I have particularly to thank you for your kind expressions
and good wishes in reference to my own more limited doings
in the West Port. You know my partialities for the local system, and have been made aware of my belief that, for a
thoroughly pervading operation, the whole territory should be
broken up into districts, each small enough to be undertaken
by a distinct and separate agency of its own—a system of
operation this which I think should be encouraged to the
uttermost.   I am therefore glad to find, that in the operations
of the City Mission this principle has been so far proceeded on,
and should rejoice if, by the extension of your resources, you
were enabled to carry it forward, even till you have reached
the desirable consummation.   Meanwhile, if, by the assumption of successive districts on the part of myself and others,
your present field shall be so encroached upon as to leave a
continually decreasing remainder in your hands, I am sure you
will find that the diminution of extent will be amply repaired
by the comfort and the efficacy of a more intense concentration.   It is thus that the local and the general might be made
to work most beautifully into each other's hands : and there is
nothing which I more desiderate than a combination of that
union and authority which are secured by the latter, with the
activity and busy interest, and thorough operation that can
only be secured by means of the former.

While I have thankfully to express my acknowledgment for
the friendly countenance and repeated civilities of the City

Mission from the very commencement on the West Port, allow me again to thank you for your present friendly allusion to it. —I ever am, my dear Sir, yours with great regard,

THOMAS CHALMERS.

No. CCCXLIX.—To CHARLES SPENCE, ESQ.

Morningside, 26th January 1846.

MY DEAR SIR,—My letter to you was prepared before I received your note requesting that I should address it to the Lord Provost. On this and on other grounds I greatly prefer addressing it to yourself. Of course the whole of it will be read, as I wish my testimony in favour of the Local System to be made as distinct and as public as my testimony in favour of the City Mission. It is well to have begun with the one, but I hope it will end with the other,—yours being the way in which you have nobly taken the lead, and ours being the ultimate landing-place.—I am, my dear Sir, yours very truly,

THOMAS CHALMERS.

No. CCCL.—To CHARLES SPENCE, ESQ.

Morningside, 28th February 1846.

MY DEAR SIR,—My experience hitherto of general bodies of superintendence makes me afraid of them, lest, in the first instance, they should be satisfied with a superficial instead of a thorough operation, which, I believe, can only be effected by distinct district agencies; and lest, in the second instance, they should, by a system of rules and forms, with the view of harmonizing all, lay an incubus upon each. I could not join in such a combination but on the principle, that the poorest of the poor should be as much looked after, and be as fully provided with the means of Gospel instruction as the middle and upper classes in society. And therefore I hold, that a system which would stop short and be satisfied with any provision beneath schools for all and churches for all, is but an apology for the thing, and not the thing itself.

At the same time, I am not insensible to the good of some sort of general surveillance, if it did not too much interfere with the independence and sovereignty that each district management should have over its own processes. For example, would they attempt only to aid and encourage, without aught like jurisdiction or control, I should think that great good might be effected by such an overseership as this. Suppose they were to collect a general fund for the purpose of aiding and supplementing the local funds raised in behalf of those districts whose management and whose objects they approved of, this would stimulate and extend the system of local cultivation without any of those hamperments and complications which I have hitherto so abundantly experienced as the fruit of my connexion with general directorships. Were such a system adopted, I think we should all hand in the reports of our proceedings and progress to you, and if we needed money, should apply to you, which of course you would only give if you approved of our doings. I can imagine too, that in course of time we might thus feel our way to a greater harmony of action than we ought to attempt laying down at the outset by authoritative rules.

Be assured that I am utterly misunderstood, if these views are conceived to have in them the least of sectarianism. It is with me a pure question of what may be called spiritual tactics, or the most effectual method of pervading our plebeian families with the lessons and influences of the Gospel. So little of a sectarian am I, that I look on the distinction between Presbyterianism and Independency, or even between your Adult and our Pædo-baptism, as a downright bagatelle when compared with the moral and Christian good of the population. My ex-

perimental feeling is, that it is impossible to act with any
degree of comfort or efficacy when overborne by the restraints
of a cumbrous and unwieldy committeeship. You mistake me
if you think I do not want some such general supervision as I
have now described, I fear, very imperfectly. I should rejoice
if, under its canopy, but without being subject to its control,
all the evangelical denominations of Edinburgh could be
brought out to this great and good work. I believe that nothing would tend more rapidly and surely to the formation of
a real union amongst us, than our being thus engaged in similar
works; yet meeting together upon the occasion of your general meetings, and there provoking each other to love and to all
that is good.—I am, my dear Sir, yours very truly,

THOMAS CHALMERS.

No. CCCLI.—LETTER TO M. DESCOMBAZ, LAUSANNE.

Edinburgh, 28th February 1846.

MY DEAR SIR,—I can assure you it is from no want of
sympathy in your great cause that I have not written sooner,
but from extreme occupation,—and occupation, let me add,
greatly beyond my strength and time satisfactorily to overtake.
Though I should not write much, then, or should not write
often, I beg you will put the right interpretation upon it, and
ascribe it to anything rather than an indifference either to
the magnitude of your wrongs or the nobleness of those pure
and high principles by which you are actuated. The same
reasons which have compelled me to retire from the public
business of our own Church, have also made it necessary for me
greatly to limit the work of correspondence. Everything, in
fact, which involves in it additional effort, or the withdrawment
of my mind from more immediate duties and cares, I must
now devolve on abler and younger men.

But while I have thus to state, and I do it with extreme

regret and reluctance, the utter impossibility of complying with your wishes for a regular or frequent correspondence, I cannot, even within the limits of this necessarily brief communication, refrain from adverting to the difficult, as well as high and honourable distinction of the position in which you now stand ; and it is my earnest prayer, that by grace and guidance from above, you might be enabled to maintain it. It were well if all Christians but knew how to combine the utmost dependence on God with the utmost diligence in the busy use and employment of means, and so as to reconcile the wisdom of piety with the wisdom of experience. Otherwise, under the guise of trusting in God there might be a tempting of God ; and therefore let me urge with all earnestness upon your consideration the necessity of speedily adopting such methods as might best conduce, with the Divine blessing, to the stability and extension of your Free Church. You may have heard the saying of our missionary Elliot, who laboured for years, and with such marvellous success, among the American Indians : He did not trust to prayer without performance, neither did he trust to performance without prayer—he was super-eminent in both ; and as the fruit of the experience of a whole lifetime, he left behind him the memorable lesson—that it was in the power of prayer and of pains, through faith in Christ Jesus, to do anything. What I should regard then as the first and firmest guarantee for the prosperity and strength of your Free Church, were the growth and effusion of serious, spiritual religion and vital godliness among your ministers and congregations. This is the object which, of all others, is mightily to be laboured and mightily to be prayed for. No organization, however skilfully devised, will supply the want of this. The best of all machinery requires to be worked ; for the attainment of its end, to be rightly and well worked. Behold then the limits of human ingenuity and power. We can set up the framework and mechanism of a church, but we are wholly dependent on the Spirit of God for the men, and should therefore pray without ceasing to the Lord of the harvest, that He might send forth unto His harvest labourers, according to His own heart, who might feed his people with knowledge and spiritual understanding. But both are best. We must not neglect the rearing of a right terrestrial apparatus below ; because without a celestial influence from above, it were the mere barren architecture of a church with none of that living spirit which should actuate, and which can alone give efficacy to all its services. It is most true that, except the Lord build the house they labour in vain that build it ; but this should not discharge the builders from their work—a work to which they should put forth their hands with all diligence while looking for the indispensable grace from on high, without which all the wisdom of man is but foolishness, and all the work of man is but as labour in the fire, and for very nought.

March 7th.—I had got thus far when I was obliged to suspend this whole communication for a whole week by the pressure of other business, and that pressure still continues ; nor have I any hope of being relieved from it for an indefinite time. I am unwilling, however, to delay any longer the answering of your letter, and can only now assure you of my readiness to obtain all the information which our experience might enable us to collect, and which might be of use for the support or extension of your Free Church. In particular, let any advice or opinion be required of us on the subject of church economics, let your wish be specifically stated, and I think I might help you to a specific answer in regard to it.

My earnest prayer is for the maintenance and spread of vital godliness amongst you—a spirituality unalloyed by any political or worldly ingredient—a real desire for the moral and Christian good of the people under your charge ; so that your interesting section of the great vineyard might, with the descent of the indispensable grace from on high, become like a well-watered garden, abounding with the fair and pleasant fruits of righteousness.—I ever am, my very dear sir, yours with the greatest esteem and regard,   THOMAS CHALMERS.

[23, *Bain's Place, Renfrew Street, Glasgow*, 11th *May* 1846.—REVEREND AND DEAR SIR,—I would take the liberty of shortly expressing to you my desire that you would use your influence in the ensuing General Assembly for the foundation of a Free Church College in this city, which, I think, is immediately called for, in order to the advancement of the Free Church of Scotland in the west of Scotland.—I am more and more convinced that the magistrate should be a keeper of *both* tables of the law, and is bound to endow and protect the Church of Christ. May the Lord hasten this in his time. With God nothing shall be impossible.—I am, yours with much esteem,   JOHN CRAIG.

The Rev. Thomas Chalmers, Edinburgh.]

No. CCCLII.—To MR. JOHN CRAIG.

Burntisland, 16th *May* 1846.

DEAR SIR,—Accept of my grateful regards for your expressions of kindness to myself. I am very glad to observe what your opinion is in regard to the duty of the magistrate, to endow and protect the Church of Christ.

I have all along said, that once our Church were sufficiently extended by means of adequate funds, that I saw no reason why we should not have as many collegiate institutions as ever the Establishment had.—I am, dear Sir, yours truly,

THOMAS CHALMERS.

[The following letter was in an answer to a very interesting communication from Mr. Barclay, in which he proposed that, instead of annual payments into the Sustentation Fund, an endowment of £100 per annum should at once be secured for every Minister of the Free Church. Tables and calculations were offered for Dr. Chalmers's consideration, from which it appeared, that if all the members of the Free Church were to give a tithe of their income for a single year, a capital sum would be realized sufficient to yield such an endowment.]

No. CCCLIII.—To J. Barclay, Esq., Tongue.

Edinburgh, 6th June 1846.

Dear Sir,—I received your valuable packet from Mr. Mac-kenzie of Farr. I appreciate very highly the zeal, intelligence, and labour in behalf of the Free Church, of which these documents give such abundant evidence. I shall lodge them with the Convener of our Sustentation Committee, to be kept by him *in retentis* till it shall be judged expedient to act upon them. Meanwhile, our great effort is to bring up the Associations; and we are fearful of every new subscription for a new object, lest it should distract the attention of the Free Church public from the necessary means for upholding and augmenting the Sustentation Fund. After the habit of supporting it is sufficiently established and elevated, then, I think, will be the time for giving effect to your magnificent proposal. I have no doubt of the capabilities of our people. They are equal to a tenfold greater achievement than all that has yet been done by them.

Allow me to say, that I doubt the expediency of ministers being employed in the work of estimating the resources of their people.

I have again to thank you for your noble suggestions, which I trust you in good time will find are not to be thrown away upon us.—I ever am, my dear Sir, yours truly,

Thomas Chalmers.

No. CCCLIV.

Edinburgh, 17th September 1846.

Sir,—I received both your letters. The first I laid aside, because of my great aversion to any direct application for my autograph ; and in virtue of which it is my general practice to leave all such requests unanswered.

Your second letter of May 6th, I placed among the letters to which I might reply ; because I felt a wish at the time to let you know the grounds of my antipathy to a practice which I think is not in accordance with good taste.

I find, however, that I have not time for the full statement of these grounds ; and shall only say in the general, that I feel as if, on the one side, the making of such a request implies a certain degree of indelicacy ; and on the other side, that in the granting of it there must be a certain sense of awkwardness, as the very act involves at least the semblance of vanity.

And yet the desire of having autographs is legitimate and natural; but the right way to go about the formation of a collection is to seek, and not from the person himself, but from any of his correspondents, such letters or fragments of his handwriting as can anywhere be found. I should imagine that to every man who feels as he ought, a naked request for his autograph must be extremely distasteful. In sending you this autograph, it is a relief that I should have something to write about ; and all the more so, that along with the autograph you have my testimony against the method in which they are sometimes sought after both by individuals and by such public bodies as you represent.—With best wishes for the prosperity of your museum, I have the honour to be, Sir, yours truly,

THOMAS CHALMERS.

[*Bombay*, *25th June* 1850.—DEAR DR. HANNA,—I have just finished the perusal of the first volume of the " Memoirs of Dr. Chalmers," which, like his " Posthumous Works," not only maintains, but elevates the high position which his name and character occupy in the admiration and veneration of Christendom. It has suggested the propriety of sending to you a copy of a very touching and affectionate letter addressed by him to my young friend

Dhanjibhái on his leaving Scotland on his return to India, and also of a copy of an introductory note to M. F. Monod, which he had intended him to deliver had he taken Paris on his way. Dr. Chalmers took a very special interest in the wellbeing of Dhanjibhái from the time of their first interview, and he was greatly attached to him. At the conclusion of the session of 1843-4, he addressed to me a note of the following tenor :—" My dear Sir, I must do myself the pleasure of informing you that I have been greatly pleased with the interesting pupil whom you have brought to me from the far East. His appearances in his examinations and exercises have been of a first-rate character throughout the session." I felt much his kindness to me in voluntarily tendering to me this testimonial which he knew would be very gratifying to my heart.

With much sympathy with all the family of Dr. Chalmers from Dhanjibhái and myself, I am, my dear Dr. Hanna, yours very truly,

JOHN WILSON.]

No. CCCLV.—To REV. DHANJIBHAI NOWROJI.

Morningside, 14*th December* 1846.

MY DEAR SIR,—The three enclosed letters are to friends in Paris, which you may deliver or not, just as you find convenient. If you have not the opportunity of these being useful to you in Paris, I beg that you will keep and open them, and an occasion may cast up when you might shew these as the testimonials of my friendship and esteem for you. I wish I could recollect any of my acquaintances in Bombay to whom I might write aught that could be of service ; but you will, at all events, offer my best regards to Mr. Nesbit and Mr. Hislop when you meet with them.

And now, my very dear Sir, let me commend you to the providence and grace of our common Father in heaven. May He be your guide and guardian amid all the perils and perplexities of your great enterprise. He has promised that He will not suffer His faithful servants to be tried beyond what they are able to bear, but will provide a way of escape that they might be able to bear it. May the aids of His Spirit never be wanting to comfort, and strengthen, and sustain you, and richly may you experience the truth of our blessed Saviour's declaration, that though in the world you shall have tribulation, in Him you shall have peace ; and may you abundantly prosper in that work and labour of love upon which you have entered. May you have many souls for your hire, and the precious fore-tastes of that bright and happy period when the Sun of Righteousness shall arise over the face of a regenerated world. It is my earnest prayer for you, that after a life of great Christian usefulness here you may be admitted to the city that hath foundations, and obtain a crown of glory that fadeth not away. Let me entreat a part and interest in your prayers ; I have great need of them, and beg that you will remember me in your intercessions at the Throne of Grace. "The Lord bless thee and keep thee : the Lord make His face shine upon thee and be gracious unto thee : the Lord lift up His countenance upon thee and give thee peace."

With the heartfelt regards and wishes both of myself and family, ever believe me, my very dear Sir, yours most tenderly and truly,   THOMAS CHALMERS.

No. CCCLVI.—To Miss MACKEAN.

Edinburgh, 2d January 1847.

MY VERY DEAR MISS MACKEAN,—I return you my most cordial thanks for your donation in behalf of the West Port.

I have great reason to bless God for the liberality which He has put into the hearts of His people in behalf of that great object, of which I am most thankful to say that hitherto it has prospered and is promising.

I had received copies of Dr. Edgar's tract, which expresses what I have long thought the only hopeful method of dealing with Ireland. What an incubus is their Popery on the terri-torial system and everything that is good !

But what fearfully harrowing accounts there are of want and extreme agony in that unhappy land to be yet aggravated tenfold ere the seasons come round again, and not even then, unless the Lord of the seasons shall open His liberal and ever giving hand.—Ever believe me, my dear Madam, yours most gratefully and truly, THOMAS CHALMERS

No. CCCLVII.—TO REV. ALEXANDER ANDERSON, ABERDEEN.

Edinburgh, 20th March 1847.

MY DEAR SIR,—I shall be at all times happy to see you on the subject of your proposed gymnasium. But do come to breakfast, for it is only then that I can answer for being disengaged. Do persevere in your good work. The greatest amount of philanthropic service is secured by leaving each man to ride his own hobby. Your object is one of vital magnitude; and I would much rather that you concentrated your whole energies upon it than that you should become a man of all works—the tendency to which I look upon as a very great failing. There is little good done by your mere universalists. Do therefore persevere, and may God prosper you.—I ever am, my dear Sir, yours very truly, THOMAS CHALMERS.

[*Claydon House, Bucks, 28th April* 1847.—MY DEAR SIR,—Am I taking too great a liberty with you, and presuming too much on my former acquaintance with you, if I request some information as to your views on the Government Education Scheme ?

I have read with much interest the speeches of Dr. Candlish and Mr. Begg in the Free Presbytery of Edinburgh, on the 7th inst., as reported in the " Scottish Guardian" of the 13th, and especially your letter of the 3d, read at that meeting.

In paragraph No. 1, you say,—" I believe that there are modifications upon their scheme which might be made, and which would give no other character to the movement on the part of the State, than a desire for the elevation of the people in general intelligence and scholarship ; an object which we should no more resist," &c. &c.

Am I trespassing too much on you, if I ask you to tell me what those modifications are ? I desire to know whether any suggestions could be made to the Government which, if adopted, would render their plan unobjectionable in your opinion.—I am, my dear Sir, yours very faithfully and truly, HARRY VERNEY.

To Rev. Dr. Chalmers.]

No. CCCLVIII.—To Sir Harry Verney.

Edinburgh, 4th May 1847.

My DEAR SIR HARRY,—I have read your letter with the greatest interest, and regret that, on the eve of setting out upon a distant journey, I cannot reply to it at any length. The modifications that I should like, would be that the Government were to drop the requisition of any certificate from the managers of the school, that they were satisfied with the religious progress of the scholars ; and I should further like that there was no power granted either to the Church of England, or to any other denomination, to force their peculiar Catechism upon scholars against the will of their parents, and still less to force attendance against that will on their own places of worship.—I am, my dear Sir Harry, with the greatest esteem, THOMAS CHALMERS.

No. CCCLIX.

ON VISITING A FAMILY IN WHICH A SUDDEN DEATH HAD OCCURRED.

My DEAR SIR,—I am so particularly taken up by previous arrangements to-day, and, I fear, also to-morrow, that I shall not be able to see you again so soon personally as I could wish. But the scene of last night makes me very desirous of communicating with you some way or other. I was very thankful

you invited me to witness it, for it was a truly impressive
one, and eminently fitted to stir up in the heart of every be-
holder a salutary feeling of the vain and transient character of
our present pilgrimage ; and I trust I felt that it is better to
go to the house of mourning than to the house of feasting, for
that is indeed the end of all men, and that the living may lay
it to heart. In a disaster so big, and at the same time so
sudden and unlooked for as that which has come upon yourself
and family, it is impossible to minister any effectual consolation without you go to the root of the matter—everything short
of that argument which embraces the great elements of religion,
and eternity, and the soul, and its meetness for the enjoyment
of God in Heaven, is but superficial and vain. The healing
influence of time will bring round the mind of an afflicted man
even without Christianity to its wonted tone ; but how desirable that our comfort should be secured on a better foundation,
that it should come to a place in the heart not by the mere
wearing away of sorrow, but by the firm suggestions of an
understanding exercising itself on the realities of faith, and
fetching from the Divine Word such considerations as will
bring peace and the peaceable fruits of righteousness along
with them. You feel now what you never felt so nearly and
so experimentally before, that the world ought never to be
counted a place of rest. It is indeed a great delusion ever to
feel otherwise ; but still it is a delusion which is always hanging about us, and that attaches to the fallen and estranged state
of our natures from God. At this moment the delusion is in
your case for a time broken up. I prophesy that it will again
return if there be no visitation of grace from on high—no
anointing which remaineth—no favourable and abiding demonstration of the Spirit of God to advance your present feeling into a practical habit and principle of the soul. You are at
this moment made most intimately and effectually to under-

466 CORRESPONDENCE OF DR. CHALMERS.

stand, that to lean upon the world is to lean upon a foundation of dust; that to build your tabernacle here, is to build your house upon the sand; and that nothing will fill and satisfy the soul and enable it to stand all the changes and vicissitudes of this eventful pilgrimage, but a renouncing of the world as our home, and taking the inheritance that endureth for ever as our portion. I know nothing that more effectually hinders a man from venturing his all on Christ than that divided state of affections in either of which he would like to reserve a portion to himself. "You will not come unto me that you may have life." You never, my dear Sir, were in more favourable circumstances for an unqualified resignation of all into His hands than at this moment ; to whom else, alas, can you go ? you never got so buried to the world as now when the dearest of all its objects has been torn away from you— when the desire of your heart has been cut down by a stroke— when your family are all in sad grief, desponding under the pressure of a great unlooked for and overwhelming visitation. Do improve the favourable season with all your might to be a new creature in Christ Jesus ; let all old things be done away, and all things become new; the very retirement will animate and bear you up under the heaviness of your present circumstances, and present calamity will indeed be a blessing in disguise if it lead you to a close alliance with Him who, though a God, is also a Saviour.—I am, &c.,   THOMAS CHALMERS.

No. CCCLX.—To MRS. M'CORQUODALE.

Glasgow, 6th October 1817.

DEAR MADAM,—I should have replied long ago to your kind letter, but I have of late been a good deal occupied. It gives me sincere pleasure to be informed of your earnest desire after that which is right, and more particularly of your high sense of the necessity of religiously training your young family. I pray that you may be directed by Him who is the Father of Light, and will give wisdom to all who believingly ask it.

There is a very leading and prominent doctrine of the Bible, without the belief of which, and influence of which, I fear that all our longings after excellence will turn out to be vain and impotent aspirations,—I mean the doctrine of salvation by a crucified Saviour. To think of obtaining this favour of God by mere unaccompanied exertion, and that too in the face of God's own declaration, that without Christ we can do nothing, is in fact to insult Him by a vain and polluted offering.

Let us accept of forgiveness on the footing that is held out to us—even that Christ died for our offences ; and let us render obedience in the strength of that Spirit which is ever in readiness to be given to the prayer of believers, and we shall serve God with a holiness, and a love, and a spirituality that do not enter as ingredients at all into the tasteful morality of the world ; and the whole course, and motive, and character of our virtue will be so different from what it was before, that all old things will be done away, and all things will become new.

I beg your indulgence for these observations ; they come from one who is deeply sensible of his shortcomings from what is right. But I trust that through earnest attention to the Bible, and prayer for that Spirit who alone can enlighten us in the discernment of its doctrine, and above all, steadfast confidence in Him who casteth out none who come unto Him, we shall each of us be enabled to maintain that walk of faith and of holiness which leads to the Jerusalem above.

Give my best compliments to Mr. M'Corquodale, in which Mrs. Chalmers joins ; and with best wishes for yourself and family, believe me, my dear madam, yours most truly,

THOMAS CHALMERS.

No. CCCLXI.—To Mrs. M'Corquodale.

St. Andrews, 17th October 1827.

My dear Madam,—I very sincerely condole with you on the heavy bereavement which you have been called upon to suffer, the first loss I understand in your family, and which, in the absence yet of all personal experience myself upon the subject, I should regard as far more trying to nature than the dissolution of any other relationship. Affection points more strongly downwards—as from a parent to children—than in any other direction; and when I think of the suddenness of your daughter's death, her interesting age, and the many cares and attentions which the delicacy of her health has required from you, and which all go to strengthen affection and add to its tenderness—the shock you have experienced must be of no common severity. And what other comfort has one liable to the same visitations to offer, but those considerations which are familiar to all, though practically felt by few, even the evanescence of our present world, and the bliss and brightness of that invisible Heaven, where sorrow and separation are unknown.

We hear on these occasions of melancholy of the healing influence of time, and refuge is often taken in such expedients, as business, variety, and entertainments. These may soothe, but they do not sanctify. They drown the painful recollection; whereas the recollection should be kept alive and made the instrument of weaning our desires and expectations from a scene so transitory. The worldly would stifle the thought—the Christian softens it by pointing his eye upwards to God and forwards to eternity.—I am, yours, &c.,

THOMAS CHALMERS.

No. CCCLXII.—To Miss M'Corquodale.

Morningside, 24th December 1843.

My dear Miss M'Corquodale,—It is of great consequence to me that I should remain all this week in the country; but I am unwilling that it should pass without converse of some sort with your family.

I am very far from wishing to overtask Mrs. M'Corquodale with too much in quantity. Such is the preciousness of Bible truth, and such its power of application, that a single verse might often suffice for a sustaining and comforting exercise to the mind for hours together; and I think I cannot do better than draw up a brief list of texts for you to read, and for her to dwell upon.—Matthew xi. 28, 29, 30. She might lean the full weight of her dependence on a Saviour who thus calls upon her.—Matthew xxiii. 37. Who can doubt after this His longing desire after all who have any desire towards Him?—Matthew xxviii. 5. It is not a sentiment of terror, but of confidence and comfort that we should associate with the thought of a Saviour, and with the attempt to seek an interest in His salvation.—Mark x. 14. Such an exhibition of our Saviour as should lead us to place all reliance on His benignity and grace.—Luke vii. 13. Another most attractive representation of the Saviour, and fitted to assure our hearts of His feeling for the distresses of men.—Luke xi. 10, 11, 12, 13. A mighty encouragement to prayer, and that whether for ourselves or for those near and dear to us.—Luke xv. 20. A most striking demonstration of God's willingness for our salvation, and of the welcome from Him which awaits all His returning children.— John i. 29; iii. 14, 15, 16, 17. A most inviting call on us to look to the Saviour on the cross; and His errand, which was not to condemn but to save, should dissipate all our fears.— John xi. 25, 26. John xiv. 1, 14. Romans x. 13. 2 Cor.

v. 19, 20, 21.   Hebrews iv. 16 ; vi. 18, 19.   James i. 17.   1 John
i. 7, 9 ; iv. 8, 9, 10, 14, 16, 18, 19.

It is my earnest prayer that the heavy trials which now lie
upon your family may turn out to be blessings in disguise ;
and that though for the time not joyous but grievous, they
may prove to be those light afflictions which are but for a
moment, and which work out for us a far more exceeding and
eternal weight of glory.

With best regards to Mr. and Mrs. M'Corquodale, and to all
of your household, I am, my dear Miss M'Corquodale, yours
very truly,   THOMAS CHALMERS.

P. S.—The fifty-third and fifty-fourth chapters of Isaiah.—
T. C.

No. CCCLXIII.—To Miss M'Corquodale.

Edinburgh, 19th January 1845.

MY DEAR MISS M'CORQUODALE,—I beg to return my best acknowledgments for your New Year's letter.   It was very
acceptable to me.

I am particularly glad that these Scripture texts should be
so much prized by you.   We are on safe and sure ground when
dealing honestly and rightly with those words of which it is
said, that Heaven and earth shall pass away ere they can pass
away.

It gives me great pleasure to hear of your sister's restoration to health.   May she ever have great peace and joy in
believing, and attain to that perfect love which casteth out
fear.   When the great question between us and God is settled,
all is well ; and the ills of life may annoy, but they will not
sink us to despair.

Let me commend you to that Bible from which I rejoice to
observe that you derive so much comfort.

Were I asked in one sentence to describe the likeliest process for becoming wise unto salvation, I should say that it was a prayerful reading of the Bible. Let the Spirit but open our understandings to understand the Scriptures, and then shall we be enabled to draw water out of the wells of salvation, for there, and there alone, have we the words of everlasting life. Give my best regards to both your sisters, and to your brother, whom I have not seen for a long time ; as also to your father, now well stricken in years. May He, whose providence has spared him to a good old age, shower down upon him the blessings of His grace, that every hour bringing us all so much nearer to death may find us meeter for that eternity on which we are so soon to enter.—Believe me, my dear Miss M'Corquodale, yours very truly, THOMAS CHALMERS.

No. CCCLXIV.—To MRS. RUTHERFORD OF EDGERSTONE.

Glasgow, 8th November 1822.

MY DEAR MADAM,—I should have acknowledged your great kindness to me long ago, and have given some expression to those feelings wherewith the truly memorable visit* which I paid to Edgerstone has inspired me. They ought to be the feelings of deepest seriousness ; but it is woful to think of our obstinate tendencies to earth and earthliness ; and how soon it is that the solemnity awakened by death, even in its most appalling form, goes into utter dissipation.

This melancholy experience of our own heart should teach us our dependence on that grace by which we are forgiven, and on that Spirit by which we are sanctified.

It demonstrates the utter vanity of trusting to our own righteousness, and ought to humble us down into the attitude of being clothed upon with the righteousness of another.

It is delightful to think, that he on whom the Saviour per-

* See Memoirs, vol. i. p. 365.

formed a remarkable cure, was not only found clothed but in his *right mind.* And in like manner there is still an insepar-able union between our being covered with the righteousness of Christ, and our being cleansed by the washing of regenera-tion and renewing of the Holy Ghost. Let us not however wait till we are made holy ere we trust in the Saviour; but a better and more encouraging process for the helpless sinner, is first to let us trust in the Saviour, and then shall we be sealed with the Holy Spirit of promise, (Eph. i. 12.) What a precious freeness and fulness does this view confer on the Gospel ! How near does it bring salvation even to those who are farthest off in alienation from God, who calls upon us even in this stage to have confidence in Himself as God in Christ reconciling the world ! This confidence would in fact put a new spiritual feel-ing into our hearts—it would emancipate them from the servile spirit of bondage—it would draw them freely and affectionately out to God as our reconciled Father. It would implant love where before there was jealousy, hatred, and distrust. And under the impulse of this heaven-born affection, will we go spontaneously forth on the walk of new obedience.

Let us therefore hold fast the faith whence all these bless-ings flow, not casting away our confidence which hath great recompense of reward.—I have the honour to be, my dear Madam, yours with the greatest esteem and regard,

THOMAS CHALMERS.

No. CCCLXV.—To MRS. USHER.

Glasgow, 19th November 1822.

MY DEAR MRS. USHER,—I have been desirous of writing you ever since I saw you last at Courthill; and indeed, upon that occasion would have wished to talk to you, and to sympathize with you alone, entering, as I do, into your deep sorrow with all the feeling of a most devoted friend, and anxious, if I could, to contribute anything to lighten the visitation wherewith it hath pleased a good but mysterious Providence to exercise yourself and your dear family.

And the great alleviation in all our calamities is, that God reigneth, and that, if we bow in resignation to Him, He will raise us up again. It is often a good thing to have our hearts rent asunder from the world, even though it should have cost us the pain of a most violent laceration. He who wounds can heal, and be assured that there is no depth of wretchedness from which He cannot lift us up, and set our feet again on a sure place, and establish all our goings, and put a new song into our hearts, even glory to God.

This is a vale of tears, and you have had full experience of it. Look onward to a bright and peaceful termination. In a few years, and we shall all lie mouldering in our graves. But, meanwhile, a pitying Saviour calls upon us to approach Him, and announces to us the power of His sacrifice, and bids us trust in His atoning blood for the forgiveness of all our trespasses, and offers to put a spirit into our hearts whereby they may both be consoled and purified, and invites us to enter through Himself into reconciliation with God, and promises that, if we will abide in Him, He will abide in us, and make all things, even the darkest events of our history, work together for our good. This is a way which lies open to us all, and great will be our peace, whenever our feet are established therein; and we shall even count it all joy when we fall into divers tribulations—looking onward to the calm and smiling haven where all sorrow and sin and separation are unknown.

It is indeed my earnest prayer that God would both sweeten and sanctify to you the cup of discipline. There is a great work before us ere we die—to become holy here, that we may be meet for being happy hereafter. Christ will enable us to do this work if we rely upon Him, and it is in the perception

2 R

of its readiness for eternity that the soul finds its best refuge from the sorrows of time.—Believe me, &c.,

THOMAS CHALMERS.

No. CCCLXVI.—To MRS. HENRY WOOD, EDINBURGH.

St. Andrews, 13*th September* 1826.

MY DEAR MADAM,—I only reached St. Andrews yesterday, and was very much affected by the intimations from Edinburgh, the melancholy subject of which was altogether new to me. Mrs. Chalmers and my family share with me in a sorrow which must well-nigh overwhelm yourself, but which, I earnestly pray, may be soothed and sanctified by the God of all comfort. My daughter Anne was particularly solemnized by the recency of our visit, and her recollections of all the kindness that we had gotten under your roof. The walk from Great King Street to the Register Office is powerfully and touchingly present to both our minds; nor do I remember, in the whole compass of my experience, a more impressive manifestation of God's mysterious sovereignty, and of man's duty to be humble, and watchful, and mindful of death.

To yourself this is one of those sudden and awful revulsions by which the heart is agonized, but by which the heart is often made better. When the nearest and dearest of all earthly relationships is dissolved, the soul, thrown loose, as it were, from its wonted dependence, may be led thereby to keep more tenacious hold upon an enduring relationship. How precious that Gospel by which we are invited to enter upon its privileges, and to come under its full protection. God in Christ offers himself to all in the capacity of a friend who sticketh closer than a brother: He is a husband to the widow, and a father to the fatherless who put their trust in Him. An earthly prop has fallen. Lean the whole weight of your dependence upon God. Put full confidence both in His wisdom and in

His mercy. Be thankful for all the recollections that you have of that evident interest which your husband felt in the truths of the Gospel, and let us be followers of them who through faith and patience are now inheriting the promises.

We deeply sympathize with your afflicted family, and sincerely hope that the health neither of them nor of yourself will permanently suffer by the shock which you have sustained. The same God who hath inflicted the wound can also heal it, and fill up the desolate void of this sore and sudden bereavement by a livelier faith than ever in the hopes and promises of the Gospel. We beg our most affectionate condolence to all the members of your afflicted household ; and with earnest prayers for your own comfort and sanctification under this heavy calamity, I entreat you to believe me, my dear Madam, yours very affectionately, THOMAS CHALMERS.

No. CCCLXVII.—To WILLIAM BUCHANAN, ESQ., GLASGOW.

St. Andrews, 11th April 1828.

MY VERY DEAR SIR,—I received our friend Mr. Brown's letter with its most affecting intimation, by which both Mrs. Chalmers and I have been moved in no ordinary degree. The desire of your heart has indeed been cut down by a stroke, and the dreary and desolate void created there will continue an uneasiness almost insupportable till replaced by the love, and the light, and the positive consolations of the gospel.

And this, my dear Sir, is one great use of affliction—one great instrument in the hand of a loving and just Father by which to reclaim our wandering affections to Himself. The heart must have an object ; and often does our wise Master in Heaven tear away the earthly object of affection that He may fill up the vacancy by Himself. It is thus that I understand John xv. 2 ; and it is thus that the chastening hand of God, though not joyous but grievous for the time, yieldeth the peaceable fruit of righteousness to him who is exercised thereby.

And what rich consolation you have in the manner of the death ; what gratitude you owe for the testimony that she has left behind her ; what a sweet blending even of the affections of nature with the hopes of religion in the precious thought that she is now among the saints in Heaven, and that a re-union with her will be one ingredient of that blessedness which awaits you when you shall enter into rest.

I feel greatly for poor Miss Marshall—offer to her our respectful sympathies ; and I do entreat, that under this heavy visitation you will know that " God is the Lord, and be still."

I beg further to be remembered to your mother, Miss Taylor, Mr. and Mrs. Allan Buchanan, and Mr. and Mrs. Walkinshaw.—I am, my dear Sir, yours most truly,

THOMAS CHALMERS.

No. CCCLXVIII.—To WILLIAM BUCHANAN, Esq.

Edinburgh, 31*st January* 1847.

MY VERY DEAR SIR,—We all hear received with the deepest sympathy and feeling the very melancholy intelligence of your son's death—one of so much promise cut off so young, and to me so unexpectedly, for I had hoped that he was in the fair way of regaining confirmed health. We enter into all your grief on this truly affecting occasion ; and while both Mrs. Chalmers and I are fully aware how painfully this bereavement must be felt by every one of the sorrowing relations in your household, we particularly advert to Miss Marshall as among the chief mourners and sufferers under the visitation which the mysterious yet merciful and all-wise God hath seen meet to lay upon you. We beg that you will offer our most affectionate condolences both to her and to all your family, and the assurance of our prayers that an event so fitted to strike and to solemnize might be sanctified to one and all of you. The chastisements of our Father in Heaven are not for the time joyous but grievous ; yet do they yield the peaceable fruit of righteousness to those who are rightly exercised thereby.

Oh, that these numerous instances of mortality would at length practically and influentially tell upon us. Strange that the lesson which is the oftenest repeated should be also the oftenest forgotten, so that we need to be ever and anon reminded that we live in the land of dying men. May the sorrow of nature be ripened and transmuted by Divine grace into the sorrow which worketh repentance unto salvation. We have only to look back on the last thirty years of our acquaintance to be impressed by the changes of a world that will soon pass away from all of us. O that we sat more loose to the cares and interests of time, so as to have our affections weaned from the things which are beneath, and wedded to the things which are above. There death and separation are unknown ; and it might well mitigate our sorrows when we reflect in faith on that place of unfading bliss where friends shall meet to part no more, and be for ever happy with the Lord.

It is my earnest prayer that God would take unto Himself His own power and reign over our hearts ; for nothing in nature, though operating with its utmost force on nature's affection and nature's sensibilities, will of itself arouse us from the incumbent carnality and earthliness that weigh so heavily upon our hearts. May this regenerating influence be brought to bear with effect upon us all ; and then shall we be translated from the walk of sight to the walk of faith, and not only look forward to, but live by the power of a world to come.

With all our united regards to yourself, Miss Marshall, Miss Buchanan, and the rest of your family, ever believe me, my dear Sir, yours most truly, and with great regard,

THOMAS CHALMERS.

P.S.—I have not yet written poor Mrs. Brown. I have many intimations lying by me unanswered. This month I shall have written twenty such replies. May we be wise and understand these things, and consider our latter end.—T. C.

No. CCCLXIX.—To Mrs. Campbell.

St. Andrews, 3d September 1828.

My dear Madam,—I received the account of your venerable husband's* death with great emotion. He has left few equals behind him in the Church of Scotland, and I shall ever cherish a pleasing remembrance of all the fatherly aid and kindness which I received from his hands.

As a theologian, he was distinguished by the extent of his learning and the depth of his views. I cannot forget a conversation I held with him in a stage coach from Glasgow to Edinburgh, and the admirable judgment which he evinced on some of the most arduous speculations which are ever attempted by the human understanding.

But your brightest comfort now must be in your recollection of his piety. May the God of all consolation bear up you and yours under the weight of this afflictive visitation, and may we all feel how salutary it is to be made to drink of the cup of His discipline, and to be the objects of His chastening love.

I beg my kindest regards and the expression of my sympathy to the Misses Campbell; and with every assurance of respect and attachment, I am, my dear Madam, yours most truly,

Thomas Chalmers.

No. CCCLXX.—To Miss Young, Burntisland.

Edinburgh, 15th October 1831.

My dear Miss Young,—It was the firm purpose both of Mrs. Chalmers and myself to have made you a visit either the

* The Rev. Dr. Campbell of Edinburgh.

last or present month ; but her delicacy and my sprain have prevented it. She is confined to bed, and I am under the necessity of travelling to Glasgow, so that we must postpone our visit for a time.

We often think of you, of the loss you have sustained, but of the many comforts at the same time which must bear you up under it. I never in my life witnessed a more peaceful old age than that of your father ; and to me it formed always a most interesting peculiarity in his case, that amid the suspension of all his other faculties, there survived in so much freshness and feeling his sense of religion. All his natural lights grew dim with age ; but that light which cometh from the sanctuary, the candle of the Lord, never was extinguished, and hence the sacredness as well as the serenity of his closing years.

Mrs. Chalmers desires me to say, that though we have not been able to make out our purpose in visiting you, we do hope that you and Miss Betsy will come to us in the course of the winter.—With best compliments to her, in which Mrs. Chalmers joins, I am, my dear Miss Young, yours very truly,

THOMAS CHALMERS.

No. CCCLXXI.—To Miss Young.

Craigholm, 2d April 1837.

MY DEAR MISS YOUNG,—We are here in great comfort and quietness, though we feel it a great blank that your house is shut at present; but you must not think of hastening your journey homewards ; and, erring on the safe side, it were better that you made the movement later than you might, rather than earlier than you ought to do.

It is one great comfort in affliction, that it draws towards them who are exercised thereby, a greater tenderness of regard from their friends on earth ; and this may well assure us of what Scripture tells, that it in like manner draws a more special regard from our kind and merciful Father who is in Heaven. And accordingly we are told that it is in love that He chasteneth—that He afflicts not willingly—that He has no pleasure in our death—that His Son, who is the express image of His own person, is touched with the fellow-feeling of our infirmities ; and surely with such a Father and such a High Priest at His right hand, we may well rest in the quiet confidence that we are in good hands, and that all things will work together for good to them who love God.

The great object with you at present is not to fatigue yourself with care of any sort, but to cast that care, whatever it may be, on Him who careth for you. The defects and infirmities of one's own spirit may well grieve us ; but even this cause of uneasiness is best disposed of by rolling it over upon God. "Take this heart, such as it is : make it such as it should be." Let us commit our souls unto Him, and He will keep that which is so committed. He will bless us with a present as well as a future salvation, making us holy by grace here, as a preparation for being happy in the eternal glory that is to be revealed hereafter.

May the Bible be felt by you in all its preciousness ; may its verses be more and more prized as pearls of consolation and great worth. Take in all the comfort of them ; and instead of exercising your mind upon them, so as to exceed the strength of your attention, let them rather say unto you, " Peace, be still." Thus may you enjoy the repose of a spirit that is staid upon God, and experience that in quietness and in confidence ye shall have strength.

It is my earnest prayer that He who in Christ Jesus is reconciled to all who have faith in His blood, may stablish and strengthen you, and make you perfect.—I ever am, my dear Miss Young, yours most affectionately, THOMAS CHALMERS.

P. S.—I am reading Buchanan's work with great satisfaction. Our elder brother was made perfect through suffering.—T. C.

No. CCCLXXII.—To CHARLES COWAN, ESQ.

Edinburgh, 19th December 1831.

MY DEAR SIR,—Mrs. Chalmers unites with me in every feeling and expression of sympathy with you and Mrs. Cowan on the occasion of this afflictive bereavement. I am glad to observe that you are deriving comfort from the only true source ; and I cannot believe that the Saviour who evinced such attachment to children upon earth, who took them in His arms and blessed them, who rebuked the apostles for forbidding their approach to His person, who declared that of such is the kingdom of Heaven—I cannot believe that the infant flower, which so soon lies withered upon its stalk, is not transplanted into those unfading bowers where it will flourish in all the bloom and vigour of immortality.

With kindest regards and condolences to Mrs. Cowan, and to Mr. and Mrs. Menzies, if still with you, I am, my dear Sir, yours very truly,   THOMAS CHALMERS.

No. CCCLXXIII.—To THE REV. DR. SOMERVILLE OF DRUMMELZIER.

Kinghorn, 22d August 1832.

MY DEAR SIR,—This is truly a sad visitation to you and poor Mrs. Somerville as parents of one of the best of sons, and to myself in having lost a pupil of whom I may honestly say, that none stood higher in my personal regards.

I might expatiate on his great and interesting and superior talents as a scholar, but these are unavailing now. Your strong consolation lies in what we all know of his faith in the Saviour, and decided piety ; and I do hope that these precious recollections will sweeten the cup of discipline both to you and your sorrowing family.

It is an appalling scourge that has come upon our land, and death, I am told, in its most hideous and revolting form, is the consequence.* Never than in such a peculiar case is the comfort of the following passage more applicable, and I trust your faith will prevail over sense and memory in appropriating it :— "Sown in corruption, raised in incorruption ; sown in weakness, raised in power ; sown in dishonour, raised in glory." May you both rejoice in the prospect of that day when that fine form and countenance, in which you witnessed so grievous a transformation, will again be restored ; when the grave will deliver up its dead; and they who, once near and dear to us, are now mouldering there shall be invested with the bloom and vigour of immortality.

Your son's death has awakened great emotion among us all. He was a general favourite among his fellow-students ; and from the first time I knew him I loved him. The grief he has left behind him in your family must be deep.and tender. Nor would I have ventured to obtrude on the sacredness of your sorrow but for the sake of unbosoming my own. May He who inflicted the wound, and alone is able to heal it, pour abundantly into your hearts of the balm of His consolation, and bid you look with the believer's eye, and the believer's hope, to that everlasting home where sorrow and separation are unknown.

With kindest and most sympathizing regards to Mrs. Somerville, and to the other members of your deeply afflicted family, ever believe me, my dear Sir, yours most truly,

THOMAS CHALMERS.

No. CCCLXXIV.—To Dr. Somerville.

Edinburgh, 23d April 1843.

MY VERY DEAR SIR,—I have been much affected and concerned by the melancholy intimation of another breach in your family.

* Dr. Somerville's son was cut off by cholera.

To use the language of Paul, you have been "in deaths oft;" and God has been pleased in His sovereign wisdom to exercise you in your old age by sore and heavy bereavements. May you have ample experience of succour and support from Him who has a fellow-feeling for all our infirmities and sorrows; and in the peaceable fruits of righteousness may you realize the truth of the precious declaration, that all things will be made to work together for good to them who love God.

The two admirable young men whom you have lost were both my students, and both of them very much valued and loved by me. Were it not for the hopes and comforts of the blessed Gospel, what a desolation would such deaths leave behind them!

God abundantly bless and sustain you, my dear Sir, under the truly afflictive dispensation. Take refuge in Christ and in His righteousness, which opens up a better and abiding world to all who believe in Him.—I ever am, my dear Sir, yours with sincerest regard and every feeling of condolence for yourself and your daughters,　　　　　　THOMAS CHALMERS.

No. CCCLXXV.—To MISS SOMERVILLE.

Morningside, 12th May 1844.

MY DEAR MISS SOMERVILLE,—I heard the melancholy intelligence of your venerable father's death with great emotion—having long had the highest respect for his character, and for his great services on the field of argument to the cause of Christianity. So long back as 1817, I was introduced to Lord Grenville, who spoke to me of Hume's infidelity, and of the desire he felt for an effective refutation of his sophistry on the subject of miracles. I told him of your father's work as the best then extant upon that subject; and I afterwards saw a high-written testimony from him in its favour, he having perused it with a high estimation of its value and power. But I am sure that it is not so much the recollection of his talents or

scholarship, but of his great faith and the love which he bore to
the truth as it is in Jesus ; it is this last which can minister
the only effectual consolation in this season of your bereavement, and cause you to rejoice even in the midst of a sore
tribulation.   There is a sanction and a sacredness given to the
sorrow of nature by the example of our Saviour, but you have
great reason to sorrow not even as others who have no hope ;
and let the deaths of the wise and the good that are so fast
thickening around us, let them incite us all the more to be
followers of them who, through faith and patience, are now
inheriting the promises.

You have had many and severe family trials.   The first of
your brothers, who was my student, and cut off while at
college, was my most favourite pupil, and I had the greatest
liking for him ; and he, after the interval of some years,
was followed by another who promised to be of great service in
the Church.   When to these I add dear Mrs. Somerville, you may
truly be said to have been " in deaths oft."   Heaven grant
that they may teach us true wisdom, that they may lead us
solemnly and practically to consider our latter end, and that we
all withdraw our affections from a world that passeth away to
that enduring world where there is joy at God's right hand and
pleasures for evermore.

Give my best regards to your sister and brothers.   May this
visitation be sanctified to the mourning survivers ; and with
sincere and affectionate condolence for you all, I entreat you to
believe me, my dear Madam, yours most truly,

THOMAS CHALMERS.

No. CCCLXXVI.—To MRS. CHARLES NAIRNE.

Morningside, 29th *January* 1837.

MY DEAR MRS. NAIRNE,—The same infirm health which
prevented me from joining in the last melancholy offices to

your departed husband, has forced me out to the country, where I am now spending a Sabbath of complete retirement and repose. I feel that I cannot better spend one hallowed hour of it, than by weeping with those who weep, and telling you in particular how deeply I sympathize with you under that awful and affecting visitation, by which the nearest and dearest of all earthly relationships is broken. This is truly a sad and sudden bereavement, and fitted of all others to overwhelm the sinking spirit, were it not that we are in the hands of a God who is as merciful as He is mysterious ; and of whom we may feel assured, that though clouds and darkness are round about Him, there is wisdom in all His ways, and tenderness in all His visitations.

May this, my dear Madam, be your own ample experience on this most trying of all occasions. May your refuge and resting-place be in God ; may you be led to confide in Him as your reconciled Father through Jesus Christ our Lord, who, touched with the fellow-feeling of your infirmities and your sorrows, knows how to succour the afflicted, and is truly as willing as He is able to help you. May He open a way to your now desolated heart ; and, making it alive to the charm and the efficacy of His own peace-speaking blood, may He carry forward your hopes and your affections to that enduring world, where sin, and sorrow, and separation are unknown.

May I beg that you will offer my kind and condoling regards to Mrs. Marshall ; and I entreat you to believe me, my dear Madam, yours with deepest feelings of sympathy and regard,

THOMAS CHALMERS.

P.S.—I cannot close this letter without the expression of a fervent and heartfelt benediction on your dear boy. May he arise to manhood and call you blessed ; may his progress through the world be unstained by the infection of this world's spirit ; may he be spared to bear you up under the weight of declining years—at once duteous to his surviving parent, and duteous to his God.—T. C.

No. CCCLXXVII.—To Dr. Begbie.

9th December 1838.

My dear Sir,—We all here deeply sympathize with the severe family affliction under which you labour. And our feeling is not the less sincere that we cannot speak experimentally to the depth or the pungency of that grief which is awakened by the loss of children. I can well conceive it to be one of the sorest agonies wherewith our Father in Heaven is pleased to try and to exercise the hearts of His people here below ; and it is my earnest prayer that, bitter and well-nigh overwhelming as the visitation is under which you and Mrs. Begbie now labour, it may be sanctified to you both, and yield in abundance the peaceable fruits of righteousness.

It is quite wonderful that, living as we do in the midst of a most precarious world, and experiencing almost every day some new instance of the unsparing and universal law of mortality, there should still adhere to our nature such a cleaving and constant tendency to forget eternal things, and live here as if here we were to live for ever. May the Giver of all grace superadd the demonstrations of His Spirit to the warnings of His providence, and effectually teach one and all of us to consider our latter end.

I grieve to hear of your own confinement ; and with my fervent wishes and supplications for the comfort and wellbeing of you all, particularly of the bereaved and suffering mother, I entreat you to believe me, my dear Sir, yours very truly,

Thomas Chalmers.

No. CCCLXXVIII.—To MRS. M'CLELLAND.

Burntisland, 14*th June* 1840.

MY DEAR HELEN,—You may well believe that I have been in a sad state of helplessness, both from external causes and from my own personal state of utter languor and disability, else I should have been at Kelton last week, and failing this, should have written you before now on the subject of your sore and melancholy bereavement.

The sad intelligence was received by us all with great emotion. For myself, I always had a strong liking and respect for Mr. M'Clelland, and that founded on his own personal qualities—a kind, friendly, generous heart, and withal an exceedingly sound and well-informed understanding, with an amount of erudition not very common among the ministers of our Church. I really do not wonder at the regrets of his neighbourhood, and the well-merited testimony which I read the other day from one of our public journals regarding him; but all this enhances the magnitude of your loss, and of our sympathies with all the grief and desolateness of feeling which you must suffer because of it.

It were well if these frequent and most affecting instances of the mutability of all that is below, would at length send our thoughts in the habitual direction of upward and heavenward, if we at length learned the wisdom of considering our latter end, and laying hold on Him who came to destroy death ; if we learned to cast all our confidence on His sacrifice, and give ourselves wholly up to His keeping and His guidance during the remainder of our days. Mrs. Chalmers and I are both most anxious to know what your wishes and purposes are in regard to the future. And depend upon my help and co-operation, if spared, in all that can be of use to you. I know you will not ask me to undertake the journey to Kelton, unless some ma-

terial service requires it ; but if it should, I beg you will feel
no delicacy in letting me know ; for I shall feel it both my
duty and inclination to forward your views.   You of course will
spend some time with us prior to any permanent arrangement
that may, after proper counsel and deliberation, be fixed upon
as the best.—I am, my dear Helen, ever yours most affectionately,   THOMAS CHALMERS.

No. CCCLXXIX.—To Mrs. BRYCE, ABERDOUR.

Burntisland, 23d *September* 1841.

MY DEAR MRS. BRYCE,—I hesitate to intrude on the sacredness of your deep sorrow, yet cannot refrain from the expression of my sympathy both with yourself and all the members
of your bereaved family on this day of solemn visitation.

May He who is at once the Husband of the widow and
Father of the fatherless, be the refuge and sure portion of you
all.   He afflicts not willingly any of His children ; and it is
my earnest prayer, that this mysterious and unlooked for
visitation may yield to you and yours the peaceable fruits of
righteousness.

That meek and gentle Saviour who wept at the tomb of
Lazarus, gave thereby a sanction and sacredness to the sorrow
of nature.   May He further sanctify this emotion by the Spirit
of all-grace, and withdraw our affections from a world, the nearest and dearest objects of which can be so speedily withdrawn
from us.   It is well that we have His righteousness to plead
for our entrance into that better world where sin, and sorrow,
and separation are unknown.   May you, my dear madam, and
all of your household, obtain that precious faith which gives a
part and an interest in all the blessings of His mediatorship,
and unites you for ever with that spiritual family of which He
is the Head, who alone hath the gift, and who alone hath the
words of life everlasting.

With best regards for one and all of your afflicted circle, in which Mrs. Chalmers most sincerely joins, and begging you will accept of our united condolence on this touching occasion, I ever am, my very dear Madam, yours with great esteem,

THOMAS CHALMERS.

No. CCCLXXX.—To MISS BURNS.

Edinburgh, 8th January 1843.

MY DEAR MISS BURNS,—We are much interested by your letter respecting dear Miss Edie. At present I write you rather than her, that she might be saved the trouble and fatigue of reading more than she is quite able for. You will judge how far the reading of this and such like passages as I shall recommend might be prosecuted so as not to draw too much upon her attention. She is in the hands of one who knows her frame ; and I should like that her own gentle spirit reposed upon Him as all her desire and salvation. May He who has so invested her with the ornament of a meek and quiet spirit, perfect the work which He has begun, and ripen her more and more for the full enjoyment of that heaven where holiness and charity shall ever reign.

The twenty-third psalm I should think well suited for her. The green pastures, the still waters, the goodness and the mercy, are all images of bliss and goodness fitted to solace and give refreshment to her soul.

The last half of the Book of Isaiah is replete with encouragement ; and the forty-fifth chapter, particularly in its closing verses, is inestimably precious. And in the 8th verse there is an immense comfort in the expression of " the Heavens pouring down righteousness." How delightful to think of righteousness as a ready-made investiture given to them who believe, and so to be exempted from all the fears of legality, and all its fruitless and fatiguing labours. It is only of such righteousness that the prophet speaks in Isaiah xxxii. 17. May the patient sufferer take up with this righteousness, so as to work peace in her heart, and with the blessed effect of quietness and assurance for ever. The next verse too (verse 18) is very soothing. The fifty-third chapter, one of the most illustrious in Scripture, is well fitted to call out in our hearts the love of the Saviour.

The whole of our Saviour's conversation with His disciples, John xiv.-xvii., particularly xiv. 1-3, she will find to be an elixir to her soul. But she must not be overtasked. Do give her my tenderest regards. My heart bleeds for poor Mrs. Edie. Say all that is affectionate and kind both to her and to your much loved patient, both from myself and from all our family.—And with our united regards to you, I ever am, &c.,

THOMAS CHALMERS.

No. CCCLXXXI.—To Mrs. Elliot.

Edinburgh, 11th February 1844.

MY DEAR MRS. ELLIOT,—The intimation of dear Mrs. Usher's death has awakened in my breast no common sensibilities ; my acquaintance with her—on my part a constant and cherished friendship—being now of forty-three years' standing. In 1801, I was a frequent visitant at Courthill, and ever treated with the utmost kindness by both of your much loved parents, whose attentions to me at my first outset in public life have never been effaced from my memory, and, I will add, have never been effaced from my heart. The maternal care which I experienced at her hand, I always felt to be peculiarly soothing ; and from the days of Dr. Charters downwards, (but my intimacy with her began more than twenty years before his death,) I have never ceased, amid all the varieties through which Providence has conducted me, to cast an eye of pleasing remembrance on the place that gave you birth, or to think of your dear departed mother with every feeling of the most grateful and affectionate regard.

But far the most interesting visit I ever paid to her was in 1833, when she told me that she had reached seventy; nor can I adequately express the joy which I felt on finding that the truth as it is in Jesus was so congenial to her heart. She had quite the tone and aspect of one who was ripening for Heaven, and I trust has now entered upon its glories. Let us, my dear Mrs. Elliot, be followers of them who through faith and patience are now inheriting the promises; and then shall the friends who loved each other on earth, and loved the Saviour, hold everlasting converse together in that region of blessedness where sin, and sorrow, and separation are unknown.

Christ casts out none who come unto Him. His blood cleanseth from all sin. God through Him beseeches us to be reconciled. He says, " Turn ye, turn ye ; why will ye die ? " He promises that if we turn unto Him, He will pour out His Spirit upon us. These are precious sayings; and both you and I are abundantly welcome to the full benefit of their accomplishment in ourselves. Let us believe in them to the saving of our souls. Let us venture our all on that foundation which God Himself hath laid in Zion. Let us give ourselves up unto Christ to be ruled in by His Spirit—to be ruled over by His law. Give my best regards to Mr. Elliot and your brother ; and ever believe me, my dear Mrs. Elliot, yours with sincerest condolence and regard, THOMAS CHALMERS.

No. CCCLXXXII.—To MRS. ANDERSON.

Edinburgh, 5th May 1844.

MY VERY DEAR MRS. ANDERSON,—This is a truly desolating stroke. God has been pleased thus to cut off the desire of your eyes, (Ezek. xxiv. 16,) in mercy, however, I trust and believe, and not in judgment. You have great reason, my dear Madam, to rejoice even in the midst of this sore tribulation, though one of the sorest on this side of death, it being the breach of the nearest and dearest of all earthly relationships.

All here have been saddened and solemnized by it. We feel that we have lost a much valued friend. Every recollection I have of the dear deceased enhances my sense of his worth and goodness and the greatness of your loss. Never in the whole circle of my acquaintanceship did I experience a more uniform flow of all that was kind and gentlemanly. But the greatest charm of his society then, and incomparably the most consoling now to look back upon, is the evident value he had for the truth as it is in Jesus, the ardent love he bore to the Saviour.

This is a mighty alleviation ; and to the force of it I am confident you must feel alive. Blessed be God that while, with the example of His Son, who wept at Lazarus' tomb, He has given an impressive sanction to the sorrow of nature, you have such abundant reason to sorrow not even as others which have no hope. Let us but withdraw our affections from a world the nearest and dearest objects of which can be so speedily withdrawn from us, and transfer these affections to the world which endureth, where sorrow, and separation, and sin, are unknown.

It is my earnest prayer that the heavy bereavement may be blest and sanctified to you all. Give my best and kindest regards to the dear Miss Andersons and the rest of your sorrowing family. Oh that we at length learned wisdom—that the oft-repeated lesson of our mortality at length told upon us, so that instead of living here, as if here we were to live for ever, we became followers of them who through faith and patience are now inheriting the promises.

And what a comfort to think of the errand on which our Saviour came into the world, even to destroy death and him that has the power of death. Let us comfort one another with these words,—assured that all who slept in Jesus, all who loved the Lord Jesus Christ in sincerity, will meet again and be for ever with the Lord. In the contest between faith and sense, let faith have the victory. Take a firm confiding hold on the promises of the Gospel. Be persuaded of them and embrace them, and let them be your songs in the house of your pilgrimage. Cast your care and confidence on Him who is the husband of the widow and the father of the fatherless. And amid the changes of this eventful and ever-shifting world, let us steady our hearts upon the blessed assurance of that record which God hath given of His Son, even that God hath given to us eternal life, and that this life is in His Son.

The Bible-mark which you gave me I still use, and it is daily in my hand. The precious text that you wrought into it I often recall with the greatest interest, and I would present it now to your notice along with some others, Num. vi. 24, 25, 26; 2 Tim. i. 10; 1 Thess. iv. 13-18; 2 Cor. iv. 14, 17, 18; Psalm xc. 12; John xi. 25, 26; 1 Cor. xv. 53, 58; Phil. i. 23; Rev. xiv. 13; xxii. 1, 5, 17.

Mrs. Chalmers and my daughters join in most affectionate condolence with yourself and the Misses Anderson; and with most affectionate and earnest prayers for Heaven's blessings on you and yours, I entreat you to believe me, my very dear Madam, yours with the greatest esteem and sympathy and regard,

THOMAS CHALMERS.

No. CCCLXXXIII.—To MISS ABERCROMBIE.

Morningside, 17th November 1844.

MY DEAR MISS BARBARA,—This striking and unlooked for death never ceases to occupy my feelings and thoughts. It is not that Dr. Abercrombie filled so large a space in the eyes of his countrymen, but it is that apart altogether from his public and general celebrity, there was so much of genuine goodness and real Christian worth; and then what a mighty influence on the side of truth and righteousness that he held out through life, and a noble and consistent testimony, and in all his publications gave such evidence of an intense affection for human souls. But over and above his claims to my reverence and regard as a religious philanthropist, there was such a uniform kindness to myself, and his offices of substantial friendship to my family have been so important and numerous, that beyond the circle of my own immediate relationship there is no removal from the world of any other acquaintance I have in life that could more affect or solemnize or warn me. It is well to speak and think of it as but a removal—not a dissolution or final breaking up. May you and all the family be enabled to realize this bright and cheering conviction, and look forward to that joyful morning of a blessed and glorious resurrection, when you shall meet again in that inheritance above which fadeth not away.

In John xv. 2, there is the intimation of a process in the spiritual husbandry of God, which I have often looked upon as especially applicable to a case of bereavement, when the nearest and dearest of all earthly relationships is broken ; when a branch beareth fruit, God pruneth it that it may bring forth more fruit. The vegetable juices are made to take a more healthful direction when all the luxuriant overgrowth is taken away. And it is so in the moral and spiritual economy. Our affections are apt to run sidewards and downwards to an earthly object, and this tendency God in His wise and righteous discipline is often pleased to arrest or to shift, by dissevering the object, and so causing the stream or current of our affections to arise from the things that are beneath to those which are above. How delightful to believe that this change in the bent of your affections may take effect upon you all, and this without losing sight of their wonted object, but by following it upward to the place which he now occupies, thus causing you to feel as it were another tie to Heaven, an augmented interest in that eternal home which should henceforth be the grand object of all our aims and all our aspirations.

Give my most affectionate regards to your sisters, who one and all of them are the objects of my sympathies and prayers. I might have addressed this broken and imperfect effusion to Miss Abercrombie ; but on her, as the eldest of the family, the main burden will fall of this sad and trying dispensation. Forgive me, my dear Miss Barbara, for having singled out you as my correspondent for the expression of feelings which I cannot restrain, yet am unable to utter but in a way the most inadequate and feeble.—Ever yours, most affectionately and truly, THOMAS CHALMERS.

[*Midmills, near Inverness, 9th January* 1850.—REV. SIR,—I cannot deny myself the satisfaction of saying how much I felt gratified at finding, in the first volume of Dr. Chalmers's Memoirs, my husband's name so remembered in connexion with a family he so greatly esteemed.*

I have often heard him, in after years, refer to the warm kindness of Captain George Chalmers, who even tried to find amusement for him when returning strength fitted him for a little exertion. A bottle would be slung at the yard-arm to serve for a mark at which the invalid subaltern might fire ; and having been fortunate enough to hit the object several times, Captain Chalmers accounted him so expert a marksman, that he declared, should they encounter a hostile ship, he would station him " to pick off the man at the helm."—I am, Rev. Sir, your obedient servant,

MARGARET MACKAY.
The Rev. Dr. Hanna, Morningside.]

No. CCCLXXXIV.—To MRS. MACKAY.

Edinburgh, 16th March 1845.

MY DEAR MRS. MACKAY,—I received the affecting intimation from Hedgefield a few days ago, and not, I can assure you,

* See Memoirs, vol. i. p. 99.

without emotion. Your dear and departed husband I became acquainted with so far back as 1806, when he spent some time with me and my brother George at the manse of Kilmany, when my brother was languishing under an illness which carried him soon to his grave. At the commencement of our acquaintance neither of us was adequately impressed by the momentous realities of an eternal world ; but I rejoice to think of him in a more advanced life, and of all the converse that he had with yourself, and of the love he bore to one whose works declare that she loved the Lord Jesus. I have finished, and on the last Sabbath of last year,* the perusal of your affectionate testimony and tribute to the cause of the Saviour. May the precious truths which you there deal out to others, soothe and sustain your own spirit under this heavy visitation of Providence; and by which the nearest and dearest of all your earthly relationships has been broken asunder. May He who is the Husband of the widow be your support and consolation

---

* *Edinburgh*, 29th *December* 1843.—MY DEAR MADAM,—I offer you my grateful acknowledgments for your "Sabbath Musings," of which I mean to read one for every Sabbath of the coming year.

I am very sorry to hear of poor Col. Mackay's severe illness.

With every prayer for the best interests both of him and of yourself, ever be-believe me, my dear Madam, yours very truly,   THOMAS CHALMERS.

In a letter to Colonel Mackay, dated 11th December 1837, Dr. Chalmers referred to a previous publication of Mrs. Mackay in the following terms :—

I read the "Family at Heatherdale" with great pleasure, as did also my daughters. I think it a beautiful tale, and written in a pure and scriptural style of sentiment. Its simplicity is a great charm to me, though I would have you to be apprized, that this very property, though in my estimation a very high one, may operate adversely on the sale of the work, or on the amount of public demand for it. Such is the depraved taste now-a-days for excitement, that nothing but a story of great incident and bustle will satiate the appetite. The work, however, must have its select readers and admirers notwithstanding ; and, at all events, you have obviously great reason to felicitate yourself as being associated with one of such an accomplished, but, above all, of such a Christian mind as that manifested by its author.—With my best regards to Mrs. Mackay, I ever am, my dear Sir, yours most truly,   THOMAS CHALMERS.

in this your day of trial, and fill your sinking heart with the bright and elevating thoughts of that enduring world where sorrow, and suffering, and separation are unknown.

What a blessed consideration that we have a Friend on high who is touched with a fellow-feeling of our sorrows. May you be filled with a realizing sense both of His power and His willingness to save you. May you enjoy the manifestations of His love, so as that you may learn to glory not only in the hope of that inheritance which He hath purchased for all who believe, but even to glory in tribulations also. (Rom. v. 23.) Through patience and comfort of the precious Scriptures may you have hope, nay, abound therein, through the power of the Holy Spirit. (Rom. xv. 13.) The last of these two verses is truly precious; and may you have full experience of the blessings there prayed for by the Apostle,—peace and joy in believing, even on Him whose blood cleanseth from all sin; and why not from your sin?—Ever believe me, my very dear Madam, yours with great esteem and regard,

THOMAS CHALMERS.

No. CCCLXXXV.—To JAMES CUNNINGHAM, ESQ., EDINBURGH.

Anstruther, 18*th May* 1845.

MY DEAR SIR,—I should have replied much sooner to your melancholy and affecting intimation of the 2d of May. I have been advertised lately of many deaths, and some of them my own relatives. But this, though it has occupied my time, has not diverted my sympathies from you in the bereavement which you have been called upon to sustain by the tearing asunder of the nearest and dearest of all earthly relationships.

Yet I rejoice to think of your many alleviations. Our Saviour Himself has given the sacred sanction of His own example to the sorrow of nature. But what a call for gratitude that you sorrow not even as others that have no hope. What

2 T

a precious consolation is the remembrance of that faith and its fruits, which give you the blessed assurance, that when she fell asleep she slept in Jesus. And what a preservative against being swallowed up of overmuch sorrow—when our affections, instead of being desolated, are only transferred from that passing and present world, the nearest and dearest objects of which are taken away from us, to that bright and enduring world where sin, and sorrow, and separation are unknown. Let us therefore comfort one another with these words. As friends drop away from us, let us draw nearer together as the followers in one common pursuit of those who through faith and patience are now inheriting the promises.

It is my earnest prayer that this heavy affliction may be sanctified and made the vehicle of the richest spiritual blessings to you and to your children. They are deprived of a mother's presence, but not, let us confidently hope, of the fruit and efficacy of a mother's prayers, lifted up by her while on earth, and the reward of which is upon high.—Ever believe me, my dear Sir, yours very respectfully and truly,

THOMAS CHALMERS.

No. CCCLXXXVI.—To FREDERIC ADAMSON, ESQ.

Gourock House, 25th *July* 1845.

MY DEAR SIR,—I am not sure if I could state so well in conversation as I can attempt to do in writing, the very deep interest I feel in you, and my earnest desire that these brief and casual meetings on this side of death should be followed up on the other side of it in that reign of perfect blessedness where sorrow, and sickness, and separation are unknown. Believing as I do in the solemn realities of a coming judgment and coming eternity, I beg that you will consider it to be from no other cause than the strength of my affection for you that I venture to remind you of the everlasting weal or the everlasting wo to which we are fast hastening. If I did not think that there is a patent way of transition from death to life, from a state of condemnation to a state of acceptance, I would be the last man to offer any disturbance on a matter which, if altogether hopeless, had better be let alone ; but confident as I am that there is no want of good-will on the part of our Father who is in Heaven, that He is waiting to be gracious—nay, beseeching one and all of us to enter into reconciliation, I cannot refrain from pressing the assurance upon you of the perfect readiness wherewith your very first approaches will be met and rejoiced in by Him who dwelleth above, on that throne which is at once the throne of grace and righteousness. Let us be very certain that Christ will cast out none who come unto Him, and that God will cast out none who come unto Him through Christ. It is true that He is determined, and that in the most authoritative and peremptory manner, that this is the only footing upon which He will receive us, and that there is salvation in no other way than by the name of Christ. But let us only recollect that He is the party sinned against, and that it is for Him, and not for us, to dictate the terms and the treaty of reconciliation ; and so He has expressly said, that no man cometh to the Father but by the Son. It may look stern and repulsive the being told that out of this way we shall never meet with acceptance from God ; but surely this is all made up for, all most fully and generously compensated, when we are further told, that in this way of it we shall never miss acceptance with God. He who out of Christ is a consuming fire, is in Christ a reconciled Father. (2 Cor. v. 18-20.) By this open door of access, the worst and ungodliest of men are invited to draw nigh, that our sins may be washed out in that blood which cleanseth from all sin, and why not our sin ? He who hath the Son hath life ; he who hath not the Son hath not life. The acceptance of Christ, then, may be called the turning point of our salvation; it is the great act upon the doing or not doing of which there hinges our eternity. On the one hand, if we receive Him by faith, we shall receive all that is needful, whether for the preparation here, or the enjoyment hereafter of life everlasting; but on the other hand, how can we escape if we neglect so great salvation? (Heb. ii. 3.)

May the Spirit, whose office it is to bring home the word to our hearts—may He open our hearts to the truth and tenderness of these sayings; they are simple but sure, and would we only place faith in the gracious promises and calls held out in the Gospel, even to the farthest off in rebellion, then should we find that according to our faith so will it be done unto us.

Do indulge me, my dear Sir, in all this, and put it down to the right cause, which is, my sense of the duty I owe to a much loved friend; for although we have not met often during half a century, I have ever entertained a very strong affection towards you. I remember well the strength of those amiable and deeply felt affinities which bound together, as with all the force of mutual instinct, our family; and which often since I have witnessed streaming forth, as first one and then another of your desolated household in St. Andrews was taken off by death. In a few years we shall all be mouldering in our coffins; then be wise and join us. May Heaven grant that we shall be found side by side, sharing together in the resurrection of the blessed; and He who saith, " I am the resurrection and the life," now stands with open arms to receive all who come unto Him, and declaring this unto all in words of deepest pathos—grant that unto us they may prove words of power—" He that believeth in me, though he were dead, yet shall he live; and whosoever liveth and believeth in me shall never die."

May the Giver of all grace pour forth His best blessings upon you and yours, upon dear Mrs. Adamson, and upon one and all of your much loved family. Farewell, my dear Sir; I leave this by Monday's boat at eleven o'clock, and I can say truly, that far the most interesting visits I have made since I left home were those to yourself and Mr. C. I cannot express how much I was delighted by his state of mind—not only patient in tribulation, but rejoicing in hope. Let me die the death of the righteous, let my last end be like his.—Ever believe me, my dear Sir, yours with best and greatest regards,

THOMAS CHALMERS.

No. CCCLXXXVII.—To MISSES WALLACE.

Burntisland, 14th May 1846.

MY DEAR MISSES WALLACE,—It grieved me exceedingly to hear of your brother's death, and it grieves me still farther to hear of your sister's illness.

Short of religion and its blessed hopes, no adequate comfort can be given under the sore and afflicting bereavement which it has pleased the Almighty God, though often mysterious in His dealings with the children of men, to lay upon you. Yet poor and ineffectual as all other considerations are, I must affirm the sufficiency of the gospel of Jesus Christ to meet the calamity which else might overwhelm you. Not that I would forbid your tears, for our Saviour himself, who wept at the tomb of Lazarus, gives to the sorrow of nature the sanction and the sacredness of His example. But let us not forget that when He went up to Heaven He took up along with Him all the sympathies and all the tenderness which He manifested upon earth. Nor can I name a passage of Scripture more endearing or more fitted to soothe and alleviate even the deepest of our sorrows than that in which He is set forth to us as touched with a fellow-feeling of our infirmities, and as having been tried in all points even as we are, and so able to succour and sustain them who are so tried.

Cast then the whole burden upon Him of this heavy visitation—" Cast thy burden upon the Lord and He will sustain thee." It is not willingly that He afflicts the children of men ; and let us assure ourselves both of the wisdom and the goodness of a Father in every chastisement that He inflicts, and every ingredient, however bitter, which He pours into the cup of discipline.

If poor Jessie can bear to be read to, I know nothing more precious than our Saviour's last lengthened discourse to His disciples. The fifteenth chapter of John has long been a particular favourite of mine. The 2d verse is peculiarly applicable to those who mourn the death of relatives, as making known to us the purpose of the great Spiritual Husbandman in pruning the branches which have been yielding some fruit, even that they should bring forth more fruit.

Offer my affectionate condolence to Mrs. Thomas Young on this sad occasion ; and ever believe me, my dear Misses Wallace, the sincere and sympathizing friend of you both,

Thomas Chalmers.

P.S.—You must know Dr. Buchanan's work on affliction. I have more than once recommended it as a fit companion in houses of mourning.—T. C.

No. CCCLXXXVIII.—To Miss Wood.

Edinburgh, 5th July 1846.

My dear Miss Wood,—I should have acknowledged much sooner the affecting intimation from Elie of your sister's death, which I felt much at the time, and have borne the impression of in my heart ever since. There are not half a dozen surviving acquaintances in the world whom I have longer known,— the period of my recollections as a visitor in your house going back to very early childhood. It must have proved to you a very desolating stroke ; but what precious alleviations in the blessed assurance that she was one of God's own people, whose life throughout has been one of consistent discipleship, and who carried in her very aspect the expression of great peace and great joy in believing. May the thought of this comfort and sustain you under this heavy bereavement, and may it wean your affections still more from a world the nearest and dearest objects of which may at any time be withdrawn from us. It is thus that the great spiritual Husbandman, (John xv. 1, 2,) in the exercise of a wise and salutary discipline, draws the affections of His children upward and heavenward to Himself; and, superadding the lessons of His Providence to the lessons of His Word, teaches us a greater diligence and devotedness than heretofore, in being followers of those who through faith and patience are now inheriting the promises.

I feel quite sure that her most frequent and favourite volume must have been the Bible. I should like to know if there were any of our great old popular authors in whom she took peculiar delight. The truth is, that I am getting fonder of these every day; and the very books which formed the spiritual aliment both of my father and mother in their declining years, are now prized by me as, next to the Scriptures, the wisest and the best. I rejoice, for example, in "Marshall on Sanctification," and am pleased to think that he was one of my father's greatest favourites. But I have a far more vivid recollection, and had indeed the opportunity of more closely watching and observing my mother's deathbed than his; and she died, I would not say in the triumphs and ecstasies, but in the calm and settled assurance of the faith. I never understood so perfectly as from the view of her last hours, the expression of the Prophet—the peace which is as a river.

This intimation from Elie, now lying before me, carries me back into a far retrospect of the years of my boyhood. Your father and mother, Dr. and Miss Reid, Miss Anna Wood your aunt, the venerable Mrs. James Wood, Mrs. Peter Chalmers, her son and daughters, are one and all of them pictured on my remembrance, and I should add Mr. and Mrs. Alexander Wood and their sons, to complete my enumeration of a living society which has wholly disappeared. Truly this is not our abiding city. May we look to the city which hath foundations, whose builder and maker is God ; and may the gracious manifesta- tions of our reconciled Father in Jesus Christ brighten and cheer to both of us the remainders of our earthly pilgrimage.

May I beg my kindest regards to Mr. and Mrs. Walter Wood, as also to my good worthy Christian friend Mr. Archibald.

Mrs. Chalmers and all here join in kindest wishes.—Believe me ever, my dear Miss Wood, yours very truly,

THOMAS CHALMERS.

LETTERS TO MRS. KEITH DUNLOP.

No. CCCLXXXIX.

Edinburgh, 2d February 1829.

MY DEAR MADAM,—I have great pleasure in assuring you of the success and the great benefit that attended the institu- tion of the Catholic schools in Glasgow. The priest, on the one hand, insisted that they should be taught by schoolmasters of his own persuasion ; but, on the other hand, he consented that the Bible should be one of the school-books. I have repeatedly visited one of these schools, and rejoiced in the opportunity of such an approximation to a sect with whom I hold it most de- sirable that we should have free and frequent intercourse. I always experienced a most cordial reception, and have even been asked to address the children, which I did, and was after- wards thanked by the teacher for doing so, although the address

was in the very spirit and sentiments that I should have reckoned the most appropriate for the children of any Protestant
school.

In short, I hold an institution of this sort to be in every
respect a wise and a hopeful one in every neighbourhood where
you have a number of uneducated Catholic children. I would
rather have a reading than a non-reading Catholic population
at any time ; insomuch, that even did they refuse our Bible as
a school-book, I should esteem the setting up of a school a
step in advance in the cause of philanthropy.—I have the
honour to be, my dear Madam, yours most respectfully,

THOMAS CHALMERS.

No. CCCXC.

28th July 1842.

MY DEAR MADAM,—We are still in Ireland, where we expect
to remain a few weeks longer ; but if God will, I trust we shall
be in Scotland before the expiry of the month of August.

Your letter came to me some time ago ; and I was much interested by the perusal of it. I should like you to attain a
settled comfort, and that, notwithstanding the defects of which
you complain, in sanctification and personal meetness for
Heaven. It is the very faith which gives the first sensation of
peace with God that must ever be recurred to and kept hold
of in order to perfect our holiness. " Hold fast your confidence and the rejoicing of your hope firm unto the end." I
wish that you could fall on the habit of repairing daily and
currently to the atonement by Christ, for keeping up your
peace with the God against whom you daily and currently
offend. It is not one great act of mercy alone that Christ hath
purchased for us ; it is mercy in every time of need—a piecemeal and ever-recurring mercy through Him who is our daily,
morning, and evening sacrifice. " If any man sin, we have an

2 U

advocate with the Father in Jesus Christ, who is the propitiation for our sins." It is thus that we should draw from
His mercy as well as from His grace, as we stand in need of it.
And let us not be afraid lest under this economy of a daily forgiveness for our daily offences, we shall be encouraged to sin
afresh that we may be pardoned afresh. "These things," says the
Apostle John, " I write unto you that ye sin not." (See 1 John
i. and ii.) The man who is truly desirous of mercy to pardon,
is as truly desirous of grace to help him. Let us have faith for
both, and we shall have the fulfilment of both. The great
secret, it has been said, of practical godliness, or of the Christian life, is to keep up peace in the heart, yet along with it a
vigilant care of our walk and conversation. Thus do we combine the security of the Christian faith with the diligence of
the Christian practice.

I am very glad you have written me ; and I shall be most
happy to reply as I can to all your communications. I feel that
I have still much to say, which, at present, I have neither time
nor space for. Let me at present conclude with the Apostolic
blessing, " The very God of peace sanctify you wholly." I have
often been struck with the juxtaposition here of *peace* and
sanctification. There is a way of combining and harmonizing
both.—I ever am, my dear Madam, yours very truly and with
much regard, THOMAS CHALMERS.

[*Largs*, 12*th June* 1844.—MY DEAR SIR,—The last day I was in your
house, a trifle occurred that gave rise to feelings I would in vain attempt
to express. I noticed two beautiful salvers on the table, and said something about them to one of the little girls, who said,—" Yes, papa got them
in remembrance of somebody near Glasgow," and turning one up she read,
—" Mrs. Glasgow of Mountgreenan." What delight would it have given
my dearest earthly friend to have known she was so affectionately remembered by one she looked up to as the means of her present peace, her hopes

for eternity !   I have ever since determined to tell you a circumstance that
occurred two days before her death.   She said to those attending her,—
" Let my situation be a warning to you ; you see that the moment the
agony of pain is relieved, I am so exhausted that sleep overpowers me—
had I now my peace to make, what would be my situation ?   But I know
in whom I have trusted, and my heart is at ease."   Oh ! my dear Sir, how
often have I wept with gratitude to you on thinking over this scene !
Before her knowledge of you her mind was quite at sea, and domestic
affliction quite unhinged her ; you brought her peace and fortitude to turn
to other objects ; and I have often wished to tell you what I was sure would
give you pleasure, but I could not without a degree of emotion one does
not like to exhibit.   I got, however, a message two days ago, to be ready
to go home at a moment's warning, being deprived, not of my consciousness, but of my physical power at once.   The Doctor was with me almost
immediately, and I am now nearly well, but put on very short allowance of
meat or drink for some time ; yet I have little doubt I shall soon be well
again, and only wish that I may retain the still, solemn, confidential feeling
of immediate dependence that at present soothes every emotion of my mind,
and diffuses over it something deeper than the tranquillity of a summer evening,—I could almost say something holy.   Think of me, dear Sir, where the
prayers of a good man avail much, and believe me, under every circumstance,
with the most grateful respect and affection, yours,   KEITH DUNLOP.]

No. CCCXCI.

Edinburgh, Morningside, 14*th June* 1844.

MY DEAR MRS. DUNLOP,—I received your deeply interesting
letter this morning.

I have long cherished the recollection of dear Mrs. Glasgow,
as being indeed among the kindest and truest friends I ever had
in this world ; and rejoiced in her growing congeniality with
all that is most spiritual and substantial in the gospel of Jesus
Christ.   There is nothing which I have oftener recurred to in
looking back upon the past, than the delight wherewith one of
her elegant and cultivated literature could peruse the homeliest
authorship of the good old Puritanic writers, whom she at one
time would have recoiled from as utterly distasteful.   Her
dying testimony to the faith is indeed most precious.   It is

new to me ; and I feel peculiarly grateful for your statement
of it, which I shall reserve as one of the most valued *memora-*
bilia in my possession.

We are all greatly concerned to hear of your illness ; and
shall be most interested to hear, by however short a notice, of
your state of health ; only do not make any exertion beyond
your strength. I rejoice to hear from you of your mental and
spiritual state—that of still and confidential dependence.   Be
assured that the stronger and simpler your reliance is, the more
acceptable to God. He likes to be trusted. Without faith it is
impossible to please Him ; but, on the other hand, the more
unfaltering our faith, or the more like it is to the unstaggering
faith of Abraham, the better is He pleased.   In other words,
our comfort and His glory are at one.   In quietness and confidence then may you have strength.   " Be still, and know that
He is God."   (Ps. xlvi. 10.)   " May the God of hope fill you
with all peace and joy in believing."   (Rom. xv. 13.)   " Acquaint thyself with Him, and be at peace."   (Job xxi. 21.)
I have often thought of a verse in Deuteronomy as peculiarly
applicable to the case of one who is physically helpless, but
still in that condition is thus encouraged to trust in God :
" The Lord will repent himself for His servants, *when He seeth
that their power is gone,* and that there is none shut up or left."
(Deut. xxxii. 36.)

It is my earnest prayer that whatever may befall in the wise
and merciful providence of God, you may be upheld in the
gospel attitude of looking unto Jesus.   One apostle tells us of
the meekness and gentleness of Christ ; another tells us that
God is love.   Surely in the face of such declarations it were
wrong to refuse that confidence for which so deep and solid a
foundation has been laid.   " Rejoice in the Lord always : and
again I say, Rejoice."   (Phil. iv. 4.)   May the 6th and 7th
verses also be abundantly realized upon you ; as also Romans

v. 11—" joying in God through our Lord Jesus Christ, by whom you have received the atonement."

Our whole family, including Mrs. Hanna, who is with us, unite in kindest and most affectionate remembrance. " The Lord bless thee and keep thee. The Lord make His face shine upon thee, and be gracious unto thee. The Lord lift up His countenance upon thee, and give thee peace."—I ever am, my very dear Madam, yours with the utmost regard,

THOMAS CHALMERS.

No. CCCXCII.

Edinburgh, Morningside, 23d *June* 1844.

MY DEAR MRS. DUNLOP,—We have great pleasure in sending our two girls to you, and are sure that they will be quite happy if they can contribute in any way to your help and comfort.

Any benefit or gratification you may have received from my last letter must have been in the proportion of its being charged with precious and pertinent Scripture. I could have no hope of saying anything effectual apart from that volume, which is indeed the Book of Life to all who read it with the docility of little children ; but it does give one a confidence in writing when he feels that all which he ventures to state or to affirm is solidly grounded on the Word of God.

There is no continuous passage which I read with greater delight than the fifty-third of Isaiah ; I remember when I made at least one perusal of it a daily task. The very cadence of its sentences is dear to me ; and I feel something inconceivably sublime in that strain of older inspiration first uttered in distant antiquity, and coming down through successive generations to elevate and sustain the faith of those on whom the latter ends of the world have come. There is to my mind an inexpressible charm in the substance of evangelical doctrine couched in the phraseology of those holy men of God whose writings served to irradiate those periods of an earlier dispensation.

Instead of particularizing certain verses as I did in my last, let me specify two or three more of those continuous portions which I would signalize by a particular recommendation.

The next then which I would mention is our Saviour's discourse to His disciples in John xiv.-xvi. There are many individual germs in it which I forbear pointing out. The passage in it which interests me most is the first half of the fifteenth chapter. Again, nothing can be more overpowering than His prayer in the seventeenth chapter.

The substance of the gospel condensed within the space of a few verses we have in the last half of 2 Cor. v. Nowhere are the calls to reconciliation more free and open; and nowhere is the regenerating effect of our compliance with these calls affirmed more distinctly or more peremptorily.

My especial favourite is 1 John iv. The love of God, the manifestation of that love in sending His Son to be the propitiation for our sins; the belief of the apostle and His disciples in the reality of the object thus presented (verse 16); and, lastly, the effect of this belief in working a love unmixed with terror;—these all evince the precedency of faith to love, and they imply, moreover, the faith of appropriation, a lesson further and very decisively told us in the next chapter, verse 11,—a precious lesson truly, and which I rejoice to observe that you so prized in the reading of Anderson's " Essay."

" Now, the God of hope fill you with all joy and peace in believing, that ye may abound in hope through comfort of the Scriptures and power of the Holy Ghost."

I think Clarke's " Scripture Promises " a very precious collection; and I know not a more satisfying evidence of the Spirit being at work with us than when the power of Scripture is felt by us.

All here join in best and most affectionate regards. Mrs. Hanna is with us. She is better; and Mrs. Chalmers convalescent from a late attack.—Ever believe me, my very dear Madam, yours most truly and with great regard,

THOMAS CHALMERS.

No. CCCXCIII.

Edinburgh, Morningside, 21*st July* 1844.

MY DEAR MRS. DUNLOP,—I feel exceedingly interested by your last letter, and all the more, that it makes me feel so gladly and hopefully of your spiritual state. There is not a more satisfactory evidence of the Holy Ghost having been at work with the soul, than that the Scriptures come home to it with a feeling of weight and preciousness greater than wont to be expressed in other days. It is not Nature that effects such a manifestation, but a light from on high—not a light which beams direct upon the mind, so as to evolve upon it other truths than those which are to be found in the Bible, but a light which shines through the Bible as the great medium of conveyance between the Spirit of God and the spirit of man. It was evidently such a light that shone upon the Psalmist, and of which he tells so much, both of its power and its enjoyment, throughout the whole of the 119th Psalm. In this view the 19th Psalm too is exceedingly to be prized. It is true that there is no direct or palpable mention here made of the Saviour; but there are manifold recommendations of that word which testifieth of the Saviour. For when it is said that the Spirit taketh of the things of Christ and sheweth them unto us, I understand by this that He taketh of the things which are told of Christ in Scripture, and sheweth them unto us. And it is truly delightful to meet with so much of Christ in the Old Testament—as in Psalm lxxxiv. 9, where the Psalmist prays substantially just as we do for justification;

and Psalm lxxxiv. 11, where he looks just as we do to the right quarter for sanctification. "The Lord will give grace and glory"—grace here and glory hereafter—the "earnest of our inheritance" (Eph. i. 14) on this side of death, and the inheritance itself on the other side of it. See also Acts xxvi. 18. Then we have Psalm lxxxv. 10, where we have the blessed union of the attributes in the work of our redemption ; and in the alliance between peace and righteousness we recognise the doctrine of God being just while the Justifier of them who believe in Jesus. (Rom. iii. 26.) Or which is identical with this, and going back again to the Old Testament, we read of God being at once a just God and a Saviour.

I exceedingly rejoice in that the Scriptures which I last pointed out have come so powerfully home to your heart—which they could not do unless in your mind there was a sense of their reality. You are right in the conclusion, that such feelings and emotions could not have been awakened without faith in the glorious truths by which they have been called forth. Some talk of the reflex act of faith, and try to ascertain its existence by a sort of direct consciousness. They may succeed in this, though I should apprehend, that we are not so sensible of faith itself as of its fruits or effects ; and that the Saviour's test is applicable to this too :—" By its fruits shall ye know it." May the love, and the peace, and the joy, and all the other fruits which are enumerated in Galatians v. 22, 23, grow every day upon you in brighter and more discernible characters. At the same time, never forget that it is not by looking for them that you create them, but by "looking unto Jesus." (Heb. xii. 2.) In other words, while not forbidden, but the opposite, to look inwardly, (2 Cor. xiii. 5,) I would still say, look much oftener outwardly than inwardly. Look more *to* the object of faith than *for* the act of faith. Or, in the language of good Richard Baxter, for every look you cast inwardly and downwardly upon yourself, cast ten looks outwardly and upwardly upon the Saviour.

All here unite in most cordial regards to you.—Ever believe me, my dear Mrs. Dunlop, yours with great esteem and regard,

THOMAS CHALMERS.

No. CCCXCIV.

Morningside, Edinburgh, 8th September 1844.

MY DEAR MADAM,—I have not been in church for four weeks, with the exception of the afternoon of this day. But there is something very enjoyable in a Sabbath at home, though I do not think that even it is an enjoyment that should be courted at the expense of duty—I mean the duty of not forsaking the assembling of ourselves together. But when one can have a quiet and solitary Sabbath with a clear and quiet conscience, I know few things more exquisite. The chapter which chiefly engrossed and interested me has long been a favourite one— 2 Cor. v. It ranks with me among what I call the superlative passages of the Bible. I know not where a greater richness of evangelical truth is to be found condensed within narrower limits than in its eight concluding verses, where we are presented with the principle of Christian obedience, the mighty transition which all undergo who are in Christ, the free and urgent entreaties of God Himself to enter upon this blessed union, and lastly, the firm and sure guarantee of our safety, and of His favour in that double exchange which He has instituted between the sinner and the Saviour, by which they were made, as it were, to change places—our sins laid to His account, and He bearing the full burden of them—His righteousness laid to our account, and we admitted to the full reward of it. What stupendous blessings are thus placed within our reach. " Open thy mouth wide, and I will fill it." " Ask and ye shall receive ; seek and ye shall find ; knock and it shall be

opened unto you." Other assurances equally precious are to
be found in 2 Cor. vii. 2, 17, 18, Isaiah i. 18, 1 John v. 11,
with innumerable other passages in the Psalms and Prophets
of the Old, and in the Gospels and Epistles of the New Testament.

The Hannas, including Tommy, and accompanied by my
daughter Margaret, are now on their Fife expedition, whither
I meant to have gone too had I been quite well. I find that I
do not agree with locomotion, and the necessity under which
I am laid to refuse applications for all sorts of service wherever
I go, is excessively irksome to me. Grace is now in Kirkaldy.
Mrs. Chalmers is in her ordinary health ; and all unite in the
expression of their warmest regards to you.

I had a very agreeable call the other day from Miss Maria
Vans Agnew, who has kindly undertaken to aid us in the West
Port.—I ever am, my dear Madam, yours very gratefully and
truly,   THOMAS CHALMERS.

No. CCCXCV.

Edinburgh, Morningside, 22d *September* 1844.

MY DEAR MRS. DUNLOP,—I am gradually coming round by
repose and retirement ; but it is altogether out of the question
that I should again so implicate myself in public business as
I have done hitherto.

I rejoice that your theological views should be so clear and
satisfactory ; or, instead of using a term so scholastic as theological, I should rather say, I rejoice that you are enabled to
make such a confident personal application of the undoubted
truths of Christianity to your own case in particular. And be
assured that there is the fullest warrant for this in Scripture,
which abounds in such terms as fully entitle the reader to
transmute the general into the particular and the personal ; as,
" *Whosoever* will, let him come and take of the waters of life

freely,"—therefore may I so come. Or, "Whosoever calleth on
the name of the Lord shall be saved,"—let me therefore thus
call. Or, "Look unto me, *all* ye ends of the earth, and be
saved,"—let me therefore confidently look unto Jesus for salvation. Or, "*Every one* that asketh receiveth,"—let me therefore ask in the full belief of the truth of this saying; and,
according to my belief, so will it be done unto me.

The same thing is admirably made out by Dr. Anderson,
author of the first of the "Three Essays on Saving Faith," which
you so much liked. And the mention of him suggests Cudworth, the author of the third of these Essays, and which
consists of so many aphorisms. If you have access to the
"Free Church Magazine," and I think there should be copies
of it in Largs, then let me recommend an article in the present
number (September) on the Religious Experience of this Mr.
Cudworth, who, late in life, underwent a remarkable enlargement in his views; and that on the strength of that very faith
which, in all its simplicity, he so well expounds in the aphorisms which you have read.

The dread of Antinomianism has led some to cast an obscuration on the freeness of the Gospel, and to view with jealousy
the representations of those who set forth this freeness in all its
simplicity and fulness. It is thus that many speak suspiciously
and with apprehension of a Tract, recently written by Horatius
Bonar of Kelso, entitled, "Believe and Live." I confess that
I do not sympathize with them. Should you get the Tract, I
am persuaded you will find the same comfort and refreshment
in it that you derived from the "Essays on Saving Faith,"
which I put into your hands.

But it is a great thing that we have Scripture itself at all
times to repair to, whether we have these human expositions
of Scripture or not. It alone is able to make wise unto salvation through the faith that is in Christ Jesus. May you ever

continue through the comfort of these precious records to
abound more and more in hope by the power of the Holy
Ghost, being filled with all peace and joy in believing.—I ever
am, my dear Madam, yours very truly,   THOMAS CHALMERS.

No. CCCXCVI.

Edinburgh, Morningside, 13th October 1844.

MY DEAR MRS. DUNLOP,—In the absence of all sensible
tokens for good, we should not let go our confidence in the
efficacy of prayer.   What a large and liberal warrant is
held out for intercession in the Scriptures.   God willeth intercessions to be made for all men, and on this ground,
too, that He willeth all men to be saved, and to come to
the knowledge of the truth, (1 Tim. ii. 1-4.)   Were our faith
equal to God's faithfulness, we should find a glorious verifica-
tion of the saying, that all things are possible to him that
believeth.   (Mark ix. 23.)   It is my confidence in the efficacy
of believing prayer which leads me to acquiesce in the prophecy
of a nation being born in a day.   In the same Evangelist, Mark,
we have a still stronger declaration of the mighty power of
faith ; xi. 23, 24.   There is much to be gathered from the
juxtaposition of what is said in verses 25 and 26.   No man
who reads all the four in connexion could possibly have the
faith described in the two first, if conscious that he failed in
the forgiveness enjoined in the two last verses—a proof that
faith, in one of the very highest of its exercises, could not
possibly lead to Antinomianism.

I do hope and pray that you continue to have great peace
and joy in believing, and further, that the joy of the Lord is
your strength.   His very promulgation of the law that we
should love Him, and His assigning to this law the highest
place in His code, making it the first and greatest of His commandments, is evidence in itself that He has presented us with

adequate grounds and objects for that faith without which it were impossible to love, as without which it is impossible to please Him. May your faith grow exceedingly, working more and more by love, and abounding more and more in all the fruits of righteousness.—I ever am, my dear Madam, yours with great esteem and regard,   THOMAS CHALMERS.

No. CCCXCVII.

Edinburgh, Morningside, 10*th November* 1844.

MY DEAR MRS. DUNLOP,—I cannot adequately express the amount of reflex and secondary pleasure which I feel in the recital you have given me of those manifestations that contribute so much of true, and solid, and most warrantable enjoyment to your own heart. If I have in any way been an organ of conveyance for those Scripture and scriptural views which so evidently have told upon you, and in a way so legitimate and so desirable, I sincerely rejoice in it. But it is not an unfrequent thing, that one should be the minister of a peace and an enlargement to others, of which he himself is very far short ; and therefore convinced, as I am, of the sovereign efficacy which lies in the prayers of a believer, I would cast myself on the intercession of all my Christian friends, and of you in particular, that God would bestow upon me in fuller measure than I have ever yet experienced, the spirit of love, and of power, and of a sound mind ; and cause His Gospel to enter my soul in the demonstration of the Spirit, and with much assurance. The kingdom of God may come to the mere theologian in word only and not in power, so as to make it a possible thing that he should deal but in the vocables of orthodoxy, and have no part in the life or substance of it. Our resort, when visited by any anxious suspicion of this kind, is in the faithfulness of God— He will not put us off with a semblance or a counterfeit of the pearl of great price, if the pearl itself be what we honestly and earnestly pray for. On this subject I have often felt that there is great comfort in Matt. vii. 9, 10. When we ask a loaf, He will not put us off with a stone, or with a serpent if we ask a fish, or with a scorpion if we ask an egg. He will not impose upon us or mock us with a vain similitude of the thing, if we in good faith ask the very thing itself; and I very heartily rejoice in the assurance, that the good work which God has begun, and is carrying on within you, is the sacred pledge of your coming inheritance—the preparative and the precursor of heaven in your soul.

But let us never forget, that the way to be kept right inwardly is to look right outwardly. Let us ever be looking unto Jesus, that we may hold fast our confidence in Him ; and that we may realize the continued fulfilment of His gracious promise, that if we abide in Him, He will abide in us, and cause us to abound in much fruit.

I feel greatly obliged by your most generous proposal in regard to the West Port. Forgive me if I do not avail myself of it, at least now. Should we be in difficulties I will let you know; but I have the comfortable expectation of being provided with the requisite supplies for this great object.

There are two things connected with this operation, each of which will give you pleasure :—

1. I anticipate as much benefit from Mr. Hanna's proposed monthly week, as I could have had, had he settled in Edinburgh.

2. Miss Maria Vans Agnew promises to be a most useful auxiliary in the West Port—efficient and wise.

All here are in about a medium state as to health. I am tolerably well.—I ever am, my dear Mrs. Dunlop, yours with the greatest regard, THOMAS CHALMERS.

P.S.—All unite in cordial regards. Tommy goes to school, and is well enough at present for it.

In regard to the apprehension you express of your ever learning and never being able to come to the knowledge of the truth—this I should apply to such as are carried about with every wind of doctrine, but not to such as are fixed, as I trust you are, upon Christ as their all in all. Such will have new views and larger views of the truth as they grow in the Christian life ; but this is not to be confounded with the vacillations of those who are unstable and unsettled in the faith. Progress is not fluctuation ; and that progress forms a part of Christian experience is indicated by the following verses :—Col. i. 10 ; John xiv. 21 ; 2 Pet. iii. 16 ; 1 Pet. ii. 2 ; Heb. v. 13, 14. The variety of Scripture is exhaustless ; and you must not wonder at the brighter complexional manifestations you may be privileged to enjoy of its single truths at one time than another, as well as the new relations which you discover betwixt these truths, with their new applications to the desires and wants of the now awakened spirit.—T. C.

No. CCCXCVIII.

Edinburgh, Morningside, 5th January 1845.

MY DEAR MRS. DUNLOP,—I cannot suffer the holidays to pass without sending you the compliments of the season ; not formally, I can assure you, but feelingly ; for I do feel the sincerest joy in believing that the unction of the Holy One is upon you—the anointing which remaineth, (1 John ii. 22, 27,)—the earnest of your future inheritance, (Eph. i. 14,)—that better part which shall not be taken away, (John x. 14.)

What a precious writer John is, both in gospel and epistle. I feel nothing better fitted to soothe and to comfort one than the gentleness and sensibility, and deep as well as tender piety of this Apostle. The whole of his First Epistle is instinct with spirituality, and in most beautiful keeping with the last discourse and prayer (the most solemn and elevating passage in the Bible) which He Himself has recorded.

I both rejoice in your experience, and have the utmost value for your prayers. I stand greatly in need of them, and therefore entreat a continued part in your intercessions. Every day convinces me more that the Spirit in the Word is the only source of light and comfort, and of all saving influences both on the understanding and on the heart. But the Spirit is given to prayer, and given too most freely and willingly; for the very ground on which God requires intercessions to be made for all men, is that He willeth all men to be saved, and to come to the knowledge of the truth.

We have had a second West Port visit from Mr. Hanna of nearly a fortnight. He is of the greatest use to me; and there is distinct progress making in our enterprise. But here too we are made experimentally to feel our need of grace from on high; for truly when it comes to an attempt upon human souls, we are made to feel our own helplessness, and to find that man is nothing, and God is all in all.

Mrs. Hanna's cold still lingers; and I begin to dislike it. Tommy is expanding rapidly; he has got a set of carpenter's tools, and among other things has made a most respectable wooden stool. He has the organ of constructiveness.

All the rest of the family are in their average health, and join in best regards.—Ever believe me, my dear Madam, yours most affectionately,   Thomas Chalmers.

P.S.—Miss Maria Vans Agnew is a most efficient member of our West Port agency. Mrs. Mowat, a very generous friend to the work, died a few days ago, to the very great grief of myself and of all who knew her.—T. C.

No. CCCXCIX.

Edinburgh, Morningside, 9th February 1845.

MY DEAR MRS. DUNLOP,—There is nothing to be regretted in the felt unsatisfactoriness of human authorship on any topic of religion, if light and comfort break in upon it directly from Scripture. I could desire no better result from any embarrassment into which you were thrown by reading Dwight, than that it was all cleared away by the 17th chapter of John.

Theologians often do perplex their readers, and more particularly in the handling of objections ; all of which, however, might be overborne by the self-evidencing power of the Bible, when we sit down to its lessons with the docility of little children. There is a sufficiency in the Spirit and the Word which might well make us independent of all uninspired writers ; and yet in their written statements from the press, just as in their spoken statements from the pulpit, there is often a very powerful influence. The reflection of inspired truths from other minds than our own, has in it a peculiar virtue, derived, I am apt to think, from the force of sympathy with the experiences and the impressions and the felt wants or comforts of fellow-sinners like ourselves. Certain it is that God has been pleased to annex a great power to human agency in the business of christianization.

The four short epistles from Galatians to Colossians are among the most precious compositions in the New Testament. I have been dwelling on them with great interest.—I am, my dear Madam, yours very truly,   THOMAS CHALMERS.

No. CCCC.

Edinburgh, Churchhill, 23d November 1845.

MY DEAR MRS. DUNLOP,—The case you mention is not uncommon—that of a good man of society trenched in self-suffici-

2 X

ency, and inaccessible to every argument for convincing him of
sin. The only way in which it can be logically treated, so as
if possible to gain over his understanding, is to reason with
him on the two distinct standards of morality, the terrestrial
and the celestial. He will scarcely refuse that surely something is due from the creature to the Creator ; and then he
may be closed with on the question, whether that something
has been really given or really withheld. The more we can
convince him how much is due, and the more we can lay bare
to him his deficiency therefrom, the greater is the likelihood of
our carrying at least the intellect, if not the conscience and the
heart. The Bible uniformly regards the world in the light of
its being God's world ; and it treats the question between God
and man as hinging upon this,—What has he done unto God ?
It views God as the Being with whom we have to do ; and it
resolves the controversy between the parties into this,—that
throughout the vast multiplicity of our doings, little or nothing
is done unto God. The charge or the complaint against us is,
that it is not His will, but our own will that we follow—not
His way, but our own way (Isaiah liii. 6) that we walk in.
These ways are exceeding various—a way of profligacy, or business, or amusement, or science, or even philanthropy and
patriotism. Some of these therefore estimable, useful, lovely,
and of good report ; yet what Luther would rather coarsely,
and revoltingly it may be, but in substance truly, denominate
courses of splendid sin, because one and all of them destitute of
godliness. It is thus that a man may rank very high on the
terrestrial standard of morality, and on the celestial may be at
the bottom of the scale ; so that, when met on the awful day
of reckoning with the question, What have you done unto me ?
he may be left without a speech and without an argument.

This is the sort of reasoning wherewith a good man of the
world might be plied ; and it is right that he should be so

dealt with. But sensible as I am of the need of a higher illumination, he should not only be pleaded with, but prayed for, that the Spirit may convince him of sin, and cause him so to feel his need of a Saviour, as that Christ shall no longer be lightly esteemed by him, nor the preaching of His cross sound any longer as foolishness in his ears.

When looking upon ungodliness as the great master sin of humanity, reaching deep into the heart of man, and pervading the whole system of his habits and desires, I have often gathered from the contemplation a fresh argument for the completeness and sufficiency of the gospel ; and this I would fain address to yourself for the purpose of comfort and confirmation. For, though this ungodliness be the very acme or extremity of human guilt, I am told of a far reaching power in the gospel-remedy that overtakes as it were and goes beyond it. In this view I hold the phrase in Romans iv. 5, to be of special importance—" justifieth the ungodly." Here, then, is a justification that overmatches the deepest and deadliest of our crimes. And of kindred encouragement to this is Romans xi. 26—" He will turn ungodliness from Jacob." Here there is a sanctification which does away the most virulent of these moral and spiritual maladies under which we labour. Thus there is that in the gospel which makes head against both the guilt and the power of our deadliest transgression, and is commensurate to the salvation of the chief of sinners from the chief of sins.

It is my prayer and hope that you may more and more experience of Christ that He is the power of God unto salvation from all your distempers, erasing your name from the book of condemnation, and making you alive to the sense and the enjoyment of God as your reconciled Father. May He shed abroad in our hearts the love of Himself by the Holy Ghost ; and what a precious assurance for us to pray over, that as He has already

given for us His own Son, much more will He with Him freely
give us all things.

I shall be most happy at all times to hear from you.   Our
family here are a good deal colded, and I myself am slightly.
Grace will be delighted to receive a letter from you.   The
college enrolments are going on faster this year than they did
last ; and there is the promise of a larger attendance at the
Hall than we have ever yet had.—I ever am, my dear Mrs.
Dunlop, yours most affectionately and with great esteem,

THOMAS CHALMERS.

No. CCCCI.

Edinburgh, Morningside, 4th January 1846.

MY DEAR MRS. DUNLOP,—I beg that you will not scruple to
write me at all times.   The labours of my correspondence have
been greatly lightened by the employment of an amanuensis
whom the Free Church kindly allows to me ; so that I have
far more leisure and liberty than I formerly enjoyed for writing
with my own hand to my own more special and personal correspondents.

I feel greatly obliged by the kind invitation of your nephew,
though I do not purpose being at Liverpool.   I have the greatest desire for the object of the meetings there ; but I cannot
undertake any distant locomotion in its behalf.   All my extra
attentions are now confined to my local enterprise in the West
Port—in which, if I succeed, and am followed up by the imita-
tions of other philanthropists, I believe I shall do more good
than by distracting and dividing myself between this and other
objects however excellent.

From the interest which Mr. Dunlop takes in the moral and
religious state of the people in Liverpool, it occurs to me that
he may perhaps like to see what progress we have made in our
Edinburgh attempt.   I therefore beg to enclose for him the

"Witness" report, although it be an imperfect one, of the speech I delivered the other day upon the subject.

I most thoroughly accord with your aspirations for greater love and enlargement than you feel you have yet attained; and you have, indeed, singled out the best expedient for the accomplishment of your wishes—which is prayer, whether it be our own prayers or the intercession of others. I believe that the most advanced and cultivated Christian upon earth will persevere to the end in the very attitude which your letter evinces—not of satisfaction with present graces, but of longing expectancy for more. It was quite so with Paul. So little did he think of having yet attained, or being already perfect, that he counted all that was behind as nothing, and so pressed onward. The very progress of one's discipleship makes him more alive than before to his yet remaining corruptions and deficiencies. And it is my belief, that Paul to the last half-hour of his history would have complained of his vile body, and said, "that in me, that is in my flesh, there dwelleth no good thing;" and exclaimed, "O wretched man, who shall deliver me?" And yet he could follow up this sad and desponding utterance regarding himself with an expression of the most grateful confidence in the Saviour: "I thank God through Jesus Christ my Lord." It is the experience of all Christians. When looking to ourselves, there may be great discomfort and disquietude—to make our escape from which, we should look unto Jesus. This was the constant habit and exercise of the Apostle. (See Phil. iii. 3; 2 Cor. xii. 8-10.) It is in the maintenance of this habit, that in spite of all our fears and all our short-comings, we are enabled to make progress—more advanced than before, and yet more humbled than before, under a sense of manifold infirmities now more clearly seen, and now more painfully felt, in virtue of the very additions which have been made to our knowledge and to our growth in grace. The summit of creature-perfection, says good old Riccalton, " lies in bringing our own emptiness to the fulness that is in Christ Jesus."

With best and most grateful acknowledgments to Mr. Dunlop, I ever am, my dear Madam, yours most affectionately and truly, THOMAS CHALMERS.

No. CCCCII.

Edinburgh, 15th March 1846.

My very dear Madam,—I should have replied sooner, but the last month of the Session is always a busy one. I can, however, assure you that your letters are always most welcome, insomuch that I do hope you will often write, irrespective of my replies, which, at the same time, I feel the greatest pleasure in making.

Your statement of the benefit derived from what I write, and similar statements from others, is to me an experimental proof of the reality of the Spirit's operations. I have long felt this to be a striking evidence ; and many are the clergymen who depone to the same thing, when told, and most credibly told, of the good that has been done to hearers by their sermons, and to correspondents by their letters, and a good that often outruns and goes far beyond the influence which the things said or written have had on the preachers or writers themselves. It may be all true, and most importantly true, what we give forth ; yet with us it may only be the wisdom of the letter, while with those whom we address it may be the wisdom of the Spirit—as if He had taken up our utterance by the way, and given it an impression on the minds of others to which those from whom it came are altogether strangers. This has been the frequent experience of clergymen ; and perhaps it is well that it should be so, to keep them humble and prayerful, under the sense of as great dependence on illumination from on high as the veriest babes in learning or intellect.

I know not if you are acquainted with the works of John

Newton. I think that you would thoroughly congenialize with them. I am reminded of him by a passage in your letter regarding your deeper conviction of the sin of ungodliness now than you ever had prior to your experience of the comforts of the Gospel. Newton was consulted by an inquirer, who thought that ere he was warranted to lay hold of Christ, he should have a more tender sense and fuller view of the evil of sin than he had yet attained to. Newton told him he was wrong, bade him repair to the Saviour immediately; and stated to him what had been his own prayer—" Reveal to me Thy Son, and after that what Thou pleasest."

It is said of Jonathan Edwards, that long after his conversion he had prayed for a more adequate sense of the malignity of sin, and got such a view of it as was like to overwhelm and unhinge him altogether, that he would never repeat such a course of prayer over again.

God knows how to temper and proportion His various manifestations in the way that is best for us, so as that we shall not be tried beyond what we are able to bear, but with the trial will provide a way to escape, that we may be able to bear. It is well that your mind was pre-occupied with the doctrine of Christ's atonement ere getting such a view of the evils of sin. I rejoice in your felt comforts, and pray that they may more and more abound. I perfectly share in your dislike of narrow sectarianism, and do hope that the cause of union will prosper and prevail over it. There are certain points, however, of direction and management—a line of procedure which still requires to be laid down; and I do not think that it has yet been fallen upon.—I ever am, my dear Mrs. Dunlop, yours very cordially and truly,   THOMAS CHALMERS.

P.S.—All join in affectionate regards, and Tommy, who is here, among the rest.

No. CCCCIII.

Morningside, 11*th September* 1846.

My dear Mrs. Dunlop,—I am reading the Diary with deepest interest ; but it will require a day or two ere I can finish the perusal of it. It is all most impressive, and some of its passages are to myself peculiarly affecting. As a record of the breathings of a mind in earnest, it is one of the most touching I ever read.—I ever am, my dear Madam, yours with great regard, Thomas Chalmers.

No. CCCCIV.

Morningside, 15*th September* 1846.

My dear Mrs. Dunlop,—I send back the Journal. I feel it a great privilege that I have been permitted to read it. It endears the writer* more than ever to my heart, and places her very high in my estimation both for her intellectual powers and spiritual attainments. Permit me to say, that it has given me a livelier interest in all her surviving friends ; and now that I have identified the niece to whom she makes such repeated and affecting allusions with the present Mrs. Robertson, I cannot but feel for her all the regards which are due to a relative and friend.

May the providence of God go along with you. May His grace operate powerfully and savingly within you. Do write and let me know your address, that I may have the pleasure of converse with you when replying to your letters.—I ever am, my very dear Madam, yours most cordially,

Thomas Chalmers.

* Mrs. Glasgow of Mountgreenan.

No. CCCCV.

Edinburgh, 22*d October* 1846.

My dear Mrs. Dunlop,—I earnestly hope that my reply to your most interesting letter of October 6, is not so late, but that it may reach you by the London address. I perfectly enter into your pleasurable feelings amid the glories of such a landscape as you have described, and still more into the sentiments which you experienced on your visit to Cambridge—a place which I have now visited three times, and at each time with a more intense gratification than before, associated as it is with the highest names of English philosophy and literature ; and over and above this, rich in that architecture which with me is the most impressive of the fine arts. I have gone over King's College with old Simeon, and expatiated in moonlight both with fellows and under-graduates through Trinity and St. John's, and what to me is a perfect gem, though but a miniature, Caius College. Its walks and academic groves, and all the relics and memorials of Newton, are every one of them most dear and precious to my heart.

It rejoices me to find that however dissatisfied with your own personal Christianity, you keep a firm hold of the atonement. Let nothing dislodge you from this ; and I speak not merely for the sake of your peace, but for the sake of your progressive meetness in mind and heart for that inheritance which Christ hath purchased for all who believe on Him. Sure I am that it is looking unto Him, and keeping fast and firm hold upon Him, which constitutes the right attitude for receiving from Him all the needful supplies both of light and grace from the upper sanctuary. And I would not measure my own state by another man's experience. The Spirit is exceeding various in His methods of dealing with believers ; so that, instead of looking to others and measuring myself by others, I would recommend a simple yet steadfast regard towards Him who is not only the Saviour, but the Sanctifier of men, alike able to prepare a place for us, (John xiv. 2,) and to prepare us for the place.

I know not if I ever spoke to you of " Marshall on Sanctification." He is at present my daily companion ; nor do I know an author who sets forth the gospel in a way so suited to promote the conjoint interests of peace and holiness.

I need not say how much I am gratified by your account of the English parson. You may well believe that such instances are most genial to my feelings. I would almost wish to make him more specially acquainted with our objects and views. But I perceive from your statements that he is abundantly intelligent as well as zealous ; and I can perfectly understand how both he and his family should be in that state of happy enjoyment which you have so impressively described in your letter.

I forget whether you received a copy of the accompanying lithograph, which you ought to have gotten long ago, as it was prepared for my West Port subscribers. Perhaps it is well fitted to give any English philanthropist whom you may meet with some general idea of our objects and proceedings.

We often hear of the delays of law ; they are not more provoking than the delays of architecture. We shall not get into our new church till January. The masonry, however, is completed ; and it really makes a fine appearance.

The services of Miss Anna Maria Vans are invaluable, and above all praise.

I do hope to see Mrs. Robertson occasionally this winter.

The Hannas are now with us ; and little Tommy, I am glad to say, goes forthwith to Merchiston.

Do, my dear Mrs. Dunlop, allow me to hear from you frequently. Your letter, as I go over it again, is a mighty solace to me ; for, amid discouragements and a thousand moral discomforts, it is an immense emollient to know of truth and friendship in this world.

All join in warmest regards ; and I entreat that you will ever believe me, my dear Mrs. Dunlop, yours most cordially and with the greatest regard, THOMAS CHALMERS.

P.S.—Pray, what is the name of the French *town* nearest to the place where Mrs. Glasgow was buried ?

No. CCCCVI.

Edinburgh, 22*d November* 1846.

MY DEAR MRS. DUNLOP,—I should have replied sooner to your very interesting letter of the 6th. I beg that you will not think it too much for me to meet your letters with an early answer to each, as I have real pleasure in keeping up this correspondence, and felt an especial interest in your last communication.

But I have first to thank you for a small note of still later arrival than yours of the 6th, and from which I have obtained a very distinct idea of the site and geography of dear Mrs. Glasgow's burial-place—a document highly prized by me, and which I shall place in my personal and family scrutoire beside the former memorandum that you gave me of your beloved sister.

You ask me if it is superstitious to feel the lesser movements of one's life as if coming from on high ? I think not. There is a charm altogether natural, and I am sure altogether fitted to tranquillize and reconcile us to whatever may cast up in the minutest applications of the doctrine of a special Providence. It is well to recognise God in everything ; and I know not a more memorable or precious verse in the Bible than where it is said that there is a diversity of operations, but it is God who worketh all in all.

I wish that, along with Elliot's book on the Apocalypse, you would get Dr. Candlish's reply to his very rash and ignorant attack on the Free Church. Altogether I hold his work to be the best and ablest exposition of the Book of Revelation I have met with. But he went sadly out of his way when he made his onslaught upon us. Dr. Candlish's pamphlet may be commissioned from London, I should think, by your nearest bookseller ; and I should be well pleased if it could be made known in your present neighbourhood.

But I am most interested of all by the expression of your self-dissatisfaction towards the close of your letter. I will not promise to relieve you of this feeling so long as you are in the body ; but I think that the Gospel is very clear as to the direction which this feeling should impress on all who experience it —a lesson that has been made all the clearer of late to my mind by my perusal of a book which I think I recommended to you, " Marshall on Sanctification." The Apostle Paul was haunted through life by the very feeling of which you complain. He called out in agony, " O wretched man ! " He counted all as nothing. He spoke of his vile body ; and would, I believe, have so spoken of it to the last hour of his history. Nay, let us look onward to the judgment-day, and we then find the unconscious disciples on Christ's right hand, asking what good thing they had ever done for Him. They forgot or made no reckoning of aught which they had rendered Him in the way of service. But He did not forget—He reckoned in their favour, not unrighteous to forget their work and labour of love. The upshot of all is, that under a sense of our own nothingness in ourselves we should cast our case upon Him as the Lord *our Strength* and Sanctifier. We should subordinate our holiness as much as our pardon to faith in Him who has undertaken for both, to work in us as well as to do for us. We should put the one case, the one necessity, as much into His hand as the other,

saying, " Lord, take me such as I am, make me such as I
should be." I think it was because of this attitude habitually
kept up that Paul said of himself, " I am dead—nevertheless I
live, yet not I, but Christ liveth in me." Let us do the like,
laying no confidence in ourselves, but rejoicing in the Lord
Jesus ; and as the sure result of this, He will put forth upon
us the hand of a Sanctifier—He will perfect His own work in
our souls, and see in us of the travail of His own soul and be
satisfied, even as He will be on the day of judgment with those
on His right hand. Let us, therefore, at all times bring our
own emptiness to Christ's fulness. Henceforth let the life
which we live in the flesh be a life of faith on the Son of God ;
and thus will our peace and our holiness keep pace the one
with the other. In quietness and confidence we shall have
strength ; and the very God of peace will sanctify us wholly.

Should Mr. Pope be still at Torquay, give him my best regards. I made his acquaintance at Leamington in 1835.—I
ever am, my dear Mrs. Dunlop, yours very truly,

THOMAS CHALMERS.

No. CCCCVII.

Edinburgh, 13th December 1846.

MY DEAR MRS. DUNLOP,—Our Free Church Committee have,
by an advertisement in the " Witness," and I should think in
other papers, given forth an invitation to all who might choose
to co-operate in their work of charity, and also their willingness to merge their collections in a general fund, to be administered by a general and all-comprehensive Committee. Meanwhile all remittances ought to be sent to Archibald Bonar,
Esq., of the Edinburgh and Glasgow Bank, Edinburgh.

What an awful state Ireland is in ! They are now dying in
dozens of hunger, and in a little while I believe they will be
dying in hundreds. It will be the same thing in our High-

lands soon, unless a far greater effort be made on their behalf than people have yet thought or felt to be necessary.

I am truly glad that you have caught the spirit and design of Marshall, and not less thankful that it has come home of late to the heart and good liking of Mrs. Chalmers. She has been very low, and though better for the present, yet I would say that hers is a frail and precarious condition.

I do not wonder, for it is by no means rare, that you should have received Christ more for pardon than for sanctification. All do so at first ; and it is often much later that they recognise Him, and still later that they make habitual use of Him, as the Lord their strength. I look on 1 Cor. i. 30 as a very precious verse, in that it gives a full view of Christ's salvation in the various parts of it. I have great value, too, for Phil. iii. 3. The order in which Paul enumerates the three habits of the believer is reverse, I think, to the order in which they take place in his spiritual history. He first has no confidence in his own strength, feeling all that he does in the way of new obedience to be so miserably abortive. He then rejoices in the Lord Jesus, (Phil. iv. 13 ; John xv. 4,) on perceiving that His office is to sanctify as well as to justify men. And lastly, as the effect of this compound attitude, if it may be so termed, that of distrust in ourselves and confidence in Christ, are we enabled to serve God in the Spirit, " striving mightily according to His grace that worketh in us mightily." (Col. i. 29.)

I quite agree with you in thinking that all other collections should be postponed at present, rather than the collection for famine should suffer. They are acting practically upon this in many places. With earnest prayers for your continued peace and joy in believing, I ever am, my dear Mrs. Dunlop, yours most affectionately,   THOMAS CHALMERS.

No. CCCCVIII.

Edinburgh, 10th January 1847.

MY DEAR MRS. DUNLOP,—I am much gratified by your approval of my brief letter on the Sabbath. I can have no objections, but the contrary, to your throwing off copies of it. I doubt very much, however, if your sentiments in regard to it will be very much sympathized with, however much I agree with you in thinking that a great and vital interest for Scotland hinges on the right determination of this question.

I rejoice in your exertions for our suffering Highlanders. The public are beginning to arouse ; but they are yet very far from an adequate view of how great the destitution will be ere harvest comes round, and what the extent of our liberalities, unless we can make up our minds to thousands and thousands more dying of starvation both in Ireland and at home.

May He who hath said, they who wait on the Lord shall renew their strength, fulfil in you all the good pleasures of His goodness, and cause you abundantly to experience that in quietness and in confidence ye shall have strength.—With the kind regards of all here, ever believe me, my dear Madam, yours most affectionately,   THOMAS CHALMERS.

No. CCCCIX.

Edinburgh, 31st January 1847.

MY DEAR MRS. DUNLOP,—Be assured that there is nothing in the mere intensity and elevation of your religious feelings, and nothing in the strength of your convictions, though amounting to assurance, which of themselves bespeak aught like illusion. For such manifestations and impressions as you now seem to experience have been often realized, and on the most solid grounds, by the most advanced and enlightened Christians of whom we have ever read in the history of the

Church. Witness the religious experiences of Doddridge and Halyburton, and Boston, and Jonathan Edwards ; and, better than all, let us only bethink ourselves of the declarations of Scripture which inform us of such enlargements as are perfectly genuine, and which are occasionally vouchsafed by the Giver of all grace as the foretastes and the glimpses of our coming heaven. If we but put their inspired meaning on such verses as the following we shall not have any doubt of these spiritual illuminations :—Ps. cxix. 18 ; Isaiah lviii. 18 ; John xiv. 21 ; 1 Cor. ii. 10 ; 2 Cor. iii. 18 ; iv. 4 ; Eph. i. 17, 18 ; iii. 18, 19 ; Phil. iv. 7 ; 1 Thess. i. 5 ; 1 Peter i. 8 ; 2 Peter i. 19 ; 1 John ii. 27 ; Rom. viii. 16 ; xv. 13.

There can be no doubt of such enlightenments and enhancements of spiritual feeling, given in greater and less degree to Christians in various stages of their discipleship. Many who have the faith, and are therefore in a state of safety, are destitute of the sensible comfort which is sometimes given to others, and springs from the bright and exhilarating views that they obtain of Divine truth. They are greatly to be prized and longed after ; but it were a mighty discouragement on many, of whom I believe that they are the real children of God, to represent them as indispensable, or to set them forth as indispensable.

I cannot perceive any delusion in the mental state of which you have written me. The ultimate and decisive test is Scripture ; and so long as the ideas which fill and elevate your mind are scriptural truths, now seen by you more largely and luminously than heretofore by the Spirit shining still more brightly than He wont to your eyes upon the Word, you have every reason to bless God and to rejoice. Certain it is, that without going forth of the Bible there is ample material within it for sustaining and justifying all the high emotions which you have expressed—nothing more being necessary than to deepen our convictions of Bible doctrine, and to brighten our assurance of Bible prospects, in order to bring the mind to a state of elevation, nay even of ecstasy. And still the Bible is the test-book, the grand touchstone by which the spirits are to be tried ; for, " to the law and to the testimony, if they speak not according to this word, it is because there is no light in them." (Isaiah viii. 20.) My judgment is, that you speak altogether according to this Word. But my observations and even references are perhaps too general for your case ; and let me therefore conclude with a few more specific references, serving to prove that Jesus Christ does, by His Spirit, dwell in man, and presides over his movements, actuating, and strengthening, and directing ; and in virtue of the close and intimate union which takes place between him and the believer, revives him and makes him faithful, even as the vine communicates life and fertility to all its branches.

John xv. 1-8 ; Rom. viii. 9-11 ; 1 Cor. vi. 19 ; Gal. ii. 20 ; Rom. viii. 3 ; Eph. iv. 16 ; Heb. viii. 10, 11 ; Jer. xxxi. 33. Observe that God dwelling in you is as much part of the promise or covenant under the economy of the gospel, as is the forgiveness of your sins.

Pray for all in whose spiritual state you take an interest, that they, too, may be made to experience these higher attainments of experimental Christianity, for many, many are they whose doctrine outruns their experience, or who have not verified in their own personal state and history, what, nevertheless, they know to be true.—I am, my dear Mrs. Dunlop, yours very sincerely and affectionately,   THOMAS CHALMERS.

No. CCCCX.

Edinburgh, 24*th March* 1847.

MY DEAR MRS. DUNLOP,—I send Mrs. Glasgow's paper with the deepest interest, and your observations on your own state

I look upon as being exceedingly just and important. We must not expect to realize at all times the same bright manifestations. But though they come to us only in passing yet precious glimpses, the recollection of them is most helpful for the sustaining of our faith, on which faith it is that, under all the variations of our sensible comfort, our safety hinges. It is by the power of faith that we are kept unto salvation.

I know not if you ever read Samuel Rutherford's "Letters." There is a passage in one of them which reminds me of your present experience. He experienced, when in prison, a most remarkable season of spiritual refreshment and illumination, during which he wrote an account of it to one of his correspondents. Among other things, he says that he was quite sure the present transport and elevation and sensible comforts were not to last, but that a time was coming when they would take leave of him, and then what he should do would be, "believe in the dark." It is quite competent to believe even in the duller and darker frames of the mind ; for belief does not look inwardly upon the frames, but stays itself by looking outwardly upon the word ; see Isaiah l. 10. Nevertheless, such manifestations are mightily to be prized and longed after, as the most precious cordials on our future way ; and the recollections of those which are past are confirmatory and comforting to the soul.—I ever am, my dear Mrs. Dunlop, yours very truly,	THOMAS CHALMERS.

EDINBURGH: T. CONSTABLE, PRINTER TO HER MAJESTY.

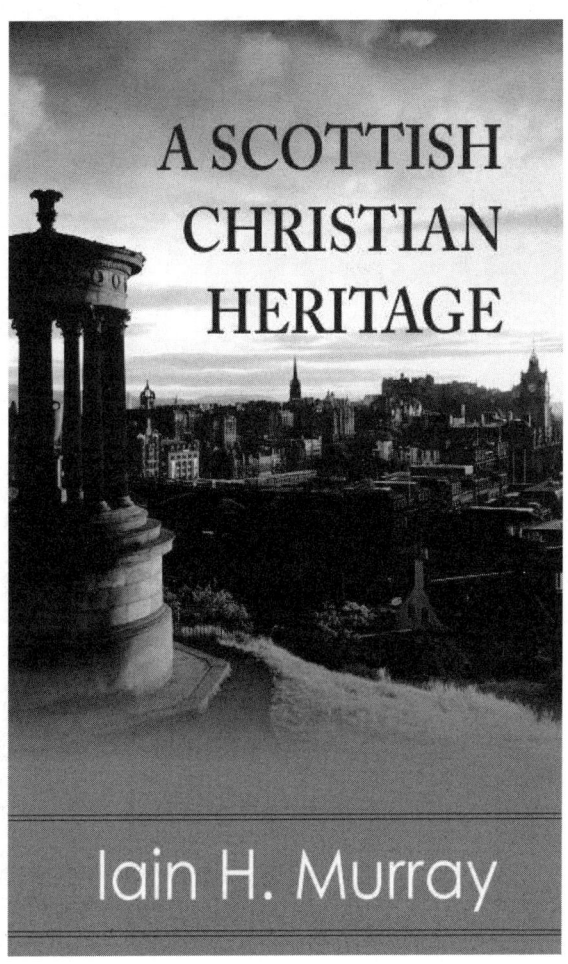

ISBN: 0 85151 930 x, 416 pp., clothbound

Memoir & Remains of
ROBERT MURRAY
M'CHEYNE

Andrew Bonar

ISBN: 0 85151 084 1, 664 pp., clothbound

ISBN: 0 85151 432 4, 554 pp., clothbound

THE PREACHERS
OF SCOTLAND
From the Sixth to the Nineteenth Century

William G Blaikie

ISBN: 0 85151 805 2, 368 pp., clothbound

THE
LIFE OF
JOHN DUNCAN
A Moody Stuart

ISBN: 0 85151 608 4, 256 pp., clothbound

A print of Edinburgh showing the North Bridge, connectin the Old and New Towns, by I. D. Swarbreck, October 183